Campaigner Against

Parkes–Wiener Series on Jewish Studies
Series Editors: David Cesarani and Tony Kushner
ISSN 1368-5449

The field of Jewish Studies is one of the youngest, but fastest-growing and most exciting areas of scholarship in the academic world today. Named after James Parkes and Alfred Wiener, this series aims to publish new research in the field and student materials for use in the seminar room, to disseminate the latest work of established scholars and to re-issue classic studies that are currently out of print.

The selection of publications reflects the international character and diversity of Jewish Studies; it ranges over Jewish history from Abraham to modern Zionism, and Jewish culture from Moses to post-modernism. The series also reflects the inter-disciplinary approach inherent in Jewish Studies and at the cutting edge of contemporary scholarship, and provides an outlet for innovative work on the interface between Judaism and ethnicity, popular culture, gender, class, space and memory.

Other Books in the Series

Holocaust Literature: Schulz, Levi, Spiegelman and the Memory of the Offence
Gillian Banner

Remembering Cable Street: Fascism and Anti-Fascism in British Society
Edited by Tony Kushner and Nadia Valman

Sir Sidney Hamburger and Manchester Jewry: Religion, City and Community
Bill Williams

Anglo-Jewry in Changing Times: Studies in Diversity 1840–1914
Israel Finestein

Double Jeopardy: Gender and the Holocaust
Judith Tydor Baumel

Cultures of Ambivalence and Contempt: Studies in Jewish–Non-Jewish Relations
Edited by Siân Jones, Tony Kushner and Sarah Pearce

Alfred Wiener and the Making of the Wiener Library
Ben Barkow

The Berlin Haskalah and German Religious Thought: Orphans of Knowledge
David Sorkin

Myths in Israeli Culture: Captives of a Dream
Nurith Gertz

The Jewish Immigrant in England 1870–1914, Third Edition
Lloyd P. Gartner

State and Society in Roman Galilee, A.D. 132–212, Second Edition
Martin Goodman

Disraeli's Jewishness
Edited by Todd M. Endelman

Claude Montefiore: His Life and Thought
Daniel R. Langton

Approaching the Holocaust: Texts and Contexts
Robert Rozett

CAMPAIGNER AGAINST ANTISEMITISM
The Reverend James Parkes, 1896–1981

COLIN RICHMOND

Foreword by
Tony Kushner
University of Southampton

VALLENTINE MITCHELL
LONDON • PORTLAND, OR

First published in 2005 in Great Britain by
VALLENTINE MITCHELL & CO. LTD
Suite 314, Premier House,
112–114 Station Road, Edgware, Middlesex HA8 7BJ, UK

and in the United States of America by
VALLENTINE MITCHELL
c/o ISBS,
920 NE 58th Avenue, Suite 300, Portland, OR 97213-3786, USA

Copyright © 2005 Colin Richmond

www.vmbooks.com

British Library Cataloguing in Publication Data
have been applied for

Library of Congress Cataloging in Publication Data
have been applied for

ISBN 0 85303 573 3 (cloth)
ISBN 0 85303 574 1 (paper)

All rights reserved. No part of this publication may be reproduced in any form or by any means, electronic, mechanical, photocopying, reading or otherwise, without the prior permission of Vallentine Mitchell & Co. Ltd.

Printed in Great Britain by
Antony Rowe Ltd, Chippenham, Wiltshire

Contents

List of Plates	vi
Foreword by Tony Kushner	vii
Preface	xxi
Introduction	1
1 Guernsey and Flanders 1896–1919	20
2 Oxford and Geneva 1919–35	50
3 Barley Before the War	106
4 Wartime Barley 1939–45	145
5 Barley: The Post-War Decade	189
6 Crises Surmounted at Barley: 1955–64	211
7 Barley: The Last Five Years 1959–64	231
8 The Final Years: Iwerne 1964–81	245
Coda: James Parkes and the Shoah	291
Index	303

List of Plates

1. James Parkes in his garden at the bungalow, c. 1914
2. James Parkes, Molly and Theodore David Parkes
3. 1916
4. Messines, July 1917
5. Theodore David Parkes
6. Molly Parkes
7. Oxford, 1921
8. James Parkes, 1924
9. Sonntagberg, 1925. Hans Becker, James Parkes, Franz Schmal
10. James Parkes, 1926?
11. James Parkes and Dorothy, 8 August 1942
12. Henry Parkes with one of his yachts, c. 1935
13. James Parkes, 1945?

Foreword: The Legacy of James Parkes

Richard Harries, Bishop of Oxford and the leading Anglican in late twentieth-century and early twenty-first-century Jewish–Christian relations, identifies three key experiences that shaped his outlook and determined his interest in this area. The first was witnessing a newsreel on the Belsen concentration camps in 1945. The second was witnessing antisemitism aimed at a fellow pupil in his secondary school. The third was a visiting speaker at Cuddesdon Theological College, where Harries trained in the early 1960s. The impact the speaker had was profound:

> One week we had James Parkes to talk to us, the man whose pioneering work revealed the extent of antisemitism in Christian history and who strove for a new relationship between Church and Synagogue. It was only many years later that I became aware of the true importance of Parkes. But it was symptomatic that what he had to say to us should have been, as it were, fitted in as an optional extra.[1]

For those now involved in Jewish–Christian dialogue in Britain and beyond, the Reverend Dr James Parkes is regarded as a pioneer, although the full significance of his role and energies in the period from the 1920s until his death in 1981 has rarely been fully acknowledged. Those of far less talent, originality and risk-taking have assumed ownership of ideas and institutions that originated with Parkes. Outside this particular and small field of activism and scholarship, what Richard Harries refers to as 'the true importance of Parkes' is simply not recognized. Since 1981 Parkes has largely been forgotten, including by the body of which he was a clergyman for many decades

– the Church of England. Even his birthplace, Guernsey, has little or no knowledge of the man. In contrast to the progress made recently by its rival Channel Island, Jersey, Guernsey has struggled to come to terms with its history of collaboration in the Second World War, including the deportation of three East European Jews. As Madeleine Bunting has suggested, Guernsey's subsequent response to their deportation has been 'grudging at best'. When a small plaque was unveiled in 2001, the Bailiff of Guernsey 'referred only to the fact that the Jews on Guernsey were foreign-born and their deportation was implemented by Germans (a factual inaccuracy)'.[2] Parkes stands as a heroic figure in Guernsey's past, a total contrast to the moral ambiguity and worse revealed in such deportations. Yet he is as obscure, as written out of history, as those responsible for the island's tiny contribution to the enormity of the Holocaust.

More generally, returning to Richard Harries, Parkes' radical message has yet to be widely conveyed within his own faith:

> It is still the case that the radical reappraisal that is required of Christianity's approach to Judaism is not reflected in the main curriculum of biblical studies, in Church history and systematic theology. Most ordinands, in most denominations, still go through their training with the old stereotypes about the Pharisees, Jewish legalism and with Judaism simply presented as a foil to Christianity.[3]

James Parkes is thus overdue a biography. His account of his own life, *Voyage of Discoveries* (1969) is, while covering all elements of his public career, unsatisfactory in getting close to the man and his motivations. In many ways, as Colin Richmond's account indicates, Parkes remains an elusive figure. Richmond's detailed interrogation of Parkes' voluminous correspondence gives greater shape to the man and reveals his dynamic and persistent character. It shows the unending effort that Parkes devoted in his career to make the world, as he demanded, one in which it was safe to be a Jew.[4] Yet whatever lay behind Parkes' energy and vision, his efforts to that effect deserve much greater recognition than has so far been the case.

Parkes, as will emerge in the chapters to follow, was not always an easy man. He was sure that he was right, especially when challenging contemporary wisdom and practice.

Unfortunately for many of his contemporaries and their reputations, his nonconformist views were often justified either at the time or with hindsight. Parkes, it seems, relished being the outsider. His refusal, at times, to join 'mainstream' organizations and to influence them from within is, as will emerge, often frustrating, verging at times on the irresponsible. But perhaps to be so radical in his vision, and to say the unsayable, James Parkes needed to avoid too much contamination by bodies, international and national, governmental and public, whose outlook was so different from his own. And yet, for all his stubborness and refusal to conform, Parkes was, in the final verdict, a creative force, a person who confronted real problems and found solutions that were aimed at both short-term relief and long-term resolution. By all accounts Parkes was a likeable, charming person; 'clubbable' is a word that I have heard used on many occasions by those who knew him. Parkes was not, however, for all his massive contributions to existing and new organizations, a team player. In his defence, many of the 'teams' of his time were exclusive or had membership that was conditional. Ultimately, his clarity of vision was such that he needed independence whether it was financial, institutional or intellectual. That he was able to achieve such independence at least partially in all three areas is a tribute to his more enlightened contemporaries. It is also an indication of the strength of the man and his ability to persuade some to take risks and do the right thing. It is hard, for example, to think how Parkes would have survived in the Britain that has evolved since his death, with its increased managerialism and corporatism and the mediocrity it demands and rewards. Sadly, there were far too few James Parkes in the twentieth century, but his era, for all its intolerance, had, at least, a place and (limited) respect for dissenters.

The purpose of this foreword is not to replicate the detail and the discussion that will follow in Colin Richmond's interpretative study of James Parkes. It is simply to outline the legacy and achievements of the man. The amnesia about Parkes sadly necessitates such a gesture – one that is made with full knowledge of the dangers of producing an apologetic or hagiographic approach. In this particular case, such dangers are neutralized by the critical engagement with Parkes that Colin Richmond has provided. James Parkes made a lasting impact in many different areas. Separating them out under neat headings is in many ways an artificial exercise. Parkes, as Colin Richmond concludes, had only a limited cultural and private life. His was very much a public, selfless career and his research, writings, collecting, activism and even friendships were part of a whole – a single-minded devotion to removing the murderous threats posed to Jews and, beyond that obscenely limited but, given the context of his work, absolutely essential goal, to normalize their position in the everyday world. Nevertheless, while recognizing the interrelationship of all Parkes' work, it will still help the reader, especially one not familiar with the man, to understand its scale and significance by dividing it into specific categories.

The first is in the area of scholarship. Parkes was educated at Oxford University where, with his usual unorthodox approach and refusal to conform, he managed (just) to achieve his undergraduate degree and then a doctorate. Later he had connections to Cambridge University through geographical proximity when he was based in the Cambridgeshire village of Barley. In the late 1950s and early 1960s, Parkes tried to find a physical and intellectual home for his extensive library. Oxford, Cambridge and University College London (at this point the largest, as well as the oldest, Jewish studies centre in a British higher education institute) were not interested. Here the point is to emphasize that although Parkes was the author of dozens of scholarly books and, in total, some 329 publications,[5] he was, until belatedly recognized by the University of Southampton when he had effectively retired, an outsider in British academia. Curiously, certainly from the perspective of the early twenty-first century, Parkes kept his faith in the importance of universities and their ability to change the world for the better. The irony is that Parkes, who did not receive the recognition he deserved from academic institutions, probably achieved far more as a gentleman scholar than by working inside them.

The most obvious contribution of Parkes to scholarship is in the study of antisemitism. For many Christian writers before Parkes, the history of the Jews and hatred towards them were closely interwoven, indeed, inseparable – the Jews, because of their devious nature and concomitant pariah status, created their own misfortune. The persistent mythic figure of the 'wandering Jew' from the early modern period onwards, doomed endlessly to tread the earth in homeless misery, was not drawn out of Christian sympathy, but was intended to represent the deserved fate of those who had murdered the son of God with full knowledge of what they were doing.[6] Parkes reversed the causality of Jew hatred. It was the fault of Christians that Jews were persecuted and reviled. To Parkes this was a deep stain on the reputation of his faith and the only response was for Christians to combat antisemitism wherever they found it. Freed from such past theological blinkers, Parkes was able to confront a secret and shameful history. Being a pioneer, and with the added burden of coming out of a lingering Victorian self-confidence that a huge sweep of human experience could be incorporated in a single study, Parkes set himself the formidable task of covering over two millennia of history. Now, coming up to three-quarters of a century later, no historian of antisemitism can fail to start with Parkes' work. In spite of Daniel Goldhagen's attempt to bastardize what he wrote, Parkes was no believer in a straight line of antisemitism from Christian teaching of contempt to the gas chambers of Auschwitz.[7] Later scholarship has nuanced Parkes' chronology and queried some of his assumptions about early Christian and medieval attitudes towards Jews. Yet what is remarkable about Parkes' writings on antisemitism generally is how well they have lasted. He was clear about the importance of 'race thinking' from the nineteenth century onwards and how this changed the nature of the debate, giving antisemitism its genocidal potential. Indeed, he was one of the first progressive writers in the early 1930s who wrote against the politicization of 'race' by totally dismissing the reality of the category 'race' itself. Hesitant to identify himself in later life with the mixed bag of sublime and ridiculous that has become Holocaust studies, Parkes nevertheless wrote some of the first historical writings on the subject, which are notable for their clarity in outlining what had happened and how. He was also prescient enough to anticipate later debates, including the place of modernity in the implementation of Nazi genocide and the question of human choice in the destruction process.[8] Put bluntly, subsequent scholars of antisemitism of the distinction and sophistication of Gavin Langmuir simply could not have produced their works without the firm foundation established by James Parkes and the wisdom he afforded the subject.[9]

Yet it would be sad and misleading if Parkes' scholarship was recalled only for outlining and analysing the negative. His presidency of the Jewish Historical Society of England after the

Second World War was in recognition not only of his efforts on behalf of the Jewish community generally but also of the detailed historical work he had written on the history of the Jews, in many different settings and eras. Indeed, Parkes could write well about antisemitism because he understood the dynamics of Jewish communities past and present and the impact that hatred had upon them. At worst, Parkes' work on the history of the Jews was apologetic. At best, it showed an understanding of the diversity and richness of the Jewish experience, one that was not confined and defined solely by non-Jewish responses and actions. From here Parkes' inclusive approach enabled his most significant scholarly legacy – his recognition of the importance of studying 'the wide field of relations' between Jews and non-Jews.[10]

In outlining the study of Jewish–non-Jewish relations, Parkes wanted all periods to be studied through as many disciplines as possible – he was in support of inter-disciplinary research before it had become the cliché of academic funding bodies. His particular, though not exclusive, focus was on Jewish–Christian relations, and Parkes recognized that the two faiths were critical to one another in the ongoing and complex processes of self-definition. On a crude general level, Christians throughout the ages needed the Jews to hate, or, more rarely, to love. In addition – in better days at least and on an everyday level – elements of theology and praxis were often borrowed as much by Jews from Christians as by Christians from Jews.[11] Parkes was insistent that antisemitism made 'normal' relations between Jews and non-Jews impossible, but he was too good a historian and scholar to accept that antisemitism itself was 'normal'. His insistence on studying 'the wider field of relations' anticipated the best of modern scholarship, which incorporates reactions and responses, ambivalent as well as purely negative and positive, to Jews, whether real or imaginary. He was interested both in the world of ideas and in everyday behaviour manifested by elites and ordinary people. Yet studying Parkes is not antiquarianism. As questions of 'ethnic' diversity and migration become ever more urgent, Parkes' pluralistic outlook and also his intellectual approach have much to offer, whether inside academia or outside it.

It is appropriate at this stage of the foreword to bring in the University of Southampton, where work in Parkes' field is now most intense. Accident played its role in the moving of the Parkes Library to Southampton in 1964, although the importance of chance should not be overstated. Claude Montefiore, the founder of Liberal Judaism and a key figure in early Christian–Jewish dialogue, was, in the first decades of the twentieth century, integral to the survival and development of what was then University College, Southampton. Montefiore's input provided an intimate connection between Southampton and broadly defined Jewish studies. Montefiore, as a friend and through his writings, was important to James Parkes and the commemoration of the man, through the Montefiore Lecture, provided the link for the offer by the University of Southampton to create a permanent home for his library. But Parkes wanted much more than a physical space for his unique collection, one that he had assembled in order to bring about greater understanding of Jewish/non–Jewish relations across the ages.

In the late 1950s the Parkes Library was formalized into a Centre. Parkes was adamant that any institution that took his collection of books, journals, pamphlets and archives from the sixteenth century onwards should see it as a 'live' organism. Such a demand ruled out interest from Oxford and Cambridge. The material was brought together by Parkes neither for the sake of satisfying an urge towards obsessive collecting (although Parkes certainly had such acquisitive traits, as this study will illustrate), nor simply for scholars to use to further their careers. Its purpose was to inform and influence contemporary debate and improve relations in the future. Parkes was lucky that the University of Southampton, an independent body since 1952, was in a period of innovative expansion. Its south coast rival, Sussex, was also seriously considered, but Southampton was chosen by Parkes because it had the background through the Montefiore connection, as well as the 'newness', to enable it to understand the intellectual excitement and social worth of developing a centre devoted to Jewish–non-Jewish relations.

Parkes wanted his Centre at the University of Southampton to be one of international importance. He had, I have been told by one of its former librarians, a vision of scholars coming off the transatlantic liners in the Southampton docks, jumping into a cab and heading straight for the Parkes Library. This foreword was begun when the *Queen Mary II* left on its maiden voyage out of Southampton. I doubt whether any of its passengers from the

USA will ever visit the Parkes Library in the manner envisaged by this maverick Anglican clergyman. Nevertheless, in a circuitous way, with points of despair and decline as well as progress, his ambitions have, in 30 years, begun to be realized. The Parkes Library itself has been transformed, more than doubling in size, through the diligence of its staff and the generosity of external donors. It has been supplemented by huge collections of archives, making it one of the largest Jewish documentation centres in Europe and beyond. It must be stressed, however, that in all this expansion of printed and archive material, the special and still unique focus of Jewish–non-Jewish relations has been maintained. It has been strengthened by the work that now takes place linked to the Parkes Library through the Parkes Institute.

James Parkes in the 1950s wanted a centre to be created where 'non-Jewish sociologists, historians, theologians, and other scholars can work in the wide field of relations between Jews and their neighbours, and between Judaism and other religions, and can meet with Jewish scholars engaged on the same work'.[12] In 1996 the University of Southampton formally accepted the creation of the Parkes Centre for the Study of Jewish/non-Jewish Relations, which four years later became the Parkes Institute. Currently there are ten scholars employed by the university in a range of disciplines – history, literature, cultural studies, music, archaelogy, anthropology and religious studies – connected to the Parkes Institute. They focus on a chronology ranging from the Graeco-Roman period to the twenty-first century. Their geographical scope and academic approaches are equally broad. Undergraduate and postgraduate courses are offered in areas that were central to the concerns of James Parkes. The Parkes Institute is also a major centre of doctoral and postdoctoral research. Three academic journals and a book series are produced in conjunction with the Parkes Institute.[13] Yet, for someone like myself intimately connected to this expansion and apparent success, there is still a lurking question: would James Parkes himself have approved of all these activities which take place in his name?

In the mid-1970s I was part of a group of teenage boys who were going out with a group of teenage girls in suburban Manchester. We were horrified to discover that we were being judged by our female counterparts on a scale of one to ten for looks, personality, dress sense and so on. Several of my (male) friends were in a new-wave band, The Still, who responded to this ranking by recording their only ever record, which included the line 'How come I only get 9.5?' So far, so adolescent, although the song came highly recommended by the then Radio 1 disc jockey John Peel. Close to 30 years on, I find my undergraduate and postgraduate teaching assessed by students who give it marks ranging from one to five. Furthermore, I am being asked, as head of history, to rank in importance my colleagues' research, giving them 'marks' of between one and four stars. Unlike the primary school teachers of my four-year-old son, however, I am not provided with gold stickers to reward them appropriately (or not yet). I cannot believe that James Parkes would have had any time for this self-important academic nonsense where work is churned out for its own sake and labelled 'internationally significant' because that is what the funding councils want to hear, and regardless of its frequently ephemeral quality. To Parkes, scholarship had to have a social and political purpose, it was to inform and be part of the process of education that would, in the long run, help remove the abnormality and dehumanization caused by racial prejudice. Those in the Parkes Institute take that imperative seriously. The pressure to publish, and careers now depend upon it, is never far away, but we hope, in however small a way, that the work of the Institute will make a difference. Certainly the need for outreach work beyond what are still laughably labelled the 'ivory towers' of academia is taken seriously. Those in the Parkes Institute are involved, as was Parkes, in advising a wide range of governmental and non-governmental bodies. They also talk, as did Parkes, to many different types of groups. The impact of such outreach may not be as powerful as that experienced by Richard Harries when he heard Parkes speak, but the effort is made and its importance recognized.

In 2000, the Arts and Humanities Research Board gave a grant totalling close to £1 million to develop research projects linked to the Parkes Library. This was official recognition of the academic credibility of the Parkes Centre and led to the support of research ranging from the Greek Bible in translation, Jews in Victorian literature and culture, Port Jews, the legacy of the Holocaust, and 'Race, Ethnicity and Memory in Britain'. The award, by far the largest ever granted by the major national humanities body in Britain to a Jewish studies project, reflected a sea change in attitudes. Jewish studies, and in this case the particular focus that Parkes originated – the study of Jewish–non-Jewish relations – has come in from the margins and effectively become part of the mainstream. James Parkes may not have been comfortable with the removal of such outsider status. The dilemma now is how to maintain the vision of the Parkes Institute while making the work associated with it as radical, ethical and challenging as when Parkes himself was active and writing. It is once again a tribute to James Parkes that it is not only his library, but also his vision that have stimulated a new generation of scholars to devote themselves to the subjects that he pioneered. Undoubtedly there are areas and approaches with which Parkes, were he alive today, would be unfamiliar. Moreover, he might not agree with every conclusion drawn by those working in the Parkes Institute. Overall, however, I hope that there is nothing he would find alien and alienating in the current work of the institute that bears his name or in the Parkes Building, where those in the School of Humanities at the University of Southampton are located. In a world increasingly torn apart through ethnic hatred, the need for an outward-looking and inclusive Parkes Institute has never been greater. The biggest challenge is to keep its social relevance in a world where academic institutions increasingly resemble public limited companies.

Finally, I want to turn to the legacy of James Parkes, the activist. For some academics, and some in the Church of England, Parkes' public role and his devotion to the fight against antisemitism made his scholarship suspect. Yet rather than undermine its importance, it must be argued that its commitment gave an urgency and power to Parkes' writing. It was backed up by a phenomenal organizational capacity that allowed him to engage in a vast amount of reading and writing alongside a career in (non-conventional) politics. Norman Bentwich, who met James Parkes through his international refugee work in the 1930s, recalled in his memoir that Parkes was 'a Peter Pan among scholars and a Puck in any administration'.[14] In the 1920s and early 1930s, Parkes revealed tremendous patience and diplomatic skill in his work for the Student Christian Movement and the International Student Service. By the later 1930s Parkes was perhaps less malleable. There again, the crisis he was confronting had grown horrendously and his increasing stubbornness did not stop him playing a central role in organizations new and old, most obviously the Council of Christians and Jews (CCJ).

The CCJ was formed in 1942, stimulated by news of the Holocaust reaching Britain. This precise location in time does not reflect the hard work over many years that had been put in more informally to the furthering of Jewish–Christian relations. Without the determination and tact of Bill Simpson, its first secretary, the CCJ would never have come into existence. Its survival in the war years was largely dependent on the equal perseverance of Parkes' mentor, William Temple, by then Archbishop of Canterbury. Nevertheless, without Parkes' intellectual input the CCJ would have failed to materialize. The body that was initially created was not fully to Parkes' liking: its initial years were undoubtedly flawed and its impact limited. Parkes' insistence that modern antisemitism had its roots in Christian prejudice and his belief that it was wrong in principle for Christians to want to convert Jews was too strong for almost all of his Christian contemporaries to stomach.[15] At least Parkes, by stating the hardest position clearly, set a gold standard that bodies dealing with Christian–Jewish relations would have to meet. Subsequently, political and theological compromise has hindered the full acceptance of Parkes' position, especially with regard to the theoretical if not practical implementation of the conversionist ethos. The Lambeth Document on Christian–Jewish relations, *The Truth Shall Make You Free* (1988), produced by the Church of England seven years after Parkes' death, owes much, in its positive direction, to his influence, communicated especially through those he had a direct impact on such as Marcus Braybrooke and Richard Harries. The resistance to abandoning any missionary zeal towards the Jews in the discussion leading up to the creation of the document, as Richard Harries has outlined, reveals how far ahead James Parkes was (and is) of his fellow believers, even within the liberal theological environment of Britain.[16] James Parkes was honoured by the International Council of Christians and Jews by a conference at Southampton a few years before his death. It remains true, however, that his impact on Christian–Jewish relations in the post-1945 world has still to be sufficiently recognized.

The last section of this foreword will deal, as does the last chapter of this study, with James Parkes as an activist on behalf of European Jewry during the Nazi era. There is an irony in ending here: Parkes in his later years, as Colin Richmond highlights, could hardly bear to remember the Holocaust. As has been noted, Parkes was one of the first to historicize the event and he did so in his usual unpretentious but authoritative manner. Alongside his reticence about recalling the horror was an equal lack of desire to explore, let alone celebrate, his own role in rescuing Jews and publicizing their flight. In the 1990s and 2000s, there has been a desperate desire in Britain and beyond to discover 'heroes' of the Holocaust, local versions of Oskar Schindler who 'saved' Jews. One doubts whether Parkes would have wanted to have become known as a 'righteous gentile' or to be feted as the 'British Schindler'. At the end of his life he clearly found distasteful what was to develop more fully as the 'Shoah Business'. At the same time, he did recognize, if modestly, his own role in helping Jews to escape Nazi persecution. I would argue, any misgivings about the title set aside, that because his rescue, relief and aid extended from the later 1920s through the whole Nazi era, and because his career and limited means were wholly devoted to 'making the world safe to be a Jew', the epitaph 'righteous gentile' fits James Parkes better than most.

In the 1970s, Edith Weisz, the mother of the actress, Rachel, wrote to Parkes about the rescue of her father, Alexander Teich. Parkes, along with Bentwich, had been responsible for bringing Teich out of imminent danger in Vienna. Parkes then looked after Teich, a prominent Jewish activist and educator, for several years in his house at Barley. Parkes characteristically downplayed his role in this individual rescue when explaining the situation to Edith Weisz: 'Norman Bentwich and I had to get him quickly out of Vienna.' No further information was given about how he did this. Instead, Parkes simply related to Edith that she had 'a father to be proud of, a man who was greatly loved by a very wide group of people throughout Central and Eastern Europe'.[17] There were other refugees whom Parkes helped in a similar matter-of-fact way; many of them he had met before the Nazis came to power in his international student work. Moreover, during the war, Parkes worked to change the antipathy of the British government towards the rescue and relief of European Jewry as he quickly grasped the reality behind the 'Final Solution'.[18]

Does Parkes figuratively and literally deserve a posthumous medal for such work? A case could (should?) be made for an award by Yad Vashem. But the patient (and impatient) work of James Parkes deserves greater recognition. His work is still *live* work today. His life and career deserve critical engagement, and this is provided by Colin Richmond in the study that follows. It is not the final word on James Parkes, nor is it intended to be. James Parkes' legacy is too significant, too open-ended and too vital for any attempt at closure to be made. The reader may find, at times, that Parkes was exasperating, as does his biographer, Colin Richmond. There is also (and above all) a greatness to be found in these pages that makes it worth confronting and remembering James Parkes: the man, it remains, was a *mensch*.

Professor Tony Kushner
Southampton, January 2005

NOTES

1. Richard Harries, *After the Evil: Christianity and Judaism in the Shadow of the Holocaust* (Oxford: Oxford University Press, 2003), pp. 1–2.
2. Madeleine Bunting, 'Our part in the Holocaust', *Guardian*, 24 January 2004. Chaim Chertok's forthcoming biography of Parkes will confirm the lack of knowledge of Parkes in Guernsey today.
3. Harries, *After the Evil*, p. 2.
4. Parkes, in a sermon in Oxford after the outbreak of war, stated: 'Our immediate duty to the Jew is to do all in our power to make the world safe for him to be a Jew.' In Parkes papers, University of Southampton archive MS 17/10/1.
5. Sidney Sugarman and Diane Bailey, *A Bibliography of the Printed Works of James Parkes* (Southampton: University of Southampton, 1977). The bibliography, with selected quotations, is available through the Parkes Library at the University of Southampton.
6. See Alan Dundes and Galit Hasan-Rokem (eds), *The Wandering Jew: Essays in the Interpretation of a Christian Legend* (Bloomington: Indiana University Press, 1986).
7. Compare James Parkes, *Antisemitism* (London: Vallentine Mitchell, 1963), p. 60 with Daniel Jonah Goldhagen, *Hitler's Willing Executioners: Ordinary Germans and the Holocaust* (London: Little, Brown and Company, 1996), p. 52.
8. Tony Kushner, 'James Parkes and the Holocaust', in John Roth et al. (eds), *Remembering for the Future: The Holocaust in an Age of Genocide* (Basingstoke: Palgrave, 2001), pp. 575–86.
9. For Parkes' influence, see Gavin Langmuir, 'Theorising tolerance and intolerance', in Tony Kushner and Nadia Valman (eds), *Philosemitism, Antisemitism and 'the Jews'* (Aldershot: Ashgate: 2004).
10. 'The Parkes Library: A Centre for the Study of Relations between the Jewish and non-Jewish worlds' (leaflet, Parkes Library, 1958), pp. 3–4.
11. For a later study see Michael Hilton, *The Christian Effect on Jewish Life* (London: SCM, 1994).
12. 'The Parkes Library', pp. 3–4.
13. For current activities see the Parkes Institute website: http://www.soton. ac.uk/~ parkes
14. Norman Bentwich, *Wanderer Between Two Worlds* (London: Kegan, Paul, Trench, Trubner, , 1941), p. 235.
15. See Tony Kushner, 'James Parkes, the Jews, and conversionism: a model for multicultural Britain?', in Diana Wood (ed.), *Christianity and Judaism* (Oxford: Blackwell, 1992), pp. 451–61.

16. Harries, *After the Evil*, chapter 6.
17. Parkes to Edith Weisz, 21 March 1974, Parkes papers, University of Southampton archive, MS 60/33/29.
18. Kushner, 'James Parkes and the Holocaust' and the Coda to this study.

Preface

> Kisses, Mum. Jewish is good! But what is it?
> (The postscript of a letter from Betty Scholem
> to her son Gershom Scholem dated Berlin 29 April 1919[1])

Did these two utterly different men, James Parkes and Gershom Scholem, ever meet? It is hard to imagine their conversation if they did, harder still to envisage what they might have said to each other about the First World War. In 1919 James Parkes went up to Oxford. Evelyn Waugh knew Parkes there as the friend of a friend and wrote of him in his autobiography, *A Little Learning*: 'one of the last of the ex-service men, he was of rugged appearance, who [it was said] had been the model for the bronze statue which stands as a war-memorial in Paddington Station'. If this indeed were the case it would be entirely fitting. During the war Parkes had been heroic in his untypical way, just as he was to be throughout his life. He has no other memorial.

Two further comments might be offered at this point. First, that James Parkes, who unlike Gershom Scholem lost his mother when he was still a boy, shared with Betty Scholem, at any rate once he had left Oxford, the preoccupations she expressed so succinctly to her son: 'Jewish is good! But what is it?' Whatever it was, Parkes knew it was good. For the rest of his life he tried to tell the world (which believed otherwise) that Jewish always had been and continued to be good. Second, James Parkes shared Herman Melville's belief that 'we are blind to the real sights of the world; deaf to its voice; and dead to its death. Not till we know that one grief outweighs ten thousand joys will we become what Christianity is striving to make us.'

There are a number of people who have helped to make this book. Without the constant support of Professor Tony Kushner it would not have been written. A 'biography' was his idea; it was also his idea that I should write one. I hope he will not feel his trust has been misplaced. For his willingness in the midst of a busy Jewish and academic life I am deeply grateful to him for taking the time and trouble to write the Foreword. In addition, Mag, Jack, and Sam Kushner are to be remembered for the forbearance they exhibited when I stayed in their Southampton house while studying the Parkes Papers.

At the Special Collections Division of the Hartley Library, the University of Southampton, I am in debt to a number of devoted staff; many hours were spent in their company while I combed through the Parkes Papers in their care. I am particularly grateful to Amanda Thom, who seemed to deal with more of my requests than did other archive assistants. Nevertheless, my thanks go to all those who had a hand in producing the relevant files and in copying as much of them as I needed. To Dr Christopher Woolgar, Head of the Division, I am especially grateful for a courteous welcome and continuing interest in my progress. Dr Woolgar is to be thanked for recommending me for a University of Southampton Hartley Fellowship, as are the university authorities for awarding me one. I also thank him for permission to reproduce the photographs that feature in the book.

My wife Myrna has entered into and enriched many a dialogue about James Parkes, a ghostly but substantial presence at our discussions over a number of years. More ghostly, but present none the less, was Myrna's Jewish grandfather: he was from Tyneside; his immediate forebears were from Lithuania. Of her goodness I have personal evidence for close on fifty years. I do not have to ask what it is, only is it Jewish?

Colin Richmond
Woodbridge
Lent 2005

NOTE

1. Anthony David Skinner (ed. and trans.), *Gershom Scholem: A Life in Letters, 1914–1982* (Cambridge, MA, 2002), p. 104.

Introduction

If this is a biography, what kind of biography is it? Not the current kind, not the kind savaged by Roger Scruton. I quote from *The Philosopher on Dover Beach*:

> As the demand for biographies increases, so does their quality decline. For reasons that have little to do with the love of literature, and still less with the love of life, biographies are now comprehensive, packed with trivial detail, and burdened by a scholarship which, through its obsession with fact-finding, raises up an insuperable obstacle to truth. Modern biographies are generally opposed to any conception (other than a sentimental one) of the heroic, and are therefore unable to justify the interest they arouse. All are very long, and all explore – with the impertinence of an age for which no human greatness must be allowed to obscure the fact of our littleness, and for which no human character must stray beyond the bounds of the cosy and the frail – the most intimate features of their victims' earthly journey. Most are written in an easy-going, middlebrow patter, reminding their readership that the lives of the great can be described in terms of the very same conceptions as rule the feelings of the gullible. In short, the modern biography is an exercise in vicarious living.

If it is not modern, it is also not post-modern, not at any rate the post-modern as defined by the Italian writer Claudio Magris, 'in which everything is interchangeable with its opposite and the Black Mass and its junk is placed on the same level as Saint Augustine's thought'. That sort of post-modernism might just as well come out of the closet and call itself by its proper name: post-moralism. It would have shocked James Parkes as much as it disturbs his biographer.

James had been upset in 1950 by an early example of another

variety of meretricious writing. Victor Gollancz sent him Arland Ussher's *The Magic People* in proof: what did he think? 'It was', he replied, 'a fair specimen of the new genre of writing on this subject', in which was displayed a 'fascination with playing tunes on the psychological dictum that, whatever I am doing, I am really doing the exact opposite, and whatever motives I think I am doing it with are the exact opposite of the motives with which I am really doing it'. Facts, he said, were 'made cokernut-shies for the artist's psychological imagination'. Nine times out of ten that psychological imagination is unsubtly post-Freudian. This writer, on the other hand, is resolutely post-Nabokovian: he will have none of the Viennese trick-cyclist's sleight of hand. What James Parkes did was what he said he was doing; what he said was what he thought; what he thought was what he believed. And we should believe it too.

Not that what he believed, thought, wrote, said and did was always right; like most great men he got a good deal wrong. He was wrong, for example, about Gershom Scholem's biography *Sabbatai Sevi*. He thought its one thousand pages too many. 'As a work of reference', he wrote, 'this volume will prove invaluable: as a biography it is to be hoped that a shorter – and lighter – version may prove possible.' One cannot have too much Gershom Scholem. One can have too much James Parkes. This biography, therefore, will be short and light. Nor should it be thought anything other than *tam ve-lo nishlam*: finished but not completed. The over-worked 'definitive' is not applicable. The opposite has been my aim: presentation, commentary, elucidation, but not definition. Definition, like completion, is in the eye of the reader. Moreover, as my approving citation of Roger Scruton suggests, I am able to address James Parkes in the words Yosef Hayim Yerushalmi used in his 'Monologue with Freud', the epilogue of his masterly *Freud's Moses*, 'I have not rummaged through your life in search of flaws'. James is indeed flawed. What master is not – a flawless master being a contradiction of terms: he or she would have nothing to teach. But I have not trawled for those flaws in the manner of so many contemporary biographers, whose only occupation seems to be that of dredging.

The biographer is no more a judge than he is the jury. Neither is he a policeman or a priest. He or she must avoid being any of those things for the simple reason that the subject of a biography can be known only in part. Above all in the person of Charles

Swann, although by no means in him alone, as the impossibility of knowing anyone fully is one of the themes of his dazzling book, Proust has shown how deluded we will be if we think we can even imagine the whole from the fragment:

> He knew perfectly well as a general truth that human life is full of contrasts, but in the case of each individual being he imagined all that part of his or her life with which he was not familiar as being identical with the part with which he was. He imagined what was kept secret from him in the light of what was revealed.

Between October 1933 and May 1934 there is a series of lengthy, empathetic, and confessional letters between James Parkes and a Miss Rose Strachan. James was in Geneva, Rose wrote once from London but at other times wrote from her home in Aberdeenshire. They appear never to have met: 'I wonder', Rose said with feeling, 'whether we are ever going to meet on this earth.' She offered him money for the work with German Jewish refugees he was doing with the International Student Service; she was engaged on the same task in Britain. If I were a trawler-man of a biographer I would have gone fishing for Rose Strachan. But I have not. I do not believe she was or became important in James' life. There is no obvious evidence of it. Yet I might be wrong. The Rose Strachan I have in mind and whom I have dismissed from the book is an imaginative compound of the other women in James' life. She may have been utterly unlike any or all of them. She may have had an influence on him or significance for him that my 'obvious evidence' does not allow for. She may be a secret I am incapable of revealing.

There is another Proustian point worth consideration. Proust makes it in this fashion:

> The truth is that similarity of dress and also the reflexion of the spirit of the age in facial composition occupy so much more important a place in a person's make-up than his caste, which bulks large only in his own self-esteem and the imagination of other people, that in order to realise that a nobleman of the time of Louis-Philippe differs less from an ordinary citizen of the time of Louis-Philippe than from a

nobleman of the time of Louis XV, it is not necessary to visit the galleries of the Louvre.

Proust was a great one for appearances. James Parkes, as the photographs of the 1920s and 1930s (and beyond) clearly show, was not. Or perhaps he was, and men of his sort cultivated the appearance of casual informality as earnestly as did city gentlemen with their pin-striped suits and bowler hats. Was James, therefore, more of his period than one is inclined to think? 'Men of his sort' is what is critical: an anti-establishment man of the middle class is what we might think when viewing the post-Oxford photographs. There was, however, far more to James than the cut of his shorts or the colour of his bandanna. His 'facial composition' for one thing does not seem to me to be 'of the period'. Of what period was it then, we might well ask? This is not to be dwelt upon; if it is, we will soon be into the shallow waters of 'racial' characteristics, and asking silly questions about the Englishness of James' nose, or whether he has Guernsey eyebrows. More important is his haircut. Not only does he keep his shock of fair hair throughout his life, it is invariably cut in a boyish style. The boy in the man perhaps, yet as we shall see the man was already in the boy long before he went to war in 1915.

I am sure James did not conform to the Proustian model. He was less like his contemporaries than most men and women are. It was his thinking that made him so, his cast of mind we might say, faintly echoing Proust's 'caste'. He did not think like the overwhelming majority of his contemporaries: that is mainly why he did not look like them. Think of Stanley Baldwin's homespun suits, think of Neville Chamberlain's wing collar and umbrella. They look more like characters out of *Alice in Wonderland* than anything else. They look absurd because in some profound sense they were. If they looked like that because of the age they lived in then the 1930s too were absurd. We now know they were. James knew it then, and (we might say) dressed accordingly. Proust is thinking about those who conform to their epoch in ways he would have regarded as more defining than the opinions they held. He is not wrong. In our eyes Dreyfusards and anti-Dreyfusards look alike. Can we nowadays when looking at a group photograph from the 1930s tell the drawing-room antisemites from the cultured philosemites (if there were any)? So: we have to do more than look. We have also to read and think. Especially we have to read James Parkes. He did have some of the tastes and attributes of his epoch, and I would have thought membership of the Athenaeum was one of them until the other day when standing on that Club's steps Lord Putnam passed me to enter with a familiarity that marked him out as a member. James Parkes refused a peerage: I suppose that does mark him out as a man of his time. But: James Parkes was too rare a bird to have more than the superficial plumage of his period. He was a non-conformist in more than appearance. The inner man was thoroughly rebellious, highly original, and inordinately cantankerous. From 1915 onwards he was usually out of step with the rest of the world. How else would he have become more Jewish than most Jews and still contrive to be a practising Anglican?

One of the difficulties of writing about such a man is trying to grasp what he was up against. Those times, though recent, are past times; the 'spirit' of that age is not the 'spirit' of ours. Many of the causes James fought for are either won or, not having been won, have been transmuted into different, not always easily recognizable, shapes and forms. Are there still Christian missions to the Jews? If there are, they have not the power and influence they had when James fought against them. It is virtually impossible in a multi-cultural, multi-ethnic, multi-religious Europe to understand the strength of that widely diffused Christian feeling of the years before 1939 that Jews were second-class persons who, if they had any sense, would not be Jews. It was, as James knew only too well, a 'hang-over' from the Middle Ages, but like every other hang-over it was both potent and mind-numbing at one and the same time. The shock that one can sometimes get from a discovery of what the men and women on the Clapham omnibus really thought occurred to me one morning recently in the crypt of St Paul's Cathedral. I came across the memorial to Major Frederick George Jackson of the East Surrey Regiment, Polar Explorer and Soldier, Commander of the Jackson–Harmsworth Polar Expedition 1894–1897. The inscription continues: 'He discovered, mapped in, and named the greater part of Franz Josef Land and rescued Dr Nansen who was lost.' Major Jackson died aged 78 on 13 March 1938. The memorial has a quotation from his book *The Lure of the North Pole*. It is the quotation that gave me pause. It reads:

> Then there is the feeling of ownership, the right of possession, which the man earns who lifts a new land or a new sea out of the darkness of the unknown and fixes it for ever upon the chart – the feeling that the savage, splendid scene before him is his because he has earned it by work of brain and body, won it by sheer force of clear head and clean muscle.

I have resisted the temptation to italicize certain words and phrases, albeit coming close to succumbing over 'his' in the fifth line. Faced with a statement as preposterous as this, one understands what James was up against, realizes how much against the grain his thinking was, and grasps just how great was his achievement in altering so many hearts and minds. What the quotation also serves to remind us of is that the English-speaking world James inhabited for the greater part of his life was an utterly different world to the one we have found ourselves in. Although less than a century in the past it might just as well have been a thousand years ago: it requires its annalist to be as much anthropologist as historian.

I have also attempted to keep in mind Fontane's plea for the incidental in art. The master novelist said: 'The incidental is obviously nothing if it is only incidental, if it conceals nothing. But if it conceals something, it will be no less than the essential, for it will always give you what is truly human.' James Parkes, whatever else he was, was truly human and it shows in the incidental as much as the essential. Finally, in this introduction to the Introduction, it should be said of the book, as it was said by T.E. Lawrence in the preface to *The Seven Pillars of Wisdom*, 'It does not pretend to be impartial.'

In the National Portrait Gallery there is a splendid painting of Eleanor Rathbone. There is no portrait of James Parkes. He is the absent man of the recent English past. It is as Benny Green has said about Lester Young: 'The original thought of one generation becomes the commonplace of the next. It is the forgotten revolutionaries who are the truly successful ones.' In what was James 'truly successful'? I think he was successful in making English antisemitism disreputable. He achieved this almost single-handedly. It is true that the Shoah has been the single greatest cause of antisemitism's loss of respectability. Anti-Israelism has perhaps taken its place, and some might want to argue is only antisemitism under another name (or flag). Antisemitism is unlikely ever to die; that, however, is beside the point. The point is, is it respectable or not to be an antisemite? It became respectable in the course of the nineteenth century, especially in Germany, but also in England. Its respectability in Germany was one of the reasons for the success of the Nazi Party. James witnessed that development from Geneva and on his European travels in the 1920s and early 1930s. He was also aware of the widespread, if rather more casual, acceptance of antisemitism as normal (possibly as natural) in England. Its 'normality' lingered on at Oxford in the 1950s, but by 1939 antisemitism had become, or was well on the way to becoming, a dirty word for most of the younger generation. James had a good deal to do with the transition of antisemitism from gentility to scurrility through his writing and lecturing.

He knew what he was up against. Here he is in 1934 on 'that most popular of all kinds of fiction – the detective story':

> The Jew is rarely anything but an unpleasant character therein, and if he is a virtuous person, he is not called a Jew. I mean that if Solomon Levi buys stolen jewels he is called the 'hook-nosed semite', if he values the duchess's emeralds after their recovery he is referred to as 'an honest merchant', but not 'an honest Jewish merchant'. But I am extremely puzzled as to what I could do with my collection of notes of Jews in detective fiction, for I very much doubt if Dorothy Sayers, Freeman or the rest are consciously prejudiced against Jews.

Because detective fiction was popular it reflected popular taste, at any rate among the reading classes, that is, the middle and upper classes. But antisemitism went deeper and further than that. It was not just 'Mrs Snooks of Stamford Hill', to whom we shall come in a moment, who was antisemitic, consciously or unconsciously. What about the respectable citizens of the Isle of Man? Here is Frank Kermode in his autobiography *Not Entitled* on his father:

> Although we never met Jews, they nevertheless had a place in our insular fantasies, figments to be feared and despised.

> I remember my father coming home from work for his midday dinner and announcing that yet another shop in the main street had sold out to the Jews. I was already suspicious of such claims, and sure enough it turned out that the shop, like many others, had been sold to a non-Jewish English business. What he meant was that the shop was no longer Manx; the English and Jews were alike in not being Manx, and in being too crafty and acquisitive for us to deal with, gentlemen though some of them might superficially seem to be.

While it is salutary to be reminded that to some people English and Jews were interchangeable, it is also unnerving to be reminded of how careless ordinary folk could be in their thinking about Jews. Here we arrive at 'Mrs Snooks of Stamford Hill'. She was a 1940 creation of James Parkes and 'Mrs Snooks', he said, 'may be cured of dislike of the Jews':

> Mrs Snooks dislikes the Jews because a Jewish neighbour has a wireless set and is very inconsiderate with the noise of it, because she does not like the Jews she meets shopping, because she was done by an instalment-wallah who was a Jew, and her husband was done by a business colleague who was also a Jew. Mrs Snooks is probably curable by antidote and other means ... I am a pedestrian person, and perhaps too apt to limit my activities to the field in which I believe results can be achieved. I don't try to do anything about the incurables ... a Streicher, a Hitler, even a Drumont, or a Douglas Reed ... I am sure they are too difficult for me! But I think it would be fatal for either Jew or Gentile or Christian to accept the idea that the whole business was incurable. It would be as bad as for doctors to sit helpless at all growths because they could not cure certain cancers.

In writing and talking clearly, logically, and persuasively about antisemitism James did much, certainly more than any other single person, to render English antisemitism powerless. Handbills, like those of the Portsmouth Jewish Truth Society (to be found among the Parkes Papers) with their claim that 'Jews are folk just like ourselves ... friendly, sincere, loyal, intelligent, religious, moral, possessed of a keen sense of humour and of a ready sympathy for the underdog and the unfortunate', are nowadays redundant as well as 'dated'.

What sort of a man was he? That, I hope, will emerge from the book itself. A few preliminary remarks, however, will not be out of place. In 1974 James told Robert Everett: 'to identify myself at Heathrow, I shall be wearing a green shirt with open collar and a green pullover. As I told you I have a shock of white hair, and I will probably be wearing spectacles.' He will have stood out in the crowd, in any crowd. What did this 'Peter Pan among scholars and a Puck in any administration' (as his old friend Norman Bentwich described him in 1941) enjoy, besides writing and talking? He liked drinking wine, especially the wines of the Loire and Rhone valleys. He adored East Suffolk: 'I love every corner of the country which you are now in', he wrote to a relative, Margaret Bell, who lived at Friday Street in the village of Benhall, near Saxmundham. He went to those corners often. He also adored the Channel Islands, where he had grown up before the First World War, and Provence. Having walked through Southern France as a young man, he went back to stay with friends as often as he could spare the time to do so; when recovering from serious illness in the mid-1950s it was at Menton that he choose to convalesce. After he had settled at Barley in 1935 he seems only once to have gone elsewhere in Western Europe. He preferred North America, where he lectured, and after the Second World War Israel, where as a supporter of the new state he was enthusiastically received. He never went to Italy or Spain: their totalitarian regimes had deterred him: 'On principle I never spent holidays in dictatorship countries because I liked to sit in the pub in the evening and discuss things with the locals,' he said in 1975. Nor did he ever return to Eastern Europe. In 1965, when Naomi Meyer, a former student of his from the 1920s, got in touch with him again, he said that she seemed to have led 'as much a wandering life as I have. Cracow I know, also Lvov, but I never penetrated to Oswiecim'. But he had not wandered in those parts for over 30 years and showed no inclination to do so: Holocaust tourism was not in vogue in his lifetime, and if it had been, he would probably not have participated in it.

Of course: he hardly had any 'spare time'. He seems not to have done any sketching after 1930, may, though may not, have continued embroidering after he no longer had to endure the agonising committee work he underwent while he was working at Geneva and does not appear to have added to his collection of architectural postcards and pictures after 1935, when it had reached 27,000 items. He did, however, continue to collect English domestic brass candlesticks of the period 1680–1880. The collection of architectural drawings he gave to the University of Melbourne in the 1960s. The brass candlesticks he donated to Birmingham City Museum – 100 in 1968 and another 100 in 1977 – such generosity was characteristic of him (as we shall see again shortly). He gardened every day with the enthusiasm and devotion only an English person could bring to that activity, until his strength gave out at about 80. He and his wife Dorothy seem always to have had a dog; in 1948 it was a mongrel bitch named, appropriately in one sense and inappropriately in another, Rassenschaende.

One reason he had such little 'spare time' was that he was as generous with his time as he was with his possessions and money. Being a committed Christian and Socialist (of a sort) it is no great surprise that he was so generous, even if it was no guarantee that he would be. There was virtually an 'open house' policy at Barley, and not only for established scholars using its unique library; first-year students were made just as welcome, train timetables for Royston having been dispatched and arrangements for being met having been made well in advance of the projected visit. Nothing was too much trouble for this meticulous and generous man. Before the Second World War refugees stayed in the house. During it, the house was filled with evacuees from London. From 1939 to 1945 therefore, James and Dorothy (whom he married in 1942) rarely had a moment to themselves. The strange idea that time might be 'his', or that he was entitled to his 'own space' did not occur to him. It was not his world; it was God's. As for money: he did not have much of it and most of what he had after 1935 was given him by Israel Sieff. He had, therefore, to husband his financial resources. After the death of his father during the Second World War he had for a while money of his own and with this he was generous. Let us take a single example. In 1951 he wrote to the Secretary of the London Poor Clergy Holiday Fund:

> My wife and I would like to give a fortnight's holiday to a

London parson – really as a thank offering for a delightful and unexpected holiday we have had ourselves ... The village of Barley lies in the hills between Royston and Saffron Walden, overlooking Cambridge and the Fens. There are very pleasant walks around Barley, and we have a very pleasant garden. We can offer hospitality to a man and his wife, and a child, or if very small, two ... I would undertake to collect visitors from their door, and deliver them back afterwards ... I do not know what arrangements you make for duty on such occasions, but, if necessary, I would go up and give his congregation a communion service, matins and evensong ... p.s. we have a well-stocked library, grave and gay, serious and frivolous!

I have said he had to be careful with money. He insisted (and rightly so) on being paid for lecturing. Here he is writing to the Rev. Leslie Edgar of the Liberal Jewish Synagogue at St John's Wood in April 1947:

Now as to the difficult problem of honorarium. I will be honest with you. Because I would like to give these lectures I would in the last resort give them free. Because it would take me a considerable time to prepare the lectures and to come to London to deliver them and because I have to live, it is absurd to give them free. I think that a fair honararium would be £10.10.0 a lecture, and I will accept whatever it is possible for you to pay, hoping that you approximate to that as nearly as you can.

He gave three lectures on 'The Relationship between Church and Synagogue since the First Century C.E.' in January and February 1948, and received for doing so a cheque for £21.00.0: a fee of £15.15.0 and travelling expenses of £5.5.0. No further comment is required.

What else was he, besides being a scholar and a gentleman? Proust says that 'men who are governed by an idea are not swayed by self-interest'; it is a truth to be observed of James Parkes. There are other quotations that also apply. One is Psalm 84, verse 6: 'who going through the Vale of Misery use it for a well'. Which is reminiscent of the Hasid Zusya of Hanipol: 'My

Sufferings? What Sufferings?' We need also to bear in mind what was said to Daniel Deronda: 'You have a passion for people who are being pelted Dan.' Or what that *zaddik* of our time, Rabbi Aryeh Levin, said in a devastating comment on Officialdom: 'It is better to work at cleaning sewage than to become an official.' The Jews were a 'pelted' people; James had a passion for them. James never worked in a sewer, but he resisted becoming an official. Power, apart from the spiritual sort, did not tempt him; not after 1915, when aged 19 he had had a 'conversion' experience. The light that then dawned was that power corrupts and was corrupting him as a school prefect. Persuasion was preferable, and it was persuasion by word and example that thereafter governed his conduct.

What were his failings? He may have been prim and proper, though probably not more than was normal for one of his generation and class. He certainly seems not to have been overly interested in sex. Yet how can we really tell? Like others of his generation and class he had all the makings of a confirmed bachelor, until, that is, he got married in his mid-40s. Sometimes one fancies him a prig, but wrongly in the sense of the dictionary's definition of 'one who cultivates or affects a propriety of culture, learning, or morals, which offends or bores others, a conceited or didactic person'. As his biographer, James does sometimes strike me as arrogant. There is little evidence, however, that he struck his contemporaries as such, although in certain aggravating situations, such as being on a committee, when, having to deal with the officious and slow-witted, he would become impatient and express his views with some force. He was not, however, conceited, although he can come across as being so in his autobiography, *Voyage of Discoveries*. Reading *Voyage of Discoveries*, one might think that he was a self-obsessed bore; on the contrary, there is overwhelming testimony to what delightful company he was. Laughter, not didacticism, was what the visitor discovered in the study at Barley. He did offend from time to time, but it was either towards those who deserved his scorn or who were liable to take offence very easily. It may be that he treated a few friends in a cavalier fashion: Bill Simpson for example. It is not easy to penetrate the good manners of that distant age, when courtesy was still a way of life. He *might* have hurt Bill Simpson; other notable casualties there were none, unless I have been forgetful and they have been forgotten.

An unexpected oddity is his apparent lack of spirituality; this appears to be as obscure as his sexuality. We need to stress 'apparent' and 'appears', a person's spiritual proclivities being an even more private matter than her or his sexual inclinations. Take, for instance, the one surviving Christmas Circular Letter that I have been able to find. It is from December 1954. It is not in the least religious (let alone spiritual). The content is thoroughly, not to say resoundingly, secular. There is not even a 'God Bless You' or a 'Peace Be With You'; all that the friends of James and Dorothy are given are 'greetings' and 'best wishes for the future'. Can it be used in evidence against them? I believe it can. After all, though it is sometimes hard to believe, James was an ordained priest. When he told a Miss Brade of Kurrajong, New South Wales, in 1961 that she 'had passed right out of [his] sphere of understanding with Ouspensky and Gurdjieff' and that he was 'convinced that although they are fascinating from the standpoint of first-century Judaism and archaeological discovery', the Dead Sea Scrolls 'are very unimportant in relation to the history of Judaism and Christianity', we appear to have found James' blind spot. The English mystics, let alone Jewish ones, seem to have had not the least resonance for him. In this he is very much a child of his late Victorian generation. Rationality and reason guided his approach not only to life, but also and more importantly to religion, his own practice of it and the accounts he wrote of it. Might he, therefore, be said to have failed to understood it? In the final analysis, I think he might. Because he did, could we go further and say that in consequence he misunderstood the nature of the world's principal problem: that men and women love each other insufficiently? I think we could. 'We will abrogate reason and love one another' would in some quarters be regarded as a recipe for disaster. St Francis, following Jesus, and Jesus following the Torah, would have seen it as the only way to salvation. A reviewer, writing in 'The Plain Dealer' of Cleveland, Ohio, in May 1931, about James' first book, indeed his first published piece of writing, *The Jew and His Neighbour*, said the author argued 'that with patience and good will, the [antisemitic] question can be unravelled and resolved'. His tone was critical. Was he not right to be? Had he not identified the humanistic fallacy at the heart of James' thinking?

This is not at all the same thing as saying that his writing, whether on antisemitism or anything else, is not worth bothering about. Far from it: James has many truths to tell. Moreover, his flight from other forms of knowledge than the rational, his emphasis on knowledge as non-mystical and (above all) non-quietist is in the circumstances understandable. Everywhere he turned in the 1920s he saw backs being turned on the idea of the achievability of human good by the ordinary human devices that had apparently served Europe so well until 1914. God, he came to believe against the grain of contemporary religious thinking, worked through men, men in political, social, and economic communities. He did not send angels any longer to tell us how to behave. He described this development to Professor W.D. Davies of the Union Theological Seminary on Broadway, New York, in December 1965:

> From the trenches in the first world war onwards, my whole life has been concerned with the attempt to find a solid and acceptable basis for Christian action in the social, political and international fields. Not only was it impossible to find this, but I witnessed, at a time when men desperately needed to discover and uphold moral foundations for their political activity and responsibility, the whole non-Roman world slide into the hideous heresy of Barth and his followers. And the Romans were no more positive. It was at this stage of my career that I was forced, quite unexpectedly, to study post-Christian Judaism ... The failures of Judaism were as obvious as the failures of Christianity. But more and more I was brought to realise that I was studying, and coming to understand, not an incomplete Christianity, or an archaistic *preparatio evangelica*, but a different religion, based on a different quality of divine action. And it was only very slowly, and with many years of study that I came up with the answer: this is how God works in the natural community. The chosen community of Christianity does not replace it. The two are meant to live in creative tension with each other.

The 'complementarity' of Judaism and Christianity did not appeal to all. It did not in fact appeal to many. Because Judaism preceded Christianity, it was easy for Jews to argue that it could stand on its own: God had no need to reveal himself again. What, in other words, had Jews to learn from Jesus? Christians, on the other hand, could (and in the case of Dorothy L. Sayers most cogently did) ask what had he done with the Incarnation. She wrote James an 11 page letter in August 1944, which deserves the closest attention. 'I have noticed', she said, 'that when anybody starts by throwing St Paul into the waste-paper basket, the next casualty is apt to be St John, and thereafter the rest of the N.T. piecemeal, till nothing is left of the Incarnate Word except a few rabbinical sayings. (At which point, no doubt, it becomes easier to equate him with the Torah!)' James resorted to being patronizing in failing to answer her telling observation: 'No wonder, dear lady, that you like the smooth imaginings of Berdyaev and Maritain ...'. In other words, in seeking to reconcile the two old enemies, he fell, as was often observed, between two stools. But then, he was never content to be merely comfortable.

He was particularly uncomfortable with 'smooth imaginings', those of Karl Barth above all others. Karl Barth he held responsible for the conversion of many young Germans of the reading classes to Nazism, and as Nazism produced the Shoah, it could be said that Barth's advocacy of political disengagement was not uninfluential in shaping the twisted path to Auschwitz. James Parkes and the Shoah is a topic reserved for the conclusion. Here, however, one thing should be said, and it ought to be in the words of Ralph de Groot, who in 1948 had chaired a meeting at which James had spoken about antisemitism. Ralph attended a talk I gave on James Parkes at Mamlech House in Manchester in 1999 and afterwards he wrote to me:

> The gradual shift from the traditional 'We accuse you' to 'We forgive you' after the Vatican Council, and to 'Please forgive us' since the fiftieth anniversary of the Holocaust, has been a remarkable phenomenon. James Parkes would have rejoiced.

So he would. Nor should we forget the part he played in the genesis of that 'remarkable phenomenon': the good men do lives after them. What would not have pleased him is the transformation of the Holocaust into an Academic Bandwagon. How has Holocaust Memorial Day been celebrated at one English university? With a 'Drinks Reception' followed by 'Poetry and Song'.

He could not have foretold so crass and insensitive a development. James was not a prophet. Take, for example, a paper he wrote for a meeting of the Saffron Walden discussion club, the Duodecimos; (its monthly meetings were 'one of the pleasures of local life', he wrote in *Voyage of Discoveries*). His paper of July 1961 was entitled 'So Why Not Be A Communist?' It begins:

> If [only] the politicians of the world were adult, or, it may be, if the public opinion and press of the world desired that its politicians should be adult ... But politicians are not adult ... and it does not seem that the press and public opinion of the world want them to be different ... So we have to reckon with the world as it is, not as we would like it to be. And, looking at it as it is now and is likely to develop during the next half-century, would it not be much more sensible for us in the West to accept the inevitable, and all become communists? For, as things stand, all the trumps in both politics and economics lie with the communist powers.

He was far from being alone in holding such views: in the 1950s I was taught in history classes at school that Stalin's Five Year Plans of the 1930s were among the Wonders of the Modern World. Unless, that is, James was right: perhaps the world would now be a better place had we all become communists (of a sort).

By the 1970s James was pinning his hopes for a Brave New World on the universities; we can see and hear him doing so in a video recording of an interview he gave in 1974 to an American television journalist. He put particular trust in the theology departments of English universities; this was precisely at the point when the overwhelming majority of them were either being reduced in numbers and influence, or were being closed down entirely. In the new universities of that and the two succeeding decades no departments of theology were conceived of, let alone founded. If James had been able to see into the future his hopes would have been drastically curtailed: Islamic fundamentalist terrorism was already coming to maturity at the University of Cairo, while in the United States colleges of a certain kind were cultivating a Christian evangelicalism, usually as fundamentalist and sometimes as violent as the Islamic variety.

In fact, the world of 'the next half-century' has not become the world James had hoped for. It is more like its opposite. James looked for a universal culture, but he could never have anticipated the globalization we now have. If he had been more of an economist he might have done, although not even an economist could have predicted the rapid subjection of nine-tenths of the world to a 'culture', which Rabbi Jonathan Sacks has described as being:

> as powerful as Greek and Roman civilizations, Islam and Christianity, but the first to have no ideology or state or religious backing. It is as devastating of local cultures as any of its predecessors. It's a globalization brought about by the market, by international corporations and the global economy and it's another leviathan which is causing great economic inequalities and instabilities, and threatening to replace all local cultures with a kind of Coca-Cola MTV substitute.

James would also have agreed with Rabbi Sacks' view of the Jewish role in this Cowardly New World: 'Every time a universalist culture has demanded a price in human suffering. I think the single most important thing the Jews have had to tell the world is that we need the courage to be different and the tolerance to make space for difference.' Were he alive now James would have agreed: it all comes back, at least in the Western and Middle Eastern Worlds, to the Jews. Those of us who desire to be different, those of us who want to resist the American Corporate version of *1984*, those of us who will have to become the ideological guerrillas of the twenty-first century, what better example is there to follow than that of the Jews. We are all Jews now, I once sermonized my students.

What James would have made of the decay of Christianity in Western Europe it is hard to say. Proust thought that at some future date 'caravans of snobs' would arrive at the cathedral cities of France to admire their architectural and artistic remains, all knowledge of religious ceremonies having been lost. The caravans that do indeed arrive at such places these days are of a particular sort of snob, the touristic variety, and their knowledge of religious ceremonies is indeed in most instances exiguous. Churches have become museums, religious objects and ornaments have become cultural artefacts, priests, monks, and nuns have become objects of suspicion and derision. James would have found this, to say the least, incomprehensible. On the other hand, he might have found consolation in the fact that of the two million Muslims in Britain a great many are devout. I doubt, nonetheless, that he would have regarded the failure of Christianity (a process he had been proclaiming from the 1930s at the latest) as the end product of the Copernican Revolution, the Renaissance, and the Enlightenment, for all of which he had such a pronounced admiration. Towards the end he possibly may have done, at any rate according to the formula in which the religious commentator Karen Armstrong has expressed it: our rational, logical, scientific culture makes 'perception of the sacred psychologically impossible', for we have lost 'the mythic sensibility' of the pre-Reformation mind, given up trusting in our own perceptions, and put our faith in self-styled experts, among whom the last and the worst are so-called business managers. Where there was once correspondence, there is now disjuncture.

Not that James ever lost hope, either in God or in Man (I am less sure about Woman). It was not in his nature, or his nurture, to do so.

It is a bleak outlook. Nonetheless, it is one that a friend of James and a far greater historian than he, Sir Lewis Namier, shared with the wife of the Venetian detective. 'The complexities of man-created problems', wrote Namier, 'now transcend the capacities of men.' It is true that Namier, as his widow relates in her biography, could interpret the behaviour of a single rude and officious ticket collector at London Road railway station, Manchester, as representative of 'the collapse of civilization' and 'the destruction of urbane living', but many a sensible man might do likewise. James would have made more allowances: for the young, for the situation, for his own forgetfulness. He did not come to see the world as in terminal decline, but then he travelled so much by car, had servants and/or a wife for all of his adult life to minister to his needs, and towards the end, unlike Namier, is not to be found rushing about from one meeting to another between London, Manchester, and Oxford.

Sir Lewis Namier, at the close of his life, would have been in agreement with Hamlet (Act II, scene 2). James Parkes would not have been:

> Ham. What's the news?
> Ros. None, my lord; but that the world's grown honest.
> Ham. Then is dooms-day near.

Not that his vision was in the slightest apocalyptical. He continued to say, until he stopped speaking altogether, that humans were in their infancy and that God, because he had created them, would be forgiving until they became adult, however long that took. He was fully alert to the world's pollution, but dying in 1981 did not live to witness the ecological desert unstoppable human greed was making of God's creation. Would he have changed his mind? It is a silly question even to ask: no one can live entirely out of his or her time. What Benny Green has said of jazz musicians is also true of the writer on Jewish–Christian relations: 'Once a musician matures he is saddled for the rest of his life with the nuances of his formative period.' James remained an early twentieth-century thinker until the end.

Unless, at the very end, after he had ceased to be a public figure making public pronouncements, he went through a second conversion experience, as, for example, Thomas Aquinas appears to have done. The Aquinas *oeuvre* fills about six feet of library shelves: looking back Thomas declared it was 'as so much straw'. I have not measured how much library shelving it would take to house the more than 300 written works of James Parkes: I think it would need to be over six feet. It is unlikely that James shared Thomas's realization that there is a certain (and very real) absurdity about a life's work devoted to thinking and writing and not to prayer and contemplation, for he was not a medieval but a modern man. He would, however, have agreed with Wittgenstein, who wrote in a late notebook that he was 'by no means sure that [he] should prefer a continuation of my work by others to a change in the way people live which would make all these questions superfluous'. For James the most important question had been the so-called Jewish one; he had not made it 'superfluous', but by getting us to understand it, he had put it in its place. 'Perhaps one day', wrote the Czech rabbi Michael Ber Weissmandl in September 1938, 'a future method of writing history will determine the value of each nation by the way it has treated its Jews.' That indeed will be the day.

1
Guernsey and Flanders 1896–1919

James Parkes was born on Guernsey in 1896. The fact that he grew up a Channel Islander may have made all the difference. He complained that he was not of full Guernsey descent (both his parents being English), but he was not transformed into a complete Englishman by virtue of an 11-year public school education at Elizabeth College, Guernsey. What happened outside school was more important than what happened within it, so that by the time he was nineteen and departed the Channel Islands, never to return save on holiday, James had become an independent, bloody-minded Channel Islander. It was a characteristic that prevented him from being the stock establishment anti-establishment figure commonplace in English society. From the start James Parkes was culturally a European.

Reminiscing as an old man, the early years before the death of his mother presented themselves idyllically to his imagination. In *Voyage of Discoveries* and in an unpublished essay entitled 'Holidays in my Childhood', written ten years later in 1976, he elaborated on the theme of the pre-tourist Guernsey of his boyhood, 'a most gorgeous place in which to be young'. It is easy to believe that it was. Not only did James have an elder brother and a younger sister to play with, he also had an ingenious father who made boats for them to paddle out to sea in and model yachts for them to sail: 'David had a lugger schooner, I had a fore-and-aft schooner with top-sails, and Molly had a ketch. Their steering was so beautifully adjustable that we could sail them out to sea, knowing they would, perhaps half a mile away, either luff or fall into irons and return according to how we had set their course.' Henry Parkes, ex-civil engineer turned tomato and melon grower, never did anything by halves. His second son took after him in that respect. In 1977, a year after 'Holidays in my Childhood', James wrote to the Editor of *The Guernsey Magazine* of his father's business:

> My father came to Guernsey in 1894 or 1895 in order to grow melons and tomatoes ... He bought Gorseland Vineries and Les Fauconnaires, which goes with it, from the Miss de Jersey's [sic], who had already built more than a dozen greenhouses. My father was a pioneer in grading his tomatoes, so that the fruit at the bottom of the basket was guaranteed to be equal to those at the top. I think I could still grade the fruit, so many hours did I spend as a boy squatting before the baskets, separating *specials* – perfect in shape and size – from A's, larger, B's, smaller, C's, irregular in size. My father profited, when there was a glut, by the fact that Covent Garden would always take baskets marked 'Gorseland'. We usually employed 8 men and, so far as I remember, they were paid between 18 and 22 shillings weekly. The foreman had 25s and a cottage, and part of the greenhouse for his own use ... The stoker came next in pay, as he had to keep the fires in for twenty-four hours a day, and seven days a week ... There was a very careful preparation and rotation of the soil. It was brought in from the top soil of successive sections of a field, stacked and enriched, and left for two or more years; then it passed for a season into the greenhouses; and then back to the field for several more years ... My father gave up several years before the first war, and his average income then stood at considerably less than £500.

Henry Parkes seems to have given up market gardening at about the time Annie Katherine Bell, his second wife and the mother of his three children, died in 1910. Holidays also came to an end with her departure; James wrote that the death of his mother left his father 'very poor'; it is a relative term. Henry Parkes lived until 1944 not ever having worked again. He had an income derived partly from shares and from properties in London and partly from a life settlement made on his second marriage in 1894. Nonetheless, the widower sold Les Fauconnaires and he and his three children shifted to a bungalow he built for them on a nearby hill. James relates that it was a haunted house: the real ghost was his mother's.

He does not tell us much about Annie Katherine Bell in *Voyage of Discoveries* save that she was 'deeply religious', had 'a very independent mind', and 'left a powerful influence on me'. He was 14 when she died and had just been confirmed into the Anglican Church. James was not sentimental, no keeper of mementoes. The books he used for his work and the copies of the letters he wrote in connection with his work he kept, but not much else. He did, however, keep his mother's note to him on his confirmation day. It is dated Les Fauconnaires 4 October 1910. She was probably very close to death. 'My dearest Jim', she wrote, 'I don't know what profession you will choose in the end, but don't let yourself get absorbed ever in your work that you forget to take your share in making the world a happier and holier place.' Over 40 years later a Miss Darke wrote to him, 'Are you the Jimmy Parkes of Guernsey Days?' She had known his mother and sister and had been very fond of both. After James had replied, Miss Darke wrote again: 'I had not known you were ordained; how very glad your mother would have been. She always hoped that one of her sons would be a priest.'

James chooses to tell us no more about why he was ordained (indeed of his ordination itself he makes something of a joke) than he does of why he volunteered to fight in the Great War, his part in which he also takes lightly. Where the fighting was concerned he did, he informs us, 'as all my contemporaries were doing'. Not all his contemporaries joined the priesthood. James Parkes was in every way un-clerical; he might even be said to have been anti-clerical. A dog-collar no more became him than did a tie; he seldom wore either. Looking at the photographs of him as a young man at large in Central and Eastern Europe in the late 1920s and early 1930s it is impossible to believe in him as an Anglican clergyman. Yet that is what he had become in 1923. He wrote, when commenting on Philip Toynbee's critical review of *Voyage of Discoveries*: 'I imagine he would be happier if I had led a frightful life of sin before I discovered religion. It was too tame for our Philip to have taken to religion naturally.' James was probably naturally religious; if he was not, he naturally took to religion under the influence of his mother, and after her death under that of his cousin, Christine Ozanne, daughter of the rector of St Martin's, the church of the parish neighbouring that of St Andrew's in which Les Fauconnaires was situated. He says as much in *Voyage of Discoveries*.

Can one also naturally become an Anglican priest? A young man, on his own admission, formed before 1916, and not entirely transformed by the war he then fought in, might have been ordained in 1923 without thinking much about it. Religious young men of that generation, or like William Temple of the generation immediately preceding it, often found themselves in clerical orders without overly reflecting upon the matter. James Parkes, nonetheless, was not like such young men in other ways. Why should he have been like them in this? His elder brother having been killed in the War, was he, therefore, doing what his mother had wished one of her sons to do? He says in *Voyage of Discoveries* that during his last 18 months at his school, Elizabeth College (where incidentally he acquired no religion whatsoever), a period 'unquestionably the most formative in my life', he 'had no thought of being ordained'. He cannot, therefore, have given his mother a promise, or made a vow to himself, for example, at the time of his confirmation.

James relates that he had many more serious discussions at St Martin's rectory than he ever had with his father. Not, he says, that there was enmity. The distance between them had to do with his not being a games-player like his brother and sister. He tells us that he was too frequently ill to take part in compulsory games at school and too timid and shy to take part in games organized outside school. Henry Parkes apparently had little time for a son who went 'constantly to bed with appalling headaches', wrote poetry, and knew 'where every flower that grew in the island was to be found'. Moreover, 'my brother and sister adored bathing, and became first-class swimmers, but I was such a skinny little creature that I became blue in five minutes, and was willingly hauled out of the sea to get on with my next [sand] castle'. James was, as we shall see, a first-class builder of sand-castles. However, although early photographs clearly show his small stature and thin frame, he was to fill out before he left school. His filling-out during his final school year we shall come to shortly: it was the making of him. His lack of interest in team games lasted a lifetime. I can find no evidence of him playing or watching football, rugby, or cricket.

What James missed by being non-participant in team games is amply demonstrated by a failure throughout life to be able to engage with others in any cooperative enterprise. He could run things, he could organize others, he could direct, he could delegate, but he never was any good at being one of a team, his brief encounter with the Common Wealth party in the Second World War proving the point. Moreover, he knew as much. In a conversation recorded by Dorothy in November 1956, when it looked as if James, having suffered a second heart attack while recovering at Menton from the first, might die, he was in an uncharacteristically self-reflective, and even more uncharacteristically self-pitying, mood:

> I went into details of James's past history with him – starting from his childhood and the fact that in a sense he had had 'no home upbringing' due to his Mother's death when he was 10 [sic] – his sister being torpedoed in the first war – his brother being killed at Passchendaele – his own war service – gassing – his invalidism when he left the army – his career at Oxford (spent mainly in an invalid chair) – his brilliance – his later career – his return to England and the struggle afterwards – sense of vocation – and all the time, in a sense, his craving for 'a group' or colleagues to work with him, to share the responsibility which he knew he could not continue to carry alone. Dr Mac told me that, for a man of his temperament, the conditions imposed upon him by circumstances (and I am not now blaming anyone) had increased his strain, by keeping the 'spot light' on him all the time. It has made him the leading figure in his own line – but at the price of too great a *deformation proffessionnelle* for his health to stand longer.

His inability to work with others, it has to be said, was supplemented by the inability of others to work with him. That said, the non-sharing of responsibility he subjected himself to is of crucial importance, because for James Parkes the idea of responsibility, whether of a man for himself, of man for his fellowmen, of God for man, or of God for Himself, was central to his conception of creation.

The skinny little runt may not have been a games player. He did, nonetheless, lead an outdoor life and become sturdily self-reliant. The 'no home upbringing' contributed to the self-reliance, as did the cooperative that the Parkes' household became at the Bungalow after the death of Mrs Parkes. The cooperative is well described in *Voyage of Discoveries*. In this instance, James had willy-nilly to be a member of the team: his 50-year-old father did the shopping, cooking and some of the housework, David kept hens and sold eggs, Molly did the rest of the housework, and James (always the lynch-pin) was treasurer, supervised the school homework of a neighbour's sons for two hours, six nights a week, for two shillings and sixpence, taught a man six miles distant Latin at a shilling an hour, bound books for cash, and did the garden. Responsibility was thrust upon them all; James was evidently happy to accept more than his share. He also became a gardener. Gardening would be a lifelong enthusiasm. It was his sole relief from intellectual endeavour. In the Second World War at Barley his gardening skills not only supplied the extended household with produce, but earned him the money to keep it financially solvent. It is not likely that he reckoned the gardening he did as a schoolboy relaxing; he may never have done so, relaxation not being in either his schoolboy or his adult nature. James came earlier than most to grief, to responsibility (both self-responsibility and responsibility towards others), to hard work, and to an understanding of money and its uses. As a result he came earlier to manhood than most.

Elizabeth College had its part to play in that development. After a year at a Dame School, James went at the age of 8 to the Lower School of Elizabeth College. He was at the College until he was 19. 'We were horrible little snobs,' he is pleased to inform us, and even when no longer little it is likely that snobbishness survived. Less in him than others no doubt: his circumstances at home were at once too earthy and too unusual to make him into the proverbial public school snob. Not being a games player and being a 'complete little swot' he was saved from becoming one of those 'Hearties' who were such a blot on the landscape of public school and university education before (and after) the First World War. He never rowed. He only paddled the box-like 'punt' his father had made for him.

It was in other ways that he was insufferable. Opinionated and a know-all, good at everything he put his mind and hand to, one cannot imagine he was popular. Indeed, only two friends are mentioned. Most boys, even when very ancient, can recall more friends than that. By the time he was 18 he evidently had a better opinion of himself than some of the masters, knowing better than they did on a variety of matters. As Senior Prefect in his final year he knew how to run the school better than the Headmaster did, which he proved by caning the whole of form 4B to bring them into disciplined line. When the Headmaster protested, James argued his case with irrefutable logic; 'from then on I ruled the school unchallenged till I left to sit for my scholarship and join the army'. It is a good story and loses nothing in James' telling of it. Nonetheless, it appears from other evidence that under a weak Head the school had badly disintegrated. There is that indefinable flavour of another age about a story involving the 'whacking' of junior boys by the Senior Prefect. By no means a worse age, yet one in which it is hard to recognize the later James Parkes.

If the boy had already become a man at 14 or 15, he went through two later transmutations, the first in 1914 transformed him into a saturnine Stalky, the second, occurring in 1915, turned him into something completely different. Here is James on the subject of his first metamorphosis:

> Had you asked me in 1913 to say Boo! to a goose, I think I would have been uncertain of my ability to do so. In any case, I would have preferred not to. I was extremely shy, thoroughly timid, played no games, though I was (fortunately as it turned out) an inoffensive lance-corporal in the O.T.C. [Officers' Training Corps], and I was a complete little 'swot'. Had you made the request in 1915, I would have had no difficulty in making the goose perfectly aware of my intentions, and perfectly amenable to them, without having to take the trouble to say Boo!

His analogy of the goose reminds me of the Lithuanian story of the fox who became a Christian. Encountering a goose one day he ate it. A goose should not trifle with saints said the fox. James Parkes was not unlike that Lithuanian fox. He converted to Christianity, setting out on a saintly path, in 1915, but any geese he subsequently encountered needed to beware: there was still a good deal of the old 1914 fox about the post-1915 James Parkes. In 1914 it was two hefty privates at an O.T.C. camp who felt the full force of the new James Parkes. They disobeyed the promoted senior sergeant's order. On being sent for, the two sixth-formers turned up 'full of bounce' to tell him he could not beat a sixth-former. He gave each of them 'a sound beating'.

Thereafter, says James, 'the camp viewed me with a kind of mystic awe'. Getting his way in such a fashion seems not to have long outlasted his subsequent thrashing of 4B. He found another way of getting done what needed to be done, one by which, so to speak, one might have one's goose and still cook it. At this point we need to listen to James once more, and with all the attention we can muster.

He is writing to Richard Acland on 2 September 1943. In an explanation of why he has found the Common Wealth party an invigoratingly new departure and why he has given the movement his support, James writes about what he himself calls a 'conversion':

> not by reading the Bible but, as you would expect from a nasty little swat, from a chance remark in the *Agricola* of Tacitus. At that time my ambition was power, and I had discovered that I could obtain it and wield it – oh, of course with the most benevolent intentions – by imposing my will on others. There is no difference between being dictator of a public school and being dictator of an Empire ... and then came Tacitus [sic] chance remark of a Governor of turbulent Britain who kept the peace not by imposing his will but by the kindliness of his manners and his respect for people ... [This was] before I joined the army as a private, and I tried to carry out my new principles in army life. I discovered it was very difficult and dropped a lot of bricks – I still do. But I also found out that it worked, and did create something quite different from the power dominion I had enjoyed before. And then along comes one Richard Acland and proclaims it as the ideal of a new political party...

No better example of the benefit of reading the Classics need be offered. Nor was Tacitus only instrumental in providing James with a fresh insight into his own conduct. As every man's image of God is humanly conceived, I believe we may discern here a crux in James' image of God. It was crucial for him that God was a responsible God, responsible for what He had created, caring for His creation responsibly. God was not apocalyptic; what He had created He was responsible for seeing through to a good conclusion; a constructive God does not stand by and watch His creation destroy itself. Although not in the slightest mystically inclined, James was in one respect not unlike Julian of Norwich, arriving at her conclusion, 'All Will Be Well', by a completely different route. A responsible God also got things done 'by the kindliness of his manners and his respect for people'. Such language may sound overly reductive: it is not, after all, the kind normally used by James Parkes to articulate his theology. The point I am making, nevertheless stands. James not only re-invented himself for a second time in 1915, but also re-invented his God. Both re-inventions lasted him a lifetime.

'I was', he writes in *Voyage of Discoveries*, 'the last boy to receive a full Victorian education in the classics.' The importance of this cannot be overestimated. James was not the only young man to survive the First World War with 'a full Victorian education in the classics'; he was, however, the only one who was James Parkes, that is a young man already formed before 1916, a young man who had grown up in particular and peculiar circumstances, and who was a Channel Islander. His experiences in the war, as well as the deaths of his brother and sister, have to be taken into account in any assessment of the personality of the ex-officer of 23 who eventually arrived at Oxford in 1919, yet it is my belief that James carried with him into the post-war years a great deal more of his pre-1916 character than did the majority of those of his generation who had fought in the war and survived it. It is a commonplace among contemporary historians that war is trauma. Such a view seems to me to be mistaken. James was neither scarred by the war nor much altered by it. School had altered him; the death of his mother had scarred him. His classical education had been far more character building than the trenches of the Western Front.

What this meant was that James was not a Modernist. There is no trace among his papers of an interest in Modernist literature or art. But then there is precious little interest in literature or art of any sort; James never shed his schoolboy philistinism. Even his early love of Greek and Roman literature did not last. Perhaps the war did have an impact: it did for whatever culture he had in him. This may be a harsh view, however, nor are a man's papers, largely working papers it has to be said, an infallible guide to his cultural interests. Yet, I can recall no reference to music, let alone modern music, to painting, to a novel, to poetry, to philosophy even, in the hundreds possibly thousands of letters I have looked at. There was not a single correspondent with whom he discussed any cultural matter. He may have listened to music on the radio and never thought to mention it. In later years he had a television but seems only to have used it to watch the news. There seems some unaccountable black hole here, not in his humanity so much as in his cultural formation. He was always too indefatigably busy for art or literature. He had built sand-castles and he became architecturally learned, building up a picture collection that in true Jamesian style was more comprehensive than many institutional collections. He also drew in pastels and sketched in pencil. Here his mother's example might have been influential: he gave four of her watercolours of Walton-on-the-Naze done in the 1890s to Essex County Council in 1958. All this, however, was more by way of his doing whatever he set his mind to better than anyone else, than it was art for its own sake: such a concept escaped him. Eleven years at an Edwardian public school receiving a Victorian classical education was the cause of that.

In other words, James never shook off a sense of mission, of the imperial English idea of duty, of the words used by his mother in her note to him at his confirmation, never to forget to take his share 'in making the world a happier and holier place'. The strange form her son's endeavours took to improve the world may have been due to his being a Channel Islander; the impulse behind them stemmed from pre-1914 middle-class England. None of this is to imply that James knew nothing about literature. He certainly knew the contents of the Elizabeth College library intimately. In the 1950s, 40 years on, he recalled his experiences in greater detail than he subsequently put into *Voyage of Discoveries*:

> I have the happiest memories of the Elizabeth College Library, from the days when Mr Rolleston, History Master and 4A, made the extraordinary discovery of a boy who was spending his holidays dusting the books and polishing those with leather covers (not to mention rebinding the Henties, Brereton's and such like which were in fragments) all by himself, having charmed the keys out of the porter. I was the actual discoverer of the Second Folio of Shakespeare ... I found it, covered with cobwebs and dust, shoved down behind the books on the bottom shelf of the end book-case in the sixth form ... I have no idea whether

> the old catalogue still exists. If it does, you would find the oldest part written in a beautiful, rather florid hand ... The next part, in school-boy handwriting is mine ... After Rolleston had discovered me happily engaged, he came in on it, and we did the whole library ... So all the subsequent treasures were our joint discoveries.

With William Rolleston, James 'formed a lasting friendship'. How relevant was the friendship to his becoming an historian? It is not easy to pigeon-hole James Parkes; he resists categorization. He was, however, without doubt an historian, of antisemitism first and foremost, of early Christianity and of First Century Judaism, and of Palestine. He became an historian, as he more than once informs us, because he wished to understand twentieth-century antisemitism in order to do something about it. As we would expect from a man who could not take culture for the sake of it, history was not to be studied for itself, but for what lessons it taught. A functionalist approach was also the one he took in the school library; he did not spend his holidays reading there, he spent them dusting the books and putting them in order. In the same frame of mind he became an historian, reading so that he might put things straight, shaking the dust out of the past so that the future could (would? should?) be happier and holier.

Dusting certainly made him think. It made him think about God. Two of his earliest published pieces, appearing in the *The Student Movement* in 1931, were called 'God and my Furniture' and 'Revelation and a Duster'. Beneath the surface whimsicality they display a Zen-like freshness. Housework turns out to be God's work in much the same way as washing-up is a means of communicating with the Buddha. Both essays begin with the bang that is the hallmark of all James' first paragraphs:

> My home and its contents are my corner of the Kingdom of God – in so far as material things are concerned. There are only two Christian doctrines of possession, both equally difficult to attain, to have nothing, and to have beauty.

> Unless even the Barthians have under-estimated the effects of the Fall, God is not primarily interested in theology.

Hence: 'God and my Furniture' is about making one's home beautiful; 'Revelation and a Duster' is about only having what one uses and keeping it cleaned and polished. Much else of good sense is said. Daily housework, for example, is 'a God-given correction of our professional perspective. It is a time for meditation.' The battle against possessiveness has to be 'perpetual' and an aspect of it is not to lock up those things we do not use: 'A locked door keeps out God more effectively than a burglar.' Harmony is the key to a beautiful home, but (and here speaks the Pre-Modernist) 'harmony does not mean uniformity'. Indeed, in describing the furniture of his Geneva flat James is revealed as positively antiquarian, having around him as he writes chairs and tables designated 'Queen Anne, Louis Treize, Elizabeth, George, [and] old Swiss'. His instructions on home-making are specific; they come under a variety of headings that demonstrate how distant he was from the Art Deco world of 1931: 'Beware of colour schemes', 'Expel the egoist', 'Avoid imitations', 'Harmony must include your ornaments'. Comfort is a secondary consideration to harmony. It had to be. A reader might raise her eyebrows at God being equated with a beautiful home; faced with the idea of God in association with that shibboleth of the twentieth-century world, Comfort, she would rightly run a mile.

There is a quaintness, not to say a homeliness, to these two pieces, which even if, or even because, they were written for Christian students, ought to make us pause. For one thing they put us back before 1914, as who after the First World War but someone formed before it would talk in so paternalistic, not to say avuncular, a fashion to young men and women at university? For another, the thinking teeters on the edge of absurdity. When we are told that 'material things are made to be broken', or that 'striped things' are to be avoided, 'patterns which are sincere' being preferable, one begins to see how precisely the designation eccentric suits him. We are clearly not face to face with a man who was influenced by St Francis, let alone by Zen Buddhism, or, so far as I can see, at any time by Hasidism. If James takes ideas to an extreme ('material things are made to be broken') it is to a logical extreme, not a mystical one. He was proud to be called a humanist; he was also a rationalist. He was as rational about God as he was about collecting coins, building castles in the sand, or about hanging sincerely patterned curtains. He must have been severely aggravating to some, a comical character to others. What saved him from being utterly ridiculous was an intelligence of such powerful authority that one was bound to listen to what he had to say, and so infectious a sense of humour that one entirely overlooked the fact that he took himself seriously.

Lastly, and essentially, the two essays are commonsensical. If God might not have intended things to be broken, he surely wants them to be thrown away from time to time:

> It is quite true that the Kingdom of God in the home means lots of other things [than the beauty of the creation], prayers before breakfast, and the sex education of children. But it just as truly means: for *God's* sake get rid of that beastly antimacassar, and that wool mat, and that silly ash tray, and that badly framed and somewhat faded group of the hockey team at your preparatory school.

Unlike modern historians God is not preoccupied with memory. And He undoubtedly does not care for clutter. Nor does He want us to work all the time, computers and mobile phones our constant companions:

> In the office His Kingdom is often something infinitely remote, to be achieved by endless struggle and combat. We stand as watchmen looking over the desert man has made of the world and society, and are conscious only of the difficulties and the immensity of the task. But the Kingdom of God is not merely a Problem. It is also something to be realised here and now; something to be enjoyed; something intensely real, something intensely simple and every day.

Alongside a schoolboy desire to scandalize, the Victorian liberal's rationalism, and all that middle-class, middle-brow good taste, is a grasp of what religion has to be if it is to be truly religious and (therefore) truly attractive.

I have dwelt on the two 1931 pieces at this point not only because they harmonise with the 19-year-old James dusting books in the school library. They also chime with the nine-page play he wrote (almost certainly in 1914) entitled 'Mrs Motherley's Spring Cleaning'. This ends with a confession from a Mr Brown: 'What I say is, I always thought spring cleaning was a beastly business, but we've had some fun out of it, and no mistake.' The remainder of the cast exclaim 'Hip Hip Hooray'. The same green-covered exercise book contains a Platonic dialogue of 15 pages, dated 26 July 1914 and entitled 'Should a clergyman be a soldier?' War, concluded Socrates, because it was not recreational but was dangerous, was not cricket; it was not to be undertaken by the clergy under any circumstances. Even before Britain had declared war, it seems that it was on James' mind to fight in one. Had it also entered his mind to be ordained?

Another exercise book contains poems. James called it 'The Black Book' and continued to write poems in it during the war and immediately afterwards. He stopped doing so once he had gone to Oxford. Why he should have kept the book is a mystery. Most poets destroy their early work. Non-poets certainly ought to. I propose to impose none of these *juvenilia* on the reader. A short list of some of the titles will show why. 'London from Hampstead' was written in 1914 and dedicated to A.K.C; 'To A.K.C on his Legs' is dated 1915; 'To Belleraphon (my Bicycle)' was of the same year; 'On the sinking of the Lusitania [written in over a crossed-through Titanic]' was also of 1915; 'To a Lady who sent us some Cigarettes (on the train from Rouen to St Omer 1916)'; 'To G.Y.B.T (during an adjutant's lecture)' of the same year; 'On the all important subject of Men's clothes (Daily Mirror)', dated June 1917; 'To an Unknown Damsel (written for a brother officer in hospital)', also of 1917. The verse is so light it is flimsy. It ranges from the moralistic-picturesque ('London from Hampstead'), and the sentimental-picturesque ('To a Lady who sent us some Cigarettes') through the humorous ('To Belleraphon'; 'On the all important subject of Men's clothes': about trousers) and the comic ('To A.K.C. on his Legs'), to the mock romantic ('To an Unknown Damsel'), the maudlin-patriotic ('On the sinking of the Lusitania'), and the nostalgic ('To G.Y.B.T': about Scotland and Guernsey).

The only poem hard to place is 'Francis (buttered on both sides) (during an adjutant's lecture 1916)'. Francis' eyes are celebrated in the first stanza: 'the grey of the seas in autumn / Of the woods in evening / And the grey of the dawning sky / Are dull and dead to the kindly light / That plays in his wise grey eyes.' The second stanza is more obviously homoerotic, as the sunlight on the waves and the flushing dawn 'Were made from the smiles that he / Shed on me / When I was sad and forlorn.' The third and final stanza plumbs the depths: 'What of his voice? / His voice is the music of waves that ceaselessly call to each other / Or the measured monotone / Of some great King of the forest pine / Aloft on his mountain throne.' Aside from splitting his sides, what is a commentator to do with such mirth-making nonsense? This poem does not have the tone of the mock romantic 'To an Unknown Damsel'; it is pretentiously serious stuff. Might Francis be a dog? If he was, the 'obviously homoerotic' applied above to the second stanza will need to be changed. The longer one is acquainted with that third stanza, the more likely it becomes that Francis, otherwise unknown to me, was a grey-eyed, barking canine. Perhaps he had been left behind in Guernsey, and being out of the blessed war had his bread buttered on both sides.

A.K.C., whose legs James commemorated in verse, was Archie Campbell, one of the two school friends on whom he 'could depend absolutely'. Campbell, who by the time *Voyage of Discoveries* came to be written was a Canon of the Episcopal Church of Scotland, and the other friend, William Spiller, were athletic and popular. They, says James, 'constituted a bodyguard when I needed one, not because I might be attacked, but because I had to have quiet when I had a splitting headache'. Two themes here coincide. The first has been touched on above: the homoerotic element in James Parkes' schooldays. Sex is a fashionable subject. I doubt, however, that the homosexual version played much of a part in the close relationship of the three young men. Sex and violence in association are even more fashionable topics, and at first glance the wholesale caning of 4B that James had gone in for when Senior Prefect appears promising. At second glance it looks more likely that beater and beaten were (innocently?) engaged in the culture of physical discipline then current in schools of every kind. On the other hand, young women do not seem to have featured in James' young life as other than helpers and companions, Christine Ozanne and the 17- year-old Baronne de Coudenhove, at whose farm James convalesced after his breakdown in 1915, falling into that category. His sister Molly, 18 months his junior, went off to school at Cheltenham when he was 16 or 17: he appears not to have missed her. In James' male world women, young or old, were second best.

The other theme, one that would turn out to be consistent if not continuous, is that of illness. James was a sickly child, so much so that aged 11 or 12 he had a whole term off from school. As an adolescent he endured severe headaches and suffered 'a serious collapse' when faced with a trial Oxford Scholarship paper in his last year at school: 'I think I had quite a long time before I was able to get up again.' Yet, as senior-sergeant in the O.T.C, he says that he 'never lost a field day ... My scouts and signallers were mostly country boys like myself ... A dozen of us could ambush a battalion and then scatter unseen, to reassemble a mile away'. At another camp he 'was a runner from the hour dot in the morning and the only food I had to eat was a kipper which I snatched from the chap who was taking a dish of them to throw away'. There may be no mystery, simply that James like many young persons was up and running one month, and prostrate the next. The mental breakdown was, so far as one can tell, the only one he ever had; his later collapses were physical and were entirely due to overwork. It is to be noted that his prostration in 1915 occurred *before* his 'conversion' of that year. The two may have been connected.

When it came to scholarships, typically James knew better than his teachers. He would not take a Channel Island scholarship, 'which would have been quite easy':

> In fact, there were often more scholarships than candidates. David had collected one the previous year; but I intended to try for an Open one, and I wanted to get one at Hertford College. This was not only because it was one of the best to be got – it was £100 a year for four years – but because Mr Penney [the Headmaster] was always boasting that he was a scholar of Hertford College. It was foolish of him to deny that I had brains; for it would have been more sensible to have told me that brains were not everything. But, as he did deny it, I intended to place before him the dilemma of either stopping to boast of his Open Scholarship, or of admitting my intelligence.

James 'duly got the scholarship ... and Mr Penney did not say or write a word of congratulation, though it was the first Open Scholarship the school had collected for twenty-five years'. When a boy gets to 19 he is likely to be both too old to be at school and too big for his boots, his school boots at any rate. He is also likely to be at loggerheads with his headmaster if only because the headmaster represents authority in a way that form and subject masters no longer do. I was always at loggerheads with mine. Besides, at such an age disrespect for authority is healthy as well as natural. Everything changes at university, where a different kind of authority is encountered. James did not, however, go immediately to university. He went to war, where he encountered senior officers, the majority of whom were like Mr Penney, less intelligent than himself yet giving him orders which were often silly, sometimes mad, and at the Front dangerous to execute. As he said of the generals he came across in France and England: 'they were a remarkable collection of absurdities'. Whether each one was is not the point; James perceived them as such. Later, he was hardly less critical of bishops (William Temple excepted) than he had been of generals. This distrust and disdain of those who took on authority, rather than had it thrust upon them, became second nature to him. Importantly, it meant that he himself shied away from positions of authority. It was not responsibility he disliked; quite the contrary. Nor was it that he did not have an authoritarian cast of mind, for, as we have seen already and will see over and over again, he could and did take command as well as the initiative, often over the heads of his 'superiors'. What he would not do was join the ranks of the so-called great and good. He could never have become a headmaster. He could not be a political party leader. He would not accept a peerage when one was offered him. He would never have become head of a college. He was adamantly not a professor. As for Honours, they had to be declined. When James commented in *Voyage of Discoveries*, that Mr Penney's 'hostility probably did more to allow my character to develop than his friendship would have done', he was speaking nothing less than the truth.

There were plenty of Penneys in the army. The second chapter of *Voyage of Discoveries*, 'Studies in Black and White: Soldiering in the First World War', is full of them. Seeing the First World War through James' eyes one is bound to wonder how that war was ever won, until one realizes it was won by the Americans. Like Solzhenitsyn's indictment of the Old Regime in *August 1914*, James' chapter on his experiences as a soldier serve to underline the moral and mental bankruptcy of the British elite. The treatment the 300 privates of his battalion of the Artists' Rifles received at Rouen in March 1916 beggars belief: 'we, who had been 300 on arrival, were only 146 when we entrained for Saint Omer ... Five were dead, and the rest were in hospital.' It was not all bad ('Black'), as James, bending over almost horizontally backwards to be fair, immediately redresses the balance with a good ('White') story about a civilized Commanding Officer and a humane corporal at the barracks in St Omer. Historians cannot be so particular; they have to generalize. Observing senior English officers through the eyes of James Parkes, a highly intelligent outsider of a very special kind, enables one to understand why twentieth-century Britain was already in steep decline in 1914. This in spite of his reticence, indeed the humility, with which he treats his own front-line experience, if he may be said to have treated it at all.

James' war was divided into four phases. A first brief period as a private in the Artists' Rifles began on 5 January 1916: he went overseas on 3 March 1916 and was invalided home on 19 May 1916. Like the confirmation letter from his mother, and his sketchbooks, Army Book 439 was among the few items James bothered to retain throughout his life. As it contains two errors on two pages, and his demobilization papers (on a single sheet) contain another, it is yet further testimony to the incompetence of those who ran the British Army. It had not been heroics that had landed him in hospital for three months, life at St Omer being 'delightful', but a *citron au vin blanc* with water straight out of the canal':

> The poisoning that resulted was extremely complicated, because I had just been inoculated against typhus, and it had half taken. All the glands of my neck swelled up until I could not open my mouth. For three weeks I more or less lived on aspirin and three daily doses of medicine. I remarked to the sister that it was fortunate the medicine was so pleasant, as I could eat practically nothing. She laughed and told me it was just port wine! Such is the consequence of being brought up a complete teetotaller! ... About three doctors visited me daily, but they could not decide what was the matter with me. So no eatable diet! On the whole I was much more nearly killed by the R.A.M.C. [Royal Army Medical Corps] than I ever was by the Germans.

Philip Toynbee ridiculed the number of organizations abbreviated to their initials in *Voyage of Discoveries*, and the annoyance they caused the reader; he might with equal justice have pointed out the abuse of the exclamation mark: note the redundant three in the passage last cited. were they are a measure of James' autobiographical embarrassment?

Ending up at a hospital in Warwickshire, James discovered Maxstoke Castle and its tenant the Rev. David Lee-Elliott. He spent, he tells us, 'most of my subsequent army leaves' at Maxstoke, where to the father of A.O. Lukyn-Williams he was 'Little Jim'. To those who had known him in Guernsey he had always been 'Jimmy'. We must remember these affectionate diminutives: our image is of 'James', the middle-aged if not elderly man, the august sage, the statesman-like scholar, the righteous gentile, and it needs to be modified by the 'Little Jim' of earlier years, impulsive, handsome, witty and downright bolshie. When James knew Maxstoke Castle, it was a V.A.D. [Voluntary Aid Detachment] hospital; he seems to have ignored its medieval past.

The second phase of his war begins by James becoming an officer, or rather began with him training to become one in the summer of 1916. He was commissioned as a second lieutenant in the Queen's, the Royal West Surrey Regiment, in December 1916 and went overseas in mid-January 1917. After a short stay at the 'abominable "Bull Ring" at Etaples', he went into quarters at Wytschaete, north of Messines in the southern sector of the Ypres Salient. Here, aged 21 he acquired his first batman, one Johnson, 'a man about twice my age ... kindly and efficient'. Johnson was the first of a sequence of man-servants whom James employed, for he carried over the batman habit into civilian life with Thomas Thomas and John McNeilage. This was the active service phase of James' war; it lasted no more than six months but was crucial in his development; and he tells us next to nothing about it. Here *in toto* is his paragraph on the subject:

> The life of an infantry subaltern in the Ypres Salient has been described so often that I have nothing fresh to add to it. In my last period in the line I was in command of the Company for the simple reason that I was the only officer still alive. But I had, without knowing it, collected a dose of mustard gas. It was realised only when I suddenly went

blind on parade some days after we had got out of the line. By various gradations I moved from hospital to hospital and ended up in London during the zeppelin raids of the autumn of 1917. I never got out to France again.

But he did have more to say, he did have something 'fresh to add to it'. Most of what he said is of critical importance in a variety of ways and therefore needs discussion here.

The first is an incident he afterwards recognized ought to have gone into *Voyage of Discoveries*. In his own interleaved copy of the book he has made a note opposite the page on which the last citation appears: 'An experience at the Messines front should have been put in here. It is on p. 60 in *God in a World at War*.' So it is. This is it:

> I was never a very good soldier, and I was always terrified of getting shell-shock. One day I was talking to a fellow subaltern in the front line, a tough young guy, with no nerves and no imagination; and I envied him profoundly. We separated; five minutes later hell broke loose with a German barrage; and the first thing I knew was this youngster being carried towards me, the horrible sight of a man completely and suddenly shell-shocked. The suddenness of the barrage had already used up all the little store of courage I had, and I knew in my innermost heart I was going to go too – and I began to. And then something – I would say someone – which was certainly not me, just took complete charge of my inside, calmed it all down, and cooled it, and gave it back to me.

There is hardly need to comment on this description of the intervention of God in a human life. It was the closest, so far as we know, that James ever came to a mystical experience, or one that he recognized as such. Where such experiences are concerned, it is worth asking two questions. The first is: how familiar was he with the concept? His reading, so far as one can make it out from the Parkes Library, was not in mystical literature, specifically not in the writings of the English mystics. I think he was probably unsympathetic to, possibly suspicious of, such experience, whether familiar with the concept or not. Secondly (and consequently), did he have the linguistic agility to describe such an experience? His account of the incident at Messines shows that he did not. James was altogether too rationalistic, too pragmatic, too Victorian to describe, let alone appreciate, an event outside his cultural terms of reference. That said, there is no saying to what degree God's direct intervention was influential in his decision to be ordained.

Secondly, he repeated his criticism of higher command in a tape recording of the 1970s. He told Peter Liddell that once his platoon reached the front line during the Battle of Messines, 'there they sat. The staff had no idea of going beyond it. They could have walked to Berlin that day. The Germans were in complete disarray'. Whether his judgement was right or wrong is irrelevant: nearly 60 years afterwards the dim view he took of the leadership of the British army had not altered one jot. There is a photograph to confirm his strictly contemporary disillusionment. On the back of a picture of him standing beside a seated senior officer he wrote, 'this is the idiot I got a M[ilitary] C[ross] for'. He never got one for himself, although the implication of an Oxford *Isis* interview, when that magazine made him their 'Idol' in November 1922, is that had he chose to he could have had one. *Isis* reported:

> It is said that after a raid of the usual devil-knows-what-happened type, when the corps commander was asking subalterns what they had done (or imagined they had done), our idol replied that he had sat at the bottom of a shell-hole eating chocolates. Despite the courage of the answer, he was not recommended for the Military Cross.

Here is a perfect illustration of what one might wish to call 'the inverted heroism' of the English gentleman. It is not usually taken to such an extreme. It could only have been (it has been argued above) by the special kind of gentleman an English upper-class education *and* a Channel Island upbringing combined to make of the young James Parkes. The sheer perversity of such a tendency to ridicule one's own bravery needs to be pointed up, by contrasting it with, say, how a former Prussian junior officer might have described a successful raid into No Man's Land, for a successful raid into No Man's Land is, I am sure, what Parkes was translating 'by inverted heroism' into absurdity for the largely anti-war readers of *Isis*. We have encountered Parkes and absurdity above. If only he had written a full account of his war years. It would not have competed in comicality with Spike Milligan's history of the Second World War, but it would surely have bettered it as an exposé of the First World War for the terrible catastrophe it was. The only good thing about it was that Wilhelmine Germany lost.

Finally, there were other consequences of James' gassing than the obvious ones of illness, an illness from which it took him a long time to recover. He told Peter Liddell:

> I had gone home before Paschendael [sic]. My brother was killed at Paschendael, but I had got home ... As a result of the gassing I never got back to France ... There was no question of me going back to the Front. I never got out of E category for the rest of the war ... I began to question the whole thing before I came home ... I wanted a job where I was saving life and not destroying it ... when I came out of hospital I became a gas officer.

Liddell suggested that James was 'to some extent a troubled spirit', and he agreed: 'I was a troubled spirit, and as I say I realised I couldn't make a decisive move during the war. I came into the Gas work.' Liddell probing, asked: 'Quite consciously and deliberately?' James concurred: 'Quite consciously and deliberately because I was saving life.' He had said no more in *Voyage of Discoveries*; only he says it there unprompted and in his own words:

> Like a good many men in the army, by 1917 I was half way to becoming a pacifist. But I felt that I was not sufficiently detached to be able to take so momentous a decision as it would have been to become a conscientious objector after more than two years in the army. To find a job in which I was concerned with saving life and not with destroying it seemed the right path to follow, and I had had experience of most kinds of gases while at the front. I still looked so young, and I had no wound stripes, that it was quite an important factor in getting the control of men who had come back from France and were much older than myself, that I could discuss with them personal experiences of gas attacks and their effects.

If there has been repetition in this paragraph it has been for a purpose. It seems to me that James, usually so sure of himself, was as uncertain half a century later of what had happened to him in August–September 1917 as he had been at the time. Was saving life a key idea then and later? Or was the young officer who looked, as the photographs testify, more like 16 than 21, who 'was sent off to the Northern Command Gas School', rationalizing at one and the same time a desperate frame of mind and an order that had to be obeyed? A little later, in the winter of 1917, his brother David was killed. He never says what this meant to him. It is certain that it meant more than a little or nothing, equally as certain that one did not talk about such personal grief. It is not that I am wishing to argue that 'something went out of' James Parkes in 1917: probably more went in than out. It is that I feel, and without more information, one can do no more than feel, that 1917 made him one way and another a more sombre, even a melancholic, person than he had previously been. Not that it was either becoming or decent to show it. Only in November 1956 did he admit to his wife the feeling of having been a vulnerably isolated figure.

The third phase of the war for James was his spell as the Queen's Third Battalion gas officer at Sittingbourne in Kent. The stint began when he came out of hospital in the autumn of 1917 and after he had completed the course at the Northern Command Gas School. It ended in April 1918 with a mental breakdown. Familiar themes predominate. There was one 'brilliant officer', Captain Trend, who headed the Gas School at Sittingbourne; there was 'an utterly detestable upper crust of individuals who played bridge and billiards with the colonel, few of whom had been to France, and who monopolised all the extra-pay positions in the battalion without either the will or the competence to do any of the work for which the pay was intended'; there was 'a totally inefficient and unqualified captain', who blocked second lieutenant Parkes' promotion, while taking the extra pay for the work he ought to have done but left James to do. When Captain Trend became camp adjutant, James became head of the Gas School. He was supremely good, so good in fact that he was asked to join the staff of the Southern Command Gas School; the colonel refused to let him go. He tells us of the innovations he made, the special effects he designed, the attention he attracted from the experts in the anti-gas services. He tells us he was working 14 hours a day. In the spring of 1918 he caught the 'flu, but being indispensable continued to work long hours. The inevitable breakdown ensued:

> By the second week I was in a lovely mental condition. The gas officer remained 100 per cent efficient. The personal 'me' was completely delirious. When I recovered I was astonished to find my complicated records were all in perfect orde ... But the gallivantings of the personal 'me' ... astonished me still more! Apparently the M.O. had warned the colonel that under no circumstances was I to be contradicted or challenged; if I was, I would probably go straight off my head ... I had a wonderful time with all the 'high ups'. As I had no inhibitions I told them publicly what I thought of them.

Having been reprimanded by the colonel, the M.O., a 'very nice chap', intervened and James found himself once more in hospital, this time at Fort Pitt in Chatham.

At Fort Pitt it was discovered that he had Dupuytren's contraction in one foot. While being operated on he 'died' under the anaesthetic and was brought round by having wet towels flicked all over his body. At some later point James got Dupuytren's contraction in his hands: hence the necessity for him to type everything. The reader at this point might feel herself justified in exclaiming in exasperation as Philip Toynbee once did: Everything Happens To Him! In *Voyage of Discoveries* James is not only better than anyone else at whatever he does (and he does a great variety of things), his adversities appear to be greater, his sufferings more varied: he even 'dies'!

The reason for such a reaction on the part of the reader of *Voyage of Discoveries* has its origin not in the man himself but in his narrative style. I have said this before and it may have to be said again. It can plausibly be argued that the style is the man, but not, I think, in this case. Consider that Ypres Salient paragraph. It says nothing about what James did. In a culture that carps, criticizes, and seeks to find the Achilles' heel of every hero and heroine, an accusation of false modesty might be levelled at him. It would be a false accusation. It is to mistake man and motive equally to believe his autobiography to be self-celebratory. Dorothy thought it not personal enough. My own view is that in attempting to be self-effacing about his significantly good deeds, James overdoes his skilful achievements at growing tomatoes, building sand-castles, and organizing student conferences. He knew he was good at many things, better than the rest of us at most of them. He also knew he was a lonely pioneer in the utterly vexed question of Jewish–Christian relations, having detected in the 1920s that this was the gravest of issues facing Europe in the first half of the twentieth century. But he does not sufficiently concentrate on that in his autobiography. He diffuses his life into too many component parts. His judgement was not invariably sound: this the additional, unpublished chapters of *Voyage of Discoveries* on Israel demonstrate, although there too he may have been more acute than I am ready to believe, future historians being quite likely to regard Israel as the gravest of issues the world had to face in the second half of the twentieth century (and beyond). In the end, it has to be said that James got his autobiography wrong. Even its title is wrong. But an autobiography is the most difficult of all writing. Biography is child's play in comparison. *Voyage of Discoveries* does James Parkes no good at all, and good is both what he did, and what ought to be – indeed must be – done to him.

A perfect example of how not to write autobiographically occurs as we move from the Sittingbourne period to the Lowestoft period of James' war. He opens a paragraph: 'The average age of a gas officer lasted four months. When I had been a gas officer for nine months, I went down with a violent attack of dry pleurisy.' You see, he seems to be saying, I am not average and look how I suffer for it. Perhaps, he believed achievement was inseparable from suffering. I am not sure how Christian it is to believe such a thing, despite many Western Christians, by concentrating on the Crucifixion and neglecting the Resurrection, evidently having done so. James, however, was not Christocentric, and he grew less so as he became more Jewish. More psychologically relevant, is the undeniable fact of James' own suffering. Nor do I primarily or necessarily have in mind his own illnesses, disabilities and breakdowns. He came to other sorts of suffering early, his mother dying at precisely the moment when a child will feel loss the most, in early adolescence. The First World War took from him his sister as well as his brother: he had to survive more than the usual traumas of that war. How difficult it is for survivors to survive is a commonplace of psychiatry in these days; it was not in 1919, when James faced the post-war world. All this, I suspect, lay too deep for words, even and especially by the time James was 70 and writing *Voyage of Discoveries*. By then a cultural habit of reticence, strengthened by what he went through between 1916 and 1918, had long been the way James coped with the world. Better to do than think, better to think about others than to ruminate about oneself. When the moment arrived to write his autobiography, and he had deliberately waited until he was 70, it was too late: he, who knew how to write lucidly, revealingly, beautifully about everything else could no longer write about himself in that way.

It was the 'attack of dry pleurisy' that ended his career as a gas officer. 'Inevitably', writes James, 'as I was constantly in the gas testing chamber, my working clothes were saturated with chlorine.' He was obliged to resign in the late summer of 1918 and was dispatched, for the bracing air, to a camp of the 19th Queen's at Lowestoft. The fourth and final phase of his war was about to open. It began with a handshake from Captain E.S. Hall, the adjutant, 'a thing I had no experience of an adjutant doing before!' James immediately became the adjutant's assistant. The handshake had been prophetic. Not only was the adjutant's office a haven of sanity, so too was that of the Regimental Sergeant Major: 'I would as likely as not find him solving some problem for somebody.' He soon learned the reason for this unusual state of affairs:

> My first Sunday morning, when I went to the 8 o'clock service in the great parish church of Lowestoft, I discovered part of the answer. The Second in Command, the Adjutant, most of the Battalion Orderly Room, several of the Company Commanders, and a fair sprinkling of n.c.o.'s and privates were all regular communicants.

No exclamation mark was called for, as he cannot have been surprised to find that the officers and men who treated each other so well turned out to be religious officers and men. Nonetheless, one wonders whether after so many 'Black' examples over the previous three years it was not something of a revelation. Did that morning service help him make up his mind about ordination?

At Lowestoft for a few weeks he had a pleasant time. One

does not think of him as a horseman. He had, however, 'learned riding in France – learned it the hard way'. Now he rode frequently, the horse was enormous, unmanageable, and had a will of its own. He tells us that his whole platoon preferred watching him in the saddle than going to the cinema. It would. Or rather: he is bound to say it would. The end of the war brought a return to what he was used to; Captain Hall was released from the army and James succeeded him as adjutant; he was back with responsibility, which he enjoyed, and work, which he did not, as it brought him into contact once again with the donkeys who ran the army, and on one notable occasion the ass who ran the country. Naturally, he got the better of them, invariably doing so to improve the lot of the men under him. Among returning prisoners of war, whose material and psychological needs had been completely neglected by his and their superiors, he quelled an incipient mutiny by re-writing the Special Message to the Army from the Prime Minister. It had been 'the usual double-faced politician's twaddle'. Forged by James, the message was incisive and to the point, requiring obedience for the very good reason that demobilization would be all the speedier for it. It was what soldiers understood and wanted to hear. They did not in consequence mutiny. The colonel, 'an amiable antique but slow [sic] in intelligence', had to be told what to do, and did it, his amiability and stupidity on this occasion playing into James' hands. On another occasion it had not. The colonel had confused a good man with a bad, giving the good soldier a confinement of 28 days he had done nothing to deserve. James, unable to stand the injustice, became a forger again, drawing up a new army record for the unjustly condemned man, regretting only the fact that he could not transfer the 28 days to the old lag who had got off scot free.

By the spring of 1919 he had collapsed again, doing his 'best to expire in a hospital in Norwich': by now the reader is no doubt making due allowance for pardonable exaggeration. It was high time, James decided, that he was demobilized. Confronted on his return from hospital with a War Office demobilization form of 'over two hundred and fifty pigeonholes', he also decided that he should demobilize himself. It was easy enough for him to throw dust in the eyes of authorities who had no notion of what they were doing. So that was what he proceeded to do. As he was demobilization officer he could sign all the necessary papers bar one but as that one had to be signed by the colonel there was no difficulty there:

> If I may be vain for a moment, the form signed by the colonel was an appreciation of the character of the officer concerned, and an estimate of his potential value to the army if he stayed. He had to state whether the officer was capable of regular infantry work, or staff work, and up to what rank his capabilities would allow him to rise ... Mine was the only form in which he had said that one of his officers was capable of rising to any rank, that he was a good battalion officer, and that he could also rise to any rank in staff work.

We might have known it: he could have become a Field Marshal had he wanted to. As it was, James was a civilian back in Guernsey before the Army became aware of his deception.

He ends the chapter with two further illustrations of the idiocy he had come across in high places, with his 'fairly clear belief that I wanted to be ordained', and with the two habits instilled him in the war years, 'which have remained with me all my life'; these were to leave the end of his bed open, and to shave in his bath. I fear that here we reach rock-bottom Englishness, despite the exclamation marks that close his sentences. A fear of being taken seriously on serious matters, particularly serious matters affecting oneself, is among the traits used by middle and upper class Englishmen to define themselves. It is not that middle- and upper-class Englishmen did not take themselves seriously. They did. It was that they feared the ridicule of their peers for showing any sign that they did. Thus, the trivial became standard discourse: the weather, the neatness of one's lawn, what dog one should own, how to make a bed, where to shave. It is no wonder there has never existed in England what has existed in every other European nation, a genuine (and genuinely respected) Intelligentsia. It is no wonder that James Parkes, an intellectual from head to toe, feels obliged to tell us that the two things the First World War taught him were how to make a bed and where to shave off his beard.

James does not quite end there. His final paragraph is about his drawing and painting. 'I became', he writes, 'a keen and fairly competent sketcher in the army. It had started with military sketching as a scout, but it soon went on to filling sketch books with records of the towns and villages of Flanders, and of the trenches.' A number of sketchbooks are among the Parkes Papers. Beneath some of the pencil drawings are comments; here is a selection from the period January to June 1917. On a drawing of Mont des Cats done from the window of an estaminet he has written: 'By means of this sketch secured an excellent omelette and coffee after Madame had shut up shop.' On one of the Ravine, it says: 'Rudely interrupted doing this by uninvited crump. Retired to dug out.' On a drawing of a farm at Scottish Wood: 'One of the hottest woods on the south side of the Salient. Always successful in avoiding it.' On one of Renninghelst: 'In this town live the only two honest Belgians I met. Did this from Padre's billet. First met Pelham here.' On one of Cassel: 'Was spotted by Military Police doing this so had to go and get a pass from the P.M.' On another drawing done at Mont des Cats: 'Went up one evening with Paul Nash and did this.' On one done at Watten two miles from Beyenghem: 'Two Madames and a Mademoiselle much interested in sketch. Secured a vin blanc on strength of it.' On one of the church at Beyenghem: 'From C Company billet. Subsequently had tea with C Company. On the strength of these [sketches] of B. invited to take port with C.O. Accepted invitation but not port. Also invited to dinner. Did not go'. Finally, on a sketch of the 'Rat Kolony' at the Ravine: '83 Germans captured here 7 June.' Had he captured them?

If he had, he would not have told us. An uncle of mine never said a word about his four years in the trenches. It is not in the habit of survivors to speak: how can those who have not been where they have been, seen what they have seen, suffered what they have endured, ever understand? If we add to this the strength of their feelings for those who did not survive, what is there to say to those whose experiences cannot compare with their own? It is, therefore, impossible to know what the First World War meant to James Parkes. We have to ask, because it must have meant something; it probably meant a very great deal.

James was not yet an historian, so he did not write about the war as R.H. Tawney and Marc Bloch wrote about it. He was not a poet, for all his versifying, so the war did not have the meanings David Jones chose to find in it, nor was he, for all his sketching, an artist, so that it did not impose itself upon him as it did on Stanley Spencer. He would never be a philosopher or a politician, so it did not have the impact on him that it had on Heidegger and Hitler, driving the one into mysticism and the other into fanaticism. But then James was not German: neither mysticism nor fanaticism held any attraction for him. The war did not drive James to anything. Paradoxically, and despite the predominance of 'Black' over 'White', it confirmed his conviction that men, with the grace of God, could put the things they had got wrong right. It is hard to believe that experience had not knocked the stuffing out of this pre-1916 view of the world. But then James was not Augustinian either, having, as we shall shortly discover, not the least sympathy for Lutheranism. Original Sin was a notion that did not impress him. Because in wartime James could more effectively put things right, get things done, more evidently see the changes that *his* kindness, *his* intelligence, *his* acting responsibly made in the lives of others, than was ever the case in peacetime, his spiritual optimism survived not only undiminished but enhanced. It would take more than a world war to dent the confidence of James Parkes in God and Man.

2

Oxford and Geneva 1919–35

Oxford had nothing to offer James when he went up in October 1919. Nothing intellectually challenging that is, as collegiate life at Hertford no doubt eased the transition to a civilian existence. He read classics for two years and then switched to theology. Predictably, his tutors were no match for him, and he was soon playing the games with them that pass for education when clever men get together to while away the time. He provides examples in *Voyage of Discoveries*; they do not impress. In his final year, typically he took as his Special Subject a course advertised in the Faculty List that no one at the university was qualified to teach: Early Christian Art and Architecture. No one had taken it in 28 years, he tells us with the usual exclamation mark. Consequently, he had to go to the British Museum one day a term for instruction; it seems insufficient but it was all James needed. However, he caught measles just before he was due to take Finals in June 1923, and was therefore unable to impress the examiners in the normal manner. He was able to do so only at a *viva*:

> I had been an expensive item, requiring a special supervisor and a special paper ... so the examiners felt that they could examine me themselves without incurring further expense. They produced the exam paper, asked me how I would answer this question and that, until gaining confidence, they adventured in too deep ... 'Just in a sentence or two, Mr Parkes, how would you construct a dome?' I gazed at them with infinite compassion: 'I cannot tell you in a sentence or two', I replied. You must first tell me whether it is to be an in-centric or an ex-centric dome, and am I to construct it on a horizontal or vertical axis?' 'Thank you very much, Mr Parkes, that will be all', they quavered gasping, and I departed rejoicing. They thus afforded me the final joy of undergraduate life, that of flooring my examiners!

The upshot was that, though he could only be awarded an aegrotat, the examiners wrote a letter saying that from what they had seen of him, 'I had reached the level of a First'; having earlier told the reader that he 'was not fit enough to do the hard work which would have got a First', such an outcome was clearly the best there could have been. Oxford has got the better of many good men; James got the better of Oxford.

If Oxford had little to offer James Parkes, he had a good deal to offer it and he did so. For one thing he made quite a splash socially. Strikingly handsome, and equally strikingly intelligent, he duly became the *Isis* idol of November 1922; he probably wrote the *encomium* himself: it is in his self-deprecatory manner. He is mentioned in the autobiographies of Evelyn Waugh and A.L. Rowse, the latter being impressed by him. Parkes thought Rowse, 'not at all a conceited young man ... He became conceited and self-centred after he got his Fellowship at All Souls, but in my day he was rather shy and very pleasant to meet.' They were not friends. Indeed, James appears not to have made friends at Oxford; he does not mention any in *Voyage of Discoveries*, and I have come across none in his correspondence. Much is missing from that correspondence, just as not everything is included in *Voyage of Discoveries*, yet my impression is that James had no genius for friendship. Or rather, it seems friendship was something he could do without. This does not mean he did not have friends, and some of those who supported him after he came to England to live in 1935 meant a great deal to him. He did not, however, 'make friends,' as the phrase goes, or if he had made friends at school, in the army, or at Oxford, he did not keep them. He had no old friends from these early years. Had he been too hurt by loss to be able to give himself in friendship? It may not have been only a brother and sister whom he had lost during the war. Such friends as he may have made then he might also have lost, the casualty rate among subalterns being what it was. In the social whirl of post-war Oxford, James was perhaps more an observer than a participant. He was not distant, but he did keep his distance.

What he did throw himself into was the League of Nations Union. He became secretary of its University branch at a time when hopes were still high that the League might achieve the sort of international cooperation that had been lacking prior to 1914. These were also 'the great days of the Student Christian

Movement', and James before becoming secretary of the L.N.U. had been involved with the S.C.M., making his first contact with William Temple, who would be a stalwart supporter of the younger man until his death in 1944. James would become an employee of the S.C.M. when he left Oxford; meanwhile, he gave most of his attention and all his energies to the L.N.U. In a revealing paragraph of *Voyage of Discoveries* he describes those years in terms that bear repeating here:

> There was nothing inconsistent in my finding my interest in the L.N.U., rather than the S.C.M., for membership of the two bodies overlapped a great deal ... In those days neither 'liberal' nor 'humanist' was a term of abuse, and humanist and committed Christian worked together over a wide area of life. Nor were we ashamed to speak of the possibility of 'progress', nor, because we did speak of it, believe in it and work for it, were we utopians or shallow or superficial. It was a generation which had seen too much of the reality of war, and which saw too clearly the immense gaps in the Christian tradition in so far as the human community was concerned, for it to be legitimate to call it 'starry eyed'. Of course it failed to achieve the realization of its hopes ... but it was a noble failure.

It was a failure as noble as that after the Second World War. The conclusion of a war inevitably engenders hopes that necessarily turn out to be false: witness the end of the Cold War. Doomed to failure as were the attempts on the part of Utopians after the First World War to make Europe a safer place, James remained loyal to the ideas that had given rise to them. He never shed his liberalism, or his humanism, anymore than he did a Victorian belief in progress. Can it be said that he never grew up? Not quite. The point of noble failure is that it has been a noble attempt. Were there not Utopians, the world would be entirely dominated by empirical materialists for whom ethics is a dirty word. There would then be more war, more terrorism, more atrocities, more deaths at the behest of pragmatic capitalism. The end of socialism has seen the beginning of unrestricted capitalist warfare: every corporate company for itself. Once business gets ideologically free from morality no one is safe. While James was no prophet, it might justifiably be argued that he knew that without a religion of humanism, the world would take a far longer time to fulfil the promise God continued to see in it.

He worked hard for the League of Nations Union, indeed over-worked for it, as being James Parkes he was virtually bound to do, so that he spent much of the time lying prone in a chair of his own invention; once his year of office was up, the chair was where he wrote his theology essays. One wonders how good they were; his Bible has survived: it is efficiently annotated in three or four different coloured inks. He did not only write tutorial essays. Indeed, he had never stopped writing from his schooldays onwards: editor of the School Magazine, he had also edited, in the months he spent in Guernsey between leaving the army and going to Oxford, the Elizabeth College Records of the War. Before that, in February 1919, he had achieved publication with a short piece entitled 'Demobilization', which appeared in *Punch* in February 1919. At Oxford he composed 'Mary Tudor: A Tragedy in Five Acts'. This, however, was not publishable. He also continued to write light verse. His poem 'Eights' Week Invitations' appeared in *Isis* in May 1922 and is rather good, being an attack on Oxford undergraduate snobbery as seen by an Oxford working girl. More to the point was his first excursion into history.

How much of 'The first Lord de Saumarez and his diplomatic work in the Baltic, 1808–1813', published in the *Transactions of La Société Guernesiase* in 1922, was his own work it is impossible to say. The 12-page paper begins with a handsome acknowledgement:

> The materials of this paper are largely derived from an Essay on Naval Operations in the Baltic by Mr C.F. Adams, an undergraduate of Hertford College, Oxford, whose death at the age of 22 deprived the University of one of its most brilliant students of history. The essay in question was written for a competition opened by the Navy League. It won the prize, and was considered by several historians to be the best monograph on the subject in existence. It is therefore a privilege to be able to make use of it for this paper.

Lord Saumarez, born on Guernsey in 1757, was raised to the peerage in 1831, 'the first time that honour had been conferred on a Guernseyman'. The essay concludes: 'the true cause of the

Moscow Campaign was the refusal of the Tsar to deprive himself of the trade advantages which were secured to him by the presence of Saumarez in the Baltic'. This, wrote James, and it is undoubtedly him, was a view 'by no means hyperbolical'.

The turning of the prize essay into a paper for publication was a double act of *pietas* and was typical of the man we have come to know. He never displayed any such devotion to Oxford, and lost no time in shaking its dust from his feet. In June 1923 he started work for the Student Christian Movement in London. He was 27.

Although in *Voyage of Discoveries* he has divided the next 12 years of his life into two parts, London 1923–28, and Geneva 1928–35, the division in 1928 was more one of form than substance. He changed his employer, shifting from the Student Christian Movement to the International Student Service, and, as he makes plain, Geneva was not London. Otherwise, over the 12 years he did much the same things. The significant break came sometime between 1925 and 1929, when he began to learn at first hand about antisemitism. The consequences of that discovery were both immediate and prolonged: he wrote a book on the origins of antisemitism, which was published in 1934, and he became about as Jewish as a Victorian Christian gentleman could without becoming any less of a Victorian Christian gentleman. That will be the gist of this chapter. The setting for it, however, must first be outlined.

In London his work for the S.C.M. comprised a considerable variety of duties; we might reduce them down to three or four. He was, for example, sub-warden and then warden of Student Movement House in Russell Square. Because 'the House was open to any genuine student ... It was not', he says, 'the easiest place to run ... Success at the house was like liberty. It was only gained by perpetual vigilance.' He created a self-help 'Guild of Happy Carpenters' to keep the furniture and fittings – which were heavily used and abused – in an acceptable state of repair, and a drama group, where audience participation was encouraged, in order to make new members, especially foreign new members, feel at home. As he had done in the army, he offended his superiors by treating his subordinates as responsible human-beings, especially the middle-aged woman bursar, an against-the-grain appointment by James, who turned the deficit-making restaurant into a profitable enterprise. 'The House, with its financial, moral and intellectual problems had exhausted my excellent predecessor'; it did not exhaust James Parkes. He was much helped by Zoë Fairfield, when she became chairman of the steering committee, and by an honorary sub-warden, Jean Brants, 'whose understanding and sympathy rescued many youngsters, boys and girls, when life in London was becoming too much for them'.

He also devised study programmes. They were based, he tells us, 'on serious reading. I gradually collected the necessary books on current international questions, and these I was ready to lend out, if I could get them into college libraries. I tried to wean students from being satisfied with potted and popular works.' There was in addition 'a good deal of devotional work, especially in taking pre-terminal retreats ... these were the backbone of the term's multifarious activities'. By then, James had been ordained by the Bishop of London, but only after a letter from William Temple had undone the mischief James had caused by refusing to re-take an ordination examination he had found so intellectually unsatisfying he had offered answers unacceptable to the examiners. It was a contemporary criticism of Temple, the Bishop of Manchester, that he ordained unsuitable candidates: one would not be surprised to find that the Bishop of London was among the Bishop of Manchester's critics. James even had a curacy: at St Stephen's, Hampstead, where the vicar disagreed with his view that the Church of England ought to preach the need for repentance and atonement on the part of the nation for 'many things that had happened and were happening in the British Empire'. It was an early brush with a standpoint diametrically opposed to his own: that politics were the very stuff of religion and the church should get itself as involved in the latter as it was in the former. Because it had been theologically arrived at, James never wavered on this point; indeed, once he had encountered the work of the 'loathsome' Karl Barth, it would become an article of faith for him.

He came across what he considered the disastrous influence of the Swiss theologian's work when he travelled to Germany. The major part of his work for the Student Christian Movement, as it was for the International Student Service, when he joined it in 1928, was attending and organizing conferences, chiefly abroad but also in Britain, notably at Swanwick, the Church of England's conference centre in Derbyshire. Each year, having attended three conferences at Swanwick in July, he departed for the continent 'with a rucksack and a programme of travel, holidays and conferences until the Secretaries' meeting towards the end of September'. He had, he goes on:

> a unique position in these wanderings ... In addition to being a secretary of the Christian group, I was a founder of the League of Nations group at Oxford, I was a member of the executive of the National Union of Students, and I was also a member of the executive of the British Committee of European Student Relief. Whatever student group I wanted to meet, I came with a visiting card which proclaimed me a colleague.

In the summer of 1924, for instance, he was at conferences in Bavaria, Warsaw and Prussia; in between he went on holiday to Austria with his two German E.S.R. scholarship students, Franz Schmal and Hans Becker, and spent a week in Prague on his own. In the summer of 1925 he was in Gex near Geneva and Oberaegeri near Zug at student conferences, in Venice and Belgrade on other business, and at Hopovo in Jugoslavia for a conference of the Russian Orthodox Church. At the close of his 1925 wanderings he went to Provence. He had already taken to a German student mode of dress, 'hardening myself with an open collar and, where possible, sandals. This had done marvels, but I still found the English winter – to which, after all, I had never been accustomed – extremely trying.' On a friendly suggestion he tried out Provence 'to get dried out in winter sun. So began a long-drawn out love affair.'. Every year for many years to come he would seek the sun and peace of mind in 'the triangle bounded on the north by Montelimar, on the east by Cassis, and on the west by Carcassonne ... always sleeping the first night at Avignon, always renewing the magic of the South'. His travels on foot, by bus, or on a bicycle invariably ended 'at La Rolane outside Marseilles, the delightful farmhouse where Madame Cru and her two daughters lived'. One of the daughters, Hélène, he had met at a student conference, her mother had been born in Gloucestershire, her father had been a Protestant missionary. He was friendly with these people for over 50 years: the last surviving letter I have come across he wrote to Hélène in January 1979.

If Provence was crucial for James' bodily and mental health, his attendance at these international student conferences was critical for his spiritual and intellectual development. His political allegiance is not so readily to be discerned. Always a liberal and never much of a socialist, he had no affection for communism and little sympathy with pacifism. Among the Parkes Papers is a copy of the *Evening News* of 12 May 1926, a single sheet with the headline STRIKE OVER. Why did he keep it? Had it been with relief or in disappointment that he had read the announcement? He was too much of an individualist to subscribe to a straightforward, secular political ideology. He was also no Little Englander: English politics in the 1920s, stirring as they might be to some, were small change compared to the European extremes he witnessed in Vienna or Prague, Warsaw or Bucharest. Still, the General Strike seems to have caught his attention. Did he get involved? If he did, on which side was it? In a short paper called *'Peace'*, published by the S.C.M. in 1932, he wrote: 'We have solved the problem of poverty, though we can only apply the solution by producing unemployment. We have enabled men to have leisure, but we can only give them a dole to spend on enjoying it materially, and an education stopping at the age of fourteen for enjoying it intellectually.' He ought not, therefore, to have been a strike-breaker.

So much conference-going, so much conference organizing, made him an expert in the subject. His book, *International conferences: a handbook for conference organizers and discussion leaders*, was published by the I.S.S. at Geneva in 1933. It is a wonderful book, one of the earliest and best in the field, as witty as it is wise, its sagacious advice as relevant today as in the 1920s, when conferences appear to have been jollier (if rowdier) occasions than the business meetings they now too often resemble. A few extracts will enable the reader to judge for herself James' practical good sense. Here he is on the time-table, which should not be settled democratically or 'every minute not actually required for sleep' will be filled:

> When the conference is primarily composed of young people, and when evening sessions are contemplated, unhappy is the lot of the conference organizers who give way. The result will certainly be that by the third day the conference is exhausted. Those who demanded the afternoon meetings will probably cut almost all the meetings, and be

found in a neighbouring café or bierhalle, and the duty-ridden will sit in silent gloom ... A meeting may be spontaneously put upon the programme for any hour up to and after midnight, when the conference itself is vitally interested in a particular question ... but the first rule of all programme-planning is to leave adequate free time.

And here he is on excursions:

Delegates should not be rushed from a meeting to a hasty lunch, or to a distribution of paper bags, then flung into motor buses, rushed off for an hour, whirled round a castle or museum, flung back into the bus, and expected to be ready for a meeting at five o'clock ... to such enterprises certain sequelae are inevitable ... either the buses get back late and there is no time for a meeting, or the buses get back punctually at the cost of having left a number of delegates behind ... of having rushed people so scientifically that all the ladies need time to change their clothes and generally tidy up ... and of having everyone else adjourn for liquid refreshment and being undiscoverable until dinner time.

When thinking about a potential site it is 'very necessary to choose with the greatest care':

It should be in a relatively quiet place. A large town is peculiarly unsuited to any conference whose average age is under forty. Older generations may be able to resist the lure of city lights. The younger certainly cannot ... Meals, meetings, and sleeping should not be in *three* separate places ... Distances for a conference and for an individual are not the same ... just across the road or right opposite [for an individual] for a conference [means] twenty minutes ... just up the road [means] half an hour ... ten to fifteen minutes ... [means] a large proportion of the delegates will never find the place at all.

The conference leader's tasks are described with an experienced but not jaundiced eye:

His most difficult task is to deal with the loquacious, the

violent and the fractious member. It will tax all his patience and self-control ... He must also keep an eye open for the Intelligent Silent. There will be some members who are silent because they have nothing to say, and it is useless to force them to speak. Their silence should not be interpreted as boredom. But others are silent through shyness or uncertainty ... if he is convinced they ought to speak, he should see that they are invited, not in a general way, but on a point which interests them.

Finally, there is the immediate environment:

> It is rare that really ideal conditions for a group can be obtained ... Conferences are too often held in large institutions, and equipped only with hard chairs. Rooms are not conspicuous for their aesthetic charm ... It is best that the room should be small ... The temptation to meet in the open air should rarely be given way to – except on the top of a tower, where I once shared in an excellent discussion in Germany ...

And there are the conference types:

> The type of delegate who moves through a conference as though he was always in front of a press camera. He always likes to be seen Talking To The President, or to the General Secretary. There is another type which presumes continually on old friendship or special services, to demand to be in on everything and is perpetually being offended if left out. There are no fixed rules for dealing with such nuisances.

What every conference organizer had to have was 'a salvage corps ... of stalwart old friends', for 'such heroes and heroines' are the 'salt of the earth and the salvation of souls', as on them depends the sanity of the organizer and the success of the conference.

So many conferences did James attend that he called himself 'the wandering non-Jew'. He recalled doing so when replying to a letter from Sir Douglas Robb in September 1960; Sir Douglas had remembered the happier aspects of conference attendance:

> I feel sure the subject of the *Observer* profile this morning is or was my travelling companion to the W.S.C.F. near Zurich in 1923 or 1924. Do you remember calling the bolsters on the Swiss beds 'Mountains of Prejudice'? The two Wrong Girls – young Michaelis from Germany? The Saxon Lutherans in knee pants? I had often wondered what you had worked at and now I am told.

The 'two Wrong girls' demand an exclamation mark. They remind us of how much goes missing of a man's life. They might not have been of more than passing interest, as Parkes does not mention them in his letter of reply, but then again they might not. At any rate, they stand to remind the reader of the biographer's fallibility – his being in this case at the mercy not only of the documents that have survived his subject's rigorous culling but also of what his subject has chosen to say about himself in print. They also should remind reader and biographer of what is rarely recoverable, and hard to recover of an august subject profiled in later life (James was 64 in 1960) as a serious-minded scholar, namely the zest for life of a man who had been through what James Parkes had been through. These were the happiest years of his life.

They were his vagabond years, and in the photographs taken then he looks more like a pirate than a priest; looking at them it is virtually impossible to believe that this is what he was. In one of them he stands with his German scholarship students, Hans Becker and Franz Schmal. He kept in touch with the latter. Franz came to stay at Barley in 1938 and by the time they began corresponding again after the war was a Roman Catholic priest at Todtnauberg in the Black Forest. In July 1945 he was in dispute with his archbishop and in trouble with the French occupying authorities; the archbishop had pronounced him mad and the French had ousted him from the office of burgomaster:

> Now, after seven weeks' twenty-hours-a-day-work, I have been chased from out my office by methods worthy of the SS. And just when I was about to vanquish, my dear Archbishop has declared me mad!! If there were 'normal' times, he would have refrained from trying to send me into a lunatic asylum!!!!! ... Let me say that the French are complete mischief-makers here. Instead of doing their first and

foremost duty to purify the region from the virulent Nazi bazillus, they strive to regain materially what they have lost during the war ... Here in this poor and pious region, they behave as if they were to rival the devils of yesterday. And are duped by them!! ... Never, I have been so badly treated under the Third Reich as now under the Commandature de Todtnau.

Franz, who patently had caught the exclamation mark habit from James and improved on it, did not come through his difficulties until 1947. James did what he could to help from a distance, but was unable to respond to Franz's invitation in 1946 to visit him, being preoccupied with journeys to Israel and the United States. Or so he wrote: one detects that he was glad of them as an excuse. Franz was hospitalized at Badenweiler in July 1946, but in September 1947 he wrote jubilantly:

My very dear James, I am to inform you of a splendid victory. I have been invited to accept a parish 7 km from Ueberlingen, one of the smallest. Enabling me to write and to have lively intercourse with my sisters and friends ... I am unable to describe my joy to have found justice in a very difficult case. DEUS providebit.

James replied in November:

I am glad that your troubles seem to be at an end at present, and I hope you will be able to settle down happily near the beloved Überlingen. I do think about you even when I do not write, and I like to think of you near the beautiful lake on which we spent such happy days. I do not see any chance of getting out to see you for a long time to come.

In his first letter to Franz in 1945 James had written: 'You will be surprised to hear that I am now married. Dorothy came down to work with me during the war and we decided it was a good partnership.' Do the two sentences have an apologetic, even defensive, air about them? Probably not, as Franz, apparently neither surprised nor embarrassed, never failed in subsequent letters to include affectionate good wishes to Dorothy. It is more likely that the James of 1945 was the one who was embarrassed at being reminded of the James of 20 years before, or if not embarrassed, simply sad that he would never see such times again.

They became even better times when he went to Geneva in 1928. The move from an institutional flat in Bloomsbury to the attic of a sixteenth-century town house in the old *cité* can only have been deeply satisfying to a man of his architectural sensibility. In *Voyage of Discoveries* his pleasure in the place comes through strongly. Moreover, he tells us: 'The beauty of my flat was a perpetual refreshment to me in a very exacting job, concerned almost always with the ugliness which men had made of their common life.' The single disappointment, if disappointment it was, was the cold shoulder he received when he turned up at the Anglican church on the first Sunday morning: 'as soon as I mentioned the S.C.M. I received a blast of thundering abuse of everything the S.C.M. stood for'. Anglicanism's loss was the Episcopalians' gain. Thereafter he attended the American church. Its chaplain, Everett Smith, became a lifelong friend, and James gained an understanding of Americans through the many students from the United States who stayed in his flat, an understanding that stood him in good stead when he went to North America for the first time in 1932.

His colleagues at the I.S.S. were also congenial, and as he now travelled even more than he had before, he had a life in all respects to his liking. He was in almost perpetual motion between European universities:

> During my seven years in Geneva there was only one occasion on which I slept for twenty-eight consecutive nights in my flat. Much of my work had to be done by personal visits, and I spent a considerable part of each year in the universities of central and eastern Europe ... Apart from personal visits, and attending conferences arranged by others, much of my work was the evolution of 'study conferences', where we severely limited the numbers [and] spent a whole week together on a very carefully planned programme ... My conferences were designed to deal with sore spots in the body academic, conflicts of nationality, of race, and of political party. We usually met in country hotels in beautiful corners of Europe, moving north or south according to the season ...

At this distance, and despite the racial and national conflicts, it seems, and I cannot help believing was, an idyllic existence, because James was traversing a Central and Eastern Europe still ethnically and culturally pluralistic, not yet ethnically and culturally cleansed, first by Nazism and then by Communism. It is a pity that he did not have the eyes and ears of a Patrick Leigh Fermor, so that he could have written about what he saw and heard. Instead, he wrote a book about organizing conferences. Of course, James did not know that Europe would disappear and (as we have seen) he was neither prophet nor poet.

Nor was he in the least calculating. He was, as the saying goes, generous to a fault, and not only with money. It has already been made clear how generous he was with his time; he was equally open-handed when it came to his space, his flats in London and Geneva being available to anyone who genuinely needed them. As for his money, it too was at the disposal of others, not usually by way of gift, which puts a heavy moral obligation on the recipient, but in the form of a loan, which obliges him only to repay it. James, it goes without saying, loaned without interest and without term of repayment. He was practising, without yet knowing it I suspect, one of the most profound truths of Judaism. Trevor Gugeon wrote to him in 1943 from Putney: 'Long ago in Switzerland (I almost feel it was in another life) you very kindly lent me money when I was on my uppers, besides giving me hospitality in your flat.' Able at last to repay a sum he could not remember he enclosed £20. James who could not remember either was happy to accept it: in 1943 he and Dorothy probably had less to spare than Trevor Gugeon.

In this connexion it is worth noting that as early as 1934 James was looking after a Jewish refugee in Geneva. Having resigned from the I.S.S., he stayed on while considering where he wanted to be when working on the medieval sequel to *The Conflict of Church and Synagogue* and while looking after 'a refugee student at Geneva University':

> I had offered him a room in my flat, telling him that I would need his help in the domestic work. This he promised to give, and would, I am sure, have given, had he had the slightest competence in that direction. As I was living on odd earnings, and had to meet his university fees as well as his board, it turned out a difficult year ... I ended up

a very competent laundryman and sempster as well as cook. For he could not even wash up or make his bed without some completely unexpected disaster. His one thought was to get his mother out of Germany into Israel, in which plan, I am glad to say, he ultimately succeeded.

It is a revealing passage, revealing of the English side of James Parkes, for here in a hapless non-Englishman he saw a lesser breed without those tidy-minded skills that had enabled Englishmen to conquer half the world and make it into an Empire.

It is odd that a man who, priding himself on being self-sufficient, almost always had one or more persons to do his laundry, clean his house, cook and serve his food, help him in the garden and write his correspondence. It was in the nature of the age he had grown up in; it also kept men and women in work. Yet it is still odd. Needless to say, when he married Dorothy she took over the care of his clothes, but they still employed John McNeilage to do the cooking and cleaning, and another young man or woman to write their letters: it is no wonder James got so much done.

Although he was a busy housekeeper in his Geneva flat, he also took time and trouble to teach himself embroidery. There was, as ever with him, a utilitarian reason for the acquisition of a skill. His hot temper we have not yet evidenced, but temperamental he could be, 'difficult' as one former student resident of Student Movement House in London said he was known to be. The countless meetings he had to attend would have tried the patience of Griselda; the committees of the I.S.S., he writes, 'were exhausting assemblies which lasted a whole week ... my temper was usually exhausted by the end of the first day ... with the result that I was a burden to my colleagues and myself for the rest of the week':

> I was wandering through Geneva one evening contemplating with disgust the fact that the whole of the following week I should spend in committee, when I found myself gazing at a shop window full of wools and tapestries. The thought occurred to me that the people who bore with the committees best were the women who knitted. They did not talk when they had nothing to say. They had an uncan-

ny faculty for seeing the way out of a dilemma in which the rest of the committee had got itself bogged down, and their dispositions remained sweet and sunny the whole week. I could not knit ... But why should I not make tapestry? I went into the shop, bought canvas, wools and needles and became a model committee member.

It is one of the paradoxes about our subject that he is so conventional in some respects and entirely careless of convention in others. He certainly did not much mind, if he minded at all, what people thought of him: how he dressed, what he said, how he behaved. He liked to startle. He would have enjoyed quietly doing his tapestry work when all around him others argued ineffectually about what to do as Europe headed for destruction. Unlike Nero, however, he was already doing what he could to mitigate the disaster.

The years he spent in Geneva were not only happy ones; they were momentous for the direction his life was subsequently to take. He tells us as much in *Voyage of Discoveries*:

> Made to think furiously by the increasing influence of Barth, I produced in the Spring of 1929 a tentative Trinitarian theology. Accepting that God in his 'home life' was wholly other and unknowable, I argued that he had from the beginning of creation revealed himself and accepted responsibility for it, and was himself the inspiration of its development. He was its ruler and inspirer as well as its redeemer. My essay had the advantage of criticism and encouragement from people like Temple ... The real significance, however, of this attempt to sum up my thinking from Oxford onwards was that, though I conceived of the Trinity as a meaningful doctrine of the total involvement of God in the whole of his creation, yet I had not discovered any clear guidance to a theology of politics. And there the matter rested for some years.

It is significant that he kept the essay of 1929 and the correspondence with Temple that resulted. He did so, no doubt, because, while his Trinitarian theology altered over the succeeding years, he never abandoned it, indeed did not dream of doing so, for it was the motor of his thinking about the way the universe worked. As we shall see, one of his last unpublished papers, written in January 1974, was entitled 'An Economic Trinitarianism', an ecological adjustment of a theology he had arrived at 50 years earlier. If he were not James Parkes, we might be justified in considering him perverse, not only to have persisted in so unfashionable an explanation of God's relation to creation, but in selecting a Trinitarian explanation in the first place. He could not have chosen a less congenial or more uncomfortable doctrine: 'I remember a learned and very orthodox divine remarking that the Doctrine of the Trinity was sent us for our sins', is the way he opens his essay of 1929. James, however, was never much concerned with comfort or congeniality. If the truth was Trinitarian so be it.

'Dearly beloved Arch-bishop', he wrote to Temple on 11 March 1929, 'I am sending you here a document, which I am sufficiently brutal in the midst of all your other work to ask you to read.' It was he said 'the result of the last ten years of my life ... an attempt to record what those ten years have meant to me in experience':

> If you feel there is something in it, then the question arises whether it is my duty to go on and give my life to trying to understand God along these lines. This is the fundamental question I am facing, and have been facing ever since I chose (or accepted) Ordination and the kind of work I am doing. I believe that it was the will of God ... Does it justify my belief, or have I been fooling myself?

Temple, by this time Archbishop of York, replied encouragingly. 'Your angle', he wrote from Bishopthorpe on 27 March, 'is a new one as far as I know; and it is vitally important to have such portrayals as we can of the Vision of God from all the angles. Nothing matters so much as the recovery of a vital doctrine of God.' William Temple knew that of which he was speaking. He once wrote to a friend that 'one of our great troubles now is that the predominant outlook upon life is formed by scientific and not by religious categories. Causation is much more prominent in men's thoughts than purpose and judgement.' Nonetheless, the difficulty was not likely to be resolved by *any* doctrine of God: the thoughts of women and men in the West were no longer attuned to doctrines of God, however vital churchmen might consider them to be. By the mid-twentieth century most Western men and women were incapable of comprehending God, save in dire emergencies when a woolly idea of 'Another as Helper' surfaced in minds tested beyond endurance. In twentieth-century circumstances a Trinitarian explanation stood a poor chance of acceptance as a version of God; it seems a strange way to have gone about rescuing women and men from the materialistic nihilism that has them in its power.

It is a temptation to be overly critical of the essay of 1929: it is an easy target. Yet, it is as original as William Temple thought it was. There is no point in attempting to paraphrase a thesis that James outlined succinctly enough in the quotation from *Voyage of Discoveries* cited immediately above: God as wholly responsible creator, God as Christ the redeemer, and God as inspirational Holy Ghost. It should, however, be noted that in this 1929 essay of five manuscript pages, God the responsible creator occupies the first three, Christ the redeemer less than two pages, and the Holy Ghost one brief, unpunctuated paragraph: 'I believe in God the Holy Spirit for the manner in which man brings to perfection the plan which God has conceived for him [it] is that is God within us and not we ourselves who through the medium of our progress works to that ultimate perfection.' More unusual than the customary short shrift given the Holy Spirit, on this occasion all the shorter because the essay was written 'between the hours of midnight and four o'clock in the morning, is the place accorded to Christ: He comes a distant second to God. Judaism was already challenging, what it was soon to overthrow, 'my previous acceptance of a Christo-centric divine-human relationship', as James put it in the paper on 'Economic Trinitarianism' of 1974. Or, as he wrote to Temple in April 1929: 'Far be it from me to rearrange the functions of the Trinity! I am only interested in trying to understand the working of "God"' and find the Trinity the best formula of that idea.' The trouble with Christianity is that it can get by with a low-key Holy Spirit, but it would hardly be what it is without Christ.

It is true that the Middle Ages got along without Christ until about the time they were coming to an end, indeed, closure could be said to have arrived when Christ came to be directly approachable, and his mother with the rest of the saints were removed from the foreground or disappeared from the stage altogether. Early Modern Times were all about Christ on the

Cross and Christ in the Eucharist. It is remarkable, until one remembers that both men were a certain sort of Victorian Anglican, that neither Parkes nor Temple thought much, if at all, about Mary and the saints. Neither was a medievalist. Despite James' *The Jew in the Medieval Community*, he was not an historian of the Middle Ages; I believe he may rather have dismissed them. In spite of his characteristic boast that he had read not only 'the sixty-six fat folio volumes of the *Acta Sanctorum*', but also 'the lives of the saints of the Eastern Orthodox Church in Greek, and then the lives of the Arab Jacobite, the Ethiopian, the Armenian, and the Georgian Churches in French translation', he does not appear to have been influenced by the theology of others than the fathers of the Roman faith. And, come to think of it, not much by them either. Where, I wonder, does his Trinitarianism come from? He does not tell us. If he had read more Eastern Orthodox theology he might have given more than a paragraph to the Holy Spirit in 1929, or come to other sorts of conclusion, about its 'function' within the Trinity than the one that he did in later years. It is revealing that he does not think of the Trinity as a means of representing how men and women, despite (or because of) their individuality share humanity with one another in the fashion that Christ and the Holy Spirit are distinct from, but aspects of, God.

Judaism, of course, would play the major part in his subsequent thinking about God, as it did in his thinking about Christ, and for that matter in his thinking about everything else. By 1974 he could write that 'the religious picture of a determinedly Christo-centric Gospel ... has consistently ignored the realities of politics on one side and economics and technology on the other ... there is no adequate theology to guide Christians concerned with political, economic, and scientific life'. While the 'arch-heretic' Karl Barth was still on his mind (and always had been since the mid-1920s), it is clear that Christ was not. The decline of Christ is more understandable than the transmutation of the Holy Spirit into Humanism. It is an inescapable fact of theology that the Holy Spirit can be transmuted into just about anything, and in one way and another in one religion and another the Spirit of God has been a stand-in for God when it has been thought God was, or ought to have been, elsewhere. But God in the Renaissance: can that really be what James Parkes thought? If so, he was no more an early modern historian than a medieval one. We had better hear him first before commenting further.

In March 1967 he wrote to Murdoch Dahl, a canon of St Albans, that 'the doctrine of the Trinity has been my obsession for more than forty years':

> I used to interpret it metaphysically in terms of God complete outside his creation, God perfect in his creation, and God the source of the perfecting of creation. I would still use this language on appropriate occasions, but I have grown gradually to a more economic interest, expressed in the sequence Sinai, Incarnation, all that we mean by 'the scientific method'.

In a letter to the *Observer* of January 1972 he was more explicit, saying that if he was 'a thoroughly "bejewed" Christian', and 'also equally "be-humanised"', he was 'in fact, a real "Trinitarian"':

> The doctrine as applied to the nature of God has proved to most contemporary Christians meaningless and unnecessary. Applied to the activity of a responsible Creator, dealing with an intelligent humanity, it is a convincing and acceptable description of an identifiable historical process. Man is a social being, and Judaism expresses the discipline for effective social (including political) action. He is a person, unique in himself, with a destiny that passes beyond time. Such a quality requires a different discipline. Hence the Incarnation and the Christian Church. But man is also a seeker in a world of inexhaustible problems and potentialities. To that the key is neither a sensitive search for justice, nor a relationship of love, but a determination to seek truth. Hence the Humanism which was born with the Renaissance.

By this time, therefore, God the Christian Father has become God the Jewish Yahweh, a theological impossibility according to the vast majority of Jews and Christians. James never went so far as to equate Him with Allah, considering 'the simplistic theology of Islam's divine unity' a non-starter 'in comparison with the complexity of the Christian doctrine of God ... [which] is immensely enriching, its paradoxes allowing of continual fresh interpretation'. Yet, why stop at Yahweh, one has to ask in a more Islamically conscious age? No doubt Moslems, like Jews, would find these identifications odious. So, of course, do Christians. Nonetheless, if ecumenicalism is to run its logical course either there is one God or none at all. No ecumenicalist can be doing with three. Or more.

So far, therefore, we have had God becoming Jewish, Christ being moved from centre-stage to up-stage left, and the Holy Ghost turning into 'the scientific method'. The latter is distinctly odd, especially when we are confronted with the ecological arguments of 'An Economic Trinitarianism' of 1974. 'We have so used the world's resources', he writes, 'that little more than two centuries of industrialism and scientific technology threaten a disastrous collapse through the pollution of earth, air, and sea.' Even if there was 'an outflow of ambulance work, more extensive and more knowledgeable than ever before ... all of it coming, directly or indirectly, from Christian inspiration', was James not able to see that 'the pollution of earth, air, and sea' stemmed directly or indirectly from those 'enlightened' attitudes he equated with the Holy Spirit? Humanism, the Renaissance, the Enlightenment: only he could have seen something of God in these movements of the human spirit. 'What', he asks in 1974, 'of the third channel?':

> Here again I must admit to having to abandon traditional theology. It took men more than a thousand years from the full flow through Sinai before they had become ready and fit to receive another direct divine activity. And yet I was brought up to believe that the third channel – the channel of truth – came to its full flow fifty days after the passing of Jesus of Nazareth, and was given to the same people ... But if one is looking for a moment when truth suddenly moved into the centre of the picture, it is there at the Renaissance. It is at least an interesting coincidence that this interpretation brings it into line with the relation of Sinai to Calvary. Again it happens within those accepting the previous channel, and again it takes between a thousand and fifteen hundred years.

Although protesting that there is 'no inherent necessity' for the number three, 'again and again one can just as easily make the essentials less or more', and that he is no 'disciple of Joachim of Fiore', in a passage like this he is playing with numbers in a Joachimite way. No historian can help but make up a chronology of the past suitable to her reading of the present, even if she succeeds in keeping the future out of the reckoning. But it is only Christians who count in threes. They are not morally bound to do so. Why did James stick tooth and nail to his Trinitarianism? Was it his intellectual defence against being 'bejewed' into Judaism?

He ended the 1974 paper by pouring scorn on 'all the diverse voices within the Christian world from Jesus kids and Pentecostalists to the Archbishop of Canterbury's New Year Message ... [that] ... urge us to go back to Christ – back to what has proved already a complete political and ecological failure, except as ambulance work'. Yet, what we should go back (or forward) to he did not make clear, beyond stating that 'in some way ... the Church has got to learn the discipline of governing the world, and of understanding and using the world's resources'. He also says that we are living in the 'Dark Ages' between the end of European Civilization, a 'Humpty-Dumpty ... [that] ... we can never put back on the wall', and the beginning of the 'first world civilization'.

This is unhelpful. It is a long way from both the hesitancies and the certainties of the paper of 1929, and we ought not to make too much of that besetting sin of the old, the tendency to prophecy. All that needs saying at this point is that James' Trinitarianism in all its transmutations is not convincing. This is not so much because Trinitarianism is *ipso facto* unconvincing, but because he did not have an overall theology of the Trinity.

In that respect, as in almost every other, he is unlike the great Soviet scientist, theologian, thinker about aesthetics and art, priest and martyr, Pavel Florensky. This is not a book about Florensky; he crops up here because his perception of the universe was more profoundly Trinitarian than that of James Parkes, more consistently worked out, more persistently thought through. I have already mentioned his reflections on the Trinity as representing the true essence of man's being. Man is not an island. The Western idea of individual identity, a concept given an almighty boost by Abelard in the twelfth century, and again by Petrarch in the fourteenth, let alone by almost every other thinker in the Renaissance, has had, as Donald Nicholl put it, 'disastrous consequences for human life in general'. Equally, science has gone haywire since the Renaissance, having from that point become obsessed with the mechanics of life. Do we not think Leonardo's drawings of machines the very heart of the matter? How wrong we are. A machine is a thing of parts. All our scientific thinking is about parts: body parts, gene parts, atomic particles, single cells. Science is as solipsistic as any other branch of Western thought, theology included: think of Luther before the Cross. Think of how reluctant so many Anglicans are to exchange the kiss of peace. Think of psychologists and their discourse about individual space, a person's time, the necessity to find the self. Pavel Florensky believed the West had gone catastrophically down the wrong road. James Parkes would have agreed with him on that, but not on how, when, and why it had happened. Florensky's Trinitarianism is a genuinely alternative model, because it comes from outside the infected zone. Like the films of Tarkovsky, at first mysterious if not alien, Florensky's theology of the Trinity after careful scrutiny becomes perfectly comprehensible because it is so lucidly beautiful: form and content coalesce. The Trinity is the key to an understanding of ourselves and the world we inhabit, not, as in the West, a hindrance to all such comprehension, because in the Trinity, as T.S. Eliot might have put it, all things come together and converge.

It is difficult to leave Florensky for Barth. Florensky believed that the Holy Spirit went out of painting at the Renaissance: when naturalistic, humanistic images replaced iconic ones, the spirit, and therefore spirituality, departed. So dismissive an indictment of Western Art, which to Western commentators takes flight at the very moment Florensky has it plummeting to earth, is not likely to find favour with many in the West. The idea of the Renaissance and the Reformation as unnatural catastrophes would not have appealed to a humanist, liberal, and scientifically orientated Anglican like James Parkes. Compared with Pavel Florensky, born 1882, executed 1937, James seems ordinary, his life conventional, his thinking earth-bound. There is no comparison. And one ought not to be made, the reader might think, because the two men inhabited such contrasting milieu. The reader may be right. Yet, across that divide each had a vision of the Trinity that was not a shared vision but quite the contrary: their perceptions were as unlike as were the milieu in which they formulated them. I am struck by that difference, by the virtually cosmic difference between them: they seem light years apart. The greatest distance between them is in their understanding of the Holy Spirit. One has reluctantly to concede that James was labouring under the gravest of disabilities when he put his mind to pondering the ineffable; the disabilities were those identified by William Temple: a Westerner's thinking was 'formed by scientific and not by religious categories'.

What James might have made of Florensky there is no knowing. What he made of Karl Barth came close to being unprintable. No one upset or angered him more: he hated no one as he hated Karl Barth. (Trouble began as soon as James found himself at his first continental conference, at Heinrichsbad 'in the northeast corner' of Switzerland in the summer of 1923, which was a turning point in his life. I shall return to it.) First, however, there is a story about the Holy Ghost. The occasion was another conference, at Gex, also in Switzerland, but five years later, in 1928, and it was here that James reports his 'first encounter with the full blast of the abominable heresy of Barthianism':

> I was responsible for the morning meditations. The whole of the rest of the morning was given to an address in German, to be followed by translation and discussion. The lecturer was Fritz Lieb, Karl Barth's assistant ... Lieb had four periods, and his four subjects were *The Fall*, *The Incarnation*, *The Atonement*, and *The Holy Spirit*. The secretary of the conference was Louis Henriod ... at breakfast on the third morning Henriod expressed his anxiety. 'Look, Fritz,' he said. 'This is the third morning, and you have not yet finished your address on the Fall ... There are only two more days of the conference, and you [still] have three addresses to give. How much time are you going to need for the Holy Spirit?' 'Oh, the Holy Spirit,' replied Lieb, 'a quarter of an hour is enough for that.'

'This', explodes James Parkes 40 years later in *Voyage of Discoveries*, 'after five hours on the Fall, was an admirable introduction to Barthian theology!'

There are two things to note. First, that the story underlines the point made in the previous paragraph about Western theologians and the Holy Spirit, while at the same time demonstrating a further point not made there: that among Western theologians

James was something of an anomaly in paying the attention to the Holy Spirit (and to the Trinity) that he did. Secondly, he 'was responsible for the morning meditations'. At Heinrichsbad in 1923 he had been responsible for the English part of the culminating Communion Service. 'We had to compose the service. The actual words of consecration were read by a Danish pastor; I took the English part (I was not yet ordained), and a French student read the French part ... This was the beginning of what was to be a somewhat odd clerical career, conducting strange services in strange places under strange language conditions.' I am reminded of a similar culminating 'service' that myself and a young woman rabbi from New York were selected to lead in the memorial bunker at Yad Vashem. Alas, instead of the ecumenicalism in evidence at Heinrichsbad in 1923, the rabbi and I were de-selected by a vociferous claque of secular Jews from the United States: it was as if James Parkes had never lived.

That is a parenthetical point, though not an irrelevant one. The main issue is to take note that James led meditations and took communion services. This is an aspect of his life he hardly touches on in his autobiography and on which there is, in the nature of such routinely spiritual matters, virtually nothing in the Parkes Papers. Yet, the spiritual sustenance James drew from the Anglican Communion Service, critical as he was of it, and the spiritual solace he himself provided in contemplative or meditational groups, especially in the 12 years he was working with students, needs to be kept in mind. He may not have been St Seraphim of Sarov, or Rabbi Aryeh Levin of Jerusalem, or even William Temple, but that he had an inner life of the spirit there cannot be any doubt. The biographer, like the historian, is dependent on evidence: he is unable to write about what is not knowable. In this case James' spiritual life is a mystery, not because all spiritual lives are mysterious, but because his has left no trace. We have, therefore, to infer it. It can be safely inferred: for him to be invited to lead 'morning meditations' at Gex in 1928 when he was no more than 32, his spirituality must have been obvious to others; it must also have been sufficiently robust for him to have accepted the invitation.

We need to return to Heinrichsbad in 1923. 'It was', he says, 'a very moving conference, for it witnessed the first meeting since the war of the French and German Christian Student Movements.'He also discusses the 'sombre background' against which 'European student life was lived and work like mine had to be done ... a good half of the political assassinations between the wars were committed by University students ... I came later to know quite well one of the group that murdered Rathenau'. He does not say how the ten years he spent in such company uniquely fitted him to read the political situation, though he came close to doing so in replying to a letter of Professor John Conway in August 1968:

> My autobiography is due out in the Spring and naturally there I describe my years in the S.C.M. and the I.S.S. I came in in 1923 as International Study Secretary, and being directly concerned with politics, was squarely up against the Barthians from the start ... From your quotation Barth seems to admire Bonhoeffer for 'sensing the political danger first, and rightly so in 1933'. The German Jewish community had sensed the political danger several years earlier and were making fully documented appeals to the German Churches for support completely in vain. Indeed the danger was obvious to anyone who cared to think it out, though they can be excused for not realising the extent to which Hitlerism would degrade the German people. I do not think anyone could be blamed in the 1930s for not foreseeing the Final Solution.

He is certainly thinking of himself, if only of himself at the outset of his European experience, when in *Voyage of Discoveries* he comments that 'British students, in their secure a-political world, had little idea of the stresses and tragedies of their European brethren', for in the introduction to a lecture he gave at the Glion conference of 1929 he writes of the 'more optimistic Anglo-Saxon', who was 'apt to forget ... the truth [that] our German friends ... had got hold of ... the reality of sin, and its effects in the world':

> I do not agree with the attitude of those members of the German movement I was meeting from 1923 to 1926, but it has made me go over all my own thinking again, and has taken away a good deal of the rather shallow optimism with which one is apt to begin if one starts as I did from the political end in an atmosphere in which some form or other

of evolution is taken for granted.

Later in that introduction he speaks of his 'compulsion to think out the position of this group whom I was often attracted to personally, who denied the whole basis on which so far my thinking had been based', although in spite of his re-thinking he wonders if he will not still be 'a cheerful but superficial Anglo-Saxon to the continentals'. If we shall continue to worry about his cheerful and optimistic Englishness, it needs saying now that his optimism after the mid-1920s was never facile and his cheerfulness was never without an understanding of the reality of sin.

At least, he had the Barthians to thank for that. What, therefore, was the bone of contention that stuck in James' throat? 'Heinrichsbad', he says in the autobiography, 'involved me at once in the controversy with which I lived continuously until I came home from Geneva in 1935, the controversy with German Protestant theology about the nature of "the Fall"', and the basic relationship between God and man.' We return to Gex in 1928 and that 'five and a half hours on the Fall' as 'admirable introduction to Barthian theology'. Barthian theology: was there any such thing? A summary is impossible and unnecessary. An attempt would do no justice to the dense, if not impenetrable, thinking of this influential theologian. Besides it is James' perception of both thought and influence that matters here.

A point of departure, the principal one for other English critics of Barth and of the German Lutheran church in the 1930s, if not for James himself, was Barth's view of the Church. I quote from the conclusion of Richard Gutteridge's book, *Open Thy Mouth for the Dumb: The German Evangelical Church and the Jews 1879–1950*, where he discusses the ideas of Karl Barth and their impact. According to Barth:

> The Church had only one fundamental task, that of serving God. She could thereby indeed be of service to man, but it was in no way her task to be serving mankind, still less to be wanting to manipulate God in man's service. She had no abstract right to be fulfilling human interests ... Dialectical Theology, of which Karl Barth was the most prominent exponent, was instrumental in encouraging the Church to be primarily concerned with her own affairs. The Church at all costs had to remain the Church ... This certainly dis-

couraged any kind of all-embracing or liberal idealism.

Here is Barth himself in 1943; the italics are mine: 'The Church has in no way *whatever* to serve mankind nor the German people. She has alone to serve the Word of God.' The italics are also mine in the next sentence. In *June 1934* he is reported to have said the same if slightly differently, 'that the Church had no warrant to elevate herself as judge over the State'. And here is Richard Gutteridge once more:

> Barthian theology with its ethical *Weltresignation* played into the hands of the Nazis with their demand for undisputed control of secular life. John Bowden has written of the price that an approach like that of Barth has to pay: 'One longs for him to say, just once, "In the name of mankind, this is wicked", for him to show insight into what other men, women and children think and feel and suffer as fellow human beings. But this he cannot do'.

John Bowden speaks in the accents of James Parkes, although James, when condemning him in *Voyage of Discoveries* for what had happened in Germany, is concerned as much with Barth's view of the world as he is with his view of the Church:

> That this evil doctrine spread over Germany is understandable, even though supremely tragic. For young Germans had to have great courage to resist so comforting a doctrine of the universality and inescapability of human sinfulness, and of human inability to do anything about the evils of the social and political worlds. It rid them of any sense of responsibility for the war and its evils. A sense of responsibility was a very young and tender growth among members of the Lutheran tradition. Instead of fostering it, Barth's influence destroyed it, and thereby made the surrender to Hitler in the vital academic field so much easier to achieve.

This is why the resistance of the students of the White Rose group at Munich University in 1942 is all the more glorious: Hans and Sophie Scholl and most of their executed friends were Lutherans.

The key word in the last quotation is responsibility. James

believed it was not only the Church, German youth, and mankind in general whom Barth let off the hook, but God himself. He needs to be quoted again at some length. Responsibility is also the key word in the following quotation:

> I was still looking for a real theological interpretation of the divine relation to our social and political life. I could not accept any doctrine of a purposeful creation which did not include the ultimately complete responsibility of the Creator. Anything less seemed to me just immoral. Now along came Barth proclaiming a godling who, apparently, revelled in making himself totally obscure and incomprehensible to his creation ... and who accepted no responsibility for the result. He had been so inefficient or malicious a creator that man, his creation, could not understand his purpose or nature ... Barth's godling was so egotistical that he regarded it as blasphemous if man tried ... [his] perpetual insistence on the *otherness* of God merely enfolded him in a fog too thick to penetrate ...

There is another side to every coin. James Parkes found Karl Barth incomprehensible, even after he had been told what a modest, unassuming, and humorous young man he was. Only on the subject of Barth could he slip into unpardonable exaggeration: Barth's book *The Word of God and the Word of Man* had, according to James, 'a title of inherent and inescapable absurdity for a work by any human being'.

Whatever the truth of his rooted belief in Barth's responsibility for making National Socialism's seduction of German middle-class youth easier, it was James' out and out hostility to the idea of God as being beyond human reach that prevented him from having any sympathy for a theologian who wished to emphasize God's distinctness from his creation. All those negatives about God that souls with a mystical bent find attractive were anathema to James. Are we not bound to say that he saw God in human terms? His God was a humane God; in every sense he was knowable. At times one feels that James saw him behaving like an English colonial civil servant of the very best sort. How else should one take the following comment: 'For the godling who gave man freewill, and did not take into account the possibility of a "fall" was so grotesquely incompetent that he had no right ever to have created man at all'? While one can see his point, namely that if we have turned out so badly, God ought to have seen it coming long before he tried to end it all with the Flood, the tone of his condemnation is Olympian: look here, Jones minor, pull your socks up. Am I being unfair for the sake of scoring an infinitesimal point? I think not. James Parkes, it seems to me, never soars. That is his strength, especially when he is dealing with antisemitism, a subject on which everyone and anyone is prone to leaving the ground with rocket-like velocity. I am not sure in the last quotation whether it is Barth or God who has to pull his socks up. It is, however, my impression that James rather thought that if God has made a cock-up of Creation he ought not to have done, and certainly that if he had exerted stronger will-power and exercised greater self-control he would not have done. We are back with a theme we have come upon before: Creation looks a cock-up but it cannot be; God is not like that and to our rescue He will one day come. I hope this is not a parody.

Alas, we can only theologize in the language we have got (or been given): the human language, hence the attempts of mystics who have experienced God to try to describe him in terms of what he is not. James does not appear to have recognized this as a problem: for him God is describable as well as knowable, otherwise He would not be God. Yet, and it goes without saying, there are difficulties about a God interested in social and political activities. One of them is that he seems to approve of the British political system and the English social structure. It is not that James was uncritical of both, and in Common Wealth saw for the first time a political party that might put what was wrong right. It is far more indefinable than that. It comes out in his obsession with Barth and with what he saw as that theologian's pernicious social and political influence. For this writer it is as if James on this issue is what he generally is not, a didactic and self-righteous Englishman. Can one not hear an echo of the familiar English refrain: it could not happen here?

He was not right about Barth in more humdrum ways. It always pays to be careful with 'big' thinkers: they never speak with a single voice. Paul, Augustine, Luther one thinks to have 'got hold of'; then up they come with something entirely unexpected and one knows oneself for a 'small' thinker. It must have been galling, though he took it with his customary grace, when the Rev. U.E. Simon wrote to tell James in 1962 that Barth 'is your man':

> I think you would be surprised to know that you have a much stauncher ally than you think in Karl Barth. It is quite evident to me that you have not read his vols. III & IV on Church Dogmatics, now all available in English ... Yes the great KB is neither anti-rational nor anti-universal, and his work on Reconciliation is, I think, uniquely great, just because it comes from him.

Far more important is something else of Barth's that James had not read. If he had, it might have made him think again, as it must make us. I am citing Richard Gutteridge for the last time. Outraged by *Kristallnacht*, Barth 'told a Swiss audience on 5 December 1938, but with an altogether wider public in view':

> When that takes place which has in Germany now been manifestly determined – the physical extermination of the People of Israel, the burning of their Synagogues and the Rolls of the Torah, the outright rejection of the God and the Bible of the Jews as the very epitome of all that has to be regarded as an abomination to the German – an attack is being made upon the Christian Church at its very roots. What would we be and what are we without Israel? He who is on principle an enemy of the Jews, even if he were in other respects an angel of light, is to be recognised as on principle an enemy of Jesus Christ. Anti-semitism is the sin against the Holy Ghost.

Antisemitism as the sin against the Holy Ghost is surely one idea of Karl Barth's that James would have agreed with. At James Parkes and antisemitism we have now arrived.

We should note that it is antisemitism not anti-Semitism. James, as we shall discover, insisted on it: it was the one battle the pioneering campaigner against antisemitism did not win. It was antisemitism not anti-Semitism because there was no such thing as semitism, let alone Semitism. There was, however, much too much antisemitism, as James discovered on his European travels.

He tells us that it was at a conference at Oberaegeri in 1925 that he was first 'brought into ... direct contact with the Jewish problem'. He was chairman and created a typically Parkesian scene after an antisemitic speech was made. Yet, it was not until he was established with the I.S.S. in Geneva in 1928 that he began in earnest to study 'the Jewish problem'. In the interim he had travelled extensively in Central and Eastern Europe and in consequence had become extremely well informed of what the problem was, particularly in the universities where, in his view, it was most acute. Why he took up the Jewish cause and made it so famously his own seems at first a mystery. Yet in *Voyage of Discoveries* he writes that in 1924 he 'began to be conscious of a void in the middle of my activity as a promoter of the study of international questions'. The essay on the Trinity of 1929 was an attempt to fill the void, an attempt to a considerable degree successful, as his Trinitarian theology would for a lifetime underpin all his other thinking. The essay's encouraging reception by William Temple must have been all the more welcome because in 1926 he had made a false start, writing a book-length manuscript on the prophets, which those who read it had not recommended for publication. The contemporary 'Jewish problem', as he became increasingly acquainted with it at first hand and in consequence began reading about it, evidently filled what was left of the 'void'. He described what happened on numerous occasions, most succinctly in a letter of September 1955 to a Mr Sniderman:

> In 1928 I went out to Geneva as Cultural Co-operation Secretary for International Student Service. This had been a relief organization excluding all political questions, but it had been forced by its success into facing the cultural and political questions which divided European students. I soon found that one of the most deeply-rooted of these divisions arose from antisemitism. In 1930 [sic] I brought together privately a group of Jewish and antisemitic student leaders, and what emerged from this group was that there was no non-Jew to be found in the European universities who had made an objective study of the Jewish problem. It was therefore obvious that if we were to go on in this field I would have to give what time I could myself to research it. That is how my Jewish work began ... As you see, my first concern was antisemitism in the universities; that led me to a study of antisemitism; this in turn forced me to a study of

> Jewish history; and this I found incomprehensible without a study of Judaism. The growing tragedy in Europe and the growth of the National Home brought in turn a study of Israel and the Diaspora.

It sounds straightforward and it almost undoubtedly was. The intellectual satisfaction the study of antisemitism brought him is all there is to it. There was no singular incident, no particular person, no moment of revelation, which impelled James into his life's work. If further explanation is required it may readily be found in his strong sympathy for underdogs and his healthy dislike of 'overdogs'.

It is, nonetheless, probable that Geneva itself was important in the decision he took to devote himself to the Jewish issue. In a paper entitled 'Judaism–Jews–Antisemites: Thoughts of a Non-Jew', published in the *Jewish Review* in 1934, a paper to which we will return in due course, he introduces himself in this fashion:

> I am not a Jew, but during the last few years I have been meeting Jews of all kinds ... and in the intervals of wandering I have been studying Jewish history from a corner in Geneva, a corner symbolic enough, for it is the end house of the old Ghetto, the bridge to the Christian quarter of the town. And from the window on one side I can look in imagination upon the Jewish quarter, and from the other side, across the old gate of the Ghetto, to the houses of the Christians.

He is addressing a Jewish readership for the first time in print, but his introduction is not a literary device: James was incapable of artifice. With his sensitivity to place and love of historical architecture it would have been surprising if he had not responded imaginatively (and creatively) to the discovery that he was living in what had once been Geneva's Jewish ghetto.

It was in fact in 1929 (not 1930) that he organized the meeting of Jews and Nationalist students. This was the Bierville conference of late December 1928–early January 1929, whose planning and proceedings he describes at length in *Voyage of Discoveries* and which he says 'saw the beginning of my real involvement in the Jewish question'. The proceedings opened farcically. José

Jehouda, a Jewish novelist invited by James to speak about 'Jewish Mysticism' on the first evening, did so for hours on end. The Rumanian Christian delegation 'demanded an equal length of time to expound Christian mysticism – about which they knew nothing; most of the Jewish members demanded similar opportunities for denying that the speaker had represented *their* views on Jewish mysticism'. James, exercising his customary guile smoothed things over and the remainder of the conference did what it had been intended to do: have both sides listen to each other's views. Lectures on the contemporary Jewish situation and on Jewish history were given by Jews. The I.S.S. 'had combed Europe unsuccessfully for a Christian scholar who could talk objectively' on such topics. Why they had is not stated. They had not, it seems, 'combed Europe' for a Jewish scholar to 'talk objectively' about German Racism or Rumanian Nationalism. Still, the outcome of a post-conference I.S.S. committee meeting was that James 'should spend what spare time I could extract from a pretty busy life to make a study of the Jewish question!' The exclamation mark is unwarranted: he cannot have been other than entirely willing to accept what turned into his life's work.

He had many Jewish helpers. Among them were Charles Singer, Professor of the History of Medicine at London University, who would become a close and lifelong friend, and Herbert Loewe, a distinguished scholar who taught at both Oxford and Cambridge and whose influential support would be significant in the years ahead, 'in his generosity, kindliness, and deep religious conviction', writes James, 'a veritable saint of Torah'. James also tells us that he made 'an important choice' at the outset of his studies, which I find both curious and revealing. 'Should I seek to know Hebrew, or to know Jews?' he asks:

> I had not time to do both, for they made opposite demands. To do the first I should spend all the time I could spare in study; to do the second I should go out and meet people. My travelling life made the choice of the second the obvious one; but I also realised that in the atmosphere of the antisemitism of the thirties I had much better not get involved in arguments about the Talmud unless I became an acknowledged master of rabbinic Hebrew ... So I bought Graetz's *History* instead of a Hebrew grammar, and

read the whole of it in the next six months. But I also made use of the unrivalled knowledge of central and eastern Europe of Alexander Teich of Vienna, to meet as many as possible of the Jewish leaders of the day.

Of Alexander Teich more will have to be said. Meanwhile, does the reader not find the passage as curious as I do? James did not become a 'master of rabbinic Hebrew'; and he was probably wise not to make the attempt. Yet, he never learned any sort of Hebrew, and appears not to have been tempted to get even a smattering: whole-hogger that he was he no doubt rejected that option too. The Talmud remained a closed book to him. Instead, he read Graetz's multi-volume *Geschichte der Juden*. The choice he made may not have put him at a disadvantage where Jewish history was concerned; it surely did as regards Judaism. However widely he read in other languages, however generous was the assistance his Jewish scholarly friends gave him, was not his understanding of Judaism bound to be that of a linguistic outsider? And were not less friendly Jews bound to be critical of him on that score?

Was choosing absolutely necessary? Were learning Hebrew and getting to know Jews as mutually exclusive undertakings as he makes them out to be? Some scholars would have buckled down to learning Hebrew and not thought twice about it; it would simply have been something that had to be done. It is not that James was no linguist: his Latin and Greek were exemplary. Nor was he lazy. In the early 1930s he may have been too occupied with everyday matters to have the time to take lessons or find a satisfactory teacher. Whatever the reason, however, he would not have been the pioneering historian he became had he set about learning rabbinic Hebrew and grappling with the Talmud; instead he would have been a different sort of person and become a different kind of scholar.

In fact, the more one thinks about this crux in his life, the more grateful one is for the decision he made. Had he not taken the one he did he would not have published *The Conflict of the Church and the Synagogue* in 1934 and *The Jew in the Medieval Community* four years later: two influential works (one of them a masterpiece) in nine years is a remarkable achievement. They are not 'popular' books and were not intended as such. If they have been 'surpassed' it is not because they were not good, but because they were: subsequent scholarship has used them as a sure foundation for further exploration, which in almost all instances has taken the form of elaboration or re-evaluation rather than super-cession. Moreover, in 1931 he had published *The Jew and His Neighbour*, a far from negligible discussion of the 'Jewish problem', although it shows how far he still had to go before he would fully comprehend it. His choice not to learn Hebrew in 1929 was, therefore, decisive.

Although he would get an Oxford doctorate a few years later, although one of England's greatest historians, incidentally an East European Jew, wanted him in consequence to return to Oxford, and although he was in many, probably most, ways the epitome of an Oxford don, he had with that choice effectively turned his back on the conventional academic world. It was not so much the ivory tower that he then put behind him, his life at Barley after 1935 hardly being one that actively embraced the hurly-burly of a world he had got to know so well in the 12 years before he took refuge there, it was the modest rewards, solid comforts, and consoling friendships of an integrated collegiate life among the gleaming spires that he was rejecting. His subject isolated him much more than it would have done had it been the Talmud. Think how welcome in the groves of academe he would have been studying a subject regarded as even more arcane among Christian scholars than Jewish history. Once at Barley he became a twice-removed eccentric: a Christian studying Jews, and a gentleman of independent means as well as of independent mind.

Neither Casaubon-like scholar nor popularizing historian, James, already an odd fish, was about to become in addition a rare bird. Meanwhile his travels on behalf of I.S.S. continued. What he observed of the deteriorating situation at the universities of Central and Eastern Europe he intended should make yet another book. Like other intended books this one ended up as a pamphlet, *The Jewish Student*, published by I.S.S. in 1933. Very full index cards for the project are in the Parkes Papers; they remain as remarkable testimony to the staggering number of anti-Jewish incidents in the universities of Poland, Rumania, Hungary, Germany and Austria in the years between the end of the First World War and the appointment of Hitler as German Chancellor. In November 1932 James wrote that he was 'well into' the book and had realized 'how extremely delicate' it was going to be: 'I am certainly not going to be able to curry popular approval of either side for the things which it seems to me need to be said.' There were, however, chapters that 'will not be finished till next year'. Lacking the book we have to make do with his annual reports, lectures, and published papers.

In 1929 he wrote a paper called 'Some aspects of the Jewish Situation in Europe'. It was an able analysis of what he calls 'the fundamental problem', namely 'the cultural problem in relation to nationalism', especially in Germany, where 'the idea of racial purity is as untrue as it is of any other of the great European peoples, and the idea of cultural purity is perhaps more untrue than of their neighbours':

> The very idea of the cultural state comes to them from the Bible. It is not to be traced to the wandering tribes of Alemanni in the forests of central Europe. I believe that German culture is great enough to grow out of this idea, but while it lasts it will create a malaise between those who hold it and their minorities ... This will be made much easier when we are able to separate a little more the cultural life of the nation from the political life of the state. So long as uniformity is expected within an artificial political frontier in cultural matters, there is so much to be said on both sides that a solution is impossible. As we develop our own cultures, we will come to see that it is not inconsistent with others developing theirs, even if they remain within the same political boundaries, and we will also be more open to a free interchange, since in the long run no culture lives to itself, and if it is once rooted it profits by drawing into itself all the streams which can be attracted towards it.

But not those that it sets out to repulse rather than attract, one wants to add 60 years after the Final Solution was implemented. That was a 'simple solution' his reason rejected: 'Fortunately or unfortunately [sic] there are too many Jews for the simple solution of the extremists, i.e. massacre, to have the slightest chance of success.' As for England, he said he did 'not know what we have done particularly for the Jews, but if they are the ones we deserve, we must have been great benefactors of that people ... for their contribution to our life is one which most of us would not be without'.

In 1930 on 'Students and European Politics', a lecture he seems to have given to a British audience, he characterized the typical European student as a political extremist, the 'purity' of whose viewpoint was 'not corrupted by the exigencies of responsibility', largely because he did not have the advantage of the British party system, and the experience of a 'debating tradition such as the Union in Oxford ... Hence, while European politics are bad enough, and quite sufficiently doctrinaire and unstable, European student politics are far worse.' His report to the I.S.S. of the same year contains other (more unchallengeable) remarks on the Jewish predicament in Central Europe:

> In Poland ... on all sides it is agreed that though the mobile capital is in the hands of Jews to a considerable extent, their general economic situation is deplorable and getting worse. I saw the three great ghettoes of Warsaw, Wilno, and Lwow. They are not beautiful ... When one arrives in Vienna one comes under the dominance of the racial idea of antisemitism. There is even now in the main street of old Vienna a shop which sells soap and scent but only to Aryans, as it announces in the window ... Prague is also a great centre for Eastern European Jews, but so far as the Czechs themselves are concerned there is little antisemitism. It is mostly amongst the German minority, and has the same combination of race myth and economic fact as elsewhere in German speaking universities.

That 'even now' shows just how difficult it was for a rational and civilized Channel Islander to believe that unreason and barbarity were not withering away in Germany and Austria, let alone to grasp that they were blooming.

In 1931 he published 'The Jewish problem in Eastern Europe' in *The Student World*, the handbook of the World Christian Student Federation, an organization he says he had severed 'creative relations' with two years previously. It is far less valuable than the paper he submitted to I.S.S in December 1932 on 'Antisemitic riots in the Universities' headed 'STRICTLY CONFIDENTIAL – NOT TO BE PUBLISHED', and much less interesting than the piece in *The Jewish Review* of 1934 whose preamble has been cited above. Nonetheless, the 1931 paper contains a passage not only central to a grasp of Christian–Jewish relations in the twentieth century, but critical also for an understanding of James' interpretation of those relations at any time:

> There are Jews who are entirely taken up with their racial purity, others who are traitors, deserters, vulgar nouveaux-riches, communists and shady financiers; just as there are antisemites who are brutal, selfish, lying, dishonest and self-seeking. That is very regrettable, but it is not the problem. The problem is that there are many sincere and honest citizens of their respective countries who are profoundly convinced that the presence of too many Jews is harmful to their country, and that there are many fine and honourable Jews who experience all sorts of humiliating difficulties in their relations with their non-Jewish neighbours, with whom they wish to live on terms of mutual respect and friendship, in common service to a country in which both may have lived for centuries.

One's reaction to such a passage is two-fold. Surely that is not the whole story is the first. As James would soon discover, it was not. Once he had read the Church Fathers he would become convinced that the deepest roots of antisemitism went back to the origins of Christianity, were nurtured by the Church in its services, and were impossible to uproot. Those convictions, when arrived at, were unshakeable. Secondly, there is the style, which is beginning to become distinctive. 'That is very regrettable, but it is not the problem' is unexpected: nasty people are not the difficulty; good people are. It is a style that makes the reader sit up and take notice. As James' thinking gets to grips with the essentials, he develops a style to express it. There is a 'thirdly': can citizens who think there are too many Jews actually be 'sincere and honest'? I suppose it has to be reluctantly admitted that there might be, even if one shares James' view that it is not the desecrators of synagogues who are the real enemy within, but the respectable and worthy householders who cast their vote for National Front parties.

The piece in *The Jewish Review* of 1934 is far more engaging. Because he has become surer of himself, at any rate on the question of antisemitism, his natural boldness of mind takes on a finer cutting edge:

> And though Jews are often accused of thinking themselves as excessively chosen, and though the accusation is often true; though there are an abundance of unpleasant texts on the *Goyim* in the Talmud; though history has made the Jews concentrate on themselves and at times hate all the outside world; in spite of all this it is worthy of note that three thousand years ago Jewish leaders commended especially to their people 'the fatherless, the widow, *and the stranger*'. And if Talmudic scholars were frequently contemptuous of the Gentile, Christian scholars of the same epoch were much more so. Some Talmudists did not reject the virtuous Goy from Paradise. I know no Christian father who admitted anyone to Paradise except through the medium of his branch of the Christian faith.

It is a style that takes risks, the counter-point of 'That is very regrettable, but it is not the problem' taking flight. The reader not only is sitting up and taking notice; but also is wanting to stand up and cheer. Here is another example:

> Oppression has made certain unpleasant social characteristics common among Jews. Judaism has made just as many fine characteristics common among Jews ... Moreover, on the whole the unpleasant characteristics are common to all groups who have passed through long periods of oppression, and the fine ones are really more 'specifically' Jewish – not that they are exclusively Jewish, but that they are more marked among Jews. A sense of justice has already been referred to. Generosity is another characteristic which has its roots deep in the Torah. Intellectual clarity is as much the result of the nature of Jewish religion as it is of the survival of the fittest.

It is a particularly provocative final sentence. In the light of it one has to ask, as towards the end of his life James was asking: Whither Israel?

The 1934 essay contains not only good writing; important truths are enunciated. There is also a striking misconception. First the truth:

> It is characteristic of the Jewish politician to allow no per-

centage for human error or stupidity, for practical difficulties or impossibilities, in his scenting out of 'antisemitism'. All that creates difficulties for the Jews, all that offends them is a deliberate and conscious effort of their enemies. Very often he is right, but by no means always ... All are not 'antisemites' whom the Jewish press labels as such.

And again (and far more importantly):

> The tragedy of antisemitism is not the actual economic or political difficulties which may be created by the peculiar position of the Jewish communities in the world, difficulties by no means incapable of solution, but the deeply ingrained inheritance by which the antisemite sees 'the Jews' in each of these particular difficulties. As a whole 'the Jews' are a menace to nobody. But the concept acts as a mist between each separate problem and its solution. It is continually fogging the issue.

There are a variety of ways of describing antisemitism and the problems it engenders, and James would at one time and another deploy them all, but this early statement seems to me to be among the very best. Here is the misconception:

> Between Orthodox Judaism and Orthodox (i.e., Trinitarian) Christianity there is only one distinction. They both have the same idea of God. They both have the same idea of man. They both have the same idea of revelation.

Or should one say three misconceptions? It is his desire for all men and women to be in harmony that makes James ecumenical where there cannot be ecumenicalism. For a man who had almost invariably come up with the answer, whether at home, at school, in the army, or during a conference, it is to be expected that he might believe every problem had its solution. Good sense and goodwill *could* get things done. Such an attitude minimizes difference. How many Christians, how many Jews think they have the same God? How many of them *want* to have the same God? The answer in both cases is very few. To be sociological rather than theological: different cultures, different religions will necessarily come up with different Gods. The antidote to bloodshed and burnt-out mosques is not for everyone to worship the same God; it is for everyone to worship the unfamiliar God of their neighbour in their place of worship, as well as to worship their own God in His (or Her) own place.

Before taking leave of James and inter-war antisemitism we should conclude with a piece of 1936. It distils the experience of his European Years into four pages. It was published in *The Jewish Academy* and is entitled 'Post-War Antisemitism'. The countries of Central and Eastern Europe and their Jewish 'problems' are gone through one by one in what had become his standard style: brisk and acutely to the point. Germany, for instance, has no *'real'* Jewish problem; it has been entirely manufactured. Austria's 'problem' is a Viennese one of Jewish refugees from the eastern parts of the former Habsburg Empire. Hungary has the middle-class employment 'problem' of a rump state, while Rumania *'in fact'* has no more a Jewish 'problem' than has Germany: 'The feeling against the Jews comes not from a qualified graduate class ousted from jobs, but from a disgruntled unsuccessful university class, often unable to graduate, who would like to be competent for the jobs – but isn't.' Poland has all the problems arising from 'the indigestibility of an enormous minority'. It is Germany that receives most attention:

> Germany takes arguments from countries where they do apply, and pretends that they apply to her also. Austria has the problem of the Jew of Galicia and elsewhere. Germany pretends that she has been swamped by 'eastern' Jews. Rumania has the problem of the absence of a middle-class. Germany pretends that she must make the most strenuous 'scientific' efforts in race hygiene, regulating marriage, sterilising the unfit, protecting amusements, to create a national middle-class for herself. Hungary had witnessed a 'Red Terror' in which Jews were involved. Germany must pretend that she also has only by the skin of her teeth saved herself from 'Jewish–Marxistic' villains of the calibre of Streseman, Bruning and others.

The paper ends with the 'shame and tragedy of Germany', because there has been 'the creation of an immense Jewish problem, where, in fact, none exists'.

Yet, in this piece too, there is the blind spot of the reasonable, humanistic observer, with which we are becoming familiar. 'In the middle ages', he says, 'the common element was religious hostility':

> This took the place of the racial theory – with a difference; for one can believe that the ignorant and often superstitious local clergy really believed accusations they broadcast, and were sincerely though erroneously convinced that the Jews did poison wells, murder children and so on. *But by no stretch of the imagination* is it possible to believe that the propagandists of racial theories can really believe themselves – even if they convince the academic or peasant mob of their truth.

The italics on this occasion are mine. We are at the heart of the matter: the failure of good men and women, of good men and women brought up with the 'scientific categories' that William Temple identified as the bane of the mentality of the twentieth century, to be able imaginatively to comprehend that un-reason and non-science had been let loose. Pandora's Box had been opened at Verdun and on the Somme and the barbarians had stormed and taken not only universities; in Russia and Germany they had also taken the state itself. The believers in racial hygiene believed the drivel they advocated, antisemites believed in 'the Jew', Hitler believed in a Judaeo-Bolshevik conspiracy, Himmler believed in Final Solutions. It is the arrogance of modern man to consider medieval man sincere but superstitious. It is also against all the evidence, for it is the 'superstitions' of modern man, sincerely held, which caused death and destruction throughout Europe in the twentieth century. Lenin and Stalin were not cynics, any more than Hitler and Himmler were. It is the hindsight we have 60 years after the Shoah that makes this obvious. It took time for the First World War to be got into perspective: in the 1920s and 1930s, indeed until the 1960s, the suffering and grief were still too immediate; not enough time had elapsed to be able to grasp that war's universal significance. Even so, Chamberlain on his return from Munich waving a tiny piece of paper and proclaiming peace for our time was a ridiculous figure for James and those of his contemporaries who were as well informed as he was. A man with an umbrella, that most rational of impedimenta, was no match for gangsters with guns.

We need to delay a little longer before moving on to James' exploration of the origins of antisemitism. We have to 'see off' a burning topic of the time that no longer even smoulders: the conversion of Jews to Christianity. Writing now one has to add 'to Christianity'; between the wars 'the conversion of Jews' would have been enough for anyone to know what was being discussed, or rather 'the conversion of *the* Jews'. In the twenty-first century Christians in Western Europe are a minority; it will probably not be long before they become a persecuted minority, ignorance of Christianity being already as great among the young as was ignorance of Judaism among the students James encountered in the 1920s. Anti-Christianism may well take the place of antisemitism and churches, instead of synagogues and mosques, will burn. It is no wonder, therefore, that converting Jews has disappeared altogether from the Christian agenda.

James takes two pages in *Voyage of Discoveries* to dispatch Conrad Hoffmann, appointed 'first secretary of the new committee on the Christian Approach to the Jew, created by the International Missionary Council', in 1930. He is more polite in the letters he wrote to Hoffmann at the time stating his position on the matter of conversion. He was utterly opposed to it. 'Our Christian responsibility', he wrote to him on 9 December 1930 'is to give the Jew a square deal as a Jew':

> I am sorry, my dear old Con, if I seem to be simply destructively critical of your programme, but I do feel that there is an abyss between the approach I am trying to make, and that of the programme you sent me. It is not a difference of emphasis but of kind. The absolute basis of my work is that the Jews with whom I am in contact know that I have no secret desire to convert them, and therefore they trust me.

Six months later, in a letter of 11 June 1931, he said that he could never accept 'an official conversionist policy':

> It will be time to consider that when we have really cleared ourselves from the natural, honourable and inevitable mistrust felt by most decent Jews for the underlying attitude of the churches towards Judaism ... A new study of the actual relation of Jesus to the Judaism of his time is essential to see

where the difference really came, and to get rid of conventional false ideas based on Saint Paul.

He was setting out his own programme; in fulfilling it he would be very much on his own and out on a limb. 'I learned very early', he writes in his autobiography, 'that to evolve a new attitude to JewishÝChristian relations was to be a lonely job.'

The next phase of James' involvement with antisemitism may be said to have opened with the second conference on the Jewish question that he organized at Nyon in 1931. In *Voyage of Discoveries* he gives a flippant account of what was no doubt a more sombre encounter between Jews and Germans. Immediately afterwards he went to Poland; in that hierarchically fixated country he became aware that if he was going to be listened to on such a recondite issue as antisemitism he should become a *Herr Doktor*: 'It was not that any doctor was a learned man, but that, if a man was not even a doctor, he could not be a learned man.' So he went to Oxford and got a doctorate. I.S.S. tolerated his absence there for one term a year for three years, he had a 'modest' post-graduate scholarship from his old school, Elizabeth College, tenable at Exeter College, and he found a supervisor in the doyen of medievalists, Maurice Powicke. His subject was the origins of antisemitism and these he found in the earliest centuries of the Christian era. He summarizes what he found in his autobiography and in a single paragraph paraphrases his thesis and the book which it became in 1934, *The Conflict of the Church and the Synagogue*. The italics are once again mine:

> I was completely unprepared for the discovery that it was the Christian Church *alone*, which turned a normal xenophobia and normal good and bad communal relations between two human societies into the *unique* evil of antisemitism, the most evil, and, as I gradually came to realize, the most crippling *sin* of historic Christianity. It was not any particular contemporary fact on either side which led to this tragic result, nor was it any deduction by the Christians of any one period from the behaviour of their Jewish contemporaries ... antisemitism arises from the picture of the Jews which Christian theologians extracted from their reading of the Old Testament, a work for whose every word they claimed divine authority.

Very soon he would carry his condemnation back to the Gospels themselves, but for the moment the Church fathers could stand as the culprits, as they very much were. Today only a handful of scholars would question the overall thesis of *The Conflict of the Church and the Synagogue*, however inclined they might be to alter its emphases and rewrite the details. In 1934 it was a different matter and Oxford University Press would not publish the book. The Soncino Press of London did. Two thousand copies were sold, yet *The Conflict of the Church and the Synagogue* did not occasion the stir it ought to have done.

Writing from Vienna to Dr Leo Motzkin in Paris on 7 November 1932 we get James' view of things while he was still hard at work. The letter is long; it is, nonetheless, deserving of our scrutiny. 'To my mind', James writes, 'the creative period of antisemitism is the period from the fourth to the tenth centuries':

> By the eleventh century the history of the Middle Ages has become inevitable ... [and] ... by the history of the Middle Ages modern antisemitism has become inevitable. To reach its causes we must go back to the time when the Jews were a normal people living normally among others. Such they were at the beginning of the fourth century. They had no more distinguishing marks than any other group ... So far I have no evidence of any peculiarity other than religious in their conduct. Nothing in their social or economic status distinguished them from other groups. There was no specific Jewish occupation. There was nothing they did that someone else did not do too – especially the Syrians ... The economic factors in mediaeval antisemitism were due to economic abnormalities in the mediaeval Jews. But these were the result not of any fantastic oriental blood or Sombartian proclivity, but simply and solely to their exclusion from other walks of life, which, when permitted they normally followed. Apart from Jerome's dislike of the price he had to pay his Jewish teachers, I know no single reference to Jewish economic activity before the time of Agobard. And I suspect his evidence, as based on religious prejudice and as lacking in any purely economic interest ... Moreover, a very important element in the whole matter is

the 'instinctive' dislike of the Jew which naturally results from the normal teaching of the life of Christ and the beginnings of the Church. With this background, if you tell a Christian the Jew is guilty of this and that he is more disposed to believe it than if you told him similar stories of his Christian neighbours.

The fact that *The Conflict of the Church and the Synagogue* caused no stir does not matter. What matters is that it changed the way historians thought about the history of Jewish–Christian relations. Everything in the passage quoted immediately above became and remains the standard stuff of Jewish–Christian history, so standard indeed that it is taken for granted.

The radicalism of James' thinking is unquestionable. In one particular aspect, however, it is more than radical: it is revolutionary, even if that revolution has not yet, and never will, arrive. In a few years he had travelled an immense distance. 'It was not any particular contemporary fact on either side which led to this tragic result, nor was it any deduction by the Christians of any one period from the behaviour of their Jewish contemporaries ... Moreover, a very important element in the whole matter is the "instinctive" dislike of the Jew which naturally results from the normal teaching of the life of Christ and the beginnings of the Church.' We are here a quantum shift away from a disgruntled Hungarian middle class, ill-educated Rumanian graduates with their illegitimate grievances, or Polish nationalist politicians grappling with a minority reckoned to owe its loyalties elsewhere. We are also some way from those insincere racial propagandists in Germany. And where have we ended up: with 'the *normal* teaching of the life of Christ and the beginnings of the Church'.

The two themes, the teaching about Christ and the beginnings of the Church, James developed in another pioneering book, *Jesus, Paul and the Jews*, published in 1936. I am not competent to speak with even the slightest authority on Paul; James probably got him wrong, but in mitigation virtually every commentator has got that enthusiastic and infuriating convert wrong: I do not intend to join their number. The first chapter of the book, however, confirms the quantum leap outlined in the last paragraph. 'We are compelled to admit', writes James, 'that so long as we maintain that the last word has been said on the

Pharisees by the Gospel narratives ... [the "typical Pharisee" as a "pig-headed Sadist" will remain] ... But if we look to Jewish sources, and to Jewish history, we are presented with a completely different picture.' What Christian scholar had ever looked with an un-jaundiced eye to either, let alone both, before James Parkes set off on his 'lonely job'? His discovery of how wrong those scholars had been about Judaism brought out his fieriest prose:

> Theological ophthalmology – removing the motes from the eyes of others – is the hall mark of Christian writing on Judaism from Justin Martyr to Karl Barth, and from beginning to end it is as universally detestable as it is usually inaccurate. One can say with perfect security that the average Christian scholar is not only much more familiar with the less agreeable sides of Rabbinic Judaism than with the similar ideas of historic Christian theology, but that he is much more familiar with them than are 99 per cent of Rabbinic Jews themselves. If we ever desire that the Jew may make an objective study of the best in Christianity, we might surely begin by teaching our own folk the best in Judaism.

It has become a commonplace among Christian scholars that the Pharisees of the Gospels were 'the best in Judaism'. We have James to thank for that. There was one 'still more difficult task ... [than] ... to present a new and fairer picture of the opponents of Jesus and Paul':

> A further stage to be reached before the Christian can claim a clear conscience on this matter: the recognition that a living and vital Judaism has survived the separation between Judaism and Christianity, survived in the purpose of God, not as a mediaeval scholastic would claim as a permanent warning to the sin of killing the Messiah, but because of the possession of an autonomous and essential witness to the nature of the relationships of God to his Creation.

Writing before the Shoah, James was still able to imagine a time when a Christian might have 'a clear conscience on this matter'; writing after it, and discovering that churchmen talked a good deal about responsibility and repentance but did nothing to change their ways, he knew his imaginings had been fond. In a review of his friend Charles Singer's pamphlet, *The Christian Approach to* Jews, published in *The Torch* of November 1937, he identified the crux of 'this matter'. 'Jews', Singer had written, 'are well aware that in the liturgies of the Churches, passages are still read as inspired Scripture, which Christian scholars themselves recognize to be spurious', and James added, 'passages which falsely represent the Jews and Judaism, and which yet we retain'. It is the words 'still' and 'yet' which, just as much as that 'even now' we noted above, give the game away so far as the sanguine Charles Singer and James Parkes are concerned. Again we are blessed or cursed with hindsight. Aside from what was done at Vatican II to take out positively insulting references to Jews in particular prayers, has any church adequately censored its lectionary? The daily Gospel and Epistle Readings are always being tampered with, but not in this respect: 'the Jews' and 'the Pharisees' still figure daily as the villains of the piece. Additionally, the readings from the Torah and the Prophets continue to be chosen with almost single-minded attention to those passages believed to pre-figure Christ. In fact, so much would have to be done that if it were, Christianity would cease to exist.

As for putting the record straight about the emergence of 'a living and vital Judaism' he was to do that in the long delayed *The Foundations of Judaism and Christianity*, published in 1960. Others have followed in his footsteps, but this is not a book about books. It is about a man and his ideas. That said, a little more might be ventured about *The Conflict of the Church and Synagogue*, path-breaking book that it was. I have written elsewhere:

> Every historian thinks he is having the last word. He never is. No history book outlasts the generation for which it is written, if it does that. An influential history book does, however, have an afterlife in the work of the succeeding generation, and, if it is very good, in the generation after that. Then its afterlife also comes to an end. Its job is done. There are a handful of exceptions to this iron law: Burckhardt's *Civilization of the Renaissance,* Maitland's *Domesday Book and Beyond*, Huizinga's *Waning of the Middle Ages,* Tawney's *Religion and the Rise of Capitalism*, Hoskins' *The Making of the English Landscape*. The list is not exhaus-

tive. What makes such books so durable? It is as much the quality of their prose as it is the originality of their ideas.

I think *The Conflict of Church and Synagogue* should join the select band. It is written with such a high degree of clarity and in the most straightforward English that a child could understand it. Such simplicity and such lucidity are rarely found in scholarly works. They are in *Domesday Book and Beyond*. I wonder whether that is because Maitland was not an academic. Nor of course was Parkes. His books are free of academic jargon. There is no parade of erudition,; no putting on of linguistic airs or stretching of the English vocabulary beyond its limits. There is no verbal posturing. Great learning is lightly worn and effortlessly displayed, or has the appearance of being so, as a great deal of care and attention has gone into writing of such limpidity.

The other point I wish to make about the book is that among its other truths and insights (for besides the reworking of the first centuries of Christian–Jewish history, it has many of these) there are at least two that require special emphasis. The first is this: 'The burning of a synagogue by a mob is a direct outcome of the intellectual gymnastics of the learned, who themselves would rarely have dreamed of committing such violence.' Intellectuals be warned: loose speech endangers lives. Secondly, there is the following: 'It is not possible to create an inferior class and then to expect that individual enthusiasm will not overstep the bounds of legal permission. The general validity of this consequence is being abundantly proved in present day Germany.' Here, surely is a universal truth. James is also admirable on 'the religious fanaticism of the oriental religious orders', that is Simon of the Pillar and his friends and followers. They are normally portrayed as harmless freaks, doing only damage to themselves; we are reminded that because of them synagogues were desecrated. The religious fanaticism of the occidental religious orders he would tackle later. He is less than admirable on other aspects of Byzantium, or so I am sure latter-day Byzantinists would claim. For example, 'Byzantine literature presents a sorry spectacle to the modern Christian historian ... a literature marked by an almost complete indifference to ethical and moral values'. We are altogether more careful these days in what we say about 'decaying cultures' and 'oriental influence'. Perhaps the overall thrust of this great book might be summed up in a single Parkesian phrase: 'happily all Christians are not theologians'.

A failure to do justice in the early 1930s to Byzantine culture and, I suspect, Eastern Christianity is pardonable. To do the same where the history of English Jewry is concerned is less so. It is during his exchange with a Syndic of Oxford University Press, recorded in *Voyage of Discoveries*, that he makes the following strange statement. The Syndic suggested he bring *The Conflict of Church and the Synagogue* down to 1290, 'an excellent date'. James replied that 'it is a totally unimportant date in medieval Jewish history'. 'And thereon', he says as if he has made an incontrovertible point, 'we parted.' I am tempted to indulge myself in an exclamation mark. We have, after all, not only to pinch ourselves, but also to remember that *Voyage of Discoveries* was written in the mid-1960s. Forty years later there has been a book about the expulsion of the Jews from England entitled *England's Jewish Solution*. Parallels, it is clear, have been drawn: rightly so. Why, therefore, did James never draw them? What does he mean by 'unimportant'? He may be thinking globally and in millennial terms, yet all the more reason for marking 1290 as a European watershed in Christian–Jewish relations. The expulsion may have been a neglected date in English history; it was and is not in Jewish memory. Have we caught Parkes napping? I do believe we have.

We now must return to Geneva. It is 1934. James is 40 and a *Herr Doktor*. What he was to do next might not be thought unusual, at any rate to those readers who have got this far, but to some at the time it can only have seemed perverse. One of those was Sir Lewis Namier, whom we have already characterized as the greatest English historian of his day. He was a Jew from deepest Eastern Europe, which may well be why he was the greatest English historian of his day. He wrote to James from Manchester on 19 February 1934; the letter must be quoted in full:

> My dear Parkes, I dined on Friday, after one of my Ford Lectures, with Powicke, and we came to talk about undergraduates and undergraduate politics at Oxford. He told me how much he wanted to have you at Oxford and that he thought you would have a good chance of being chosen Chaplain at Oriel, if you stood for it. He added that he himself is not on the Selecting Committee – but I take it that he must know more or less how the land lies. He asked me

what I thought of it from the point of view of the I.S.S. movement, and I gave him the answer which I now repeat to you: that I think it of the utmost importance that you should stand for that post and obtain it. Oxford will in the next few years be the chief battle ground between the forces of civilization and darkness in this country. I consider Cambridge much safer, and the young Universities less important. But if there is a chance of your obtaining such an excellent vantage point, I think it is well nigh your duty towards the movement, of which I consider you the prime mover, to take it. I understand that you will have plenty of time for your research – and if you want to go to Paris or Geneva there are the vacations, and moreover there are aeroplanes. With present communications you could, I think, arrange your work in College in such a way that you might from time to time take off three days, even in term time, whenever required. In short, I urge you most strongly to stand for that fellowship. I hear the report of your Examiners on your thesis was downright 'lyrical'. Yours ever, LBN.

Here was an opportunity. Oxford as an apocalyptic battleground was an exaggeration: it had not been that since the time of John Wyclif. Yet, the university in the second half of the 1930s was a more politically exciting place to be than it had been for centuries, as appeasement became the topic of more than just conversation. A year after Hitler had come to power, Namier, one of the most sensitive of observers of European politics, on which he also wrote sublimely, was well aware of what was ahead. So, of course was James. Neither of them was a pacifist and, well-informed as they both were, neither would be an appeaser. If Oxford was to become the front line Namier thought it would be, we might have thought that James would have been tempted by the chaplaincy and fellowship at Oriel. He was not. It is impossible to be certain why not. He says nothing at all about it in *Voyage of Discoveries*. If the reasons he gave for rejecting later offers of livings apply in this case, then he was opposed on principle to being paid for doing one job while actually doing other things, that is being paid for serving as a priest when he was chiefly engaged in writing and lecturing. His scruples were not those either of medieval clergy or of modern dons.

Namier, for one, saw the advantages, we might say the virtues, of such a life. Or, did James simply run away?

For what he did do was resign from I.S.S. in the summer of 1934 and in the spring of 1935 return to England where, financed by Israel Sieff of Marks and Spencers, he led the life of an independent writer and lecturer. Barley was never an ivory tower, because on the one hand James was accessible and hospitable to all, his books being at any fellow scholar's beck and call, and on the other because he did not cut himself off from actively supporting good causes, especially that of getting Jewish refugees from Germany and Austria into England. Nonetheless, after 12 years in one front line Barley has to be viewed as a retreat. James did not see it that way: for him the work he was doing on antisemitism had to be done and done by him because no one else was doing it. If it was not actually war work, if he was not quite in the trenches, it was very much like the work he had done at the gas school in the First World war: in a grim situation he would do what he had the gift for in order to prevent the bad from becoming worse. Others, Namier and Powicke among them, may have seen things differently. Poor Powicke: he rates no more than the most passing of references in *Voyage of Discoveries*, and while James had undoubtedly known infinitely more about the subject of the thesis than had his shy and retiring supervisor, Powicke must have given James valuable assistance in clearing a path through the Oxford bureaucratic undergrowth, however slight may have been the help he could give him in other ways. Supervisors are often lavishly thanked; Powicke gets not a word of gratitude. James at 40 seems not just to be his own man, which he had been since he was a boy; he seems also to have grown so self-reliant, become so dependent on his own judgement, that 'his tendency towards self-belief, ...' while not excluding the contribution of others to a great enterprise, does on occasion fail to acknowledge it. Perhaps too many of his co-workers he came to regard as 'other ranks', even if there were non-commissioned officers among them. We need to remember that the 1915 conversion to kindness as a means of getting done what he wanted doing, was about the exercise of power. James was not arrogant. He was magnetic and dynamic, and he used his charm.

He had presumably used it on Israel Sieff, as he had earlier on various members of the Warburg family, who had given him money to augment the work of I.S.S. in 1927, and again in 1933 to pay for the work of the League of Nations High Commission for Refugees. James worked for a while under James McDonald, the High Commissioner, but they parted company amicably in the same year when there was a disagreement over salaries: James McDonald and his immediate staff were getting too much, James Parkes, his non-Jewish expert, and Norman Bentwich, his Jewish one, not enough. Israel Sieff seems to have helped financially with the publication of *The Conflict of the Church and the Synagogue* in 1934, and when James outlined his plans to him for continuing the work on antisemitism from a base in England, he agreed to underwrite the project to the tune of £250 a year. It had to be England as James could no longer afford to live in Switzerland. He preferred Cambridge to Oxford, and with good reason Cambridge University Library to the Bodleian. The house he found in the village of Barley was 15 miles south of Cambridge and two or three miles out of Royston on the railway line to London. The house, advertised at £1,250, he secured for £1,185 with the help of his solicitor uncle, Sackville Bell. Before he got to Barley, however, there occurred what has come to be known as 'The Geneva Incident'.

The incident got him notoriety in the English Press: 'Nazi Plot Against British Clergyman', 'Old Elizabethan Threatened By Nazis', 'Mystery of Geneva: Vicar's Servant Attacked', 'Man Knocked Out in Former Curate's Flat', ran the by-lines. This was the only time James Parkes ever got into the newspapers, apart that is from when his letters were published in them, when his Profile appeared in *The Observer* in 1960, and when he was obituarized. Here is what happened. He came to England in January 1935 and went on a strenuous lecture tour that took him over the following few months as far afield as Edinburgh and Aberystwyth. By the end of March he was in Cornwall recovering at the house of his friends the Singers. He had already recruited for Barley Thomas Thomas, the odd job man at Student Movement House when he had been its warden ten years before. Thomas had a wife and family so had been unwilling to work outside England. He was happy to come to Barley. Having spent ten days or so with his father on Guernsey, James went to London in mid-April; after attending to business there he went to a conference in Oxford and returning to London to collect Thomas, they travelled to Geneva together, there to pack up the contents of James' flat. They arrived on Thursday 25 April. The drama that ensued is described at length in *Voyage of Discoveries*. During James' absence his flat had been provided with police protection, threats having been made on his life (and to his books) by the Swiss Fascist Party, the *Eisene Front*. In the late afternoon of Saturday 27 April, under the nose of a sleeping policeman outside the door of the flat and with James inside it, Thomas, mistaken for his employer because he had on his best suit, was beaten unconscious on the stairs by an unknown assailant. He was so severely assaulted that he could not travel back to England for three weeks, and when he and James did get to Barley at the end of May Thomas was and remained for many months 'a very sick and disturbed man'. It is to James' credit that he persevered so long in such a trying situation with an unhappy and unstable invalid. After helping James get the garden straight in the summer of 1935 Thomas left Barley early in 1936, apparently to the mutual relief of both of them, but to Thomas's later (and everlasting) regret.

They corresponded at intervals until James and Dorothy moved to Dorset and found Thomas 'living only half an hour away'. Thomas died in 1968. There are numerous letters between them in the Parkes Papers; others are from James to friends asking for their help in finding Thomas a job or, after his wife died and his son had been killed on military service in India, asking them to call in to see how he was. An early letter from Thomas, undated but of March 1937 as that was the month James replied to it, is worth giving in its entirety. The great majority of the letters written to James were from fellow scholars, old friends who were his equals, or men and women of some standing in the world at large. The letters to and from his nephew Aldus when Aldus was at school are a notable exception, and we will make use of them later. There are a handful of others of a similar, homely nature. The letter from Thomas is pathetic. What it demonstrates is the regard an ordinary working man had for the exceptional man who is the subject of this study. This might not be the way Bunter would have written to Lord Peter, or Mr Lugg to Albert Campion, or Jeeves to Bertie Wooster, although in better days (better days that never came to pass) Thomas might have written to James as they, good batmen that they were, would have done to their gentlemen. The letter was written from Hollybush Cottage, Sandridge, St Albans:

My dear Dr Parkes, I was just ever so glad to hear from you for it did cheer me up for it was just like old times and yet at the same time it makes me feel very down hearted to think of what might have been and what is. I know you may say it was my own fault at leaving Barley – yet at the time I felt I was doing it all for the best – for as you know just at that time I was feeling very down – I know now what made me feel worse than what I had been feeling was because of some one we had stopping with you. It made me think of that bang on the head and as you know that made it worse. But as things have turned out I may just have well stopped with you for what good have I done – none. You know when I left you I was hoping to have been able to come back again – but what is the good of wishing that now for I feel some how I have not got a chance – I only wish I had. You know ever since I left Barley I have been fed up – for as I have said I have done no good only made things worse. Some people will never say they have made a mistake – but I don't mind saying I *know* I have. Well good by and God bless you – with kindest regards from Mrs Thomas and John and myself. Yours always Thomas

James had neither left Geneva nor arrived at Barley in pleasant circumstances. The only amusement to be found in 'The Geneva Incident' is the case of mistaken identity it involved. The casual attire of an unusual Englishman abroad and the formal dress of his retainer had led to the wrong man being banged on the head. It is ever the way with fascists: they get their man but it is always the wrong one.

3
Barley Before the War

The Geneva Incident at such a range as this seems almost comic, or rather one is tempted to think James' response to it risible. Take the following paragraph:

> On two occasions in my early days at Barley I went to Harwich to meet friends from Germany who were coming to stay with me, and then return to the Nazi world. I found the police, passport officers and customs men fascinated by the problem of ensuring that there was no risk of any Nazi seeing my friends meet me and so becoming themselves suspect. They devised a route by which they would see my visitor off until I could meet him safely, and held up all the rest of the passengers until he and I were out of sight.

It is better to resist temptation, best of all to be charitable and to give James the benefit of every doubt: the attack on Thomas had been unnerving; the threats he had received had not proved illusory; he was a marked man. In Nazi Germany, friends like Fritz Beck had been murdered; bestial things were being done to former opponents of National Socialism at Dachau and elsewhere; there were plenty of fascists in England, even more Nazi fellow-travellers, and enough thugs for hire. Yet, one wonders whether the police, passport officers, and customs men at Harwich did not have a good laugh together when the clergyman and his German friend had departed. All that fuss about what, they might have said among themselves. Better safe than sorry the more serious of them might have responded and we have to agree.

There is, nonetheless, another and more genuinely funny side to the way in which James behaved, not only in the cloak and dagger antics at Harwich in 1935, repeated with regard to his father in Guernsey during its occupation in the Second World War, but also in the burning in May 1940 of 'all files which showed other Christians, especially prominent ones, associating themselves in pro-Jewish activities', and even in his not travelling in Europe during the second half of the 1930s. As we have said, he was wise to take precautions, especially in May 1940: had the Germans occupied Britain, as they looked like doing, James (and most if not all of his friends) would have been dead. About this we should make no bones whatsoever. What makes the reader laugh or wince according to her level of tolerance is the manner of the telling of these serious stories. In *Voyage of Discoveries* James is his own worst enemy. Philip Toynbee was right when he said that 'what emerges from this misleading book is a near caricature of the bustling liberal cleric of our day, shallow in too many of his attitudes, impatient of everyone who differs from him about anything, and cocky to the point of insufferable boastfulness'.' I am not sure if the boastfulness is insufferable; as his biographer I have had to learn to suffer James' strong sense of self-importance gladly.

One of Toynbee's charges needs to be dealt with at greater length if only because it seems to be true: 'shallow in too many of his attitudes'. That is not quite the right phrase for what demands discussion, but it will serve as introduction to Parkes the Philistine, a topic already touched on. Where in the autobiography is there a word about art, or literature, or theatre, or film, or opera, or music? His silence has to show that they did not mean much to him. Of course, he is no more likely to mention that he had a radio or a gramophone and listened to it, than he is that he had a car and drove it to Harwich to pick up his continental visitors. Equally one does not write letters about seeing a Rembrandt, or reading Proust, or listening to Bix Beiderbecke, or does one? In the hundreds of letters in the Parkes Papers I cannot recall one that touches on the arts, of whatever variety. I have the uneasy feeling that James might have regarded the arts as frivolous, demonstrating alas that Toynbee is right, for you have to be 'shallow' not to respond to the creative and imaginative ways artists, writers and musicians enrich the world, God's creation. At the most superficial level our exclamation has to be: alas he missed so much! Beyond that is a more serious question to be asked: what sort of a man is it who finds neither instruction nor delight in imaginative and creative endeavour? That James was 'shallow' is only a part of the answer and not an important part, as James was not 'shallow' *tout court*. How is it that so well educated and such an intelligent man can be so impervious to culture? Should we blame his West Midlands bourgeois forebears, his Victorian father, Elizabeth College, or Oxford? Or is this a simple (and typical) case of Englishness, the English, by contrast with the French and Germans being noted for their philistinism: scratch an Englishman and find the Philistine. Yet, as we have been at pains to emphasize, James was not a typical Englishman. In other words, he did not have bad taste; he had no taste at all.

On the other hand, he did have the typical Englishman's eccentricity: he was a passionate gardener. As, however, he gardened with one eye to making his garden pay he was also the true son of his Guernsey market-gardening parent. Of his wartime garden he tells one of the stories that made Philip Toynbee gnash his teeth in public. It was a case of Israel Sieff to the rescue; whereas the local markets had paid James next to nothing for his fruit and vegetables, Marks and Spencers took all he could produce and paid him a good price. Soon he was organizing his fellow-villagers:

> When the accounts were settled at the end of the season, I went to the first and asked him how much he expected. He worked it out as best he could, and said that he would be very much disappointed if it was not in the neighbourhood of five pounds. I gave him a cheque for nearly twenty.

Nor could James leave it at that; he goes on, 'One of my biggest regrets is that I had to abandon, almost before I started it, my original intention to keep a diary and produce at the end of the war *A Village in Wartime*':

> I think it would have been a best seller, for I was involved in every aspect of the life of the village. I was involved in the affairs of both the parish church and the Congregationalists, for I used frequently to take the service for the minister, who was air raid warden for his village. I preached at most of the Congregational churches around Barley. I was, *of course* [my italics], involved in the whole educational life, in evacuation and billeting, and knew all the farmers and watched the agricultural changes. I was also in touch with the A.R.P. ... I was perpetually too busy, and at the end of the day, far too tired to make the necessary effort to write up a diary.

If we did not already know him better we might well believe his fellow villagers called him behind his back an interfering busybody, and that visitors to Barley returned home to complain of the opinionated bore they had had to put up with. On the contrary: the first pocketed their cheques, were instructed by his sermons, and were appreciative of his never failing generosity (one of the first things he did was to give away half an acre of his garden to make cottage gardens), while the second invariably went beyond common courtesy in their letters of thanks, making clear that they had been entertained in every sense.

In the company of friends James relaxed. Gardening seems only to have been partially relaxation. At least it was a change from sitting at his desk writing, which is how he occupied the greater part of every day. It is not, I think, a question of all work and no play: James was the very antithesis of a dull boy. He did work too hard, and in the later 1950s endured the painful consequences of his belief in the Protestant Work Ethic. It was both less and more than him taking over zealously 'the Work', as he and Dorothy would call what he was doing for Jewish–Christian relations; in explanation we have to return to his lack of culture. Painting, music, literature give heart to men and women, the arts being as uplifting as they are sustaining, and at their best they are as much glimpses into Heaven as are the rites of religion. Indeed, at their best they often *are* what make religious rites Heavenly. Why was James impervious to this aspect of the arts? The answer, at least partly, seems to lie in his inability to get out of himself, the reason for that being that he was so completely bound up in his own preoccupations and achievements he took little thought for anything outside them, as his unfortunate autobiography all too clearly demonstrates. It is, however, only half the story; his self-reliance is surely the other half. James was not only a do-everything and a know-all, he was so imbued with the ideas of duty and responsibility that he had to attempt everything and try to know all. Both nature and nurture made him the sort of man he was: he had to be doing and doing for himself

I doubt that he was ever impulsive; I do not believe he was ever rash. I am not sure that he ever fell in love. Courageous, honourable, thoughtful and never thoughtless, as well as generous, his virtues were the tried and true ones. He was also, as we have seen, adventurous of mind, going where no English gentile had either dared or wished to go, and bold of spirit, taking on all and every task, both those that came his way and those that he had to go out of his way for. He can be readily imagined on Scott's Last Polar Expedition or with Shackleton sailing to Georgia. Thus, the devotion he showed to his 'poor Jews' is no mystery. For him Jews were a chosen people, chosen because they were the last of a long line of unfortunates, whose lineage began with African slaves and chimney boys, and continued through factory workers, imprisoned debtors, and fallen women, until reaching a sort of apotheosis with the wounded of World War One. James was a Victorian adrift in a New Age. He was fortunate to find in the 'poor Jews' a cause good enough for a life's work.

Luxuries in the conventional sense he could not afford. It may be, therefore, that visits to London art galleries and attendance at London concerts came under that head, although as he was quite often in London on business or at the British Museum reading the books he did not have at Barley, he could easily have taken in one or both with little or no expense. He had, as we have come to expect, his own decided views on spending, and as he was living out of Israel Sieff's pocket he had to be (and was) particularly scrupulous. In the late 1920s he had set out his ideas on money for a fellow worker in either the Student Christian Movement or the International Student Service; in a long, undated letter to 'Eleanora' he combined conventional wisdom with idiosyncrasy. To live simply if not frugally was the aim, and as regards 'routine spending', 'When I was in London, I scaled myself I think to three pounds a week or two pounds ten, but the result was I never had to worry. I am sure many people worry themselves all the time by not doing this.' The real issue was, 'What should one do with the residue?' First there was 'the question of tithe'; here he undoubtedly took his own advice both before and after 1935:

> I think the tithe is an important thing to conserve, but not in the form of adding up to say that I have just given the Lord his tenth this year, and now I need not worry about other charities. For people like ourselves in S.C.M. and I.S.S. work it is very simple. Put it back in the work. There are always lots of things that the general funds will not stand – paying students to conferences and such like ...

> Sometimes it is in the dull things that you cannot ask people for – buying your own typewriter for the movement's work or office furniture. Don't expect it always to be romantic, or heroic.

When making a purchase pay what was asked; much 'rubbish' was talked about 'wasting money'; money, like life, 'was not made to be rationed':

> Perhaps some people will be very shocked at all this ... They will say that there is so much misery in the world etc. Well there is something in it, but money is NOT in a special category with regard to that. If that idea were logically applied there would be no civilization or culture justifiable in the world at all. We have duties to others than the poor. In a word we are to live in the Kingdom of God as well as to achieve it, and that means a certain expenditure on ourselves and our surroundings ... This sets the standard of my expenditure, though I do not pretend to live always up to it. This or that luxury would not exist in the Kingdom of God, therefore I am not justified in spending on it. I include in this extravagant restaurants, fancy prices for objets d'art and jewellery, collecting first editions, stamps and such like. But there are other things which are called 'luxuries' which are not, books, good pictures, theatres and of course beautiful furniture, flowers, holidays. On these we are justified in spending.

Is this not a passage crying out for an exclamation mark? Did James think he knew what the furnishings of the Kingdom of God actually were?

The other absurdities derive from that one. Here again is God in human form, in this instance God as Connoisseur, the God of Good Taste, but good taste according to James Parkes. What fun we could have with the passage: God mulling over the menu of a restaurant; God in the sale room withdrawing from the bidding as it goes beyond his reserve price for an objet d'art; God cancelling a holiday in Ibiza; God as Gardener pulling up the weeds; but not God the Stamp Collector poring over beautiful stamps. It is too easy to indulge in mockery. Nonetheless, the point being made is serious. There is another that James does not quite make and it can be framed in time-honoured fashion where descriptions of God are concerned: God is not a collector. Nor, one feels, should the religious man or woman be. The urge to collect might be a strong one in men and women; it is not a natural one. What is collected is irrelevant, unless it involves doing damage to others (scalps, rare bird's eggs, guns); it is the act of collecting that is, to say the least, unsocial. It is odd that the socially minded James Parkes did not see that. He collected English bronze candlesticks.

He presumably did not do so using any of Israel Sieff's annual £250. Some of this sum went, as it was agreed that it would, on books necessary for 'the Work'. By far the greater part went on the establishment at Barley. The house itself was large, being a fourteenth-century hall house much altered and extended. There were plenty of rooms and plenty of space, enough for James' books and for him to create two bathrooms; there was also a barn and a granary, and even after James had given half an acre away there were two acres of garden. When Thomas Thomas departed in 1936 James got as his general factotum John McNeilage. John did the cooking (even after Dorothy arrived in 1942) as well as just about everything else domestic. In 1936 he was engaged to a girl from the village and they soon acquired a cottage and got married. Apart from his war service in the Y.M.C.A. canteen at Ipswich, John worked for James until he and Dorothy left Barley in 1964. *God in a World at War*, first published in 1940, is dedicated to him. *Good God*, also published in 1940, was dedicated to Kenneth Dodkin, then in the Royal Artillery, but before that the other arm of what was sometimes called the 'Barley Tripod': Kenneth was James' 'personal and research secretary'. Like John McNeilage, Kenneth Dodkin was 'a local youngster'; he was, wrote James, 'not particularly brilliant', but he learned quickly and 'developed into a wonderful colleague, completely reliable in keeping both my diary and my accounts, and doing it with a generosity and loyalty which always replied to any suggestion of an increase of salary that this had better wait until there was more money in the till'. Kenneth Dodkin appears to have replaced rather than served alongside Hermann Eschelbacher, the research assistant James employed when he was first at Barley while working on *The Jew in the Medieval Community*, published in 1938. How long Rose, the village's only unmarried mother before the war (when 'handsome prisoners of war' came along to add to the tally) was James' charwoman he does not make clear. Of course it was the village outcast who had to be his cleaner; of course he paid her fifty per cent more than the going rate for local charwomen.

Such was the staff required for a scholar in the 1930s who was not the fellow of a college, or a teacher at a provincial university with secretaries and a catering department on hand. James undoubtedly did better than either: college fellows in those days seldom had a secretary *and* a research assistant, if they had either, while a lecturer at Manchester, London, or Leeds, unless he had a private income or lived in a student hostel, had usually to fend for himself. Regarded in that light, it is no wonder that James turned down the chaplaincy at Oriel for Israel Sieff's £250 per annum. He would have got a lot less done at Oxford. If he had had scruples about taking a salary for doing one thing while occupying himself with others, he was not unmindful of the ambiguities of the option he had chosen:

> In fact there never was 'more money in the till', though I.M.S [Israel Sieff] was reasonable about the inevitability of expenditure growing. But I never asked him for more than the minimum on which I could manage, for the calls upon him were far more than most non-Jewish millionaires would attempt to meet, and I was always conscious of the unfairness of a Jewish friend having to provide the necessary funds for fighting against the non-Jewish, in fact Christian, sin of antisemitism.

It was Freud who said it was not Jews who should reply to antisemitism; I do not think he is reported as saying that Jews should pay for Christians to do so. At any rate, Israel Sieff soon got the first instalment of what he was paying for. James worked rapidly: *The Jew in the Medieval Community* took only two years to write, the index being completed by the summer of 1937. The preface was written in January 1938 and the book itself came out later the same year.

It is something of a disappointment. One reason is probably that it was intended to be the second of a five-volume history of antisemitism and volumes III–V were never written. The worsening international situation from 1938 and the Second World War have to take the blame: James became deeply committed to helping Jewish refugees after the fall of Austria and once the war had begun he was also active, principally (but not only) as a prominent member of the Common Wealth party, in politics generally. At least, that is what one is bound to infer, for I have not found, or have not remembered finding, any direct statement on how the missing three volumes became a host of other books. It was also the case that James saw in the foundation of Israel the best answer to antisemitism, and being the activist he was he put much time and energy into publicising the fact. We cannot argue that Israel ought not to have diverted him from the task of writing the history of antisemitism. Israel has already lasted a good deal longer than a history of antisemitism written before the significance of the Shoah had sunk in would have done.

A second reason for *The Jew in the Medieval Community* being unsatisfactory is that it is less than half the story of medieval European Jewry. The book is sub-titled *A study of his political and economic situation*; the succeeding volume was to be called *The Church and The Jews in the Middle Ages*. As it stands, *The Jew in the Medieval Community* consists of three parts: an introduction which takes the narrative begun in *The Conflict of the Church and the Synagogue* down to the opening of the twelfth century; a long central section on the political status of Jews; and a final section entitled somewhat misleadingly 'The Royal Usurer', as it deals with loans and banking in general during the Middle Ages. All three parts are exemplary for their time. Nowadays, however, the middle section seems overdone. James had sent these 'political chapters' to Maurice Powicke. His former supervisor responded in June 1937: he thought the Church had been unfavourably presented. In reply, James agreed and left it at that. An attempt to show the medieval Church *vis-à-vis* Jews in a favourable light, especially during Powicke's beloved thirteenth century, would have been impossible. The history that was possible we never did get from James, volume two remaining unwritten (or unpublished); we are left with the politics and economics of *The Jew in the Medieval Community*, which are generally agreed to be considerably less than half the story. James was clear on that, which is why he got both topics into a single volume and was going to devote a whole volume to the sole subject of the Church. Nevertheless, the political, or rather legal, situation of Jews in the Middle Ages, for that is a more accurate description of what the second section of the book is about, is reckoned by most commentators these days to be of tertiary importance in the development of antisemitism. Religion comes first, economics second, and politics and the law third, or even fourth if sex is given the prominence some in the current Age of Sex would want to give it.

What a contemporary reader notices first about *The Jew in the Medieval Community* is the absence of a chronology, the chronology that has been accepted since the late 1940s and has become the backbone of all subsequent histories of the medieval period. Once known as the Twelfth Century Renaissance, the changes of that century are now regarded as more wide-ranging than simply cultural. They relate to urbanization, the full advent of a money and market economy, bureaucratization, suburbanization with all its tragic consequences for the displacement of rural bodies and minds, and (in short) the origins of capitalism. The 'long twelfth century' has become a catch-all for the emergence of a vigorous, outward (and in the minds of progressive historians) forward looking Western Europe, with internal colonization of pasture and woodland and external colonization eastwards as part of what some would see, under the leadership of the Church, as an imperious if not an imperial mission. The Church, once believed to have gone through a period of reform in the late eleventh and early twelfth centuries, is viewed with a more jaundiced eye these days; no longer are its self-proclaimed 'reforms' seen as much more than a ragged garment to cover what otherwise would have been naked aggression against secular rulers. The secular clergy of Western Europe were ill-mannered, ill-trained, and ill-read; until the coming of the friars in the thirteenth century they were no match for the majority of Cathar perfect and Waldensian laity. It was, as ever, chiefly women who were pious and knew what piety entailed. The old adage that the least devout man in a town was its bishop was proved over and over again, not in every generation and not in every city (take, for example, the early twelfth-century Thurstan, archbishop of York), but in most generations and in many cities. The 'short thirteenth century' was a different matter: the secular clergy and urban laymen were beginning to get on some sort of terms with the Christian faith. About the papacy the less said the better. By the mid-twelfth century popes had to be lawyers, because the Church had become a corporation and only a corporate lawyer could run it; even Innocent III, for all his largeness of vision, was a lawyer. None of this forms the background to James' discussion of 'usury', nor would it have done for the examination of the Church and Jews in the volume that never was.

The lack of an established chronology hampers the contemporary reader's appreciation of *The Jew in the Medieval Community*. It does not spoil it, but it does not help it. For what is mainly lacking is an account of how religious, economic and social change influenced the reflective man and woman's view of 'the Jew'. Indeed, such people may not have thought much about Jews until they began to think about Christianity, let us say in the decades either side of 1200. It was not until the second half of the thirteenth century that the Church's drive to make every man and woman understand the rudiments of their faith had much impact on those who were more instinctive than intellectual. Once there was a more widespread grasp of what a Christian ought to be, there came the realization of what he could not possibly be. He could not be a Jew and he ought not to have anything to do with Jews. Once the model Christian came into view, the anti-type Jew did also. Somewhere between the 'long twelfth century' and the 'short thirteenth century' the idea of 'the Jew', and the pornographic imagery that accompanied it, took root in Western Europe.

Religious reasons were not the only clay that went towards the creation of that Frankenstein. Judas was not only a renegade and a traitor, he had also kept the apostles' common purse and it was for thirty shillings of silver that he betrayed his lord. In the feudal world (and beyond it) to betray one's lord was the most heinous of crimes, as Dante made abundantly clear; to do so for money was unthinkable. To do anything for money in the twelfth century was ignoble: what men of worth did was done for land (with serfs on it), for horses, tents, swords, objets d'art, and for women. A nobleman might even betray his lord for a woman, at any rate in fiction. Money was dirty, *all* money was dirty until in the next century the friars, but not Francis, began to preach that some of it might be clean. Hence those who handled it were dirty. While there were more Christian bankers and dealers in money in the twelfth century than there were Jewish ones, with the Christianization of crafts and guilds (every craft had its guild, every guild its patron saint), Jews were excluded from all but the craft that had Judas as its patron, commerce in money. Jews once upon a time and in the not distant past had been and had done all that Christians were and did, except that they had not gone to church. By the end of the twelfth century, save in Sephardic Spain, almost every Ashkenazi Jew made a living by trading in money, or by working for those who did. The image of 'the Jew' had come into being.

Not much of this can be found in the second and third parts of *The Jew in the Medieval Community*, for James took a peculiarly static view of the history of Jewish–Christian relations once the drastic developments he had described in *The Conflict of the Church and the Synagogue* had taken fatal effect:

> For a large proportion of the Jewish people conditions remained essentially the same from the tenth century to the twentieth, and the present day has seen the old medieval insecurity affect the lives of millions of Jews who believed that it had at last become a thing of the past.

It is a sentence that has to be read twice by the contemporary reader before she can quite bring herself to believe its multiple errors, for the changes of the long twelfth century are far from being the only ones omitted. In all respects it is such an astonishing denial of history that one begins to doubt James' credentials as an historian. It may well be that some of the interpretations and explanations of historians have been overelaborated and not only in the medieval period, yet every one of them would blanch upon coming across the sentence just quoted. Not only are there omissions; there is also contradiction, the second half of the sentence contradicting the first. If the twentieth century had witnessed the revival of 'the old medieval insecurity ... a thing of the past', some degree of modern security had intervened. One has to wonder what James was thinking about when he wrote such a sentence. If history has stood still in it, geography has altogether vanished into thin air.

He is sounder on 'usury' and better on bankers. Regardless of subsequent work, the third section of the book may still be read with profit; how language betrays us: 'to read with profit' is a phrase that shows our twelfth-century capitalist origins. Capitalists in those distant days were not allowed the free rein they are in the epoch of 'Fordism', as James was well aware:

There is a point which is frequently overlooked. A modern usurer continues to collect his interest until his debt is paid. If the interest is not paid, it is added to the capital and accumulates further profit; and all the time the usurer himself is legally and socially secure. His medieval ancestor had to deal with a number of limitations. He was very rarely allowed to charge compound interest; at times his usury could only run for one year, whatever its rate, and however long repayment was deferred; and it was common to stipulate that once the usury had reached the total of the capital, it could not increase further.

He is also good on the idealistic stance adopted by the Church towards the lending of money, namely that Christians ought not to do it, that there was no reasonable rate of interest, and that the employment of money solely to make money was sinful. The Church's uncompromising other-worldliness was by 1200 a position from the past, the monastic past of pre-capitalist times: Francis performed an anachronism when he took a silver coin from one of his brothers and threw it on a dung heap. James is good also on Jews as lynchpins of the slave trade, but as he was writing before the history of the Vikings became, the sophisticated exercise it subsequently became he overlooks their role as the principal slavers of the tenth and eleventh centuries.

The Vikings are the polar opposite of the Jews: they assimilated easily, quickly blending into the contemporary foreground. The part the Vikings had played for over two centuries as Western Europe's most dreaded and hated enemies (the barbarians outside the gates) came to an end at about the time Jews in Western Europe began to be an object of fear and loathing. As Western Europe started transforming itself into Christendom, the enemy within took over from the enemy without. Jews tended to live in the heart of towns, yet they had international connections and engaged in what might be called extra-curricular activities; they appeared to be able to conjure up cash at a moment's notice and apparently had killed Christ. Were they not the prime candidates for a fifth column?

Individualized religion became important in the early thirteenth century just as the use of money was becoming widespread. Political hostility towards the Jews arrived not many years later. It was surely his non-chronological approach that prevented James grasping the significance of the date 1290 in Jewish history. Lack of a chronology also accounts for his failure in the 'political' chapters of *The Jew in the Medieval Community* to describe the change from pragmatism to bigotry on the part of rulers during the two centuries preceding 1290. Not every European ruler around 1100 was as ruthlessly pragmatic as were the Anglo-Norman kings of England, most notably William Rufus, yet none of them was bigoted in the way Louis IX of France and Edward I of England were. It was 'Christian' kings, dukes and counts, their mothers and wives, who were responsible for the deterioration in the situation of Jewries across Europe in the course of the thirteenth century. Arguably, James ought to have given more attention (as a political issue) to taxation; he was not, however, being strictly a book not a document man, a frequenter of the Public Record Office in Chancery Lane, even though it was on the site of the medieval *Domus Conversorum*: the English Exchequer of the Jews rates only a single entry in the index of *The Jew in the Medieval Community*.

Religion, money, sex: they once upon a time were the three topics to be avoided in polite conversation, unless memory has let me down and it was politics not money that was beyond the pail. Love and sex undoubtedly played a large part in gentile hostility towards Jews, at least in the legislation enacted by the Church. In practice, sexual love knew no boundaries, as in the notorious case of the deacon of Oxford, burned in 1222. In this matter there are two beautifully choreographed moments in Claude Lanzmann's film *Shoah* that are timelessly enlightening. A group of Polish women from Grabow are asked if they are pleased that there are no longer any Jewesses; the answer is that because their disappearance has removed from the scene the women Polish men best liked to make love to, they are. Immediately the film moves to the flourmill in the same town. Here Polish men are being interrogated; one is asked 'Does he miss the Jews?' We expect a negative answer but get, after a dramatic pause, a positive one: 'Yes, because there were some beautiful Jewesses.' In the Middle Ages, whatever the Church decreed, Christian–Jewish love-making came to an end only when Jews were expelled from the towns and countryside of a Christianized Europe.

The Jew in the Medieval Community is beautifully written. There are many pertinent observations and numerous memorable illustrations. For example, in the laws of Constantine a synagogue is referred to as a *conciliabulum*, Roman slang for a brothel. What could be more telling? If official language becomes that of the streets what chance of justice (let alone mercy) is there for those of whom it is used? When the language of abuse is the normal discourse of government those abused know they are doomed. We need look no further than Hitler and Lenin for confirmation of a universal truth. Agobard, for whom James has a soft spot, did not stoop to bad language, despite his knowledge of the *Sepher Toldoth Jeshu*, the Jewish Life of Jesus, a work characterised, writes James, by 'caricature', 'embittered satire', and 'contempt'. It was only to be expected: turning the other cheek is only for an exceptional handful. Had Jews been in Christian shoes and Christians in Jewish ones, the boot would have been on the other foot. James' account of the 'curious acts of violence' that took place at Eastertide in certain French towns (and at Rome itself), when Jews were set upon in a ritualised fashion, also makes one pause. When being both abusive and violent to Jews became normal Christian behaviour in the twelfth century these Easter rites ceased: what is to be learned from that? Had the boot been on the other foot, it is not difficult to imagine Christians at Passover being the object of a rite of Jewish contempt. On the other hand, it is impossible to imagine the antisemitism that took root in the twelfth century, with a tenacity which showed itself only recently in the desecration of a synagogue in London, a cemetery in Hull, and a memorial in Nottingham, would have had its Jewish equivalent.

A non-Jewish historian of the Jews is never likely to know everything about Jews, and James remained Christian in mind, if not in his heart and soul. Is it Jewish or Christian never to give up on mankind? James never did. Yet, evil is as ineradicable as antisemitism, so what is one to make of the following passage:

> Like all great social tragedies it [antisemitism] was not deliberately intended by human wickedness. Just as the nineteenth-century industrialist never intended the slums which were, in fact, the inevitable outcome of his economic policy, so the early fathers never intended the pogroms and massacres, the humiliating legislation, the insults and misrepresentations, which succeeding centuries have reared upon the foundations which they laid. None of the

other factors, psychological, economic or cultural, which lie dormant in all human relationships for good or evil, could of themselves have brought this monstrous spawn to birth, much though they may have contributed to its subsequent growth. Its 'onlie begetter' was the Christian theologian ...

A good deal of what raises the eyebrows here has been discussed above, but further discussion is required at this juncture. Harold Nicolson once said that antisemitism was hating Jews more than is natural. Did he mean it was natural to hate Jews but not to an antisemitic extent? Or that it is natural to hate Jews to the extent that one hates other people but unnatural to hate them more than that? If so, one wonders which people he had in mind. Why should it be a whole category of people that we hate? Do we hate all bus drivers when one of them is rude to us? All plumbers when one of them does a botched job? All professors when one of them turns out to be a cheat and a liar? All politicians are not tarred by the same brush anymore than theologians are. I suppose we are back with the age-old question: why pick on the Jews? What have they ever done? We can pick out class enemies, slum-creating industrialists for example, because they cause 'inevitable' social damage. The British can pick on the Germans because they seem to have wanted one world war after another. The Irish can pick on the English and we all know why. The Palestinians pick on the Israelis. The list is probably never-ending. We do, however, acknowledge that there are good Germans, just as we do that there are good bus drivers: because we often come across them. Why do not good Jews of our acquaintance have the same effect? That surely is where the unnaturalness comes in, and it does so to a greater extent today than it did in the Middle Ages, when a Christian asked why he hated Jews would have had a 'natural' answer ready: the Jews had murdered Christ.

Or was it only a psychological pretext? Did the medieval Christian have to have someone to hate? If he did, was it as a man or woman that he hated, or as a Christian? It was certainly expected that as a Christian he should hate Jews. In much the same way it was expected of Ukrainians that they would define themselves as such by a hatred of Poles (let alone Jews). Perhaps that is what Harold Nicolson means by a 'natural' hatred: if two peoples have always been at each other's throats, whatever the origins of their mutual animosity, what else is one to expect? The difficulty of trying to decide whether a Christian hates as a Christian or a Ukrainian as a Ukrainian is that no man or woman is simply a man or a woman: we are all something or other besides being women and men. To start with we are daughters and sons, often brothers and sisters, sometimes wife and husband. The difficulty is obvious. Some have even asked: do men hate women? Thus: if I want to be critical of James Parkes for trying to get humankind off the hook of hatred (original sin? psychological flaw? D.N.A. awry?), I find no logical, that is no rationally satisfying way of doing so. Logic is no match for history. Humankind has always hated as well as loved, and if there has not been sufficient cause, has invented one. The Christian fathers, upon whom James puts all the blame, had theological opponents before they concocted reasons for opposing them. Why, the reader asks, did they have opponents in the first place? As Jews did not murder Jesus what was the problem?

We have arrived at difference, the unspoken theme of the previous two paragraphs. Are the differences real or imagined? Those concocted by the Christian fathers, James appears to be saying, were imaginary. What, then, were the real ones? Is it not the different things we do that make the actual difference? In this case we need not look further than the day of the week selected for its holiness: is it Friday, Saturday, or Sunday? Yet, even in such a case other differences were already in existence before Jews, Christians and Muslims decided on their weekly holy day, for it seems holiness is defined by difference: our holiness is not their holiness. How can it be? The search for origins is a fruitless task. Where Christians and Jews are concerned one cannot get back beyond the Torah. Were the followers of Jesus to keep it or not? Jesus thought any followers of his were bound to do so, though like good Jews they should question it at all times and at every level, with every fibre of their being. Paul thought otherwise. Still: to end the story with a single culprit is thoroughly unsatisfactory. Is it necessary to hate Saint Paul?

Another aspect of the passage quoted three paragraphs back is hardly less intractable. It is the vexing one of intention. With regard to intention, James is no better or worse than the rest of us in the West, the Twelfth Century Renaissance having left its indelible mark on our culture. It was Abelard who put the idea of intention so squarely into the picture, even if Anselm had done some of the groundwork. Intention was taken into account by thirteenth-century confessors centuries before it was by secular magistrates. Culpability is less if the intention is not to harm: murder becomes manslaughter. Did the Jews intend to kill Christ, or was it only a troublesome agitator from the Galilee they wanted rid of? It was an important question. Although it seems inconceivable to those of us raised on historical sociology that the Jewish opponents of Jesus could have believed he was Christ (for if they had they would not have opposed him), it was accepted by almost all Christian theologians after Abelard's time that they did. Hence, they were more culpable than if they had only been instrumental in disposing of an embarrassingly charismatic teacher. It looks, therefore, as though James is not only condoning the behaviour of nineteenth-century industrialists, at any rate in relation to slums, but also his third-and-fourth century theologians, at least with regard to the hurt and harm their ideas gave rise to. The analogy may not be precise. Nineteenth-century industrialists did not care about the pathetic consequences of their profit-making; in those hard times so long as the margin between outlay and income was as wide as inhumanely possible, what business was it of theirs? Their obligations lay only in one direction: to the shareholders. Where did the church fathers' obligations lie?

It is odd that with his highly developed sense of responsibility James seems not to have been aware of the arguments deployable against those who regard intention as the critical component in an interpretation of action. Whatever the intention of Jews, Romans and Pontius Pilate, a man was crucified. When cars kill people are they not dead? When widows and orphans are fed, do they inquire why? Whenever we give a beggar a few coins, it does not matter what we think of her. It seems no excuse to tenants that their landlord did not intend the house they live in to become a slum. What they want is something done about it. In post-medieval times the belief seems to be that the road to heaven is also paved with good intentions, a consequence no doubt of the lack of belief in hell and purgatory. James was certainly too much of a humanist to believe in hell.

He was hard put to it, he said, to imagine Hitler there. He even made excuses for Douglas Reed, whose antisemitic book *Disgrace Abounding* was published in 1938. In a letter to T.R. Feiwel, who had sent James an article he had written about

Reed's book, he wrote that he thought it 'wisest (and incidentally I believe it to be true) to treat Douglas Reed as a victim of emotion rather than malice. I think it is a tactical mistake to attack him as a deliberate enemy; and I believe some of your paragraphs should be modified in this sense.' Feiwel subsequently 'put the article in a drawer'. I am not sure he should have done; there are times when one should not lean over backwards, even or especially at the bidding of the great. There is more in that letter to detain us, bearing as it does on intention and the idea of Jewish degradation, a theme with which both *The Jew in the Medieval Community* and our examination of it will end.

Here is the most contested ground of all, ground littered with the bodies of those who have stepped on the explosive mines that are scarcely to be avoided. In his letter to T.R. Feiwel, James writes of his Jewish friends reading no further than chapters 23 and 24 of *Disgrace Abounding*; 'but I think', he continues, 'that a great deal of the venom in his attack on [Jewish] refugees is explained in the incidents of chapter 26. One is still entitled to say that his generalizations from these incidents are absolutely unfair, but I think that their effect on him cannot be ignored.' James' readiness to find in actual fact a sufficient cause for prejudice has been noted previously, particularly in his assessment of Polish–Jewish relations in the 1920s and 1930s. In the letter he goes on, 'Incidentally a good deal of Jewish publicity is somewhat of the same character but nobody will believe me that its results create in the Gentiles the absolute opposite to what is intended.' James is about to step onto the most explosive mine of them all: are Jews responsible for the Jewish Problem? Have they been their own worst enemies? In the concluding sentences of *The Jew in the Medieval Community* James gives the impression that he thinks so:

> It is in this period that the Jew [sic] begins to be involuntarily the part-author of his own misfortunes. For the first time it became possible to use the contemporary behaviour of the Jew as an argument against him, as a justification for the hatred of him. Hatred of the usurer came in the minds of the Christian public to justify the killing of the deicide ... If the birth of modern antisemitism is observable in the usury of the Middle Ages, it was accompanied by, and directly the consequence of, another aspect of the modern

Jewish problem, the powerlessness of the Jew to direct his own destiny, with all the psychological consequences which that involves. The necessity of cringing before an owner with absolute power, and a populace moved by religious fanaticism, greed and hopeless indebtedness, inevitably produces unattractive characteristics. The Jew became what circumstances made him: his main, almost his only, responsibility in the creation of those circumstances was his desire to remain loyal to his Judaism. It was Christendom which decided that the price of that loyalty should be psychological and social degradation.

It was a remarkable way to bring a long (and remarkable) book to a close. Although there are qualifications, 'involuntarily' and 'part-author', 'necessity' and 'circumstances', for example, it is a single word that gives the game away: 'cringing'. Douglas Reed's Jews are 'cringing', the Jews in the mind of an antisemite are invariably 'cringing'; they may also be crafty, but they are not crafty in the way gentiles are, when the word is applied with more than a hint of approbation. James Parkes was not Douglas Reed. I am suggesting no such thing. But that James did share with Reed one of the most deeply imbedded prejudices of the age he lived in does appear to be the case. No one today would write of Jewish 'psychological and social degradation', let alone link it to a devotion to Judaism. Was it because some Jews were bankers, as James is suggesting? He is surely still on his old tack of a result having to have an actual, an observable, a measurable, a 'real' rather than an imaginary cause. There can be no smoke without fire, however small the fire, however dense the smoke. Undoubtedly, it has been the Shoah that has finally taught us it is the fireless smoke which is the most lethal kind, the kind that chokes you to death. This way to the gas, ladies and gentleman.

James' return to England in 1935 re-acquainted him with British politics. It was not long before he was actively engaged, although 'actively' for James meant in the main writing and lecturing. The East End, currently claiming a great deal of attention, was soon occupying his also. He wrote to Neville Laski on 30 December 1936 that in the previous October he had come 'to the conclusion that I ought to spend some time on the East End situation'. He had found, he went on, that among those who were 'quite unaffected by the wild general accusations of the fascists (Protocols, ritual murder etc.) there was an extremely critical attitude towards the Jews with whom they had come into contact':

> Their economic, social and moral conduct were all adversely criticised. They were said to be bad employers, bad commercial rivals, bad neighbours and immoral. Those who made these statements proceeded to illustrate them from examples of their own experience. You can easily guess the type of thing I mean — the clothing trade, cut price shops, Sunday trading, clannishness, etc.... What worried me very much was that I got this kind of accusation so constantly from those whom one would have expected to be more intelligent.

Evidently he had been into the East End. Can we imagine him interviewing the residents? It is more likely that he talked to those who worked among them and it is their views that he is reflecting:

> I have given in the two paragraphs above not my own views or scientific analysis of the situation, but the opinions of people whom I met in the East End. On the other hand I do think that there is enough reality in their criticism to necessitate a serious examination of their charges, for it is absolutely vital that this group should be won to whole hearted cooperation, and this can only be obtained if they are convinced that the Jews themselves are doing everything that they could be legitimately asked to do to set their own house in order.

So there it is: 'set their own house in order'. If there is a beam in the Christian eye (Protocols, ritual murder etc.), there is a mote in the Jewish one. He told Laski he would be giving 'a certain number of educational lectures to small East End audiences' in the Spring of 1937 and hoped that they might have some impact.

He had already elaborated on the Jewish mote in a paper of November 1936, called simply 'Antisemitism in the East End'. It seems not to have been published and probably served as a text for one of the lectures of 1937. 'Since it is common in all social relations only to distinguish ourselves from another group when we wish to express disapproval', he wrote:

it is natural that it was for unsociability, clannishness, sharp practice, and actual dishonesty, that 'the Jews' came to be distinguished from others in the East End, and the fact that the majority were exceptions to this estimate passed unnoticed. For example, the Jews are frequently accused of wealthy ostentation: actually, as a whole, the Jewish population of the East End is one of the poorest sections of the community, but it is the wealthy only that attract attention.

It was 'natural' too that Jews were 'peculiarly nervous and easily shaken in the present world situation; and the amount of violence which the Fascists have succeeded in setting in motion in a relatively short time, has filled them with real alarm'. Another piece dated January 1937 and called 'The Cause of Antisemitism', was no doubt the basis for a lecture he gave on 27 January organized by the Jewish People's Council Against Fascism and Anti-Semitism. When he had given this or a similar lecture to another gathering a week earlier, the chairman had thanked him effusively: 'You were magnificent last night and a huge support and comfort.' In this paper James necessarily concentrates on the plank in the Christian eye:

> I remember seeing on a page of a newspaper five references to Jews. A young Jew had given a brilliant piano recital; two Jewish youths had been awarded the police medal for bravery and assisting a police constable assaulted by hooligans; two Jews had been accused of a commercial offence. The first was referred to as a rising English musician; the next as brave youths in the East End; only the third pair were called 'Jews'.

Nevertheless, he was also concerned to point out Jewish 'concentration' on particular trades and businesses, and in particular streets, as a 'cause' of antisemitism. His list of nine of the 12 cities where a quarter of the Jewish population of the world lived in 1937 now reads for the most part like a terrible obituary: New York, Chicago, Warsaw, Budapest, Vienna, Moscow, Lodz, Kiev, Paris. If the missing three were Berlin, Lvov and Vilnius, they too have become cities of the Jewish dead. As James immediately goes on to discuss 'concentration' as a consequence of antisemitism, it seems odd that he should have seen fit to label it as a 'cause'. One hopes his audience emerged enlightened rather than confused.

In what seems to be the last of the pieces in the sequence, entitled 'Why is there a Jewish Question?', James indulged in some highly speculative, indeed highly unlikely, generalizations:

> Finally there is the charge of actual dishonest practice, when it manages just not to be illegal ... Among every group you will find more offences of one kind than of another. Some nations are prone to crimes of violence. Here the Englishman considers that it is unsportsmanlike to use a knife, the Italian considers it barbarous to use fists. French juries excuse crimes of passion which an English jury would condemn. Where groups of these nations live together each notices the crimes of the other that are different from his own, but does not notice that his own commonest crimes are not committed by the other. So in this case we notice the high proportion of Jewish cases in commercial offences, but we ignore the clean record they have in other directions.

This was, it seems, how an intelligent and informed Englishman saw things in the mid-1930s. Was it the Germans or the Swiss he had in mind as prone to crimes of violence?

In *Voyage of Discoveries* he tells us that he was not in agreement with the predictably cautious stance adopted towards Mosley by the Jewish Board of Deputies: 'it was everything that Mosley stood for that should be opposed'. Yet, in February 1938 in correspondence with William Temple he gave enthusiastic assent to his friend's recommendation of a policy of non-protest on the part of the Board with regard to the possible persecution of Jews in Rumania. The Archbishop of Canterbury, implied Temple in his letter, did not wish to rock the Orthodox boat in those parts:

> There is always the risk of making it appear that those who are already under suspicion as poor patriots are in fact the friends of foreigners. No doubt the Board of Deputies would understand all these points very well ... but it must be understood that very often an apparent hesitancy to

make public protests is really due to an appreciation of the situation rather than a failure to appreciate it.

James in his reply wrote that Temple had told him 'just what I wanted to know ... It would appear that on the matter of protest "great minds think alike"':

> for I have continually repeated to Jewish audiences which ask me the question that 'protests have an infinite capacity for irritating those against whom they are directed and a negative power of assisting those on whose behalf they are made'. I do not know whether I shall be asked about the matter but I wrote to you largely in the hope of preventing just the kind of approach which you would deplore.

No one would want to suggest that protest is a policy for all occasions: each occasion requires to be taken on its merits and given its deserts. The Board of Deputies, as James was only too well aware judging by his account of their attitude towards Mosley, was nonetheless prone to be backward on those occasions when going forward was what was demanded. It may not have been what was required in this instance and James may have been right to have judged it so, but it does come as a shock to find him expressing his ideas on non-protest in such a way as to suggest he was less a non-protester than he was an anti-protester.

James had no more of a monopoly on getting things right than he had on the truth. He certainly got Munich wrong. He did so in a series of long letters to William Temple 'after the event' in October 1938. On 12 October he reports his attendance at a meeting of what he calls 'The Club': 'Percy Dearmer's old group now meeting at the Temple.' They were appeasers one and all and 'full' of what he calls 'repentance and dope'. 'I wish', he writes, 'they could go to Prague or to hundreds of thousands of Sudeten homes and see whether they also are filled with divine thankfulness for the righteous solution found at the last minute.' What will happen now? His answer to his own question is a curate's egg of considerable proportions. We should have fought: 'there would have been immense destruction, but Germany could not possibly have won ... Now every month is in Germany's favour, and from the military point of view she will grow stronger and stronger.'. Right so far, but only so far; he continues: 'it is extremely improbable that there is any real danger of a world war ... There are widespread elements in Germany which are on our side, and who will, ultimately, count ... From my point of view I also feel it a great blessing that we did not have to fight a war with Russia for an ally ... It is still possible to make Geneva work ... Geneva is still capable of being an enormous power in the world.' Then comes the postscript: 'Oh my poor dear Jews, they are in the soup, and O how they poured it over themselves during the crisis in Golders Green and elsewhere. Poor Darlings!' The 'poor dear Jews' knew time was up; the poor, deluded Englishman who was so patronizing towards them did not.

He wrote again to Temple, 'further to my explosion of yesterday', on 13 October. Munich was 'a moral defeat', 'a spiritual defeat'. It was also 'an act of God':

> but it was not a granting of our prayers even if it was an answer to them. He gave us peace, but He gave us the peace which normally a nation receives after defeat in war, and showed His mercy in granting it without war. Le bon Dieu is full of the most unexpected surprises. Speaking in human terms, and without irreverence, it was a masterpiece of genius, but a little naughty. Dear me, and then people think that God can only be described in completely abstract terms. How dull compared with the astonishing reality.

One would have thought that Munich might have been characterized as the work of the Devil. It is extraordinary that so political a creature as James claimed to be could talk in this trivializing fashion about the lowest point in English politics since the Restoration of Charles II. In response to a letter of Temple's, he wrote again on 16 October. We had, he said, 'to turn our backs ... on ever increasing competitive armaments and seek to make the method of discussion and agreement a more effective instrument of justice and appeasement'. To that end an appeal should be made to the nation in the name of the churches 'to choose the second path':

> We may make of this opportunity either a mere readjustment of the balance of power, or the first steps to a new world-order; but whichever we set out to do, we must real-

ize that this is a last opportunity given to this generation, and that to choose the harder path will entail sacrifices on our own part, as well as on the part of others.

We have to remember that he is writing not only to an old friend; Temple, being Archbishop of York, was a prince of the church. Still, whatever allowance is made for the context and for our hindsight, James had very little idea of what Hitler was and what his ambitions were for Germany. He, who says in his autobiography that he had seen before 1933 what was coming in Germany, did not grasp the meaning of Munich. Not many people did; like them it was not until March 1939 that James understood that 'the last opportunity given to this generation' was to make war not peace. Can he truly have believed that 'a new world- order' of the kind he envisaged was possible with a Nazified Germany? Why is there no mention of righting the wrongs done to the Czechs and Jews of the Sudetenland? It seems that Barley was something of an ivory tower after all.

In *Voyage of Discoveries* James describes two episodes intended to demonstrate what an important and influential man he was. They both involve William Temple. On a visit to England in 1933 or 1934 he had told Temple of 'the anti-Jewish measures actually in force in Germany, and the threats of what was to come'. Temple had informed the Archbishop of Canterbury, who had believed ambassador Ribbentrop's false assurances and was to make a pro-German speech in the House of Lords the next day. James was summoned to Lambeth in the morning: 'The speech was not made!' In 1935 during his lecture tour of the country, he arrived at the Selly Oak Colleges in Birmingham and having talked about 'the separation of Christianity and Judaism' as 'a schism which, like all schisms, left truth divided', was told that Temple the week previously had said exactly the same. 'Then', said his host, 'we heard it from the throne, now we hear it from the power behind the throne'. Between his own view of himself and his view of the European situation in the Autumn of 1938 there seems an unnerving disjunction. Munich does not feature in *Voyage of Discoveries*.

One further piece of evidence that James was as deluded as most of his generation about the realities of European politics has to be cited. It shows that even after March 1939 he had no real notion of the racism at the cankered heart of Nazism. In his letter of 3 April 1939 to T.R. Feiwel about Douglas Reed's *Disgrace Abounding* he wrote:

> It is obviously true that persecution of the Jews gets more attention than other persecutions. There are many reasons for this and naturally Jewish knowledge of how to present their case after centuries of persecution is only a small one. I think you want to make sure of the fact that antisemitism is a pretext-weapon of totalitarian propaganda. The persecution of Czechs, Spaniards and Chinese, though horrible in itself, has no relation to any world philosophy, and is not connected with any intention to attack the civilization of the Czechs, etc., or to suppress them in any other part of the world where they exist. It is not the *persecution*, but the *defamation* which makes the attack upon the Jews unique.

It is not the everlasting debate about the uniqueness of antisemitism, and more particularly the uniqueness of the Shoah, that we should get engaged in at this point; for the moment it is sufficient to say that James is right: antisemitism is a different kind of racism, even if there may be a variety of racisms into one of which it might be fitted. It is his underestimation of the genocidal drive behind Nazi racial attitudes in general that needs emphasis. The Nazis were determined to suppress the 'civilization of the Czechs', and the 'civilizations' of the Poles and Russians, just as much as they were intent on the destruction of Judaism. If they had won the war, no doubt every culture would have suffered to a greater or lesser degree, the only 'civilization' worth having and keeping being German. James is not to be taken to task for failing to see what has only become clear 50 years later. No one in 1939 knew what was ultimately in store for Poles, Russians, Czechs, Serbs, Gypsies and Jews. As it could not be imagined, it could not be known. Nevertheless, one would think that he might have had a better idea than most of what Nazism was and the drives behind it; he had been in close contact with it before 1933 and in 1935 at Geneva had witnessed it in action. What had convinced the Archbishop of Canterbury one morning at Lambeth in 1933 or 1934 were the texts of the anti-Jewish laws James had brought along with him. It is true that the Nazi regime sent out conflicting messages before 1939; surely James ought to have been a more acute reader of them than were others. After all, he was not pro-German like most of the deluded; unlike most of them he was pro-Jewish.

Moreover, he was virtually in daily contact with Jewish refugees from Germany and, after the Anschluss in March 1938, from Austria. He was receiving, or ought to have been receiving, first-hand information. He had been officially involved in helping refugees from November 1937, joining in that month the newly formed Church of England Committee for 'Non-Aryan' Christians, the creation of George Bell, the pro-German, anti-Nazi bishop of Chichester. On 1 February 1938 in the Jerusalem Chamber, Westminster Abbey, he was one of the speakers at a conference organized by the Committee; the title of his talk was 'Our Responsibility'. James remained a member until November 1939, when he resigned because of pressure of work; 'it is very good of you', wrote the secretary in reply to his letter of resignation, 'to say that we may look to you for help at any time'. The Committee found money hard to find, Christians giving a derisory amount. Whereas British Jews had raised well over a million pounds to help German Jewry, wrote George Bell to the *Times* in January 1938, all that a National Christian Appeal, made through the Churches of Great Britain, had produced was £10,000. This, he said, was 'a lamentable truth', and he asked for better support of the Committee formed in November 1937. It is unlikely that he got it. Immediately after the Anschluss James appealed for financial help for Pastor Büsing, a 'Non-Aryan' refugee, then staying with him at Barley:

> At present in a large number of cases Christian refugees have to be told that there is no money for them in the Christian Organizations; the result is that the burden of assisting them has been placed on the shoulders of the Jews, who are already staggering under the weight of continually increasing responsibilities for refugees from every country of central and eastern Europe.

It is doubtful if he received much assistance, unless it was from his Cambridge University friend, the blind Canadian historian of medieval chantries, Kathleen Wood-Legh, who was 'very anxious to do something for Austrian refugees in Cambridge', and who with Lady Kathleen Oldfield had 'already worked very hard for different groups of refugees'.

Christian aid, in fact, amounted to very little. The story of the inability of the Church of England to demonstrate much more than sympathy, and not always that, has been told elsewhere. The Church's most recent historian, Andrew Chandler, has reached a dismal conclusion:

> The story of the Church of England and the Jews of Germany and Austria from 1933 to 1939 is one of genuine and humane, but occasional and irregular, vision and effort. There are many examples of the moral goodness which the Church represented institutionally and encouraged socially. Equally evident, however, was the genuine failure of the Church to recognise fully the moral demands which the political world made upon it.

George Bell, who asked James for an historian's help with his lectures on refugees, and was given it (even from the historian's retreat in Provence), was a tower of strength. He was very much an exception. About Roman Catholic assistance, as there was none, little need be said. 'The Catholic situation is really scandalous in matters of relief', James wrote to Bishop Bell in July 1938; 'my Jewish friend Loewe had just succeeded in placing a very distinguished Catholic orientalist in a Quaker College, and the entire Catholic answer to the request for help, was a Postal Order for ten shillings. The rest of the money came from Jews and Quakers.' He went on to say that he had completely failed to get any help from 'Catholic sources' for the 'unexpected expenses' incurred by other Jewish friends on behalf of Irene Harland, 'the chief *Catholic* fighter against antisemitism in Vienna'. The italics are mine, their purpose being to underline the miserable record of the Roman Catholic Church in Britain with regard to refugees. If the Church of England did not do well, the Roman Catholics did badly.

James himself did a great deal. All he did would take too long to catalogue here; Irene Harland and Pastor Büsing were only two of the many refugees he helped. Hugh Schonfield and Rabbi Eschelbacher of Düsseldorf, the father of his first research secretary, were others. The refugee he did most for was his old friend and colleague Dr Alexander Teich of Vienna. They had known one another since 1925, when Dr Teich had been Secretary of the World Union of Jewish Students. He had also been the Director of the Organization for the Social Welfare of Jewish Students in Vienna. After the Anschluss he was a marked man; 'we had to rescue him quickly', said James. He was brought to Barley in 1938, and when his wife and daughter joined him in 1939, the family settled into a house in the village, 5 High Street. Vienna's loss was Barley's gain: they became respected and much loved members of the community. Yet, here is a measure of the terrible tragedy of the Shoah, one relatively neglected because it has been overshadowed by death, death on such a scale that the suffering it has caused has been well-nigh limitless. Dr Teich's journey from Vienna to Barley represents the other sort of damage that was done to the life and lives of Jews and non-Jews alike in Central and Eastern Europe: an irreparable loss of its best minds and bravest hearts. James wrote in an obituary of his friend, who died in 1959, that his 'outstanding quality ... was a complete integrity and impartiality, which made him one of the most trusted figures in central European Jewish life. Everyone knew him, from the Cardinal Archbishop to the Socialist leaders; and this was true not only for Austria but for Poland, Rumania, Hungary, and elsewhere.'

It is also an indication of our ignorance of this aspect of the Shoah that it was not until 1974, when James had a research student working on Jewish students in European universities between the wars, that Dr Teich's daughter, Edith Ruth Weisz, came to know about her father's work. 'I am in total ignorance of what my father did ... and would be most grateful to learn something', she wrote to James on 13 March 1974. James replied on 21 March: 'As to what your father did, he was a key figure in the whole of Eastern European Jewish life, both political and academic. He knew everybody and was so transparently honest that everybody trusted him':

> In Vienna itself he had an extraordinary position because he was trusted equally by the University authorities and the Church. He could maintain excellent relations with both the Cardinal Archbishop of Vienna and the Rector of the University without losing touch with the Jewish students. I remember turning up in Vienna at a very troubled moment when he had just been locked up by a howling mob of students in the Rector's study. It was the Rector, not Alexander, who had completely lost his head.

'So you see', he concluded, 'you have a father to be proud of, a man who was greatly loved by a very wide group of people throughout Central and Eastern Europe.' Edith Ruth and her three-year-old daughter Rachel had paid a memorable visit to 'dearest Uncle James and Auntie Dorothy' at Iwerne on 18 August 1973. She was able to inform them of all the latest Barley 'happenings', she and her husband having kept on the house in the High Street as a second home to the one they had in Hampstead. Rachel had been 'a handful, as you noticed', she wrote after the visit: 'Thank you for being so kind and patient, the result is she longs to come again and see you – the affection you kindled was immediate and strong, I'm afraid.' This will not be the last time when we shall find James and Dorothy winning the trust and affection of young children. It only serves to point up the poignancy of their decision to have no children of their own.

Refugee scholars were not the only kind James encountered. His proximity to Cambridge brought him into contact with others, like Kathleen Wood-Legh, who would become one of his and Dorothy's closest friends, and Clifford Dugmore, the writer of a remarkable little book, *The Influence of the Synagogue upon the Divine Office*, finally published in 1944. In the late 1930s Dugmore married and moved to Staffordshire, becoming private chaplain to the Earl of Shrewsbury and rector of Ingestre-with-Tixall. He shared with James an old-fashioned, understated sense of humour. Witness the preface to his book, dated at King's College, London, and written in the third person:

> Had the opportunity (and the time) presented itself for the author to rewrite the whole book, he might have modified his conclusions on certain details ... but with regard to the Church's debt to the Synagogue in the realm of worship, the times of public prayer derived from the old Temple worship *via* the Synagogue, the content of the early Christian services, and the development of the Monastic Hours, he would not wish to change what he wrote in a country rectory while German bombers flew overhead in the early days of World War II. At least there was leisure, in those circumstances, to read, ponder, check and re-check one's references in the intervals between Air Raid duty and parochialia. In a modern university such days seem to belong to the age of Dr Samuel Johnson.

Here was a book that would never have been written had there not been *The Conflict of the Church and the Synagogue*.

James became a member of the Senior Common Room at St John's College, thus, he writes in *Voyage of Discoveries*, paving 'the way for me to get a Cambridge degree. Being modest, I asked them only to make me an M.A., holding that it was absurd to be a double Doctor of Philosophy ... Thereby I unintentionally created the precedent of not receiving the same degree as I had at Oxford, and all kinds of special formulas had to be composed for me.' Can this truly be modesty? The degree gave him access to the shelves of the University Library, and the far more precious right to take its books home to Barley. He also, naturally enough, corresponded with scholars at Oxford, notably the inimitable Beryl Smalley, who would transform our understanding of the relations between Jewish and Christian scholars in the twelfth century, as well as (in one short article) our estimate of John Wyclif. In June 1939 James wrote to her hoping these twelfth-century Jewish–Christian 'friendships' would be sorted out 'by the time I come to the third volume'. It was already being delayed, 'as I am having to write a book for an American publisher before I can settle down'. He also knew the hardly less formidable Helen Cam: she addressed him as 'James' and ended her letters 'Yours always'. Cecil Roth was more formal. At one stage Roth suggested collaboration between them: 'I was at white-heat when I got into touch with you about it in the first instance ... But I was rather intimidated by the scale and responsibility of the work, and the douche of cold Barley water finally discouraged me.' What, one wonders, was the nature of the project James so effectively stopped in its tracks. Cecil Roth wrote on 24 December 1939, and after sending his good wishes for the New Year, ended the letter: 'When I develop misgivings, I am comforted by the consideration that I would enjoy your company in the Concentration Camp.'

None of these men and women, apart from Kathleen Wood-Legh, was a friend in the strict sense. Charles and Dorothea Singer were friends in every sense. James' first letter to the Singers is to be found among the Parkes Papers, the reason probably being that it was never sent. It is dated Guernsey 7 April 1935 and was very unusually handwritten. James wrote principally in order to thank Dr and Mrs Singer for 'the enjoyments of my week at Kilmarth', which was the week he had spent with them before his return to Geneva and the attack on Thomas Thomas. The other topic of the letter is James' report of discovering on his arrival in Guernsey 'a large budget of letters from Geneva full of alarums and excursions. My flat is night and day in occupation of the secret political police.' Having learned of 'an intention to raid my flat, presumably in the hope of discovering documents which would compromise refugees or people living in Germany', the police were 'guarding it for me!' How cloak and dagger it seemed to him before the attack on Thomas brought home the reality. Despite our knowledge of the attack, how cloak and dagger it still seems, the alarums and excursions of yesteryear taking on a glamour they did not and do not have. It is our excuse for turning them into entertainment. In the agitated aftermath of the assault on his manservant the letter to the Singers was forgotten. Besides, Thomas was in no state to go to the post office.

In *Voyage of Discoveries* James takes two pages to celebrate the Singers; he particularly honours Charles Singer for the learned and wise man that he was and for the influence he had been on himself. Charles, he writes, 'made a unique contribution to my spiritual growth ... It was in the contemplation of Charles's quality that I ended up with the phrase that "Jewry is a civilization" ... one typical aspect of his "Jewishness" was his intolerance of injustice, which included injustice of thinking'. His sense of 'membership of the Jewish community *once it was attacked*' was his 'deepest quality.'. The italics in this instance are those of James himself; they are revealing: more probably than any other single person, Charles Singer was the cause of James sticking with Jews and Judaism during the gravest crisis both had undergone since the first century of the Christian Era. James also writes that it was Charles who taught him about 'the scientific method' of 'later scholasticism and the Renaissance ... What mattered was the new approach to any problem made by examining the actual data to elucidate concrete and contemporary issues, instead of seeking some previous authority.' Another 'lesson' was that, 'while Judaism and Christianity insisted on the personality of God, it was more often important for the scientist's understanding of creation to see the impersonality of truth and law. The intrusion of ideas appropriate to personality only confused the issue.'. Charles here confirmed James in his lifelong commitment to a post-Enlightenment interpretation of history, past, present and future, an interpretation examined (and criticized) above. Between us

1. James Parkes in his garden at the bungalow, *c.* 1914

2. James Parkes, Molly and Theodore David Parkes

3. 1916

4. Messines, July 1917

5. Theodore David Parkes

6. Molly Parkes

7. Oxford, 1921

8. James Parkes, 1924

9. Sonntagberg, 1925. Hans Becker, James Parkes, Franz Schmal

10. James Parkes, 1926?

11. James Parkes and Dorothy, August 1942

12. Henry Parkes with one of his yachts, *c.* 1935

13. James Parkes, 1945?

and 'later scholasticism and the Renaissance', he wrote, 'stands the barbarity of Russian Communism and German Nazism'; there is no need to rehearse the old debate about the origins of totalitarianism, yet, at the outset of the twenty-first century we are far more conscious of where 'the scientific method' took us in the middle of the twentieth. Theories of class and race, based apparently on 'examining actual data', were persuasive, sufficiently convincing to provide the pretext for the murder of millions. Men and women in the Middle Ages were killed in the name of God; in the Middle East, in Pakistan, in New York they continue to be killed in His name. Killers always require authority: if it is not the authority of a sacred text, it is the authority of a scientific theory. It is difficult to see much progression here, let alone any security for life and limb 'in the impersonality of truth and law'. Which truth? What law?

Without doubt, Charles Singer influenced the way James thought. What he could not alter was the way James lived. He certainly tried. In October 1941 he wrote saying that he was coming to London to meet Albert Napier of the Lord Chancellor's Office:

> The subject of the interview is yourself ... What I am going to say to him is that some one in office in the Church should be an authority on the Jewish Question and what about it? I suppose every sensible man sees that, with the world situation before him, this is one of the key questions and the thin end of the wedge of Nazism. Can the edge be blunted is what the Lord Chancellor's office ought to be thinking about ... Despite all you have said – and are doubtless going to say – to the contrary, I am still of the opinion that you could be more effective in this dratted question if you had something of a pulpit to which you could invite suitable speakers and something of a parish into which you could dollop suitable curates. But I know that this point annoys you and so I will not raise it further.

There is much else in a long letter, not least Singer's diverting observations on the British establishment's newly found enthusiasm for the U.S.S.R. ('what you call "the woodlice" blessing Stalin'), and especially on 'a septuagenarian Archbishop of Canterbury turning an intellectual and moral somersault in a few hours', but it must not deflect us from the main point: that James' best friend believed him to be not making the most of his talent: James had dug a hole and buried it.

Charles returned to the issue towards the end of the war. In the interim, in January 1943, they had both been caustic about Eden's speech to parliament of December 1942 on the extermination of European Jewry. Charles wrote: 'people seem to think that all that is needed to put things right is to express a few admirable sentiments ... Eden seems to me a peculiarly mean figure in this respect.' James said he and Dorothy agreed that 'Eden's speech was contemptible.' It was a pity James was still a private person; had he been the public figure Charles wished he was, an expression of the contempt he felt for the government's lack of response to the news of the Final Solution would have caused at least a slight stir in the depthless pool of its complacency. Charles returned to the question of James' lack of impact on affairs of state in March 1945; he was far more forthright and a good deal angrier than he had been in October 1941. We shall need to quote what he said at some length. He began on his theme without the usual preliminary courtesies:

> I have been thinking much about you for I have long been uneasy about your position. You know well what is, in my opinion, the right course for you to follow. I do not express that view again as you do not like to face it. But there is a question which you may perhaps ask yourself ... Can you name any living man in the English-speaking world who occupies an important position in public opinion or directly influences opinion who has no official status for doing so? I know of none ... There is no philosopher, theologian, political thinker, economist, scholar, moralist, historian, man of science of whom I can think who influences opinion save by help of the status which he holds or has once held ... What hope then is there that you, ploughing a lonely furrow, letting off from time to time stimulating though ephemeral little books and occasional articles in little-read journals, what hope is there that you will succeed in getting people to listen on a subject on which, it is quite evident they are determined not to listen, what hope? Perhaps you may elicit a friendly or angry comment here and there, obtain a convert here and there, speak on a few platforms to audiences

already convinced, and get an occasional brick or bouquet thrown at your head. What more can you hope for?

One 'small thing' he hoped James might do, was to put himself up for a D.Litt. at Oxford, albeit were he successful he did 'not for a moment believe that your power of influencing public opinion would become a jot better'. 'I have written thus', he concluded:

> because I am disturbed in mind. I am aware that I have no right to set down what is written here and that you may not be pleased with me. But I have tried to put to you the situation as it is, or rather as I see it, and not as I (or you) would like it to be. Turn the matter yet again in your mind, and in doing so think, and think again, of what your position is likely to be in five or ten years time.

He did not talk in terms of 'your responsibility', but one feels he might as well have done.

James replied ten days later, on 13 March 1945. We shall have to quote his letter at even greater length, as this is the fullest statement James ever made on the subject. 'We both appreciate very much the friendship and anxiety which underlies your letter', he wrote on his and Dorothy's behalf, 'and we will try to give it the careful reply it deserves.'. There were two points to be 'cleared fairly simply'. The first was 'employment in the Church, i.e. a living':

> I am still convinced that the solution of a living is impossible. Financially it would give me just enough money to live on, but it would still leave all real Jewish work to be financed separately. But from the standpoint of work, it would inevitably mean cutting down the Jewish work to an occasional lecture or book or article with the minimum of travel ... it would be impossible for me to go inside the ecclesiastical system and not get involved in all the problems under which I see that system labouring at present.

The last point was not an excuse. Almost exactly three years before, James had told Charles: 'Until the church faces the fact that the secularism of the last three centuries arose directly out of her incompetence to give answers to the questions which men had begun to ask I cannot see any rebirth for religion.' The second point to be 'cleared' was the D.Litt. 'He had wanted', he wrote, 'to get a D.Litt. for the two medieval volumes (i.e. vols 2 and 3) when completed. I don't think I can present volume I as it already got me the D.Phil. Vol. 3 has not been written owing to the war.' He suggested alternative books; he did not mention the possibility of completing the third volume: as we shall see, its time had passed.

'Now', he continued, 'for the main issue of my being a private person. Here we entirely agree with you':

> I have wanted for years to cease to be a private person, both because the job is far too big for one man, and for the reasons which you suggest. Now it seems to me the first factor is really even more important than the second, and that it points away from the search for a place for myself individually either within the church or the university, and points directly towards the creation of some kind of Institute. As you know, we tried to interest Israel Sieff in the foundation of such an Institute two years ago; and he replied with a general guarantee that he would agree that something was done ... after the war. We had several discussions on it last year, and at the time he was very anxious to set it in Palestine, while I felt that it had to link Palestine–Great Britain–U.S.A. But we have not split on this question.

Why, he asked, had Charles not mentioned the 'Institute solution' in his letter? Did he think it the wrong solution, or 'only that I have done jolly little to bring it into existence?' If it was the latter, 'I have to admit that pressing executive and administrative plans is not my strongest point.' He needed, he said, 'continual gingering up about the Institute ... Dorothy does her best', and he wished to know if 'the whole Institute idea is in your mind a wrong one'. The 'Institute solution' seems very like an evasion of Charles' insistence on the necessity for James to have a public position. What sort of power would he have been able to exert as Director of an Institute that no one in Britain cared about? He admitted in his letter to Charles that if 'Gentile money' was ever to be forthcoming, it would have to come 'to a considerable extent from the U.S.A.'. James was right about it not coming from Britain; when an 'institute' did struggle into existence it was Jewish money that gave it life.

We now come to the final part of the letter. James is at his most confessional. He is, nonetheless, still evading the main thrust of Charles' letter. There is also what one might justifiably describe as special pleading. Refusing to admit that he disliked leading from an exposed position, he did concede that his 'activities during the war years do look rather scattered and confined to oddments in obscure publications or of an ephemeral kind':

> But I think that, below the surface, they have gone a good deal further than that, and can be regarded as years of preparation for the time when more visible activities should be possible. In 1939 I was – alas – the leading non-Jewish expert on antisemitism and I could give a very competent lecture on the history and meaning of antisemitism and trace it to its historical roots. And I had a general feeling that the traditional Christian conception of Judaism was wrong. If there had not been the long gap in carrying on the work that I was already doing then ... I don't think I should have got much further, or got through to the position at which I now stand of seeing the problem of Jewish–Christian relations in a purely positive way in relation to the whole sweep of the world's problems – political as well as spiritual. I am a slow thinker and it has taken me some time to work out the issues of the impact of the scientific method on historic Christianity, the further relation of this to the historical identities of Judaism and Christianity, and, still further, the relations of these to humanism and the U.S.S.R; and then all these had to be related to the political realities of the situation. If I had been going along busily on the lines already laid down in 1939 ... I don't believe I should ever have thought these other points out.

It was 'a product of those years that I have sufficiently cleared my own mind'; he now had 'foundations which, out of those rather long and difficult years, I never should have got had I been apparently more "successful" earlier from a standpoint of influence and power'. In other words, he had moved from being an historian to being a commentator on the dilemmas of the Western World. It could be observed that he might have done better by remaining an historian, were it not for an unavoidable fact of human nature: a fertile mind cannot prevent itself taking off. A spur to James' mind taking wing, and one which he does not allude to in the letter, although it has been examined at length above, is that he had run into difficulties while still on the ground. *The Jew in the Medieval Community* is not the exciting book *The Conflict of the Church and the Synagogue* is. Being a survey of themes already well known, rather than a narrative of one newly discovered, it must have been less exhilarating to write. James may have felt the same when he was setting about volume three. Where others had gone before he probably had no desire to go. For 'a slow thinker' there was plenty of thinking to be done between 1939 and 1945. Some of it will feature in the following section.

Meanwhile, we should take leave of James at Barley before the war came to change life there as it did everywhere else. He played his part in village life, as he tells us in *Voyage of Discoveries*: a manager of the Church Primary School, a member of the Parish Council, Vice-Chairman of the A.R.P. when it was formed after Munich, in charge of the evacuation of adults and children from London. He was a licensed preacher of the Diocese of St Albans, in which Barley was situated, 'and did what I could in helping either in Barley or in the surrounding district'. What he could and would not do was help the rector of Barley. The explanation for that lies in a letter to Charles Singer of August 1941:

> I forget whether when I was last in Kilmarth the Rector had already put the crown on his iniquities by messing about with evacuated children. Life has been pretty well hell for the last three months ... as the charming old gentleman went all around the village dramatically swearing to his innocence and stating that it was a persecution launched on an innocent man ... However he has just been convicted at Quarter Sessions and sent to a mental home for nine months so that we are at any rate rid of him ... The parish has not only had twelve years of John Rutherford Gardiner, but for the last ten years of the previous rector nothing was done ...

If the Church at large needed to mend its ways, it could have got off to a good start by putting its house in order at Barley.

4
Wartime Barley 1939–45

James had an eventful war. He got married. His father died. Evacuees and refugees filled his house. For the only time in his life he was active in a political party. He became John Hadham and wrote widely popular and highly acclaimed theology for the people. The Council of Christians and Jews was founded, 'the first steps to its formation' being 'taken under a pear tree at Barley'. Jewish causes of all kinds occupied him. The destruction of European Jewry, a catastrophe whose unimaginable dimensions would not be grasped until it became history, filled him with an inexpressible anguish, his government's bathetic response with righteous anger. Only the prospect of Palestine as a place of asylum for those Jews who might survive the Shoah provided partial consolation.

It will be in the following order that we shall deal with James in wartime: family affairs, life at Barley, politics, theology, and the 'poor, dear Jews'. Yet, we might start, where James started, with antisemitism. On 19 September 1939 he wrote to the Home Secretary enclosing a nationally distributed broadsheet, which had turned up in the village. The Army of Today's Alright, it was headed in capitals and with a question mark. Its [sic] LED by a JEW: Isaac Hore-Belisha ... Minister of War. Its FED by a JEW: Isidore Salmon ... Catering Advisor. Its CLOTHED by a JEW: Montague Burton ... Army Uniforms. And BLED for by YOU. 'In itself', James wrote, 'it is perhaps trifling':

> but it gains importance in the present circumstances and in the countryside from two points of view. In the first place large numbers of Jews are evacuated all round us and an attempt to stir up antisemitism in the countryside is likely to create a lot of difficulties. In the second place it is scarcely the moment to create disaffection with the Army and its administration. In these circumstances I felt it my duty to call your attention to it.

One wonders what sort of impression it made in Barley, where the chairman of the Parish Council, Redcliffe Salaman, was a Jew, his vice-chairman, James Parkes, was a self-proclaimed philosemite, and where at 5 High Street lived Dr Alexander Teich and his family.

The early months of the war, indeed until Dorothy came to work for him as his secretary in 1942, were 'difficult' for James. He wrote plaintively to Herbert Loewe at Cambridge in January 1940:

> Life is very difficult at the moment, and it has been impossible to get to Cambridge. The car is laid up, and I have exceedingly little money, but, apart from that, I am all on my own, and my days are spent at the typewriter, trying to keep the work going by correspondence without a secretary. For Kenneth [Dodkin] is now a gunner in the Anti-aircraft Regiment on the East Coast, and Herman [Eschelbacher] is still trying to join up somewhere.

Later the same month, he wrote to Guy Emerson, with whom he had stayed in New York during his visit to the United States and Canada in 1938–9, that he was 'just managing to survive' without a secretary. He was busy with 'immediate Jewish questions, especially Jewish Peace Aims':

> I am doing my best to persuade the poor dears not to be more foolish than nature, or rather history, made them, but to realise that to confine themselves to demanding rights guaranteed by hypothetical federations is an irritating and totally useless procedure ... At the same time I am involved in another bit of work which might amuse you, to wit trying to make the dead bones of the Christians get a little flesh on them. I don't think we are going to build much of a brave new world without a rather more intelligent and definite belief in an intelligent, competent and trustworthy God, who knows what he is doing and why he is doing it. So I have written a Penguin Special, which will be out shortly, called 'Good God' ... In the intervals of such activities, I have to look after two billeted teachers, and such domestic affairs as lighting up fires in the morning, getting breakfast, thawing freezing pipes, keeping the house clean

... So the war has not reduced me to idleness, and so far the Lord has been most ingenious in keeping the widow's cruse supplied with cash for the weekly bills!

By the autumn of 1940 his total household was six and he was looking after another eight evacuated Londoners in a cottage across the road. By that date his 'economic position' was 'not too bad': his 'lodgers' were able to pay, he had sold his greengage crop profitably, and *Good God* had sold more than 50,000 copies. He was still receiving his annual £250 from Israel Sieff, or rather during her husband's frequent absences abroad, from Rebecca Sieff, with whom James was on the most friendly of terms. His bronze portrait bust adorned her Park Lane sitting-room, he sent her his tapestry work and apples and onions from his garden, and stayed overnight at her house when he had business in London. She looked out for suitable secretaries. Her cheques, it should be said, continued throughout the war.

Early in 1941 it was Becky Sieff whom he informed of the possibility of his becoming an R.A.F. Chaplain. It was not to be: 'The chaplaincy proved impossible', he wrote to another correspondent later the same year, 'as I was not prepared to commit myself to really going full time into the air force, and I am very glad I didn't, for both James and John are fully occupied.' It was his writing as James Parkes and as John Hadham which prevented his acceptance of the living of Little Hormead, Hertfordshire, when it was offered him by St John's College, Cambridge, in 1942; 'while it is admittedly an inconvenience that neither of them condescend to provide me with much to live on, I could not reconcile it with my conscience to accept a living in order to provide an economic basis for carrying on my present work ... I would not like to take a living unless I intended to devote myself primarily to my responsibility to my parishioners.' No doubt his outspoken views on the state of the Anglican Church, voiced in a Cambridge University Sermon of April 1941, had impressed as many as it had repelled, yet it is impossible to think of James as permanently administering to a parish: in one way or another he would have upset most of his rural parishioners.

But, not in the way the Rector of Barley had. That unsavoury episode was drawing to an unsatisfactory conclusion in 1941–2. The village had been torn apart by it. Grace Gardiner, 'the excellent sister of our very unsatisfactory rector', whose 'combination of selfishness and incompetence amounted almost to genius', by this time was not only running James' household; she had left her brother to come to live with James and his 'lodgers'. Her brother had turned out to be a thief (or a receiver) as well as an abuser of boys: 'the sale of the Rectory goods – or such as had not been stolen – has been completed', James wrote to Redcliffe Salaman at the end of September 1941, 'so I am glad to say Grace has no more concern with anything at the Rectory'.' The manner in which the Church dealt with the unrepentant Rector might well have been an additional cause of James not wanting to have a benefice and be under the jurisdiction of a bishop. In January 1942 he wrote at length to Norman Bentwich of the ostrich-like stance two bishops had taken:

> The Rectory business has tailed off very unsatisfactorily; the Bishops of St Albans and Bedford have behaved with complete cowardice and indifference throughout. Apparently the only thing which matters is the economic security of the holder of the parsonic freehold, and they have sabotaged any hope they might have had of salvaging Gardiner's soul by allowing him to lie and flatter his way to a pension. In face of the court's verdict, they have completely exculpated him and not even accepted the necessity for an ecclesiastical trial or any ecclesiastical action. On top of this, the Bishop has kindly allowed the parish of Barley to pay a pension of £500 a year to a Jew-converting friend of his who desired to retire, and who is so well-equipped for dealing with a very difficult rural situation that he has not been in a parish since 1914, and has never been anywhere in the country! He has been since 1917 London Secretary for the Church Mission to the Jews, and is now on the verge of 70. A more abominable application of the accepted convention that the unfortunate people of the countryside exist for the payment of pensions I find it difficult to imagine ... On the other hand, the situation has to some extent cleared up in the village ... I think even his [the Rector's] strongest partisans, and those who are most violently opposed to Salaman, are beginning to realise that he was not the persecuted saint they have thought him. The Bishop himself came here himself a fortnight ago, but his visit was almost entirely useless, as it followed his dona-

tion of a pension to Gardiner and his recommendation of a pension to the retiring Jew-converter. Had there been the slightest sincerity in his desire to visit us, he would have come and discussed matters with the Parochial Church Council before taking either of these actions.

Is it any wonder that James Parkes detested bishops, resisted becoming a parish priest, and believed the Anglican Church to be impervious to significant change?

There was, however, one item of good news in the letter to Norman Bentwich of 9 January 1942. 'I have been given', wrote James, 'the admirable present of a first-class secretary, with the result that my output of work has been considerably increased, and the strain of domestic existence considerably reduced. I am almost becoming quite good-tempered again.' The 'first-class secretary' was called Dorothy Wickings. By July 1942 James was even better tempered. He wrote to the Rev. George Kirkpatrick: 'You asked to be remembered to Miss Wickings and you are just in time to do so, as she is shortly becoming Mrs Parkes. However, she graciously says that she hopes you will be able to come here again in the future as you have in the past as we shall be continuing exactly the same sort of life as we have been leading up to now.' How typical not only of James as James but of James as a man of his age. He was going to be married; it would alter nothing. James and Dorothy were married in August 1942. He was 46; she was 42.

Who was Dorothy Wickings? We can learn a little about her from a typescript memoir she began in May 1975. It peters out when she gets to 1945; promised chapters on their joint travels after that year were never written. Towards the end of what she did write there are some carefully chosen words on what she calls 'The Barley Rectory Affair'. It left, she said, 'a mark in the village which lasted several years, owing to the fact that James and Redcliffe had been involved in a mass of false accusations', and 'at the first elections after the war, the village threw them out' as Chairman and Vice-Chairman of the Parish Council. James, says Dorothy, 'remained something of an enigma to the villagers'. What one wonders did they say about his wife?

What we can say is that Dorothy suited James about as perfectly as any woman could. For one thing she was as strong-minded as he was. During the 1920s she had worked as a secretary for a reinsurance company in London. She lived with her parents at Hildenborough near Tonbridge in Kent and spent her free time playing hockey and tennis and acting in amateur drama groups. She seems to have been the epitome of John Betjeman's Joan Hunter Dunn. In the memoir she admits as much. 'Employment in London', she tells us, 'gave me no opportunities to develop interests some of which, with hindsight, I can see have both influenced me, and developed into interests shared by James and myself during our years together'. She began to change in the early 1930s. In 1932 she switched companies and because she had French spent much of the next two years in Paris. A bad road accident (she was knocked down by a motor cyclist), and the necessity for a long convalescence to recover from it, put paid to that job, but she at once found new employment with 'a well-known Lloyds firm: they accepted me with alacrity'. The firm had close connections with Germany. Consequently Dorothy went on a long holiday during the early days of the Nazi state. Uninformed politically before she went, she returned with a new awareness of international politics. Back in London she soon discovered that her insurance company was underwriting German rearmament; the insurance was simply a cover for arms dealing. In time-honoured fashion her superiors said: and why not? Dorothy there and then became a pacifist: 'The next thing was that I was presented with a bordereau for insurance of a shipment of arms. The premium was exactly the sum of my salary for the year. I wondered how many deaths would go to pay that salary. It was as simple as that.' When she wrote a letter of resignation to the Company Chairman, 'at that time the "Father of Lloyds", explaining that my reason for doing so was disapproval of the sale of arms being carried on under the guise of insurance, there was no reply ... I had stumbled on to more than I had suspected.' Here was the dark side of Dorothy's recreational world, the Joan Hunter Dunn world of 'the strenuous singles played after tea', 'the cool verandah with its lime-juice and gin', 'the dance at the Golf Club', 'the woodlanded ways', 'the late summer haze'. There could be no going back, either to the suburban idyll or the tainted city.

She joined the Peace Pledge Union and the China Campaign Committee, working for the latter before joining the Anglican Pacifist Fellowship and working for them. Evidently much in demand, she was soon asked to become Secretary of the Dick

Sheppard Memorial Club. Dick Sheppard had been the founder of the Peace Pledge Union and the club had been founded to continue the work he had been interested in. The premises were off Oxford Street and Dorothy continued to travel there daily from her parents' Hildenborough home. This all changed with the Blitz and with her appointment as Secretary of the Press and Publicity Committee of the Christian Council for Refugees from Germany and Central Europe. She could no longer travel safely and so came to live in Bloomsbury, James' old haunt. It was with a friend of her future husband's that she now came to work, the Rev. W.W. Simpson. The work itself also brought her closer to James' interests and inevitably she came into his orbit. The question was bound to arise and Dorothy duly asked it: 'Who is James Parkes?' It was, nonetheless, another 18 months before she met him. In the interval she became actively engaged in Jewish refugee matters, and in meetings of Jews and Christians in London. She also read *Good God*. Then, in late October 1941 she heard James lecture. He was without a secretary and immediately afterwards she went down to Barley to help him out on a temporary basis. If it was not love at first sight, it was certainly something. She resigned from her job and in her letter of resignation of 4 November 1941, reproduced in the memoir, she wrote:

> This business of taking myself off to work with Dr James Parkes does not seem, perhaps, entirely rational, but I would just like to say that I have a very deep conviction in some way, for a period at least, my most useful service will be with him. I do not know him beyond having two words with him last week, and one or two phone calls; from everything I hear he will be a very difficult man to work with. I am taking quite a revolutionary step (for me) in breaking away from practically everything to which I have been tied, including work and contacts which I value highly, to try out something which is, by its very nature, a quite unsafe job of work ... I am quite aware of all this unreasonableness, and yet the conviction remains that I am taking a step which will, in the long run, and perhaps in quite a small way, be valuable to the cause of the refugees and the Jews, and therefore that I am not leaving the work, but just transferring to another department.

Well: not entirely. She was going to work with a man once described 'as fair-haired and blue-eyed a Nordic gentleman as ever God created'.

In January 1942 she went back to Barley on a more permanent basis, though what the terms of her employment were she does not say. The rest is, as the saying goes, history. They became engaged in the Spring and were married in the Summer. As both were highly consensual adults it was no ordinary marriage. 'I expect James just booked the first free day in his diary for your wedding, didn't he?', Dorothy was asked. She stoutly denies it: 'it was undertaken with the greatest solemnity and as careful preparation as Hitler and the Royal Family would allow'. The possibility of Hitler invading East Anglia in August 1942 seems a little far-fetched for them not being married at Barley, but it is the one Dorothy gives. They were, therefore, married at Hildenborough on 8 August 1942. William Temple should have performed the ceremony; he, however, was summoned to christen 'one of the Royal babies', so that it was Dorothy's local vicar who was called upon to officiate. 'It was a good quality wedding', she writes, 'and it still wears well. I did not promise to obey.' Nor did they pray for 'the heritage and gift of children':

> We used the 1928 alternative, which included the petition that I might be 'a follower of holy and godly matrons', a nice phrase, we considered. We should have liked children, but in view of our special work, the agony of the second world war, and the refugees and the holocaust we felt that we were called to work together, but not to produce a family.

Would they really 'have liked children'? At their age? Besides: if you like children, want to have children, don't you have them, by adoption if there is no other way? If they had sex, what form of contraception did they use? The idea of the Shoah as a reason for not having children in 1942 seems not only bizarre; it cannot be true. One's feeling must be that James and Dorothy's marriage was what medieval historians call 'companionate', and good companions they undoubtedly were over the next 40 years. In defiance of Hitler, they returned to Barley for the wedding breakfast. 'The guests', says Dorothy, included three members of the Athenaeum, Dr Redcliffe Salaman, Sir John Graham

Kerr, and my husband.' It is an uncharacteristic boast. The speeches, or such parts of them as Dorothy chooses to record, were awful. The happy couple honeymooned with the Singers at Kilmarth.

They did not have much money. When she came to Barley Dorothy gave up a salary as well as a job, and she brought no money with her: Financial matters were a mystery to them both, she writes. They did, however, have a good financial advisor and after the death of James' father, Henry Parkes, in February 1944, 'the financial situation cleared somewhat'. Henry Parkes owned about 20 houses in London, in Barking and Leytonstone; their value was £4,200. The property came to James. He had been in communication with his father during the German occupation of the Channel Islands; it had been a correspondence conducted by the Red Cross and through intermediaries, James being unwilling to risk the German Security Police finding out that Henry Parkes was the father of someone on their 'wanted list'. This was not a manifestation of James' inflated ego, as Philip Toynbee believed it to be. Unlike Toynbee, James had not forgotten the Geneva Incident, nor, unlike Toynbee, did he underestimate either the vigilance or the vindictiveness of the German Security Police. Perhaps he was being overcautious, if so, it was with good reason. Better to be absurd than sorry. With his father's permission he had drawn on his London bank account when he needed to. He had also been able to let his father know of his marriage and to receive his congratulations. What he could not do was be at his father's deathbed or attend his funeral. Moreover, he had to wait until the war's end before he could learn from Ena Crocker, who had nursed Henry Parkes during his final, lengthy illness, of how his father had been towards the end:

> The conditions under which we were living and the food, at his age was all against him, he gradually got weaker and very feeble, and finally had a stroke, was taken to Hospital and passed away a week after. We had his body brought home and the Funeral Service from St Stephen's Church. We did all we could for him and gave him as much as we possibly could, he had an enormous appetite, but the food we had contained very little nourishment. Your Dad quite understood the reason you did not write directly to him, he

told me about it and said he would not dare write to you, but he was always delighted to receive news of you from my sister, it was the wisest thing to do, as if the Germans cannot get hold of the one they want, they punish the next of kin, we have had some of their dirty work here.

It was not only his father with whom he lost all significant contact. He told Ena that he had been 'warned by a friend in the Foreign Office not to write to anyone in German Occupied countries'.

The consequences of this hiatus should not be exaggerated: James had already turned his back on Central and Eastern Europe long before 1939. After 1945 he never went back to any of the places that he had come to know well in the years before 1935. It is understandable that he never returned to Germany (or Austria), and not being a Soviet sympathizer perhaps it is just as readily comprehensible why he never went to Warsaw, Budapest, Belgrade, or Bucharest. Yet, there is more to it than that, more to it than that the overwhelming majority of those he did write to (and welcome at Barley) lived in the United States, Canada and Israel, countries he was happy to visit. Karl Barth had something to do with his hostility to the continent and to continental ways of thought. So too no doubt did the enduring memory of the Geneva Incident. But also, as we shall see, he became a self-confessed Anglophile. This did not stop him holidaying either in the Channel Islands or in Provence, but most of his holidays, and he took all too few, were taken nearer home, at Walberswick, Southwold and Aldeburgh in East Suffolk. The Second World War, in emptying Europe of Jews, also played its part in this transformation of the European of the 1920s into the Anglo-Saxon of the 1960s.

Such times had not arrived in 1945. Nor should we leave wartime Barley in such a sour frame of mind. By 1944 prospects there, and not only monetary ones, were decidedly better than they had been in the first years of the war. That stands to reason in the broadest sense: the war was being won. It was true also in a narrower one, as the following extract from a letter of 1944 demonstrates. James wrote to Edwin Silcox, Director of the Canadian Conference of Christians and Jews, on 24 May of that year:

> For the last six months I have been doing little travelling, and instead enjoying the beauty of Barley in general and

> my garden in particular. I have even been able to rescue bits of it from four years' neglect, which has done me a lot of good, and is making Dorothy into quite a good gardener ... This spring the garden has been more beautiful than ever, and in the autumn it provides me with a considerable proportion of my income. My barns carry the scent of apples into the highways, and my cellars are filled with good things. Moreover, I have the incredible luck to have my old pre-war John [McNeilage] back to run the house, as he has been invalided out of the army YMCA, and we are able to keep our guest room filled with the weary or the interesting – and sometimes both. The house indeed grows shabbier all the time, but remarks placidly that it is not the first time it has been shabby in its four centuries of life. Only the constant flight of bombers overhead reminds us of war – and the idle car in the garage.

It comes close to being rhapsodic. After all the vicissitudes of politics and theology James had been through in the four years he mentions, it was undoubtedly Voltairean.

It is time to turn to politics, to James' political failure. This is the word he used in his 'Apologia pro vita mea in rebus publicis versata 1942–1944', a typescript of 23 pages of March 1944: 'in giving this a scholarly Latin title, I give at least one of the reasons why it is a record of failure'. This is not the place for a history of the Common Wealth Party, even a short history. Nor are we particularly concerned with the divergent personalities of the other participants in what turned into a predictably messy business: Richard Acland, Tom Wintringham, and R.W. Mackay. In *Voyage of Discoveries* James gives a self-exculpatory account of his less than satisfactory 18 months in politics; it is only one quarter of the truth. But what was the truth? We are not going to arrive at it now, because no one knew what it was then. Reading the letters that passed between them after James had surrendered the chairmanship of the party at Easter 1943, and again when he left the party altogether a year later, is dispiriting. How familiar to one who has sat on committees, attended departmental meetings, argued in corridors, tried to see sense and perhaps talked nonsense, how tediously familiar are these contradictory accounts of what happened at a Manchester hotel, of who said what to whom, of what he meant, of how it was intended, of what was the *real* issue. As it all amounted to nothing in the end, as it usually does, why should we spend much time on it here and now? I think we will not. For what lies beneath the calculated attitudes and the unpremeditated insults is not some exposable truth; what does lurk there is an unsolved problem and an impossible dilemma. How best to run a party, a state, an institution was debated, I recall, by Plato and Aristotle. The discussion stemmed from the question: Do you want a tyrant? And was not the answer in the affirmative so long as a good one could be found? James says that R.W Mackay was 'ambitious, autocratic, unscrupulous'. He seems to have been just the man to lead a political party, and lead it successfully. James thought otherwise. He was not going to be dictated to. He preferred the system of an 'amateurish committee, ideas, and intentions'. It had to be 'amateurish', because not one of the four was a professional politician and none in the least resembled those all-knowing, all-seeing guardians who ran Plato's Commonwealth. In fact: they no more existed than did the benevolent despot. Which brings us to the impossible dilemma, the circle James could never square.

Thomas More had been unable to do it either. The dilemma is posed in *Utopia*. No doubt it had been discussed in Rome and Athens a good deal earlier. Does a man who wishes to improve the conditions under which the people live go into politics? Unlike Erasmus, Thomas opted for participation. It is too simple to say that he made the wrong choice, although because he lost his head, he patently must have done. Politics are never black and white; they are like Primo Levi's grey zone: compromise and concession, accommodation and the hard-won bargain are of the political essence, and those are polite words, as Watergate has taught us, for what actually takes place in privy chambers and on the back stairs. Both Thomas More and James Parkes believed in what James called 'a politics of kindness'. Thomas did not believe in kindness when it came to disrupters of the King's Peace, but that is another matter: where do you draw the line with such people? How tolerant can a state be of those who wish to abolish it? Had the Nazis been proscribed would Weimar have survived? Should racists not be swept from the streets? If anti-capitalist demonstrators can be, why cannot anti-ethnic ones? Can one kill with kindness? Once in politics, Thomas More quickly discovered he was trapped. What good he could do for Englishmen and women was nothing compared to the evil done them by those in politics for reasons other than kindness. Indeed, most politicians never gave a thought to the good of the English people. Politics, he found, were not about kindness. What did James find? Because Common Wealth was founded to improve the lot of the English spiritually as well as materially, he discovered that the English were spiritually unimprovable. On resigning from the party in February 1944, he wrote to Kenneth Ingram:

> I do not believe there is any permanent place for Common Wealth in English political life except as a group who are seeking a new way of life ... The present leadership will not achieve that, nor will the present methods. I am naturally saddened so to depart. But heavier prices than that will be paid before our ancient and spiritually debauched society can renew its strength.

Can a society 'spiritually debauched' ever 'renew its strength' from its own resources? One is bound to think not, but James never did lose hope: perhaps reformation might come from without. Since his day even that hope has evaporated.

There were other equally hard facts to be faced. If at one extreme English society was beyond salvation and at the other there was R.W. Mackay's 'Neronic jealousy and suspicion', between them lay the mundane middle ground where a new political party was unlikely to make headway against those long established. Whatever the groundswell of anti-establishment, anti-conservative feeling that had developed by 1942, it was never going to be enough to carry a socialist, particularly a Christian socialist, party to power, had Common Wealth survived to fight a post-war election. Class was the culprit. James was far from being a socialist in any routine sense; 'even to secure economic change', he wrote in his 'Apologia', 'we would need to accept many new ideas in the fields of personal and social relations'. What these amounted to he spelled out later in the same paper:

> At present Sir Richard Acland, Bart., Wilfred Brown, Esq., son, uncle, cousin or something of the owners, are expected by the 'working classes' to be different, and to start higher up the rungs of the occupational ladder, not because of any

merit, but just because they are 'gentry'. Common Wealth is striving to abolish that society and neither Richard nor Brown ... had realised that the only real basis for the new hierarchy of responsibility was recognition of superior talents or merit, and that this recognition must be mutual. We were going to create a society in which the prime minister and the crossing sweeper might have been at the same school and call each other Jo and Bill. There would only be peace and creative harmony in that society if the crossing sweeper acknowledged it was his superior merit that had made the other prime minister, and if the prime minister honoured the competence at his job of the crossing sweeper, and if, outside their jobs, both could meet as friends. Incidentally, they also did not realise that it is just because this recognition exists among the 'upper classes' that their rule is so firmly established. When I meet a cabinet minister who was at Oxford with me, we slip at once back into the same relations ... One of the most difficult things with which I had to try to cope was that Richard's immediate reaction to any opposition or criticism was that 'people must have confidence in their officers' and to tell them this. Confidence is not a thing with a 'must' in it, and it is certainly not created by officers demanding it and refusing to listen to criticism or to acknowledge mistakes. It rests on this same assumption of a basic difference between the officers endowed with an inherent superior wisdom, and the 'little folk'.

Was it not Utopian to think this could be changed? Thomas More had thought so, and in *Utopia* had made his thinking plain. Gents rule all right. They did in 1516, they did in 1944, and they do today.

It is because social distinctions are inevitable and everlasting. Like the poor, gents are always with us. The 'disappearance of social distinctions in a reconstructed society', writes Proust, 'is by no means a foregone conclusion'. So it has proved from Communist China to Capitalist America. James was right in one respect: economics where social (and personal) relations are concerned matter less than the cultural deformation that seems either to be a feature of original sin or an aspect of the sin against the Holy Ghost. In this regard communes work no better than does a meritocracy. Social distinction, whether it be claimed and granted on grounds of blood, virtue, money, membership in the Nazi or Communist Parties, or the ability to kick a football, will not go away. Thus, James was wrong on the bigger issue, or rather he was looking for heaven on earth, because 'a new and socialist society' based on personal relations other than 'the present utterly artificial pretence' is unachievable. This is not to say that some societies are not more social, even if they are not more socialist, than others; or can be for a time, as was Britain in the 1950s and 1960s. But it is to say that political action, like economic change, is not going to rid us of social distinction. Other members of the committee that ran Common Wealth put their faith in the first or the second, or in a combination of the two, so were as guileless as was James. We are not talking here about social, political or economic alleviation any more than they were. They, James included, wanted Britain to be more fundamentally changed than that.

It was Kenneth Ingram who wrote most boldly, at any rate to James, of political action as the motor of social change. James had told him that he did not believe there was 'a place for Common Wealth in English political life except as a group who are seeking a new way of life'. Ingram replied:

> I agree that the religious side of C.W. is vital, but I am sure that it can't be developed in any other way than that of the political struggle ... To think of the need for new ways of living without becoming a serious political force (with all the 'Mackay' type of organization which that involves) would only – in my view – lead to that fatal deadlock at which so many religious movements have arrived. Personal relationships will remain an idea unless they are the outcome of efficient (political) action.

It was also Kenneth Ingram who wrote to James in March 1944 wondering what all the fuss he was making was about. 'I have finally been expelled from Common Wealth by Mrs Marsden', James had written to him. 'It would make an admirable novel of the Thomas Hardy type.' Ingram responded: 'There isn't a crisis ... Aren't you over-emphasizing the incident? To leave C.W. because Mrs Marsden is restive does indeed seem to me incongruous.' Here we come back to earth with a jolt. Mrs Marsden seems to have been the custodian of the Party headquarters in Gerald Road, London, where James lived from time to time. She had in some manner upset him. It was the final straw he said. Ingram wrote again, in response to another letter from James, informing him that Richard Acland had confirmed his expulsion from Gerald Road:

> You should get free from the nervous state of tension to which you have been reduced. I can sympathise with and I can understand your position. But I see also that you are attributing significance to incidents, which, in fact, they do not possess. The Gerald Road affair hasn't any relation, direct or remote, with the Mackay–Common Wealth affair. Nor, in fact, need it in itself affect your membership of C.W.

One would not bother with this, did it not show James in an unfavourable light, a light that needs in a moment to be reflected back on the more important incident of a year before when James resigned the chairmanship. We know that James could be 'difficult', might he also have sometimes been 'impossible'? Grown men behaving like children: is it a tragedy or a comedy? What is the tone of the last letter in the March 1944 sequence – comic, ironic, or tragic? Here is James writing to Richard Acland. 'My dear Richard':

> I have delayed a very long time answering your letter of 12 February. You will, I suppose, have realised that it cuts my last link with Common Wealth. I should be grateful if you would send down the various things I left at Gerald Road. There is a red road map of London in the sitting room, a grey pull-over, and (possibly) a grey sock in the cupboard of the bedroom, and my brush and comb. In the bathroom are shaving and teeth cleaning implements. You also have a collection of my photographs, and my milk bottle at Sprydon.

What hope of changed personal relations can there be when they are conducted at a level where the return of a toothbrush, a grey sock, and a milk bottle are more important than sticking together to create a New Age?

None of the above appears in *Voyage of Discoveries*. What, or rather, who does is James the Saviour and James the Martyr.

Attending a conference of Common Wealth called in October 1942 to deal with the emergency caused by J.B. Priestley's resignation as Chairman, James found himself propelled into the chair. 'My only qualification' he writes, 'was that, as a completely new member, I was not involved in any of the suspicions and intrigues which had bedevilled the situation.'. Enter James the Saviour:

> It was not an enviable position. All I knew was that the meeting was called in order to wash dirty linen in public – and my main qualification was that I alone of those present did not know what the dirty linen was, or round which corner I should suddenly find it. The fact that several hours later Common Wealth was once more a relatively united body with some understanding of its purpose, was taken as evidence that, while I did not pretend to know anything of practical politics, I did know how to take the chair, and I remained as temporary chairman for a number of months.

He had done it again! Saved the situation single-handed. In March 1943 James the Martyr makes his appearance. After criticizing R.W. Mackay for his 'big business technique', and telling us that he would have been 'perfectly willing' to hand over the chairmanship to Mackay, who wished to add that office to the one of general secretary which he already had, James continues:

> But that was not his method, and instead I was subjected to a series of false accusations, intrigues and plots which did no good to the movement. In the end I was deliberately 'framed' and had either to split the movement by defending myself or allow the false charges and what not to stand. It was less than a year after the trouble with Priestley's resignation, and I was sure another internal conflict within the leadership would be fatal to the movement ... so I retired without saying a word in my defence.

Perhaps he ought to have done. The letters and papers that have survived from a few months later (the Manchester Hotel Affair) show that he was no more James the Blameless, or was not held to be by his colleagues, than he had been James the Hero. It was one thing for R.W. Mackay to accuse him of writing 'unadulterated drivel', quite another for Richard Acland to tell him he had thrown 'a bloody great crowbar (and a bloody silly crowbar because it deals with details and not with fundamentals) from one end of town to the other'. But, as has been observed more than once, politics makes fools of us all. It is not politics that James should have got into. It was public life.

That said, and it was Charles Singer who said it, it was not easy for 'a socialist scholar', as James called himself, to live in an anti-socialist society. He was an unusual socialist, as well as a special sort of scholar. 'While I had been for some time a socialist, I was convinced more than economic change was required', he wrote in a passage of the Apologia already cited, 'and that even to secure economic change we would need to accept many new ideas in the fields of personal and social relations.' He had, he continued, 'been trying to work out these relations for more than 20 years'. It would have been 30 years if he had been thinking of his 'conversion' in 1915, when (so to speak) he had given up being R.W. Mackay to become James Parkes. Did he mean 30 years when he wrote 20? It is more likely that he was referring to 1923 when he began working for the Student Christian Movement. Beyond his being cooperative and not being acquisitive, it is difficult to see what the 'relations' between him and others were that James had been working out, cooperation and non-acquisition not being 'new ideas in the fields of personal and social relations'. It is, nonetheless, clear that James' socialism was social rather than economic, and that, being a queer sort of Christian, he was a Christian socialist only in the broadest sense. But then he was also a queer sort of socialist. In a short and not altogether coherent piece written for the *St Martin's Review* in February 1945 and entitled 'Target for 1945', he put forward some of his hopes for post-war Britain. There are almost as many blows aimed at his opponents, imagined or real, as there are constructive suggestions. I have to confess that I am not always able to follow the thrust of the former or the drift of the latter; perhaps the reader will do better. She will have to judge for herself.

'Now I quite openly believe in the new society *as a Christian*,' he wrote, 'and I quite openly detest the mugwumpery of *The Christian News-Letter* and the Ecumenical Movement':

> Today ... we are not living in normal times, but in a revolutionary period; and parties are separated by fundamen-

tally different conceptions of society ... In such a situation the church cannot be neutral ... He who does not assist the new society is positively assisting to maintain the old. If he positively and with conviction believed in the old, well and good. If he doesn't, his neutrality is cowardice and treason to God, as well as to his fellow men. There is no half-way house ... In the political issue which dominates our life, I believe there is only one side which Christians ought to support, and that for religious not 'political' reasons. The Tory Christian I respect *as an opponent*; and I do not propose to abandon my Christian fellowship with him. Equally the Socialist politician I shall support, even though I do not propose to follow blindly everything that he may desire to do. That seems to me to be a realistic acceptance of the basic fact that men are imperfect – both religiously and politically. Moreover, I shall persist in believing that fundamentally the issues before us are simple ... and the typically ecumenical love of involved phrases, 'profound' examinations into human sinfulness and general 'tieflichkeit', seems to my simple mind to be mostly poppycock.

That saw off Karl Barth and all his evil, mystifying works. Or did it? A socialist Christian might be able to respect a Tory Christian and (one hopes) *vice versa*, but mutual respect on the grounds of man's imperfectability is not the point. If the issues are simple then politically a choice has to be made. In part, the practical part of politics, this is a matter of voting, but what about ideologically? Surely, in ideological terms a Tory Christian is a contradiction in terms. Capitalism is not the message of the Gospel, even if Jesus did not question the existence of private property. Let us hear more from James:

> The issues before us are profoundly simple. We are confronted with the alternative between a society which, however humane, is founded on property and the competitive instinct in men; and a society which, however imperfect, is founded on persons, and the co-operative instinct in man. The pretended intermediate society of 'controls' seems to me to get the worst of both worlds. What we need today is unbounded creation not abounding restrictions ... I could believe Lord McGowan as an uncontrolled capitalist would

> really put his best into doing a good job of work for the community, if I believed in capitalism. I could believe that Lord McGowan would do an equally good job of work quite loyally if we said to him: 'please continue to run I.C.I for the community as a public servant'. I can't believe in his doing his best as a private capitalist wrapped up in the red tape of controls.

What happened to the economics involved in the running of a private community? Even if we followed James into a denigration of the primacy of economics, they have to be allowed some role in the relation of Lord McGowan to the community. Are not the shareholders his 'community'? Is not the making of profit on their behalf his responsibility? Does not that obligation alone tend to make him look askance at socialism? Realistically, red tape is better (for the community at large) than unbound capitalist wealth creation. It is after all an imperfect world and imperfect men and women need 'controls': self-control has never been effective.

It is not that James is being naïve. He is, however, being simplistic. He does not like a competitive society, nor does he care for one that gives priority to property; persons must 'come first', the competitive instinct must be subordinated to the cooperative one. All Christians, except Tory ones, would heartily agree. How is that new society to be achieved? Apart from condemning controls, James offers no advice, albeit in 1944 he wrote to a correspondent that one should have a determination 'to change as much as is necessary in society ... in the present juncture this means to me, work for the non acquisitive society, the society of common ownership'. He wrote in the *St Martin's Review* essay that he would vote Labour in the forthcoming election, even though he found 'the present Labour Party and some of its leaders very disappointing', yet when Labour got in he was not prepared to give them any help: offered a seat in the House of Lords he refused it. Here, surely he might have been able to become influential in public life, on Jewish causes as well as on English political and social matters. His letter to Mr Asterley Jones of 25 September 1946 is worth citing in full:

> I have thought a lot about your suggestion that I might help the Labour Party in the Upper House. I feel that the three main arguments against it are that I don't live in

London, so that much time would be taken in attending; that I cannot afford to get accommodation in London and Barley is just too far out to get to and from daily; and that the line on which I might consider myself sufficiently distinguished is both too narrow and too exacting. I *am* interested in many other questions; but I cannot spare the time I would need to be competent to express too much on them.

There are echoes here of his decision of a dozen years earlier not to learn Hebrew. If a man or a woman wants to do something, he or she does not raise objections, but gets on and does it; it is the not wanting enough that prevents the doing; the rest is apologetics.

If James did not enter public life, he took what opportunities presented themselves for public speaking. As the University Sermon he preached at Great St Mary's Church in Cambridge on 27 April 1941 is one of the fullest expressions of his theological position, certainly in relation to the church, it will detain us for some time. He used as his Aunt Sally an article by the Rt Rev. Cyril Garbett, Bishop of Winchester, published in the *Daily Telegraph* on 10 April 1941, and entitled 'What is the Complaint against the Church?' It was an innocuous enough piece, complacent where it was not bland, and reassuring where it was not complacent: about what one would expect of the *Daily Telegraph*. It was not a red rag to a bull, although the conclusion that the nation had to become 'truly Christian', a 'vague Christian emotionalism' having been 'substituted for intelligent Christian conviction', and in order to achieve it there had to be 'Christian education for all the children of the nation' may well have got James' goat. The bishop at one point said that critics of the Church might be asked 'What do you want the Church to do?' It was to this question that James addressed himself. First, however, he went onto the attack:

> The situation today is that the Church, as an institution, so far from turning the excellent average material which it receives from its confirmation classes and theological colleges into better and more educated Christians with deeper and enriched spiritual experiences, crushes in far too many cases their initiative, devitalises their faith, and

turns them into the cogs of an increasingly unwieldy machine.

Warming to an apocalyptic theme, for, he said, 'the Church, like the civilization within which its institutions and formal expressions of faith have grown, has come to the end of an age', he continued:

> And just as we know in our economic and political society that we must not only make changes of form, but must also make changes going more deeply into our individual and social personality, so it is with the Church. It is evident that the anomalies of Anglican organization, the scandal of public and private patronage, and of the parson's freehold, the autocracy of the Bishops, the selfish incompetence of Church finance, all unfit the Church, as it stands today, to play the spiritual leader in a New Age.

The Rector of Barley was very much on his mind. 'But', he went on, even were all these reformed … the malady would not be cured.' After telling his audience about God, 'the responsible creator and ruler of this world, then planner and guide of its corporate societies', he got down to what the terminal malady was.

What was critically wrong with the Church was the language she used of God. Even though 'the greatest mystic must express himself in the language of his time':

> God himself is unchanging. [But] His being is not affected by the rightness and wrongness, the competence or incompetence, of our signs. It is no proclamation of a new God, no act of blasphemy, to revise and rewrite the signs of yesterday. It is rather an act of treason to maintain signs whose inscriptions are effaced by age, whose meaning has become totally obscured by changes in the thought and expression of the men for whom they are intended, and to refuse to alter them on the grounds of Biblical authority or liturgical tradition … Here lies the condemnation of the Church of England, as, indeed of all the institutions of the Churches, from the Vatican to Central Hall, Westminster, from the Anglican form of service for the National Day of Prayer … to the extemporary utterances of innumerable Free Church

pulpits ... The clergy and the laity in their public acts proclaim, preach and worship a God who is frequently described in the terminology of a dead world, in a language which they themselves often do not believe, in thought forms which, so far from arousing awe and affection, can, among the men and women of today, arouse only repulsion, contempt, indifference or incredulity. It is a terminology created before the evolution of modern science, of modern psychology and of modern conceptions of government, justice and responsibility. It was utterly real at the time of its creation. Today it is not.

There was more to this than words. The Wittgenstein of 1941 would have agreed. 'How long', James asked, 'can we read and sing ... in our services passages from the Bible which, in the study and the lecture room, we readily admit to be corrupt, incomprehensible or inaccurate?' The answer has to be for a very long time indeed; even if the 'repetition of sixteenth-century formulas' has ended, we continue to sing about and pray to a Lord, first envisaged in feudal terms, and a King, first conceived in the image of a monarch with crown and sceptre. James believed this to be a sad state of affairs. A start had to be made on rewriting the ordinary services of the Church; they had to be linguistically updated, made to resonate with 'simplicity, modernity and directness'.

We can detect the progressive humanist in this and on cue, so to speak, he gave unmistakable voice to a humanist view of God and creation. There was 'no field of human activity' in which we had not made 'considerable moral progress since the days of those who composed the words' used in public worship. It was moral progress 'to know a world working by law', and 'to know that the measure of power is the measure of responsibility'. It seems extraordinary to me that even if what had happened in Soviet Russia was still mainly hidden from view, what had happened in Germany since 1933 was not. James Parkes, more than most, knew what had happened there, just as he surely knew what had happened in Poland in and after September 1939. Yet, on the eve of the Final Solution, he could still speak of 'moral progress', of 'a world working by law', of the measurement of power by responsibility. It took time for the immoral, barbarous, and irresponsible use of power by Nazis and Communists to sink in. In the case of the latter it was not until Alexander Solzhenitsyn and Robert Conquest put us in the picture nearly 40 years later. Nonetheless, did James really think Stanley Baldwin the moral equal of William Ewart Gladstone, Lord Halifax a better man than Lord Salisbury, Mr Chamberlain an improvement on Mr Asquith? He certainly did not consider Karl Barth a theologian more morally congenial than (say) George Herbert, theology having been bypassed in the onward march of morality. He got to this theme next:

> I do not think there is any field which calls less for complacency than that of theological developments of the past ten or fifteen years. Today one proclaims himself of Barth, another of Brunner, a third of Maritain, a fourth of Berdeyaev, and this unintended effect of the ecumenical movement in all its branches is almost totally unfortunate. We have had little compensation for this deluging of our religious life with the outpourings of continental decadence, casuistry and escapism. We have sacrificed our moral responsibility to our own people to a vain striving after emotional and verbal unity with every heresy from Rumania to Bonn; and we have congratulated ourselves on our agreement on non-essentials with those to whom we should have had the courage to proclaim that we do not believe in their God; we do not believe in their man; we do not believe in their Christ.

These are more than harsh words; they border on the hysterical. Did he blame Barth, if not the others, for the war? If 'continental decadence, casuistry and escapism' was to be found anywhere it was in the heads of the Nazi 'true believers' and in the besotted minds of those of the German people who first voted for them, and then greeted their achievements in Austria, Poland and France with something akin to rapture. James appears to have cast Karl Barth in the role of John Chrysostom: the Man Responsible For Everything. There is also more than a touch of chauvinism here. It came out more fully a little later. 'I am not ashamed', he said, 'to express my belief that in the present situation in the world's affairs the Anglo Saxon world bears not only the future of liberty and democracy upon its shoulders, but also has the heavy responsibility of re-interpreting the doctrines of the Christian faith in the light of the knowledge, and to meet the problems, of today.' In the midst of the dark days of 1941 patriotism was more than pardonable; it was essential. Still: what had happened to the Czechs and Poles, let alone the French, Dutch, Norwegians and Danes, and their claims to 'liberty and democracy' or 'the doctrines of the Christian faith'? Perhaps in those dark days, before the Americans entered the war and while the Nazi–Soviet Pact was functioning, James regarded those peoples as out of the reckoning.

He did not end on that note. He returned to his main theme of a God whom we should address in a language compatible with Modernity. It was both the language and the ideas of men, 'however saintly, who believed themselves to be living in a static world, created in seven days by a mere act of power and then corrupted by sin, and whose conception of authority was based on the absolutism of oriental despots', that we had to jettison. It was, he repeated, 'the end of an age':

> We cannot ... rest content merely with the maintenance of the past. The past can neither be maintained nor restored. But there can be no New Age without a soul. The Churches must go forward or take their place with the Churches of the East as the fossils of a great tradition and the betrayers of a humanity which, then, without them, but guided by God through other channels than theirs, will move forward to a greater future.

Well: it was a sermon. It was also wartime. It is also easy to look back 60 years later knowing that the destroyers of tradition and 'betrayers of humanity' (an extraordinary phrase) were, of all people, Germans and Russians. Because so much of the past, especially but not only the Jewish past, was lost forever between 1917 and 1989, because so many bodies and minds when not destroyed were displaced, we, whether we are Jews or Christians, or perhaps neither, set far greater store on tradition, traditional usage, and traditional language than did the generation to which James belonged. They speak to us of the past, about which we have every right to be nostalgic, even sentimental, but above all they speak to us of eternity. The language of the twentieth century turned out to be a language of violence, suffering, obscenity and murder. It did not have God in its vocabulary. Better to be embarrassed by the language of the prayers we use to ward off despair, of the hymns we sing to keep ourselves from crying, the psalms we say to prevent us going mad, than not to pray at all. As the later Wittgenstein might have said: it is not the words of the prayers that are important, it is a prayerful frame of mind. If our times are indeed the 'end of an age', it is because most of us no longer pray. It is not the right words that we cannot find; it is that we longer know what prayer is.

Besides, there have been remarkable changes in the language of Anglican services since James' day. Almost all of them have been in directions James indicated; the most recent of them might even have gained his approval. As for the changes in the liturgy of the Roman Catholic Church since Vatican II, they have been revolutionary. In one respect, however, things have not changed. Inevitably, this has been where Jews feature in the readings from the Bible. In the Cambridge sermon of April 1941, James does not specifically identify this area as one where change was required: he was not after all preaching about Jews and Christians. It was, however (and as we have already noticed), a matter that greatly exercised him. While it would be true to say that Jews no longer appear in the liturgy, either to be pitied or to be vilified, they do appear in the Bible readings set for each day. In the readings from the Gospel, the holiest of the sequence of three readings, the first two being from the Old Testament and from the Epistles, Jews almost always are referred to in derogatory fashion as 'the Jews', and as Sadducees and Pharisees they are the villains of the story. In the 23rd chapter of Matthew's Gospel, Jesus lashes into them. It is the chapter James gives as an example of a lesson read in Anglican churches, which ought to be no longer.

He did so in a letter to Cyril Garbett. There was an exchange between them after the sermon had been published in *The Cambridge Review* of 2 May 1941. The exchange demonstrates the futility of controversy, so it will not be dealt with at any length here. Nevertheless, asked to be more precise on the distinction he had made between 'Cyril Garbett' and the 'Bishop of Winchester', James in a letter of 31 May 1941 offered the following illustration:

> As a scholar in Jewish matters, I am often asked by my Jewish friends what my attitude is to Matt. xxiii. I view that

chapter, as do all scholars I know, as a series of wild denunciations which, in their present form, I can by no means accept as coming from the mouth of Jesus Christ. I know the chapter to be inaccurate and unfair. I imagine that if a Jewish scholar approached Dr Garbett, he would receive approximately the same answer. But you are also the Bishop of Winchester, the Ordinary on whom the responsibility lies for the maintenance of the Prayer Book. I note that even the book of 1928 would not allow this chapter (the 1922 lesson for the Mondays after Quinquagesima and 9 Trinity) to be omitted without your direct authority. Even more frequently I am asked about the verse from Matthew's description of the Passion (xxvii, 25), which has historically been used to justify thousands of murders of Jews – I am not exaggerating – and which is part of the Gospel for Palm Sunday. Yet even conservative scholars doubt its authenticity. Have you, as Ordinary, forbidden either of these passages to be read in your Diocese?

These are not his only examples. He told the bishop, he had 'been humbled by the generosity of my Jewish friends in helping Christian refugees for whom the Christian committees could do nothing'; he had thanked God that 'they had enabled an unhappy victim to be saved'. He did not think Dr Garbett would regard his thanksgiving as blasphemous, 'but the Ordinary receives from every candidate he ordains, his assent to the Article asserting that such an act on the part of my Jewish friends is "positively displeasing to God"; and he will not institute a clergyman into a living in his diocese until he repeats this assent'. There was also the withholding from forgiveness in the Absolution of those who did not 'unfeignedly believe' the Holy Gospel; Jews, obviously, were excluded.

In another letter, the last in an acrimonious series in which Cyril Garbett, far from showing himself to be the 'Colonel Blimp' James (in a letter to a more sympathetic correspondent) called him, keeps a cooler head than his adversary, James replies to the charge that what was true for a bishop was true for himself 'and all the clergy'. He agreed:

> I have felt the position very keenly ever since I have been ordained, and I told the Bishop of London of my feelings

> before he ordained me. I do feel compromised by the position, but I have not resigned my orders, because I do not personally view the performance of the services as the main function of my life as a priest, and because the Bishop did ordain me, knowing that I was going to fight for the change of the articles and the liturgy. I told the Bishop of St Albans the same thing when I became a licensed preacher in his diocese.

There is a revealing admission here: 'I do not personally view the performance of the services as the main function of my life as a priest.' What, we are bound to ask, did James see as his 'main function ... as a priest'? I am not sure that we shall ever find an answer to that question.

There is another equally revealing exchange in the letters. It concerns what James called his 'obscurity'. He claimed he was distressed more by Dr Garbett's 'sneers' at his 'obscurity' than he was by the bishop's 'abuse'. While 'distress' is no more than the conventional posture adopted by all controversialists and 'abuse' a word they deploy without a second thought, the charge that there have been sneers at one's obscurity is less often met with. In this case it was also unfounded: 'It is simply untrue to say', wrote the bishop, 'that in my letter there are "sneers" at your "obscurity". This is either sheer misrepresentation or the result of an oversensitive imagination which sees insults where none are intended. I am not dealing with charges made against me by some obscure young curate, but they are made by a Doctor of Divinity, an author of several books and a preacher before the University of Cambridge.' The bishop was right: I can find no sneers either; James was undoubtedly sensitive on the matter; he could not leave it alone. The postscript to his last, and most conciliatory, letter reads: 'I am more obscure than you say. It is the humble D.Phil., not the majestic D.D.!'

What further observations are to be made on the sermon of 27 April 1941? Two will suffice, one platitudinous, the other a little more profound. First, the platitudinous: to read the contents of the 'Calendar' that immediately follows the sermon in *The Cambridge Review* of 2 May 1941 is to realize how little, on the surface, has changed in Cambridge over 60 years. The films on show have different titles, but the titles promise the same sentimental content (with less violence and little sex). The lectures on

'Abyssinia of Yesterday', 'A new Metope Head from the Parthenon', 'The Situation in China' sound familiar. How many attended? The cricket at Fenner's, 'C.U. *v.* Mr. J.A. Witherington's XI': how different would it have been? As a theo- logian might put it: is it the substance or the accidents that have changed? I myself know most about cricket. Its substance has changed as utterly as does that of the Eucharistic bread. Only the accidents remain. Is it the same with the services of the Church?

The second observation is in the form of two questions. Can Christianity exist without 'the Jews'? Are not 'the Jews' at the very heart of Christianity? 'The Jews' are certainly no accident: this is what James demonstrated once and for all in *The Conflict of the Church and the Synagogue*. Christianity was antagonistic if not quite from the beginning, as near to it as makes no difference, except to the scholar. Judaism developed in the same fashion, in opposition to a whole host of rival religions and other gods. Islam also soon came to define itself by what it was not: it was not Christianity, not Judaism, not Zoroastrianism. If competition is central to religion, these three religions at any rate, then it must be to life itself. James Parkes has to have his Cyril Garbett. Especially he has to have his Karl Barth. When Matthew put those words into the mouth of Jesus in the 23rd chapter of his gospel he was doing what comes naturally to man. And to woman. It is by antithesis, not through synthesis, that our minds work, and our hearts too, for loving is (or seems to be) inseparable from hating. If, therefore, religion, which ostensibly is devoted to the cooperative principle, is itself competitive, if the religious among us, save for a handful of saints, contend and argue with one another, what chance is there of a New Age? Or, phrased a little differently: why should God bother? There was more to Barth than met James' eye.

John Hadham's, that is, for in the early years of the war the subject of this study was as much, or as often, John Hadham as he was James Parkes. In *Voyage of Discoveries* he devotes two chapters to this theological *persona*, which he adopted in the second year of the war. The Cambridge sermon of 1941 was, in his view, given by John Hadham. For me, however, John Hadham is very much James Parkes. There are six John Hadham books spanning the 20 years from 1940 to 1962. During the war there were also a number of John Hadham broadcasts. Radio is barely less ephemeral than is television: what is heard and seen one day is forgotten the next. When they are not being used to propagandize and advertise, radio and television are by and large means of entertainment, and things entertaining never generate more than a passing interest. This is even truer of what used to be called 'serious' radio and television than it is of a comedy half-hour or a night at the circus. The John Hadham broadcasts may have helped some, perhaps many, of those who heard them in the dark days of 1942 and 1943, that after all was their propaganda purpose, but they quickly went into oblivion. The same is true of the books. Like the romantic novels of the day before yesterday, they are virtually impossible to read these days, save as period pieces. Nothing ages as fast as 'new' theology, the theology presented as necessary for a new age, theology as prophecy. By now we are familiar with most of the themes of the theology of John Hadham; this, therefore, will be a short section.

The first book, *Good God*, was by far the most successful. James tells us in *Voyage of Discoveries* how many copies it sold and what his royalties were. The paper shortage of 1940, he suggests, prevented even greater sales. The later books sold less well, the last two, *God at Work in science, politics and human life*, published in 1952, and *Common Sense about Religion*, published in 1962, apparently sinking without trace. They carried James' Trinitarian message. Even the second book, also published in 1940, *God in a World at War*, was not well received. It was particularly not well received by William Temple. In *Voyage of Discoveries* James writes that he sent Temple a copy of *Good God* and that Temple had 'told I forget whom, but it was not me, that he considered it the most important contribution to theology for the past fifty years'. In the letter Temple wrote to James in April 1940 while he was still reading *Good God* he said he was enjoying it 'immensely': 'it is a very vivid and racy account of the sort of thing I was brought up to believe'. James, although saying he was 'terribly busy with a dozen jobs for my poor dear Jews', replied at length. It was Israel Sieff who had 'persuaded' him to write the book. The remainder of the letter was very much a rehearsal for the Cambridge sermon of a year later, apart from a paragraph on universal salvation, a topic that he may well have dropped from the sermon because Temple had not agreed with it. Here is another combative passage from the letter Temple found disturbing. The tone is familiar, the odd capitalization is presumably due to a 'lack of staff':

I feel that the Anglo-Saxon religious world is beginning to feel its way towards the necessity for this fundamental reformulation on the basis of fundamentally new discoveries about the nature of God. The continental world, Protestant, Catholic and Orthodox, is miles away from it. On secondary issues the Berdayeffs, the Maritains, the Barths and the rest of them have a lot to teach us. On fundamentals they are merely playing with new patterns woven out of old cloths, very pretty, frightfully attractive, and opium, opium, opium all the time ... Opium which makes the Anglosaxons consider it even conceivable that they should entrust a key position in the Christian world to a Visser t'Hooft in spite of all his intellectual understanding of Anglo-Saxondom. The ecumenical movement has meant that a very large proportion of the time and strength of people like your noble self ... is given to seeking a common basis with those with whom I believe immense agreement is possible on secondary matters, but who are fundamentally wrong about God.

Like some of the paragraphs of *Good God*, which Temple, having finished his reading, found 'perverse', a passage such as this, of which there were any number in the next book, *God in a World at War*, displayed a contempt for other theologians that the archbishop, to say the least, found distasteful.

In that second book James wrote, *inter alia*, that Christian theologians had the 'moral courage of wood lice', that 'Germany's greatest tragedy was Martin Luther and the Lutheran Church', that 'a few extra prayers or petitions inserted into the outworn services' were not what were wanted, that the 'institutions of the churches ... behind their imposing facades, their vast budgets, their huge nominal membership [were] but dry bones and words, words, words'. Having read *God in a World at War*, in July 1940 Temple wrote to James outspokenly. They had also recently talked. As a result of his reading and their talk the archbishop said that he had 'settled down to a conclusion which I must pass on though it may fill you with despairing rage'. It was to James' treatment of his opponents that Temple so strongly objected. In a first letter Temple got no further than writing that James was 'perhaps a little arrogant'. In a second, responding to James' defence against the charge, he was more explicit:

> When I spoke of arrogance, a horribly harsh word, I couldn't find another ... You call a number of fairly competent theologians 'little' so and so. Why little? For myself I am sure the 'continental' outlook has a lot of truth that we tend to miss. I should be quite happy if you denounced Vidler for so writing that the multitude is bound to misunderstand, though I believe you exaggerate that. And I could not complain, though I regret it, if you denounce what he really means. In fact, you denounce him for saying what you know he does not mean; and that strikes me as unfair. Of course, the danger of your whole method is that you so emphasize the intelligence of God that you obscure His holiness. I did not think that happened in 'Good God'; I did feel it in 'God in the War'. Well, well. I have said my say privately. Now you say yours publicly.

'Your God', he had said in the first letter, 'becomes too like H.G. Wells' "Invisible King" for my liking.' Archbishop Temple had also closed that letter with 'Well, well': 'Well, well. You must prophecy as you are inwardly moved.'

The trouble with prophecy is that it disappears overnight. The couplet in bishop Christopher Wordsworth's famous hymn, 'Prophecy will fade away/Melting in the light of day', is especially true of prophecy apostrophized by its stridency. James had stigmatized matins and evensong as 'medieval'. William Temple had said he liked them and that they were for the 'instructed'. Medieval or early modern, they continue to be said or sung by the 'instructed'. It is not that James was theologically in error, or even that he 'obscured' the 'holiness' of God (which he does). Where James goes wrong is in believing that the uninstructed may be brought to understanding by modern methods, as if Modernity would not also pass away. His 'arrogance', it seems to me, ultimately resides in his humanistic, progressive belief, that his age was getting it not only better but 'righter' than the ages preceding it, that, for example, the language of today has greater authenticity than the language of yesterday. What about the language of tomorrow? Does it not make the language of today the language of yesterday? This debate is sufficiently antique to need no further pursuit here.

Instead let us look back on the schoolboy John Hadham. Here

is an episode recounted in *Voyage of Discoveries* that, so to speak, says it all:

> While we were still at Les Fauconnaires and I shared a bedroom with my elder brother, David, I remember coming back from church full of rage at the meaningless and unacceptable psalms which we had been singing. David was always a good conservative, and at once defended the psalms on the grounds that we had always had them, and I replied that we had had the psalms of David long enough, and it was time we had the psalms of James! It is only due to lack of time that I have not attempted to fit our liturgical use of the psalms to intelligent twentieth century beliefs ...

I think I should like to italicize 'only' and 'intelligent' in the last sentence. David must have had to put up with a great deal.

We can move fairly effortlessly back from John Hadham to James Parkes by way of letters he wrote to Alan Richardson of the Student Christian Movement in the Spring of 1941. He had refused an invitation to speak at the Movement's summer conference, doing so on the familiar ground of his theological differences with it: 'I shall merely be a fish out of water at your gatherings.' In his present circumstances it was also 'very difficult' for him to do much travelling: 'I am constantly having to refuse invitations to lecture either as John Hadham on Religion, or as James Parkes on Jews'. He went on:

> I'm afraid I must appear rather disgruntled and cantankerous. I find being John Hadham very difficult, and I cannot imagine why the Lord wanted to add that existence to the already busy James Parkes with a family of sixteen million Jews to look after, which is surely enough for any man!

Within the next 18 months his 'family' was to be drastically reduced. James, like almost everyone else, had no inkling in April 1941 of the catastrophe that was to engulf the Jews of Europe after March 1942. The Russian War had not yet begun (although it was already far beyond the planning stage), while whatever schemes projected for the extermination of European Jewry were still merely sketches if indeed they were even that) in the minds of Himmler and Heydrich. The Shoah could not have been foreseen: death and destruction in Poland was one thing, the Final Solution was altogether something else. What happened on the killing fields and in the death camps, how much James knew of what was happening, and how he reacted to that knowledge perhaps should be dealt with in a chapter covering the years of war, but 'James Parkes and the Shoah' is too important an issue to be tackled *en passant*. It has, therefore, been deferred to a conclusion.

Meanwhile, the complexity of the issue might be exhibited by two examples. They are placed at this point as evidence of the difficulties of interpreting the reaction of a man who wrote tirelessly about a wide range of intellectual matters, yet whose reticence about his own emotional life by the middle of the Second World War was a deeply ingrained way of conducting himself, probably of protecting himself, in a world that twice in his lifetime had embarked on war to save itself from a raging German Nationalism. James was no longer young: he was 45 in 1941.

First, there is an illustration of how the English, who have rarely if ever experienced it, discuss suffering and evil. James wrote on 5 August 1943 to Miss Sibthorpe, Honorary Secretary of the National Committee for Rescue from Nazi Terror: 'I am awfully sorry that your letter about the Canadian broadcast [on Jan Karski's report on the Final Solution in Poland, of which a copy accompanies the letter] coincided with my greengage crop.' She replied the following day: 'Thank you so much for your letter and I hope your greengage crop was a good one. You made my mouth water as greengages are one of my favourite fruits.' On 18 August 1943 James wrote to Miss Sibthorpe again. 'I think it would be a good idea', he told her, 'to publish the talk on Jewish mass executions.' No doubt the greengages had been safely gathered in. Second, by contrast, in a May 1964 undated draft of a letter to Bill Simpson and Joan Lawrence of the Council of Christians and Jews, James wrote:

> There are two subjects on which I admit I cannot talk and argue. I can only write, because I care about them so much that I break down and weep. One is the holocaust and the other is the complete indifference of the Christian world to the real roots of Israel and its real justification, and, indeed, necessity.

Comment on such a statement is virtually redundant. If I am tempted into annotation, it is simply to draw the reader's attention to the depth of feeling expressed in it. James' belief in the 'necessity' of Israel might, however, be noted.

The reasons for the underlying tragedy of Germany, which one suspects roused him to exclamations of anger rather than reduced him to tears of distress, he articulated at some length in a letter to Victor Gollancz of 10 May 1945. Thanking the publisher for sending him 'your magnificent pamphlet on Buchenwald', he said he wished to raise an additional matter and to 'have your opinion on it'. The matter, a familiar one, bears repetition as it is enunciated here in an austerely judgemental form. 'It seems to me', James continued:

> that the academic, professional and especially religious leaders constitute a group on whom a very heavy and inescapable responsibility lies. ... Were it a question of raising such an issue from a judicial standpoint for condemnation or acquittal, I think they would be hard put to it to defend themselves. But that is not in question. It is not judgement these groups have to face, but a fact of history. As a direct result of the fact that they did not resist, a million Polish families died; a million Soviet families died; a million Jewish families died; and hundreds of thousands of Dutch, Danish, Belgian, French, Yugoslav, Greek, Norwegian, British and other families died, and by their deaths have given them a second chance. Even did we wholly acquit them and agree that they could not have been expected to risk their own lives and families deliberately as professional and religious groups, yet they cannot escape the fact that these others were given no choice, but died in their millions before Germany could be freed from the Nazis.

Because James was inflexible when it came to the question of responsibility, he could be more clearheaded than most on the issue of German responsibility for genocide. We know now that the great majority of academics and professionals not only did not resist Hitler; they were among his most enthusiastic supporters, particularly where antisemitism was concerned. Those German students of the 1920s whom James encountered, and whose antisemitism he so much detested, were in the 1930s energetic Nazis and in the 1940s the perpetrators of the Final Solution. Above all, his emphasis on others than Jews is notable, not perhaps notable in May 1945 when it was by nationality that those who had died, even (or especially) those who had died in Buchenwald, were categorized, but remarkable in later years when often it seemed only Jews had been killed by Germans. James, as we shall see, never deviated from the fact that Jews were not the only victims of Nazi racism.

Victor Gollancz, 'rather rushed' in his reply of 14 May 1945 because he had been asked to do 'a pamphlet on the Jewish aspects of the camps', enunciated a different sort of truth about 'academic and professional leaders'. 'They are', he wrote, 'too atomised, and very few of them have any realization of their political responsibilities.'. Nothing, therefore, was to be expected of them. It was 'the religious leaders' who had betrayed the past: 'in fact, I think the most notable betrayal in the whole history of the last thirty years has been the betrayal of organized religion *everywhere*'. It is unlikely that James would have disagreed.

Gollancz, on the other hand, might have found James' ideas on 'the whole history of the last thirty years' of Anglo-German relations, as he had set them out nine months earlier, not entirely to his liking. In a long and considered response to Gerald Bailey, Secretary of the National Peace Council, in July 1944 James pulled no punches. 'I have read the material on peace and Germany which I received this morning with great foreboding. I fear that the history of 25 years ago is going to repeat itself.' He had three major points. Nazi Germany had planned for war over several years. 'We were doing all kinds of silly and disreputable things, but neither we nor any of the United Nations were planning war as a positive policy of aggression.' Secondly, there was what he called 'a perfectly objective problem', namely German racism: 'the immense mass of Germans will accept with enthusiasm a Government based on the aggressive selfishness of racial superiority; so long as Hitler was winning the voices raised against him [were] exceedingly few'. Thirdly, there had been the Treaty of Versailles and 'the despair of Germany'. The harshness of the former had been overstated, the extent of the latter exaggerated. It had been more than 'the wickedness of the Kaiser' that had caused the First World War, yet, the British had fallen for the propaganda that pretended

'Germany had *no* responsibility for the war'. 'And now', he wrote, 'you are trying to do so again. But this time it is the other side which is the central problem: the question of the evil will and the misuse of power.". If there was one country and one people that James knew inside out it was Germany and the Germans.

He was equally critical of the idea in a National Peace Council document that 'the remaking of personal links with Germany will be doubly difficult because of the mental and physical isolation of Germany during the last decade'. 'Don't you think', he asked Gerald Bailey:

> it may also be made slightly difficult by the concentration camps, murders, lies and violences of the Nazi government in 'peace time'? By the rape of Czechoslovakia? By some unfortunate actions of the Nazis at war, by Warsaw, and the Warsaw ghetto? By Rotterdam and Belgrade? By Lidice and Oradour sur Glane? By the shooting of hostages and prisoners of war? By a million or two murders of Jews? By the wiping out of cities? By the feelings of Europeans who have personally suffered under these things? Even apart from the fact that the 'mental and physical isolation of Germany' before the war was, in so far as the statement is true, entirely of Germany's doing? I saw enough of the student world from 1923 onwards to be able to support that statement with all the facts you want.

It is his Europeanism that comes out so strongly here. It was the 'needs and feelings of Russians, Poles, Czechs, Danes, Frenchmen and all the rest' that merited attention.

The 'poor dear Jews' demanded a different sort of attention. It goes without saying that James had been actively concerned about them throughout the war. In a book that is about a man who had little time for institutions and who had had his fill of committees and conferences, there is no need to go into detail about the organizations James was engaged with on behalf of Jewish refugees or in response to the news of the Jewish plight in Occupied Europe. It was in such a fashion that he became acquainted with Victor Gollancz and with Eleanor Rathbone, a far more redoubtable campaigner than James and someone who was as exceptional a person of her times as he was. It is her portrait, not his, that hangs in the National Portrait Gallery. I do not think that Bill Simpson's picture is there either; probably it ought to be. The Rev. W.W. Simpson was a Methodist. He was Secretary of the Christian Council for Refugees from Nazi Germany when Dorothy worked for that organization in the first years of the war, and he became the first Secretary of the Council of Christians and Jews when that organization came into being in 1942. James was always ready to relate that the 'first steps to the formation of the Council ... were taken under a pear tree at Barley', without informing us of what they were. Why was James not secretary, people asked then and continue to ask. In *Voyage of Discoveries* the reason he gives is a trifle disingenuous. 'I would have wrecked the Council in a month', he writes. We have seen that many years before he had taken up tapestry to alleviate the tedium of committee meetings, but has he not also told us of the many conferences he saved, including that of the Common Wealth Party, by his tactful chairmanship? It would have been his want of patience and lack of tact that would have ruined the fledgling Council he declares; Bill Simpson, on the other hand, was able to endure everything: 'the frustrations, the necessary compromises, the dilatory verbosity'. He did so for more than 30 years. However energetically and purposefully James worked unofficially and behind the scenes, one cannot resist an impression that he believed his own work to be more important than that of the Council. We have come across this attitude before, and Dorothy was very soon to share it: the 'work', their work, took precedence. Proust's dichotomy between the writer's inner life and his life in the world is not what is in question. James' writing was the 'work', but that writing was not about one man's moral relation to the world, it was about the moral relation of Jews and Christians.

Not that the 'work' consisted solely of writing. James was sufficiently like Martha to be up and doing in a variety of other ways. To take one example, not I think mentioned in *Voyage of Discoveries*, there was the Jewish Hospitality Committee for British and Allied Forces. For this he wrote a newsletter in November 1944, in which he said that since the beginning of the war he had 'seen more of Jewish chaplains' work than of Christian', and that American chaplains based near Barley had much enjoyed finding 'a Jewish library in a quiet English village'. Many of those who visited or stayed at Barley wrote appreciative letters and some became firm friends. Because hospitality is one of the principal duties of religion, and because James and Dorothy held open house at Barley during the war, we can safely assume that they are to be counted among the righteous. As the heartfelt letters of thanks demonstrate, they gave freely of themselves; they are, therefore, also to be ranked among the blessed, if there is a distinction to be observed between the righteous and the blessed. Moreover, James gave of himself in another way: he lectured much and widely. It was a long time before I found in his correspondence a letter turning down an invitation to lecture, and by the middle of the war he was getting many such invitations. Unless it was the Student Christian Movement who wanted him to speak, and until ill health at the end of the 1950s slowed him down, his letters of refusal were invariably couched in terms of genuine regret. Nor did he take lecturing lightly. Virtually until the end, whatever the occasion, he always typed out what he was going to say in full whatever the occasion. We will take a single example. On Thursday 22 July 1943 he gave a lunchtime lecture at the church of St Mary Woolnoth in the City of London. It was called 'Christianity and Jewry' and lasted half an hour. Here is a taste of what he said:

> We all of us, to some extent, know the facts of the Jewish story today. Even amidst the other horrors of this war, it stands out as something more horrible than anything else. All through the sad history of man's cruelty to man there has been massacre; men in hot blood have wiped out men, women and children, and tribunals in cold blood have practised horrible cruelties over long periods. But I don't think that in all of our human story has there been such an abhorrent combination of these two things. Men have – and remember it is not the action of one or two men; there must have been hundreds, indeed thousands involved in it – week by week and month by month now for a year, been collecting the Jewish population from country after country and quite coldly exterminating them — men, women and children of all ages.

'And remember', he reminded his listeners in a later passage, 'the Jews were in this war much longer than any of us, since

1933.' One wonders what kind of an audience he had and what they made of such truth telling.

Not everything was unflagging hospitality or unmitigated horror. How could it be? There was, there had to be, humour. We have noticed before, as we will notice again, that James could be and more often than not was good company. In *Voyage of Discoveries* he tries to achieve a lighter note and fails. He does better with some of his correspondents, including his young nephew Aldus (as we shall see), although in other cases his attempts at humour might be regarded as somewhat too laboured to be entirely successful. Writing to make the reader smile, let alone laugh, is a hit and miss matter. I am not even sure that his intermittent correspondence with the novelist Louis Golding, a sympathetic and playful correspondent, gets beyond the level of the sixth-form. Yet, writing is one thing; talking is another. There is abundant testimony to what splendid company James and Dorothy were. Dorothy, while hardly qualifying as a Marx Sister, might have been as responsible as her husband for evenings which in their letters the American servicemen described as not only 'enjoyable' but 'thrilling'. There was laughter as well as enlightenment: 'I had difficulty in keeping from laughing out loud on several occasions', wrote Sergeant Meyer of the U.S.A.F. In the same letter Sergeant Meyer also commented, significantly in this context, that having read a pamphlet of Dr James Parkes, he could not 'reconcile it with the Dr Parkes I came to know'. Sergeant Meyer might, however, have been in deadly earnest, as what he was unable to match up with the Dr Parkes he had encountered was the latter's stated belief in the Incarnation as the 'central event of the world's history'. A sociable evening by definition is not a serious occasion; irreconcilable differences do not surface; it is not intended that they should. Is humour, therefore, a saving grace of mankind? Without it, would we not be at each other's throats even more often than we are? Does the world not need more Marx Brothers and Sisters than the few that it has? Perhaps, James' fault was not to take himself too seriously, but the world.   Alas, the wartime world had to be taken seriously. As he told Dr Maude Royden in June 1942:

> I find my poor dear Jews to be the most trying children in the world, and I constantly have to remind myself that any

other group put through their history would probably show still more deplorable characteristics, but nowhere are they more infuriating than in the imbecility of the political leadership of the Zionist movement.

Dr Royden, who wrote her own pamphlets on 'Jews and Christians', had been pro-Zionist until she had visited Palestine in 1937. 'I returned from it very much opposed to the Zionist State, for it is a *State* that Dr Weizmann and his friends aim at and not a National *Home*, which was promised them.' James and Dorothy were on amicable terms with Chaim Weizmann, at any rate in 1946, when they wrote telling him 'how utterly ashamed' they were 'of ourselves, our country and our religion', and to express 'their admiration of your courage and balance at this time'. 'What distresses us most', they added, 'is that personally we are without influence or power to reach those who are responsible for policy. We have tried to do what we could by speech or writing.' The reader, having got this far, will hardly be sympathetic: power and influence had been renounced on more than one occasion, indeed one occasion was that very year when James refused a peerage. Dr Weizmann replied that their note had been 'one ray of light in a world that seems almost drowned in darkness'; 'you', he went on, 'are one of the givers in this hour of our need'. Much had happened in the four years after 1942. Nonetheless, Zionism remained Zionism. How imbecilic was its political leadership? Was it any more so than that of Britain? James may be caught out here trying to face in two directions at the same time. This was what Dr Royden accused him of with regard to Christianity: if its ethical system was 'wholly Jewish', why was he so keen on the Incarnation? Or should we say that James got himself backed into a corner by trying to be fair to both religions? How could someone who believed Christianity to be so Pharisaic profess to be a Christian, was Maude Royden's unexpressed thought. Chaim Weizmann's might have been that anyone so evidently for us cannot be against us. I feel that I might be backing the reader into a corner, or heading her towards a dead end. It is in the nature of the subject we have reached: the foundation of Israel. It is pointless to say what a terrible error the Balfour Declaration was. That is like saying, what a pity the Holocaust happened, or what a shame that men kill: kill beasts, birds and fish, women and children. Israel is not a mistake; it is the 'necessity' James described it as. At least it is until it ceases to exist, if it ever does cease to exist.

James was critical of others than Zionists. Hear him on a chief rabbi and a Roman Catholic bishop. The year is still 1942; the occasion is a meeting to launch the Council of Christians and Jews, the venue was Grosvenor House in London:

> Henry Carter had got to the meeting the Chief Rabbi and the R.C. Bishop Matthews. Both clearly intended to sabotage any practical work of the Council on general lines. The Bishop invited us to contemplate together with loving reverence the home life of the B.V.M.; and the Chief Rabbi invited us to combat antisemitism. The Bishop stated quite directly the lack of any interest of Roman Catholics in Jews who were not religious, and the Chief Rabbi denounced any religious cooperation of any kind. The two worked most amusingly hand in glove, whenever anyone else made a sensible suggestion.

Is it any wonder that James steered clear of committees, where he would have been obliged to deal with people like these? It was February 1942: they were fiddling while Jews were burning at Chelmno. In the same letter, to the Rev. William Paton of the International Missionary Council, James reported on other matters: a conversation with Jan Masaryk about East European Jewry, the unreality of most American pronouncements on Zionism, the uselessness of an uncritical approach to the Jewish situation in Palestine, the undoubted fact that the British Mandate there would have to go, and that 'something on a large scale, and revolutionary, such as the removal of the Arab population, *may be* the right thing'.

The last was a theme he returned to in a letter of June 1943. He was writing to Ben Rubenstein, Chairman of the Financial Committee of the United Jewish Congress:

> I may say personally that I am not a bit alarmed about the treatment Arabs would receive in a Jewish commonwealth, nor do I think Jews would desire a compulsory exodus of Arabs in order to avoid any minority problem, although personally, I would be quite prepared to discuss the matter,

if that were in fact Jewish policy.

No doubt, James did not think Jewish policy would ever come to the expulsion of what he probably thought of in 1943 as a minority. Anyway, Jews did not do such things, which is how he put it to a Mr Hutchison, who wrote in September 1943 saying that he detested Jews and Catholics, even if he added that these were 'feelings in me that I ought not to feel': the others who wrote similarly, and there are many letters among the Parkes Papers in the same vein, entered no such apology. 'Of course', James replied, 'there are many bad Jews, just as there are many bad Protestants':

> but when you know Jewish history the amazing thing is that there are any *good* Jews. My own experience has been that it is difficult to find a better example of what we mean by humanity, culture, and civilization – and that includes honourable conduct – than is to be found among good Jews. There comes a stage in civilization when one can say 'I don't think that, as a people, X or Y could revert to barbarism.' I feel this about the Scandinavians and the Danes. It is not because progress is automatic or mechanical, but because a standard achieved has such deep roots that I do not think it could be destroyed. I do sincerely feel the same about the core of Jewry, and I think it is amazing that this is so, when they have passed in their history through every experience which is likely to twist, humiliate, and discredit a human group.

They had not, however, experienced state creation, which, it has to be said, makes barbarians of us all. The historian need only point the reader to the creation of Norway, Denmark, and Sweden in the eleventh and twelfth centuries, or to the creation of Israel after the Exodus. Of Israel after the Diaspora more will have to be said.

Meanwhile, James ought to have the last word. In April 1947 Professor Ellis Waterhouse resigned from the London Society of Jews and Christians because of Jewish terrorism; this had made it 'impossible' for him 'to feel friendly with Jews as a race'. The executive of the Society asked James to reply to the professor's letter of resignation and this is the gist of it:

> I say to you openly that when my Jewish friends condemn terrorism I am glad and I honour them for it, but that of myself, both as Christian and as Englishman, I profoundly regret it but I have no right to condemn it, and can only say with profound shame and humility: 'in these ranks but for the grace of God would be James Parkes'. If you have reflected at all on the inner torment in the spirit of any Jew today at the misery of his people; if you have reflected, not on whether the members of our present government ought to have made the promises they did before they came to power, but on the inevitable reaction of Jews in distress all through Europe to the fact that they did make those promises; if you have reflected that two years after the end of the fighting many tens of thousands of Jews of Europe are still without security or hope, then, I say, you should thank God that the tradition of Judaism is still strong enough, even in those Jews who avow themselves secularists, to have prevented terrorism from being far more widespread and far more death dealing than it has been so far, and that there are many Jewish voices, both religious and political, raised against it; and you should redouble rather than abandon your cooperation with the Society.

Or should the very last word be reserved for the commentator with hindsight? The Deir Yasin Massacre was exactly a year ahead.

5

Barley: The Post-War Decade

If these ten years were to be summed up, it would have to be in a sentence that contained the word 'work' 20 times over. What made all the work possible was what James called the Barley 'tripod'. He describes it in *Voyage of Discoveries*:

> While I wrote books and articles, and was frequently away for conferences, lectures and committee meetings, John McNeilage ran the house and exercised a general control of the vegetable garden, surrendering the reins to Dorothy for the evening meal. Dorothy was responsible for the whole secretarial and filing work, as well as being hostess to a continual series of guests. It was only by the competence and generosity of these two 'legs of the tripod' that Barley remained upright until the mid-fifties. Financially we spent all that was realisable from my inheritance, and then relied on I.M.S.

Between the mid-1940s and mid-1950s, James published five books and upwards of 60 articles, essays and occasional pieces. The books covered both familiar and new ground: *An Enemy of the People: Antisemitism* was published in 1945; *The Emergence of the Jewish Problem, 1878–1939* in 1946; *Judaism and Christianity* in 1948; *A History of Palestine from 135 A.D. to Modern Times* in 1949; *End of an Exile: Israel, the Jews and the Gentile World* in 1954. He and Dorothy spent three months in Palestine in 1946; they were guests of the Jewish Agency and Israel Sieff paid their boat passage. If the visit was not a turning point, it was undoubtedly a watershed, and a not unpredictable one for a man who looked for whatever signs of hope there were in a dark world. After the Shoah, Israel was the only hope for his 'poor dear Jews'.

As for the extent of his other work, the first fortnight of July 1945 will serve as an example. On Sunday 1 July at Bristol he preached the opening sermon in a series of five 'on the principles which should govern the Christian in exercising his vote'. The idea for the sermons was that of the priest of the church where they were preached, the Rev. Mervyn Stockwood, and James on 'God and the General Election' did not beat about the bush:

> We know by experience what the Tory type of society involves: profits before service; competition before co-operation; conflicting imperialisms; unemployed capital as an asset and unemployed human beings as a liability; production controlled by money and interest. We know that such a society has led to two world wars in one generation. We are bound to strive for a different kind of society ... the Left is striving for such a new society.

He might just as well have carried a banner proclaiming 'Vote Labour'. The following Sunday, 8 July, he was at the neighbouring churches of Whaddon and Meldreth in Cambridgeshire, a few miles across the county boundary from Barley, standing in for a vicar who was on holiday. James was on duty at Meldreth for Sung Eucharist in the morning and for Evensong in the evening; in the afternoon he had taken Evensong at Whaddon. He preached at all three services. During the following week, 9–14 July, he attended a Toc H staff conference at Oxford giving one (or more) 'Invocations'. The one he submitted in advance greatly pleased those who read it. 'You are taking immense pains on our behalf', they wrote, 'it is not too violent for us and it will not create alarm and despondency. It should challenge those who are capable of it to some straight thinking.' When afterwards the organizers wrote to thank James they said he had 'stirred our minds, refreshed our spirits and, more than once, made us conscious of our sins and failures'. They regretted 'deeply that you had reason for feeling, at any rate once, that what you said was not received with Christian courtesy that you had a right to expect'. On Sunday 15 July he was again on duty at Meldreth and Whaddon: at Meldreth in the morning for Holy Communion at 8.00 and Mattins with a sermon at 10.45 in the evening; at Whaddon for Evensong and a sermon. It should be noted that to arrange for him to 'stand in' on these two Sundays took an uncommon amount of 'fixing up', which involved a time-consuming correspondence.

As always, there was a steady stream of friends to entertain and visitors to accommodate. A number of them are mentioned in *Voyage of Discoveries*, including Fritz and Else Rosenfeld. After the death of her husband in 1947 and Else's return to Bavaria in 1952, she and Dorothy wrote long letters to one another, Else being fully as much Dorothy's friend as she was a friend of James. Nor was she the only one: Julia Namier and Kathleen Wood-Legh were two among many others. It needs to be stressed that Dorothy was a person in her own right, and that her personality just as much as her husband's engendered and sustained close and loving friendships for both of them. It was to Else that Dorothy wrote in August 1953 confessing that she and James had 'come to a turning point in our lives':

> ... for one thing, our capital really is exhausted now and we have to find out whether it will be possible either to *expand* in our own work, or pack up on it and take a parish ... If we can do it, we want to turn Barley into the Institute we have longed for: that of Jewish–Christian relations ... We hope somehow to raise funds in America for this. Then we want to build on a library and secretary's room here and to get a good secretary. We should like to dig up the orchard and turn it into a *campus* with small buildings where students of the Institute could stay. All this is taking shape in our minds, and we hope that to do it we may become a Foundation – with American capital.

Fond hopes, we now have the luxury of knowing. Dorothy and James in August 1953 were indeed fully occupied with a variety of pressing matters. One was the creation of 'some kind of "bridge group" to deal with Israel–Arab relations, and the Arab refugees (really much more of a "world" problem than most folk realise)'. As for 'the religious situation in Israel (and generally speaking in Jewry generally)' it was, Dorothy told Else, 'pathetic'.

Else Rosenfeld was a remarkable woman and James and Dorothy helped to get her story broadcast and printed. Less well known was the prelude to it: Else's breakdown at Barley in 1959 and James and Dorothy's critical role in her recovery. James told the Bishop of Coventry, the President of the Guild of Health, of the miracle of Else's healing; 'when staying with us last year', he wrote in January 1960, she became 'feebler and feebler and almost comatose':

> We learned from her daughter that this was not the first time this had happened. We got her to hospital, but they sent her home after a week saying there was no organic illness and nothing they could treat. Our doctor, who is a Christian, said to me: 'It is your job, not mine; there is something inside she is trying to escape'. With God's help and guidance we soon found it was not unrepented past sins of Else herself which were oppressing her, but the terrible memories of Nazi days and actions she had to perform, and inner withdrawal from S.S. inquisitions and continual presence. I gave her communion, and we had prayers with her, using a simple form, I suppose almost of exorcism. With Dorothy holding one hand and me the other I used to call her back: 'Else, come back to 1960' … In a very few days she was up again.

Else, as James told the Bishop, was 'a Protestant who had a Jewish father and a Jewish husband. She managed to get husband and children away in 1939, but no exit visa came for her. So she stayed, and in Nazi Germany of 1939 went and registered herself as a Jewess, so that she might help the Jews. The heroism of such an action is staggering.' Indeed, it is. It was probably Else's miraculous recovery that led Dorothy and James into the 'healing movement within the Church of England', an interest he discusses in *Voyage of Discoveries*.

Julia Namier was also Dorothy's friend. It was Lewis Namier who in 1934 had advised James to apply for the chaplaincy at Oriel College, Oxford; it was advice James had not taken. Namier, according to his wife, was a 'passionate Zionist', who was ignorant of all but the 'taboos and prescriptions' of Judaism; these, she once told Dorothy 'he finds intensely uncongenial'. Whether he and James encountered each other before the November weekend of 1948 the Namiers spent at Barley, we do not know. It seems not, as James and Dorothy do not appear in Julia Namier's intensely felt biography of her husband. The weekend, James wrote to Walter Zander, had been 'interesting'; there had been 'some good discussions along the lines of both their interests'. Dorothy was far more enthusiastic. The weekend, she told Julia, had been 'something quite special'; she looked forward 'to the development of the friendship as time goes on. I feel it is founded on solid ground, and it is a nice, warm feeling.' The remarkable Julia Namier had already written: 'How do I set about thanking you and James for laying the foundations of what both of us feel to be a true friendship of the greatest value to us. Such inceptions, whenever they occur, are too amazing to be enclosed in a formula, yet they throw so much light ahead that for a while they reduce to a shadow all the other, accompanying, details, facts, or events.' If they met again it can only have been infrequently if at all, for I have found no evidence of them doing so. As late as 1959, the year before Sir Lewis Namier's death, they were unable to arrange a meeting in London: Lewis was too busy with his work for the History of Parliament Trust and Julia was invariably out until lunchtime.

James and Dorothy were as hospitable at Barley as they had been during the war; they were also just as liberal with their money, perhaps even more so during the time they had more to be generous with. In 1948 Walther Loeb, a German – presumably a German–Jewish refugee – who had been 13 when he came from Berlin to Britain in 1933 and in 1948 was married with a young daughter, had secured a place to read Zoology at Birmingham University, provided that he pass the Higher School Certificate in Chemistry. To attend the university he needed money. James responded to a circular letter, in which Walther asked for a loan of £300 to see him through his first year, with a letter to Hanna Rosenfeld, Else's daughter, who lived, as did Walther, in Birmingham. After outlining to her Walther's case, he went on:

> As you know, Dorothy and I have not got much money, but we are trying to work out our Christian responsibilities as rentiers. The position is that Loeb wants £300 ... and that actually we could lend him this money though we could not afford to give it him. We fully recognise that lending to an individual is a greater risk than investment in government stock, but we would take that risk if it seemed right to do so from Loeb's point of view ... What I am asking you to do is to see Loeb and to give me your impression of him. Don't look at it from the standpoint of 'O dear, what shall I do if the Parkes lose their money'; that is our affair, not yours. I want you to look at it from the standpoint of what will be the effect on Loeb of his being helped through becoming indebted to a private individual whom it will be his moral

> obligation to repay … Meanwhile, I have written to Loeb, asking him to write to you and call upon you.

The Loebs visited Barley, the £300 was offered and accepted. Walther then failed the Chemistry examination. The money was returned.

Nor was it only Jewish refugees who benefited from James and Dorothy taking their 'Christian responsibilities' to unusual lengths. Herbert Ashbrook, Antiquarian Bookseller of Belsize Park, London, when 'really hard pressed for money' in the Autumn of 1949 received a loan of £25; he repaid it in June 1950. James was always buying books, as not all those he needed were in the British or Cambridge University Libraries. With his purchases he had other help than that of Israel Sieff; the bill for 'several hundred pounds' spent on second-hand books in Jerusalem in 1946, for example, was paid by Simon Marks, while 'for some years' Maurice Blinken, 'an American friend, paid our American book bills': we might well remember their generosity when using the books of the Parkes Library.

The few years of financial independence afforded them by what James' father had left him were over by the early 1950s. The idea of taking a parish then resurfaced as a possible alternative to continuing their Sisyphean labours at Barley. In May 1948 the Rev. Arthur Berry, vicar of the united benefice of Ivinghoe and Pitstone, Bucks, and recently appointed in plurality to neighbouring Marsworth, wrote 'out of the blue' to his 'Dear Brother' offering James the opportunity to be his 'assistant'. He would have the vicarage at Marsworth, 'quite nice and not too large, [with] a nice garden', and about £300 a year. James replied to his 'Dear Brother' that he and Dorothy had been 'talking very seriously over your proposal, but to our very great regret it does not seem possible with all the innumerable commitments which I have':

> I would give anything to live in a parish where I could really feel spiritually at home, and where I could share in the local life and work of the parish as much as my other commitments allowed me to do, but I do not see how it is possible for me to undertake the responsibility you would want … The one thing which the Lord forgot when He turned me into a trinity as an Anglican parson, as John

Hadham, and as a specialist on the Jewish question, was that, unlike Himself, the three would have to share the same 24 hours a day, and that one would have to stop work when the other began.

Thus, the same reservations applied to taking a parish in 1948 as they had in earlier years; the rest was the wishful thinking of a workaholic.

In December 1948 it was Barley Rectory itself that came into consideration; it was to become vacant in March 1949 and James pondered it as a possibility. It was not to be. He told his old friend Canon Tissington Tatlow, it looked 'as though the Lord wants me to go on as I am, and intends to continue His little game of cat and mouse with our economic position'. The rector who had replaced the 'reprobate' Gardiner, one Taylor Wood, had not once asked him to preach or take part in a service. All he had done was get James to celebrate early communion, 'when he does not wish to get up and because I have told him I will not take a fee for taking a celebration'.' During this or another vacancy, however, he took services of every variety; those he conducted between July and September 1951, his fees totalling nearly £17, he set out in a letter to the Bishop of St Albans. This was one of a number to the bishop between June and November of that year describing in pungent terms the chaotic situation at Barley. That situation is too complicated and too parish pump-like to describe in detail; besides, it was a drama that never became a crisis, just as the bad blood between James and the bishop was predictably made good again. Two of the letters, nevertheless, cannot be resisted: the first has James on an unusually high horse, the second has him putting the bishop in his not very exalted place. The high horse letter was of 2 June 1951. As it is highly articulate, largely true, and commendably brief it must be cited in full:

> My dear Bishop, I am always puzzled as to how to answer your highly gothicked summons to a one-day clerical conferencette. I spent twelve years of my life helping the human animal to meet in conference in such a way as to profit from it, and why the Holy Spirit should be expected to make up for indulgence in a method which no serious organization has used for the last twenty years I do not

> know. Medievalism helps devotion; it does not help discussion; and as clergy are rather more long-winded than laity, a couple of hours together do not constitute taking counsel on any subject under the sun for some two hundred individuals. I did attend your predecessor, Michael's, 'synods' when I first came here, as he had asked me to become a licensed preacher in the diocese, but for the last dozen years I have always made excuses – like the gentry in today's gospel? – but as this is the first time I have had to answer yourself, I want to say honestly that I will not come.

Dorothy made him write a more considered letter on 22 June. He made no apology, but he did invite the bishop to meet him at the Athenaeum or to come to Barley. No meeting ensued. A letter from the bishop in November reduced James 'to despair' and then, at the close of his second reply inside a week came another outburst:

> I offered to come and see you in June; you never even referred to the offer. Then I invited you here, because I became convinced that it was only in the middle of the situation itself, where others could be brought in if necessary, that the real issues involved could be discussed. My wife and I are not social climbers, anxious to boast that we have entertained the Lord Bishop. We have invited many hundreds here in the course of the years from many countries, and they have come to discuss with us religious, scholarly, educational, political and personal problems. I am bound to say that we have never before had the experience of our invitation being scarcely even acknowledged.

William Temple apart, James was unlucky with bishops, including, when he was in Israel in 1946, the Anglican Bishop of Jerusalem. Or is it that the great majority of those on the Episcopal bench either put him down as 'an embittered crank', James' phrase for what the Bishop of St Albans might have thought him on receiving the letter of 2 June, or as a cross they had not too painfully to bear? But then: he might have been a bishop himself. Ought he to have been?

Sometimes it is easy to forget that he was ever a priest. James never forgot. One of the 'invocations' he pronounced at the Toc H conference in July 1945 was that the communion service needed to be claimed 'as the centre of divine–human cooperation rather than as the individual preservation of our body and soul to everlasting life'. Here he showed his true colours as a Low and Liberal Anglican: the idea of the mMass as private was one he clearly had no time for. Communion was what its name implied, a communal experience, the coming together of a community, however idealized that community has to be. At the core of the Christian liturgy, as at the centre of Jewish life, was a meal, however symbolic, whatever its historic origins, eaten in harmony with others. The priest did not celebrate for the people; he celebrated with them. Nor did the communicant receive the body of Christ alone; he shared in it with others. It was not a private moment; it was a public one. It is, therefore, understandable that James was not an Anglo-Catholic and that he had little time for pre-Vatican II Roman Catholicism. Dorothy shared his antipathy. In a letter to Else Rosenfeld of the early 1950s she wrote:

> We in Barley have the oddest rector yet – and that is saying a lot. We attended early celebration three Sundays ago, but left before the celebration, because he had suddenly gone 'all Roman' and there was nothing to identify it with the Anglican service; he was celebrating a mass for the feast of the Annunciation of the Blessed Virgin Mary – a feast which does not come into the Anglican calendar at all – and it really was a poser for an Anglican clergyman such as James. The villagers (who get fewer and fewer) don't know one service from another. So James and I left quietly – there were only two villagers besides ourselves.

It is a picture not without its charm: James and Dorothy stealing away from an almost empty church. Nor without its significance: how many communicants make a community? This time, Dorothy told Else, 'it really means the end of our ability to attend our own village church'. They had informed the Rector of nearby Barkway that they would in future go to his church; both he and the Rural Dean 'were wholly in sympathy' and could see 'no other action that we could have taken. But it does not help us much and is sad.' It was not only sad for them; it is sad for us. What hope that Jews and Christians might see eye to eye when Christians themselves do not, when even a James Parkes feels he cannot be in fellowship with, is unable to receive Communion from, a fellow Christian priest?

Was it another example of withdrawal? It came at about the same time as he withdrew from active participation in the Labour Party. Work was the excuse. He wrote on 5 November 1952 to the Secretary of the North Hertfordshire Branch:

> There is no doubt that I have been a totally ineffective Chairman of the local party, and this situation is not likely to improve. Partly I have been very willing to do nothing because I have been very disturbed by the division within the party, and felt that my sympathies were largely on what party leadership would consider the wrong side. But that is only a minor issue; the permanent problem is that of time. We have the kind of job in which we only stop working because we are too tired to go on ... our busiest time is in the evening, when we are less disturbed from outside. Neither of us usually stop work until after 11 p.m.

Such a life was a sure recipe for disaster. Did they never relax? Did they never go the village pub of an evening? If they did not, probably they should have done. To fill every waking hour with intellectual work was not only dangerous to bodily health and mental stability, it was itself a kind of insanity, tempered only by the fact that they were not giving their lives to the creation of wealth and the making of money.

Their exhausting journeys in the decade after the end of the war brought no relief, James travelling three times to Israel and three times to the United States, Dorothy accompanying him twice to Israel and twice to the United States: during each visit they were almost continually on the move and James hardly stopped lecturing. Although they had the occasional holiday on Guernsey or Sark, went once to James' 'beloved' Provence, and from time spent a few days at Southwold, Walberswick, or Aldeburgh, they could not afford the annual holiday they evidently ought to have had; they were only able to go to Provence in 1951 because an insurance policy of Dorothy's had fallen in. In addition, James in 1949–50 was President of the Jewish Historical Society of England. For a non-Jew it was a signal honour, but there were two Presidential Addresses to be given and characteristically he did not take the responsibility lightly. It seems inevitable that something should have had to give, and that it would be James' health. In April 1953 he had an emergency operation at Charing Cross Hospital and after it spent three weeks recovering there. Almost immediately he left for a five-week visit to Israel. In October 1953 while preparing for a lecture tour to the United States he had his first heart attack: it did not stop him from going. He returned only to depart once more for the United States with Dorothy in January 1954. She drew up an itinerary of the three months they spent there; it is evidence of how exacting was their schedule, particularly for James. After two weeks in New York, they spent a week at Boston and Harvard before going on to Philadelphia, Washington, Nashville, Dallas, Phoenix (for a week's rest), Los Angeles and San Francisco. In March they were at Kansas City, Chicago and Milwaukee; in April they went to Detroit, Cincinnati and Buffalo. On 5 May they sailed from New York, first class on the *Ile de France*. James had earned the comfort, having become ill in Chicago and collapsing in Cincinnati. The sole consolation was that he had earned eight thousand dollars towards the foundation of the putative Institute.

They 'struggled on for a year' until in June 1955 James had what the doctors called 'a cerebral spasm'. 'Of the next two years', he writes in *Voyage of Discoveries*, 'there is little pleasant to say.' These were the years of crisis: of them and their immediate aftermath something will have to be said. Before it is, and James the writer and thinker disappears from view for a time, we need to comment on some of what he wrote and thought during the ten years between 1945 and 1955. What he did not write was 'the third volume of my big series on the history of Jewish–Christian relations', and the 'careful study of the Arab refugees and the causes of their flight', which he maintained he was writing in the second half of the 1940s. The plight of the Palestinians brings us to what he thought about the foundation of Israel.

On his return from Palestine in 1946 he declared himself 'a more convinced partitionist than ever', while in *Voyage of Discoveries* he speaks of the 'mental collapse' of the British administration. About what happened next, the war of 1948, the declaration of the state of Israel, the actions undertaken by the Jewish victors against the vanquished Arabs, anything said here, however hesitantly, will be offensive to one side or another, those 'sides' being even more pronounced today than they were half a century ago. The differences are best articulated in the correspondence between James and the historian Arnold Toynbee. That they conducted themselves throughout like English gentlemen makes the tragedy they were debating so much more poignant; their amicable association was brought to a fitting conclusion when they lunched together at the Athenaeum in March 1952. It was in February 1951 that Toynbee asked James to 'look at my piece on the relations between the Jews and Western Christendom and give me your comments and criticisms'. James obliged. The resulting chapter in volume 8 of *A Study of History*, published in 1954, was entitled 'The Jews and the Modern West'; the section that concerns us is the last and is headed 'The Fate of the European Jews and the Palestinian Arabs, A.D. 1933–48'. The 'comments and criticisms' that James had volunteered had evidently made little impression. Here is Toynbee:

> In A.D. 1948 some 84,000 out of some 859,000 Arab inhabitants of the territory of Palestine which the Zionist Jews conquered by force of arms in that year lost their homes and property and became destitute 'displaced persons'. If the heinousness of sin is to be measured by the degree to which the sinner is against the light that God has vouchsafed to him, the Jews had even less excuse in A.D. 1948 for evicting Palestinian Arabs from their homes than Nebuchadnezzar and Titus and Hadrian and the Spanish and Portugeuse Inquisition had had for uprooting, persecuting, and exterminating Jews in Palestine and elsewhere at divers times in the past. In A.D. 1948 the Jews knew, from personal experience, what they were doing; and it was their supreme tragedy that the lesson learnt by them from their encounter with the Nazi German Gentiles should have been not to eschew but to imitate some of the evil deeds that the Nazis had committed against the Jews ... The tidal wave that overwhelmed the Palestinian Arabs in A.D. 1948 was a backwash from an upheaval in the relations between Gentiles and Jews in Western longitudes beyond the Palestinian Arabs' horizon ... In a Modern Western Society that had come to overshadow all the rest

of Mankind, even an imperfectly and precariously emancipated Jewish diaspora in the West had become a power in the World through becoming an effective force in the political life of potent Western countries; and, in consequence, the West's unsolved domestic Jewish problem had become fraught with perils for non-Western and non-Jewish peoples who had nothing to do with this Western problem except for being in the Westerners' power.

Even in such a passage some might think 'lost' in the first sentence altogether too passive a word to encapsulate what was done by the Jewish Agency, the Jewish armed forces, and the new Jewish state to ensure that the Palestinians who fled their villages during the war did not return to them. In mitigation it has to be said that one of Toynbee's exhaustive accounts begins: 'The cold blooded systematic "genocide" of several millions of human beings in extermination camps, which had been the worst of the Nazis' crimes against the Jews, had *no parallel at all* in the Jews' ill treatment of the Palestinian Arabs.' The italics are mine.

James' fullest statement of the opposite case came in an article written for the *Jewish Journal of Sociology* in 1962 and entitled 'Toynbee and the Uniqueness of Jewry'. Before coming to it, however, the letter he wrote to Toynbee on the eve of their Athenaeum luncheon ten years previously must be quoted; in it he illuminates the divergence between them and reveals his own hand:

> Thank you for your manuscript. I have spent most of the day in consideration of it; and I am still troubled ... You know that I accept Israel in a way which you do not; but I accept that, from your standpoint, the whole development from Herzl through Balfour had to be rejected. I can see that, on that basis, the rejection by the Arabs of Palestine and the Arab states of the partition decision of the U.N. would be regarded as a morally right rejection ... Though one might accept that the rejection of partition was based on moral reasons, does this automatically sanction the decisions on the basis of that rejection, i.e. to meet it by force, and to use that force for the massacre of those in whose favour the decision was given? For that was, in fact, plainly

stated to be the intention both of the [Arab] states and of the Palestinians. This seems to me to be plain contrary to any conception of international morality ... Surely whatever standard is applied must be applied to both parties; and if you do so apply it, I still think that your analogy with the Nazis breaks down. For they willed an evil end, and predetermined evil means to carry it out. I would never accuse the Arabs on either clause. The end they willed was not in itself evil; and they were led by events into evil means; they did not predetermine them. But I would be equally confident that the Jews before the bar of history – or the judgement of God – would be acquitted on both scores. Nowhere in the planning of Zionism will you find evil intended against the Arabs; and, as with the Arabs, you will find evil means growing out of man's failure to meet the full spiritual challenge of their situation ... The true tragedy of the Arabs is that they are not innocent, neither the refugees nor the Arab states; and the same is true of the Jews.

Yet, both being guilty, which was the guiltier of the two? Virtually everyone thinks he has the answer, but the answers are never the same. On the other hand, to abstain from responding at all, while shrugging one's shoulders or roundly cursing both parties, is no answer either. Our two men were big enough to see all sides of the question; they did so without sitting on the fence.

The article for the *Jewish Journal of Sociology* repays careful reading. It is in effect an extended review of chapter 8 of *A Study of History*. Toynbee, James says, 'omits the principal characteristic of Judaism by defining the purpose of all "higher religions" as being to bring the *individual* into contact with Absolute Reality'. Judaism, however, above all else that it might be, is a 'corporate expression of religion':

> Rabbinic Judaism turned away entirely from the welter of apocalyptic eschatology which was much beloved by the eastern Christian churches. In place of it was this insistence on roots in the Land of Israel, and Jerusalem as a centre for the whole world ... Without this clue to Jewish survival during the long centuries before emancipation, it is impossible to understand the meaning of Zionism ... For it is

completely misleading to explain Zionism simply by the nationalisms of the nineteenth century, although those nationalisms largely dictated the form it took for Jews, and in which it was understood by other. ... It does not matter whether [the] attraction to an actual area of territory which has motivated two returns at an interval of over two thousand years is unique or not. The essential point is that it is real, and that it is ineradicable ... The tragedy of Palestine since 1917 is that it is the fault neither of the Jews nor of the Arabs that a romantic vision turned into a reality resting on naked force ... Historically there has been no past in which the area of Palestine was exclusively inhabited by Jews; and there is no *panache* in the Arab past save in the periods when they lived in tolerant symbiosis with other inhabitants of the Middle East, Jewish as well as Christian. Perhaps the British ought to have tried to explain more why they had issued the Balfour Declaration; perhaps it would have been different if the Arabs of Palestine had not been subjected to pressures of a pathetically sterile nationalism elsewhere in the Arab world; surely it would have been different if the Jewish return had been adjusted to the Arab capacity to understand and absorb it, instead of to the growing terror of life in Europe. But the point is that it is as totally unscholarly to lay all the blame for the result on the Jews as it is to lay it all on the Arabs. Jews have as much right to be in the country as Arabs.

Who has that sort of 'right' to the land of Palestine would be beside the point (save possibly to scholarly historians), were it not for the inescapable fact that it is in such emotive, not to say fanatical, terms that so many of the descendants of those who owned most of the fields and farms of Palestine in 1948 see the appropriation of their property by a Jewish state. The so-called 'present absentees' have never had any chance of redress for the robbery perpetrated on them. What good does it do them to make comparison with the plundered Jewry of Europe? Scholars must make connections and historians distinctions, for one catastrophe is never the same as another and the Nakba is not the Shoah, as Toynbee pointed out. Nevertheless, when an injustice is done, it behoves us all to point it out, not to find mitigating circumstances for it. Lord Acton warned against going down that path.

James sent the text of his article to Toynbee before it was published; Toynbee replied graciously but with sadness:

> One of the strange and unhappy things about the present Palestine affair is that people who, like both you and me, have no personal or national interest at stake in it, and are disinterestedly concerned for what is true and right, cannot come even near to agreement about the rights and wrongs of the case.

How does a liberal humanist explain the undoubted fact of even the very best of men having to agree to differ? Without an explanation, what hope is there for a world in which the worst tend both to predominate and to prevail? Resignation, in the form in which it was enunciated by James in his last letter to Toynbee, can hardly be regarded as a satisfactory response to so woeful a state of affairs: 'I end with the words of Stowe describing, if I remember, the eastern wall of the city [of London] which would fall into the marshes, "and so I will leave it for I cannot help it".'

He did not leave it, writing and lecturing on Israel at all times and in all seasons. He is particularly outspoken on the subject in February 1955 in a letter to Dr Luther Adams of Lennox, Massachusetts. 'The Gentile enquirer or critic', he wrote, 'must be given the real roots of Israel in Jewish history and Judaism ... To my mind they point straight to the existence of Israel.' What he called 'Anti-Israelism', to distinguish it from antisemitism, recognized that 'these roots existed in Jewish history', but rejected 'the belief that they were rightly met by the actual state which has emerged':

> Such 'anti-Israeli' usually point their answer by reference to the wrongs done in the creation of Israel – it has created Jewish terrorists, Jewish brutality and indifference to the Arabs, and so on. Their case is strengthened when Jewish publicists dodge or whitewash these incidents, and do not recognise Jewish imperfections. On the other hand, Gentile and particularly Christian, defenders of Israel are ... strengthened [in their argument] when one can say (as, happily, one can) these things are regretted, condemned and fought against by an element in Israel, just as keenly as

by anyone outside. That is one of the great tragedies in the present situation: there is nothing comparable on the Arab side, or among the pro-Arabs. They do not condemn Arab excesses, or admit any Arab responsibility for what has happened.

'Anti-Israelism' was antisemitic when it presented 'the emergence of Israel simply as nineteenth-century nationalism without any moral justification', or when it condemned excesses in Israel 'without any recognition of the contemporary situation, or the Jewish past, in Israel or eastern Europe':

> In other words, when for any reason it lays the blame for anything and everything which is wrong entirely on the shoulders of the Jews, and denies that there was any positive and moral reality within the Jewish case which explains, if it does not justify, Zionism and Israel. A hideous example of purely antisemitic anti-Israelism was the behaviour of most of the Christian authorities in Palestine during the war – broadcasting and exaggerating every excess they could attribute (often falsely) to Israeli, while keeping completely silent about any Arab excess; and this is to a large extent continued in Christian propaganda for the refugees which absolutely refuses ever to mention the facts that it was the Arabs of Palestine and the Arab states who started the war, and that Israelis have no factual or moral responsibility for a substantial proportion of the flights.

It is the final statement that requires elaboration, as, whatever James thought, it was untrue.

Two things have to be said about James' attitude towards the Palestinians. The first is that he was taken in by the myth of the Jews making the desert bloom and this meant that he saw the *fallahin* through Jewish Agency spectacles. The second is that he did suffer from 'Anti-Arabism'. It is the tone of his references to Arabs that give that game away; for example in a letter to Elizabeth Monroe in December 1953 he wrote of the Arab refugees as doing 'nothing except breed'. A third thing is probably that he did not know enough about Islam.

Taking Islam first, we find James in the letter to Elizabeth Monroe saying the following about it:

> To me one of the greatest problems in the world, if not the greatest, is the orthodoxies in religion, whether Roman Catholicism in Christianity, Jerusalem orthodoxy in Judaism, or Islam – so far as I know practically all Islam, for its reform movements are so puny. My own feeling is that this inability to get an Arab out of his skin is tied up with the nature of Islam ...

No one would be likely to disagree with him about his 'orthodoxies', which are now known as 'fundamentalisms', although Pope John XXIII was going to surprise him, and among the most devoted workers for peace in Palestine have been and are Roman Catholics, particularly Roman Catholic monks and nuns. Fundamentalist Judaism and fundamentalist American Protestantism have much to answer for, when mischief making in the Middle East is at issue. So has fundamentalist Islam. Does it have more to answer for than the rest? We are still waiting to know.

Little needs to be said about his 'Potemkinization' on the 1946 visit to Palestine, evident in the pages devoted to it in *Voyage of Discoveries*. He does not mention visiting a single Arab village. No one told him how to read the landscape as it should have been read. What we get, therefore, is the standard, sentimental account:

> We met a certain number of *kibbutzniks* whom we had first met on our trip around England or at the orthodox farm near Thaxted which was less than twenty miles from us. We paid a long visit to the group of orthodox kibbutzim, first around Tirat Zvi near Beth Shan, then in the Kfar Etsion group between Bethlehem and Hebron. Linking this visit to our subsequent stays in the country, we have been enabled to realise the splendour and determination of the planning and its realization. In 1946 we saw Holon being built. And watched with amazement, almost amusement, the dwellers bringing in barrow loads of earth to make their gardens in that absolute waste of sand. But we shall always remember the thrill when, on a subsequent visit to Tel Aviv, a lady who had met us at Holon ran up to Dorothy, reminded her of our first meeting some years previously, and exclaimed: 'My

dear, the birds have come to Holon!'
It is surprising to find him seeing only what he wanted to see, was expected to see, and was meant to see, a shock to discover him behaving not like an observant, sceptical, and discerning traveller, but like any other tourist. He had always been the first and never the second when travelling in Central and Eastern Europe during the 1920s.

His 'Anti- Arabism' did not have to be part and parcel of his 'Pro-Judaism', but, as the last quotation demonstrates, it appears to have been. On his 1946 trip he seems only to have met a single Palestinian Arab, whom he misunderstands and, in the telling of the incident in *Voyage of Discoveries*, patronizes. West undoubtedly encountered East: 'I found that I could get much more reliable information either from the British, or from Jews.' He talks of 'continuous Jewish life' carried on 'with courage and determination', but not of 'continuous Arab life', which in the countryside was equally courageous and determined. Moreover, he says the bravery and tenacity which Jews had shown in Palestine 'outbid that of the Christians'. Which Christians does he mean? The Christian Arab peasantry of Galilee appear to have slipped his mind. Nor does a comment on the 1948 war show an understanding of, or sympathy for, the Arab response: 'I have not seen anywhere an attempt to explain why, when every advantage of numbers, terrain, and support was with the Palestine Arabs, when they would have been able completely to sabotage the new Jewish state simply by staying put, their whole behaviour was so inexplicably foolish.' They deserted their villages, he rightly says, with every intention of coming back, just as they had always done when raided by other clans or the Bedouin. They did not understand that the arrival of Jewish fighters 'could only mean that they lost that from which they retired'. How were they expected to know? Even when the British had descended to punish young men and to demolish houses, they had gone away again. In the circumstances, how could he have reckoned the behaviour of the *fallahin* to have been 'inexplicably foolish'? Comparisons, particularly any that concern the Shoah, are generally best avoided, yet here is one. Jews in eastern Poland and western Russia knew all about pogroms: the only good thing about them was that they were quickly over and life afterwards would return to what it had been before. How were they expected to know that when the

Germans arrived in 1941 it would not be the same, and that this time it was going to be the end of a way of life they had always known?

The history of Palestine is the history of the world writ large. The history of Jerusalem, the city of peace, is the history of humanity, always at war with itself. A balanced account of any of those histories is impossible. Only a saint could write them and among historians there has never been a saint. What is written here will be unacceptable somewhere else. Yet, there are two aspects of the history of Palestine which are more terrible than the rest. The first is that Yad Vashem is there and not in Europe. The second is said best by Meron Benvenisti:

> The Arab and Jewish landscapes – so different from each other – which have long stood cheek by jowl, in hostility and mutual disregard, have now merged and been engulfed by a wasteland of cement, stone, and asphalt ... the struggle for the Land has become a struggle for profitable zoning. The Jewish Landscape triumphed, but it was a Pyrrhic victory.

Has justice been done in this assessment of James Parkes and the foundation of the State of Israel? My concern that it might not have been comes under the headings of anachronism and omniscience. Is it anachronistic to think that the man who was James Parkes, born when he was, educated where and how he was, having the interests and friends that he had, could have thought and written otherwise then he did? Given his Jewish sympathies, given the 'Arabism' of the British administration in Palestine and the British government, was he not bound to give his support to what the Jewish Agency was doing and what the new state of Israel did? Above all, given the Shoah, would we in his shoes have behaved differently?

Which brings us to omniscience. Here let us listen to the wisdom of a great historian, Samuel Eliot Morison, whose fourteen volume *History of United States Naval Operations in World War II* has the entirely deserved status of a classic. A quotation from volume nine: 'Writers on military subjects', says Morison, 'are in danger of contracting the occupational disease of omniscience. Years after a campaign they necessarily know more than the generals, admirals and statesmen did who had to make decisions on imperfect knowledge, and too readily conclude that everyone at the time made mistakes, nevertheless, I cannot avoid the conclusion that the entire HUSKY plan was wrong.l.' (The HUSKY plan was that carried out for the invasion of Sicily in July 1943.) Morison was writing in the early 1950s, volume nine being published in 1954. Similarly, whatever reservations I have about James Parkes and Palestine, I nevertheless 'cannot avoid the conclusion' that James was wrong.

Here is Morison on military operations in Sicily during August 1943. They can be understood, he writes, 'only in the light of what has come out since the war from enemy sources. The Allied generals imagined they were driving the enemy back by a series of brilliant offensives. Actually the Axis was conducting a series of rear-guard actions to cover an orderly evacuation of Sicily, which was carried out with complete succes.' What James believed had happened in the war of 1948 was almost certainly not what had actually occurred, that is, unless it is still too soon to know. He was not alone in his misperception and persevered in it, just as the Allied generals (and doubtless many others) continued for years, perhaps all their lives, to believe they had fought one sort of battle when it was entirely another that they had been fighting.

Morison writing once again about operation HUSKY says that 'a powerful deterrent to a bolder plan ... was British memory'. There is no need to labour the point about James' memory in relation to the creation of Israel. It is not the Shoah that is the issue; it may have been *the* issue in his mind, but what was in his memory was the whole history of the Jewish diaspora, the responsibility of the Christian Church for the persecution of Jews, and the remorse and repentance Christians were not showing for their part in that history, that persecution itself, and the culmination of both in the Shoah. Had James not always favoured the underdog? How was he to detect that the underdog in Europe had become the 'overdog' in Palestine? His memory of Jews and Judaism told him that it was impossible. If James, of all people, had been unable to predict the Shoah, how could he have been expected to imagine, and therefore to perceive, the change wrought by the imminent prospect of statehood and then by statehood itself? Memory rules the imagination, imagination governs perception, perception determines how we act.

Despite our apprehensions on the score of anachronism and omniscience, James on this particular charge, it seems, is not to be entirely exonerated. Nonetheless, let there be no mistake about James in general. Before we turn to the years about which 'there is little pleasant to say', let us remind ourselves of what he was and what he had done. When Leo Baeck wrote in 1948 to thank James for his congratulatory good wishes on his 75th birthday he said: 'Time and again I feel indebted to you, being aware of what you mean to all of us.' And in 1954 the 90-year-old Bernard Berenson in a letter to Sir Robert Mayer paid James the following tribute: 'I have never read anyone more fair minded as an historian.' These two great men had lived long, seen much, and pondered long. Different as these two remarkable Jews were, they knew a righteous *goy* when they encountered one.

6

Crises Surmounted at Barley: 1955–64

There were two crises, both major. The first was the two-year crisis of James' ill health. The second arose from the first and was of longer duration: what form should the Parkes Library (or Institute), incorporated as a charitable company on 9 August 1956, take and where could it find a home? The idea of a Parkes Institute at Barley with James its active director had to be discarded quite early on. The final solution of a Parkes Library at the University of Southampton was not arrived at until much later, and almost as an afterthought. Only at the time that James and Dorothy departed Barley for Iwerne in 1964 was the long-running second crisis resolved.

James' health first broke down in June 1955. He was 58. Dorothy wrote to Alisa and Zwi Werblowsky towards the end of that month to tell them what had happened. Exhausted by the three-month lecturing tour in the United States, it had taken James 'until the beginning of this year to begin to recover':

> ... then, since he has been working hard on the book, and we have had other problems as well, he has for the past fortnight 'completed the completion' of the exhaustion and I have had him in bed really ill. He is always rather subject to migraines; a fortnight ago he had 'the mother and father' of them all and has been laid out ever since. Today he is down for the first time. There's nothing for it but rest and sedatives ... we all hope to persuade him to go for a holiday for some weeks very soon ... Meanwhile he's just *got* to go slow ... I really don't know how 'us girls' can keep our 'Big Ones' from overdoing it.

A week later she wrote again putting off the Werblowskys'

August visit: James needed a much longer convalescence than expected, after which the doctor had ordered a month's holiday. Israel Sieff paid for the month at Crans in Switzerland; it helped them get through until the summer of the following year. On 30 August 1956 Dorothy wrote to Eric and Pearl Schrayer:

> I have some very distressing news indeed about James. He is at present in hospital, very ill – indeed still on the danger list – with coronary thrombosis, following pneumonia and pleurisy. He was in hospital for 12 days with the latter, and then returned home for 3 days and seemed to be making progress; however, the attack occurred on Sunday 19, and he barely survived. He was moved back into hospital on August 20, where he has been most critically ill for the past 10 days. I am thankful indeed to say there is some progress, but he is still far from being out of danger, and will at the very best be in hospital from two to three months, the doctors tell me ... I do not know what will happen to the newly born Institute. I am officially its secretary, but James will not be able to do anything about it for a long time to come. I am hoping that others will be found who can 'work' it.

On 2 September Dorothy wrote to the Schrayers again: James had made 'such a stride forward' and the Institute was 'showing signs of standing on its own feet'. It was a joyful letter. 'I am so thankful about this progress', wrote Dorothy, 'that I wish I had Pearl's rolling pin to wave in the air!! I made James laugh today by telling him that I had bought a hat which he had not yet seen, because I should have to try in some way to live up to Pearlie's chic little headdresses!!!' The joy was premature.

On 6 September Dorothy wrote a very different letter to Mrs Ruth Hardwick. Having made good progress, James had returned to Barley for three days; there he collapsed again. 'It was a miracle that he survived and his recovery will necessarily be very slow indeed ... I am given to understand that he will be in hospital for another two or three months at least, and will then have to go away to recuperate. I am only thankful I still have him.' In fact, such were James' powers of recovery that he came out of hospital only a month or so later. The doctors had insisted, however, as Dorothy told Professor Norman Sykes on 26 October, that James 'must winter out of England ... we depart for Menton on Monday next (accompanied by our doctor to see James safely through the journey and into the care of a doctor in Menton). The financing of this lengthy stay abroad was causing me great anxiety – when suddenly a miracle happened. For out of the blue a very charming lady whom we know, hearing how ill James had been, sent me a cheque to cover the whole expense.' The generous lady, as James tells us in *Voyage of Discoveries*, was Mrs Bryce-Salomons, who for some years had been a benefactor: the cheque on this occasion was for £200.

Dorothy had written to the Schrayers in the last week of September, when James was still in Addenbrooke's Hospital but on the point of being released to a nursing home at Hunstanton, Norfolk, that they had been 'quite right': 'it is the long sustained anxiety about the future of the work which has resulted in this most complete breakdown, which nearly cost him his life ... The main thing for the next six months is to keep James entirely free from worry and anxiety, and he must on no account talk about – or do – any work.' In Menton during the winter, probably for the first time in 30 years, he did neither.

They returned to England in the spring of 1957. In Paris on the way home they met Leon Poliakoff, to be precise at 12 noon on 10 April in the Musée Cluny; I know nothing of any importance about the meeting. Did they look at any exhibits? If so, which ones? On 2 May Dorothy told Dr Alfred Wiener that James was 'very much better', but that she had to 'act as rather a "dragon" and insist that he has adequate rest'. It was inevitably in vain. Late in June James, 'though not yet allowed to resume work', was 'beginning to do so'. Early in September they had a week's holiday in Suffolk. Then, on 3 October 1957 Dorothy wrote to Maurice and Rosa Eisendrath in New York that James 'has once again been most seriously ill'; he was back in Addenbrooke's and 'it would be a long time before he is well enough to leave':

> The trouble started with a virus infection of the larynx and trachea; then suddenly pneumonia developed; that is clearing up satisfactorily, I understand, and the penicillin injections are now discontinued. He is, however, again on sedatives and anti-coagulants, as there is a painful thrombosis in the left thigh. He is a very sick man and the doctors are puzzled at these sudden collapses, especially as we had

just returned from a happy holiday and were both feeling very well and beginning to breathe freely ... I don't know what is going to happen about Institute affairs ...

She wrote again to the Eisendraths on 30 October. On 14 October, having had her letter of 3 October, they wrote expressing their distress and enclosing a cheque of £300 for 'the Parkes Fund'; Dorothy responded with so lurid an account of the state of general medical practice in rural England that it has to be quoted:

> Nothing could have been more unhappy than the situation in which we found ourselves with a doctor, who is either (or both) a desperately sick woman and a drug addict. When I tell you that it took two hours to get her up in the middle of the night when James took a turn for the worse (with pneumonia) and it also needed half the village to rouse her (and then they found that the garage door was open, her car door open and her case of drugs etc. there for anyone to help themselves to) you will realise a little of the situation ... The district nurse – and our own doctor on her return from America on Saturday – have described the position in the village in regard to the patients as a 'shambles' ... In himself, however, James is full of life and energy; he is, in fact, very much the life of the ward in which he is ... So you see, we have real grounds for optimism; but this. letter explains a little why I have been unable to write to you much, and why I have (very reluctantly) had to take steps in regard to the wreck of a doctor herself.

The grounds for optimism were false. James had phlebitis in his left leg; he was still in hospital in mid-November. In mid-December Dorothy told Maurice Eisendrath that if James were not 'relieved of strain altogether, there is nothing to expect but another, probably fatal, coronary thrombosis'. The doctor had sent him to a psychiatrist, who had said that there was 'nothing wrong except the never-ending anxiety imposed by the situation'. The 'situation' was that of the Institute; 'something drastic' had to be done, said Dorothy, 'or we shall lose James':

> That is what the doctors tell me, and God knows they have had enough opportunity of judging. He was under their

charge during the whole of his coronary illness; and has been in hospital under observation for 9 weeks now ... We are being advised by one of the most outstanding medical Psychiatrists [at] Addenbrookes and the London Hospital. I have been approached by friends; there is a Cambridge church available for a chaplain, and they are very anxious that James should consider taking it. They say, rightly, he will never be well while the intolerable situation imposed by Sieff continues. And when he is well enough, they ask me whether he could not be prevailed upon [to] take this church and leave the Institute to be run by others?

Dorothy's deep distress is revealed by her prose. Israel Sieff, once upon a time a fairy godfather, had become the wicked uncle. Talk of taking a benefice and of giving up the work that had sustained both of them for years demonstrates what a low point had been reached. It was not quite the lowest.

That had probably been reached in the autumn of 1956 when Dorothy had panicked on a spectacular scale. She did not do so again. Having had James seriously ill for most of the subsequent year, she knew much more than she had then about the nature of his illness, and within a few days of writing to Maurice Eisendrath she had been reassured by the Consultant Psychiatrist's report: 'I found Mr Parkes to be fully normal mentally.' James was not fit enough, he wrote, 'to carry the burden of responsibility of the Institute at the same level as hitherto. He should be fit, however, to live a scholar's life.' If given a sense of security regarding the Institute, 'there is reasonable prospect that he will stay well and active in his writing and academic work for some years, although perhaps less intensely active than he used to be'. On the morning of 19 December Dorothy had a lengthy discussion with her husband about the Institute, which she minutely recorded, and on the same day she wrote to Maurice that 'after having seen the doctors' she was marshalling 'all the facts of the situation'. Immediately after Christmas she wrote to Israel Sieff, and with a decisiveness and sense of purpose she had not shown for some time set about giving James the security of mind that could only come from putting the Institute on a firm foundation. It would take years but she had made a start. We can, therefore, be precise about the timing of James' recovery: it began on the morning of 19 December 1957 with his earnest discussion with Dorothy. When she wrote to Norman Glaister in May 1958 she was in an almost buoyant mood. James after 'three years of very grave ill health' had 'resumed writing ... and so he is getting back to normal in the way of work'. Moreover, while 'not in any way out of the wood financially' the Council of Christians and Jews had 'allotted to us a small annual donation for the next three years ... This is a cornerstone on which to build.' So it was, and one of the unsung heroes of these years of crisis was the Council's secretary W.W. Simpson. To Bill Simpson, to Dorothy in panic, and to an account of the gestation of the Parkes Institute and Library we shall now turn.

We will begin with 'The Growth of Barley', a paper drawn up by James and dated 2 January 1956. It gives the financial history of the Institute To Be up to that point. Israel Sieff [IMS] first came on the scene in 1933; he gave £300 towards the publication of *The Conflict of the Church and Synagogue*. 'In 1934', writes James, 'I spent some time at Bishopsthorpe with Archbishop William Temple':

> discussing the value of my seeking to give up my whole time to this work [of Jewish–non-Jewish relations]. Dr Temple encouraged me to do so, and remained deeply interested in it up to his death. I then discussed the question with IMS, indicating that I thought it to be considerably more than one man's life time which was involved. Though an 'institute' was not then discussed, and would, indeed have been premature, the putting of the work on a permanent basis was already raised when war broke out in 1939. The plan on which we worked up to 1939 was that I raised what I could from Christian friends, and that IMS met the deficit. He did not wish me to make an appeal to other possible Jewish donors, and I have never done so. The work began on an annual expenditure of £800 and rose to about £1300 by 1939. Of this about £150 p.a. was from Christian sources.

On his 1938 trip to Canada James met Rabbi Maurice Eisendrath, a meeting, as we shall see, of great significance. During the war James 'kept the work going' as best he could with 'very limited resources'. For two years Mrs Sieff helped by paying the salary of a secretary, and in 1944 on the death of Henry Parkes James was left 'something under £10,000':

> Of this over £6000 has been spent in keeping the work going, together with gifts from time to time from IMS amounting to £1,275 between 1947 and 1950, when (in 1951) IMS, Sir Simon Marks and Mr Sacher made covenants giving us annually £750. IMS in 1953 made a further covenant, by which I received £500 in November 1953, and a further £500 in December 1954. In September 1955 IMS effected a further covenant of £500 per annum, bringing the 'family's' [contribution?] up to £1250.

As if 'The Growth of Barley' were a *curriculum vitae*, James throughout gives the titles of the books he has published and the lecture tours he has undertaken. He also lists other gifts of money received, for example, a three-year grant in 1951 of £100 annually from the Arthur Davis Trust. He ends the paper with the visit to the United States in 1954; this was undertaken at the invitation of Maurice Eisendrath and was as much a fund-raising venture as it was a lecture tour:

> We crossed the Continent to the Pacific Coast, but ill health prevented me from completing the schedule planned for me. Through the help of Dr Eisendrath we brought into England between February 1954 and May 1955 £3,615 3s 11d. On 19 December 1955 we received the balance of what he had been able to collect for us in a 'Parkes Foundation Fund', bringing the total American contributions to £4,334 in all. This has enabled us to carry on with the work, and make necessary repairs to the property.

There is an appendix on the history of the library, the manner of its funding, and its estimated value as of June 1956: not less than £7,500. A second appendix is a table of annual expenditure, headed 'Barley "basic" budget'. The full sum is £3,400. The principal expenses are the salaries of James and Dorothy, he at £500, she at £250, domestic wages and insurance £800, household costs, including coal, heat, light, and maintenance, £690, and secretarial salary £500. Does it seem too much, or too little? It is not easy to decide after 50 inflationary years. The reader will have to make her own mind up. She might consider the difference between £3,400 and £1,250 and whether an institute like that envisaged by James and Dorothy could have been had (even in the mid-1950s) for the latter.

On 9 August 1956 The Parkes Library Ltd was officially registered. Five days previously, on the afternoon of 4 August, the doctor had been called out to see James; within an hour he was in Addenbrooke's Hospital; he had pleurisy and pneumonia. On 5 August Dorothy wrote the first of a series of letters to Bill Simpson. As she told Walter Zander in a 'confidential' letter of a few weeks later, it was Bill Simpson whom she had asked 'to handle all matters in connection with the Institute on behalf of James and myself until we can return and take things up again'. A simple measurement of Dorothy's agitation, apart from the length of the letters themselves, is the manner of their address. On 5 August she writes 'My dear W.W.', as she does again on 18 September. By 28 September it has become 'My dear Bill'. But on 5 and 6 November it is 'Dear Mr Simpson'. On 16 November it is once again 'My dear W.W.' and so it remains on 23 and 25 January 1957. Bill Simpson's sole surviving letter to Dorothy (at any rate in this file) was of 23 January: we shall need to examine it closely. Before doing so Dorothy's letters must come under scrutiny.

The letter of 5 August informing Bill Simpson of James' departure for hospital was six and a half pages long. Its first paragraph ends with three exclamation marks: 'This knocks James out of any discussions for the next three weeks, at least!!!' For our narrative its most important disclosure is a letter from Israel Sieff of 27 June, which Dorothy cites in full. We need to quote only two sentences: 'Quite frankly', he writes, 'it is impossible for me to add to the very heavy burden with which I am already loaded, and my only hope is to get help from other people. I enclose a cheque for £200 as a further loan, but this is really the absolute limit to which I can go.' This was bad news. Dorothy glossed it at some length. For us half a paragraph will have to do:

> For the agreement in all our negotiations with IMS has been that he would get a group together in England who would give the basic amount of roughly £3000 odd which was necessary for the Institute (though not registered) to carry on as it has been doing for its past years, and that the

American group which Mr Eisendrath had in view (who have already, it must be remembered, contributed £4000 and to whom he hoped to add further names) should 'swing' the additional amount for expansion.

All this had been discussed with Israel Sieff before James went to the United States in 1953; Mr Sieff had subsequently done nothing. Registration, Dorothy reported, was practically completed, as indeed it was four days later. However, she wrote,'*This is still the essential before commencing operations!!!!!*' Four pages, with much underlining and further exclamation marks followed. She included a copy of 'The Growth of Barley' and proposed an immediate conference. Did it take place?

In her next letter of 18 September Dorothy is intemperate on the subject of Israel Sieff. He is no longer sociable IMS; he has become the distanced Mr Sieff; and on one occasion simply Sieff. Here is a sample:

> James' convalescence has to be for a year. And the position in regard to Mr Sieff is so intolerable, that I should not consider it right to accept 'a period of recuperation' for James from him. That is quite categoric. ... Mr Sieff's duty and responsibility is to the Institute *which he has created*. It is his responsibility to see that *the Institute* is responsible for its Director and Governor, James Parkes. And he must, in some way or other, be made to see this responsibility ... For I am becoming of the opinion that Mr Sieff has no intention whatever of helping the Institute to function. What his motives are I do not know. But I am utterly convinced of this. Whatever his position in regard to it may be, he must on no account any longer be allowed to hold this power of life and death over both James and the newly born Institute ... This sounds a very hard and ungrateful thing to say; it is not so. We have suffered so much from Sieff's control in the past, that my most earnest prayer is that we may be delivered from it now, while there is an opportunity.

By 28 September James was much better: she was going to take him his clothes and he looked 'wonderfully well' and was 'in the best of spirits'. She dreaded having 'to bring him up to date with all my "machinations" of the past weeks'. It was, nonetheless, a sprightly letter (and of one page only).

Everything had changed a month or so later. Dorothy's letter of 5 November was of three pages long; that of the following day was a page longer. In the same way as IMS, Bill Simpson had been transformed: he had become a distant Mr Simpson. Dorothy was writing from Menton. James had collapsed yet again; he was 'critically ill with coronary trouble' and in hospital at Nice. She was far from home and friends, in unfamiliar surroundings, and her steadfast nerve had momentarily given way: her 'strong feeling' was that James should take a parish and that both of them should 'withdraw from The Parkes Library Limited, leaving it to exist or fail in its own right'. she could 'no longer continue the struggle'; nor was she willing to do so:

> I know that the present situation, if left unchanged, will kill James, and will, if I am not relieved of anxiety, cause a breakdown for myself. I would like, before this happens, to get some idea of where and when we could take a living. Then, if and when James has recovered sufficiently, I will do my best to persuade him to relinquish the Jewish–Christian work ... I had hoped to have progressive news of development of the Institute during the time James has been ill ... nothing has, so far as James and I are aware, been settled since then.

The letter of 6 November repeated a good deal of what Dorothy had said the day before; this was because she wished 'to emphasise certain things':

> People have asked me every time James has broken down why I did nothing to prevent him taking on so much when I knew his health could not stand it. My reply was that I considered James' work important for the world, and that unless it became very clear indeed that he could not continue the work, I would not interfere – for each man must 'follow his star'. Now the time for my intervention (I will not say interference) has come. The whole complex of the situation is too much for either of us to cope with.

There was also a revealing paragraph on the circumstances of James' collapse, revealing for the interpretation Dorothy put upon it:

Then for James himself; what preceded the attack two nights ago was that we had contacted the chaplain of the English church here, and he and his wife came to dine – a very quiet dinner. They were with us only from 7.30 to 9.00 But it released the pent up tension within James; he talked of mutual friends and interests. *There was nothing he could say to explain himself or his position* – for all that is entirely known to both himself and myself. The doctors say that something during this conversation must just have 'blown the lid' off the suppressed anxiety and worry, and as soon as James retired for the night the coronary occurred.

It was, needless to say, all the fault of the villain of the piece: 'It is a very heavy load of responsibility which rests upon Israel Sieff!!!' She also blamed herself. She should have insisted 'long ago' on James giving up the work, taking a parish, and only writing 'as and when he could'. But she had not: 'I suppose I was intensely proud of what he was doing, and of what he is.' That was all over now. '*I will not* have this state of affairs continue.'

Ten days later, when she wrote once again to 'My dear W.W.', she was more temperate. James was 'making good progress'; they had found ground-floor accommodation in a quiet hotel with 'home cooking'; they liked the English church and the English chaplain and 'his most sensible and friendly wife'. It was in this letter that Dorothy told of her going into 'the details of James' past history with him': that too seems to have eased her mind, so that it was almost with equanimity that she was able to write of him as 'the leading figure in his own line, but at the price of too great a deformation *professionnelle* for his health to stand longer'. She had also consulted another doctor, 'a very old friend of ours from England'. He suspected that everything had 'a *physical* cause, and if he is correct', Dorothy continued, 'it would be an enormous relief, for I should feel that James would be able to do the work, with all the help now offered by the group of Governors etc. etc. And the whole situation would be entirely changed – no more talk of parishes etc. but a real return to vocational work.'. She assured 'dear Bill' that she now had 'a real feeling of reassurance, for which I am most thankful'. So must Bill have been.

Whatever sense of relief he felt on receiving the letter of 16 November, however, did not stop him writing in plain terms to

Dorothy on 23 January 1957. After thanking her for 'the several letters which I have had from you since I last wrote and for the memorandum about the Institute' that had arrived that morning, he opened a new paragraph. The italics are mine:

> All that I want to do at this stage is to beg of you *once more* to pull yourself together and to have some confidence in your friends here who are doing their best in a very difficult situation to be as helpful as they can. There is not the slightest use at the present time in continually reverting to questions which unfortunately can only be regarded for the time being as hypothetical questions. You and James are in the south of France with one purpose only, and that is to get James as fit as possible as soon as possible so that we really can make some progress ... I am sorry to write in this strain, but I feel I have no alternative but to do so. We all know that you have very heavy anxieties to carry and very many problems to face, but in this you are very far from being alone, and there are a great many people who are so very much less fortunate than you are not merely with regard to their past experience but also I think for future prospects. I repeat that you have friends. Do please give them credit for being friends and try to have some confidence in them.

Dorothy had already turned the corner of her paranoia. On the same day as Bill Simpson wrote to her, she had written to him. James was much better. He was coming off medication, was increasingly 'alert', was walking better, and taking longer walks. She had told him her troubles. 'For the first time for six months we are together in thought; this, for us, is a great thing.' She sent her 'affectionate greetings'. Two days later, having received Bill Simpson's letter of 23 January she was contrite. She was 'truly sorry' that she had caused 'pain and embarrassment'; she was grateful for his friendship during the past months; she realized that she had got 'on to a "long playing record" of "It all depends on me", which was neither the real position, nor the impression I wanted to convey; but which, no doubt, I did convey'. She had shown Bill's letter and 'this reply' to James, and believed she might now show him 'anything that comes'. 'Please believe me', she ended, 'when I say I am aware of our *many* blessings, when

I view the world around me today. God knows I am indeed grateful.' The crisis within a crisis was over.

What about the Institute between January 1957 and its final establishment as the Parkes Library at the University of Southampton in 1964? If this was not entirely a seven-year crisis, it was a trying time. James makes rather light of it in *Voyage of Discoveries*. Yet, because it is the all too familiar story of administrators in distinguished places looking a gift horse in the mouth, until the Vice-Chancellor of a provincial seat of learning had the courage and foresight to take the bull by the horns, it will not be taken so casually here.

It took time to sort things out with Israel Sieff. He could not or would not pay for what James and Dorothy so earnestly desired; they wanted what is nowadays termed 'An Advanced Institute of Learning', which houses visiting scholars for periods of study ranging from a month to a year. Tantur, established in the 1970s on a hillside between Jerusalem and Bethlehem, is such a place. James and Dorothy were thwarted pioneers. Who else shared their vision? Not Israel Sieff, not Bill Simpson. On 12 July 1957 Dorothy set down a discussion she had had the previous day with the latter. Their divergent views of the Institute come into clear focus. 'With every desire to help', writes Dorothy, 'Mr Simpson obviously found it difficult to understand the financial position.' There was much discussion of Israel Sieff, who had promised £1,000 a year, and Bill Simpson advised Dorothy 'not to worry him with all these details, but to say, in effect: "We are very grateful indeed for all the help you have given. We appreciate that there is now the Institute, and appreciate your support to the extent of £1000 per year."' 'This', she recorded, 'I consider it is not possible to do.' A long indictment of Israel Sieff follows. The differences of view also emerge from their exchange about a secretary and about books:

> I mentioned that we had been fortunate in getting a Secretary who lived nearby to work part time at £3 per week. WWS exclaimed: 'What is she *doing*? And why add to expenses when the money is not there?' I explained there was library cataloguing and all sorts of things to do. He was not convinced, believing that I was capable of doing all these things ... I spoke of the difficulty of reducing the cost of running the work, which has grown naturally, and said

> where did one begin? For example, was James not to buy any books? He implied that he must not do so; that in an ordinary organization, permission would be needed from the Governors for the purchase of books etc. I said, who is to say such and such a book is not necessary and cannot be afforded? He said it was for me to say so to James – 'If not you, who else?'

How familiar is this non-meeting of minds. An administrative mind will rarely allow that those who do the actual work, historians, teachers, librarians, secretaries, the dogsbodies like Dorothy, know best. How could one run anything with a part-time secretary (at £3.00 a week)? How could outsiders, Governors for instance, understand anything about buying books? How could Dorothy be expected to tell James what books he must not buy? 'The whole interview (especially because WWS is such a great friend) was most depressing', wrote Dorothy. She summed up gloomily: 'IMS desires to see that "the Parkes" have enough to live upon; this he calls "looking after the Parkes", and he believes that £1,000 per annum is sufficient for this.' Evidently Bill Simpson did too, even though 'the Parkes' had a £1000 overdraft.

If it had been galling to live on charity, how much more bitter must it have been to have one's realizable plans rejected by old friends, whose vision did not come up to one's own? James was more conciliatory than his wife. When Dorothy made her notes on the conversation she had had with her husband at Menton on 19 December 1957, his final words were characteristically hopeful. Because in this instance it may be presumed that we have James' rather than Dorothy's views on Israel Sieff, it is worth giving them at a little length:

> It is the breakdown of 'committal in honour' between Israel Sieff and myself about which I am saddened. At the end of the war I offered IMS to get into other work and free him from all financial responsibility. IMS refused and said 'James, the family will always look after you'. About the same time I inherited something less than £10,000 from my father; I told IMS I had done so, and that if I went on with the work I thought it right to spend this on it. This I had already discussed with Dorothy, and she was willing that

we should make the sacrifice. IMS knew from the beginning that I was spending my capital at the rate of about £1000 a year. In 1953 I told him that what was available was spent. He said 'That is alright, James; it does not make any difference.' Since then he has supported us ... But his support is always given late for our needs, and in such a way as to impose on Dorothy and me the maximum strain ... Part of the strain involved is that it is not only we who are concerned, but that with the agreement of IMS we have a number of distinguished Jewish and Christian scholars here, on the Continent and in America, involved; and that appeals for support from other people in both England and America are entirely held up by IMS not doing what he has promised ... I am still sure that if I asked IMS to see me, he would see me, and we should have the same friendly relations as we have always had, and discussions of the most serious aspects of the work; I have not the slightest evidence that this would not be so. And while I was well enough to go and see IMS personally the crisis was always staved off.

This time too 'the crisis was staved off'. The price for James and Dorothy was high, at any rate in the short term. They would not have the institute of their desire. They would have to trim that particular sail and cut their cloth according to Israel Sieff's £1,250 per annum.

Not that the money was immediately forthcoming. The stresses and strains of the association with their benefactor continued, and might be more fully documented than they have been here, as might the planning for something more than the *status quo* at Barley, which is how the remaining seven years James and Dorothy spent at Barley might be described. Here is James' description of business as usual in *Voyage of Discoveries*; it is of December 1963, but could be for almost any month in any one of the seven years:

We have one scholar from America working in the Hall on material from our periodicals; another from Jerusalem in the Garden House writing a book on the present confrontation between Judaism and Christianity; a third from Germany in the South Room preparing for publication by Gollancz her wonderful broadcasts on her life before,

> through, and after the Nazi period. A fourth is occupying a corner of my workroom checking rabbinic references to a German work which he is translating for an English publisher. Dorothy is correcting the galley proofs of two publications due to appear this winter. And I am busy on my next book! You will see I refer to the *Hall* and the *Garden House*. The Hall is the big Club house next door which was idle and which we lease. We have all our periodicals there as well as three offices. The Garden House is the old granary which we restored in 1961 with sitting room, bedroom and utility room.

Another account supplements this one. In the December 1963 description, James has taken for granted the indispensable third leg of the 'tripod' John McNeilage, whose decision to retire when he became 65 in the spring of 1964 would bring Barley to an end. He does not do so in January 1964 when he wrote to Professor David Daube at Oxford; Professor Daube had been reported 'puzzled' at James saying 'that the Centre at Barley' rested on a tripod:

> Of course if the work simply consisted of James Parkes writing books, the material for which he was able to consult in a university or college library, or in rooms separate from where he lived, then the work would depend simply on my fitness. But I did not speak of books. I spoke of a Centre which exists here at Barley and which calls <u>equally</u> for the work of three people. A large house has to be maintained, because it houses all the books and offices as well as Dorothy and myself. It has also guest rooms which are constantly used. For the midday meal there may be anything up to eight people. This is kept going by John, and it is impossible to pass over the work to either me or Dorothy, each of whom is fully occupied with our own work. Each of us, of course, has part-time help, secretarial or domestic, and that can be changed. But it is entirely unrealistic to think that the casual assistance which is all one can get in these days can replace any one of us three. ... Please recognise that this is so, and that we are not bluffing or exaggerating when we say that the Centre is going to close at the end of April. There is either an alternative by that time, or

we must start putting the books etc. into mothballs.

The alternative was not far away; the books were to escape mothballing. Within months James and Dorothy had moved to Iwerne and the 'Centre' had been transferred to Southampton University.

There had been numerous attempts to find a home for it over the preceding years. In 1960 there had been a scheme to link up with the Wiener Library in London. A dinner at the Dorchester Hotel was held on 22 February; a brochure was printed; then silence descended: the anticipated money was not forthcoming. In 1962 there were negotiations, instigated by Israel Sieff and subsequently repudiated by James, for the books to be kept at University College London. There were misunderstandings; there was recrimination; and Israel Sieff ceased to be chairman of the Governors, though he did not cease his annual payment to James and Dorothy. James, understandably, would not have his books locked up in a room with 'Parkes Library' on its door and with no one making use of them. He told Norman Cohn: 'I could only regard immurement in Gower Street as the last of all possible solutions.' In 1963 a proposal that Cambridge University Library should have the books came to nothing; it seems from the correspondence to have been a non-starter from the outset. By the end of that year, when the prospective retirement of John McNeilage created a sense of urgency, an 'Emergency Committee' was set up. Norman Cohn, David Kessler, and David Astor were three of its members. One of the Committee's achievements was to persuade Israel Sieff, though he may not have needed much persuasion, to grant James and Dorothy the £1,250 a year for their lifetimes. It was not, however, the Committee that came up with the University of Southampton.

Depending on one's point of view, Southampton University was either a fortuitous accident or a miracle. Let James tell the story. On 30 December 1963 in a letter to Robert Carvalho, Convenor of the 'Emergency Committee', James wrote:

> Dr Taverner, the head of the Geography Department at Southampton, was here [at Barley] discussing Israel and Judaism with us a week ago. We have been helping one of his students considerably, and he has written on Israel himself from a Christian standpoint. I told him of our situation and he said at once: 'I hope Southampton will be consid-

ered a possibility. We already have Claude Montefiore's Library and we have just established a full theological department. Now shall I explore this a bit more, and send results at once to you, or do you want me to lay off taking any direct action ... would it be reasonable for me to sound round a bit first?'

What happened next is described in *Voyage of Discoveries*. Invited to attend the annual Montefiore Lecture at Southampton University, James and Dorothy were happy to accept: they would be able to combine the visit with one to look at houses in Dorset, the county to which they had decided to retire. Before the lecture 'there was a reception for the guests in a long common room':

> We were at one end of it, but when the Vice-Chancellor appeared at the other end, he exclaimed across the room: 'I thought it would be Jimmy,' came across to us with his wife and explained that they had both been students at Aberystwyth when I was a secretary of the S.C.M. They even told me the title of a lecture I had given there in 1924. We were staying with Dr Ellis Taverner, a geographer who was interested in Israel, and who had visited Barley. When he came home and told us the Vice-Chancellor would like to see us after breakfast, I thought it was to reminisce on Student Movement days. But when we went into his room, he started straight off with 'I hear you are very troubled as to where to place your library. Would you consider Southampton?'

All that needed to be done was achieved smoothly and speedily. On 29 June 1964, James could tell David Astor that the University was going to make a public announcement on 8 July and he expected it to state 'that they have been offered and have accepted the collection of books known as the Parkes Library, and have agreed that they will include in the development of their plans for post-graduate students the encouragement of study of the subjects for which the library was built up (the wording is mine)'. He added that 'we are extremely happy about this solution', and that in favour of it was the university's use of the library at Barley 'for several years', the fact that they 'asked for it, and when we made encouraging noises, took the trouble to send its Librarian down to examine it'.

A few days later, in a letter of 2 July to David Kessler, James could not resist a Parthian shot at Israel Sieff. It was, however, a Parthian shot almost immediately regretted and (as we shall see) retrieved. On 2 July James wrote:

> I don't think you must worry too much about our future. IMS is being temperamental about it ... I know you refer constantly to his 'generosity', but his personal generosity since 1945 extends to one cheque for £200 given me suddenly when he found I paid out of my own pocket something I obviously need not have. Nothing else has come out of his pocket, and it would be absurd to pretend that the Israel and Rebecca Sieff fund had not had a very full return for its outlay in the work which has been done at Barley.

This is not the way to end. Two days later, on 4 July, he wrote again to David Kessler. Because this is truly James Parkes speaking let us conclude with his second thoughts on Israel Sieff:

> Looking through my copy of the letter to you about the 'generosity' of IMS, it occurred to me that, by dealing with that particular issue, I had left a negative impression which needed correction. I think that letter had to be written to avoid misunderstanding. But you might well say, simply on the basis of that letter alone: 'Well, why does he protest such affection for IMS?' The answer is that, in a pioneering and controversial job such as Dorothy and I have done over the years there is something much more important than money, and that is the assertion and protection of our independence and intellectual integrity, and there we could always count unreservedly on IMS ... It is true that, before the war, he did join financial generosity to his defence of my right to say, write, and think the things I did; and to refuse to write or propound the accepted views of Jewish organizations because they thought they had the ear of IMS. But, though we had perpetual financial headaches with him in later years, we never had any weakening of real interest in what we were doing, or in his insistence on our absolute right and freedom to do or not to do

what seemed to us proper. That was the real and unwavering fundamental of our relationship, and the natural and proper basis of my equally unwavering affection for, and gratitude to, him. I wanted you to know this, because I felt that I had to make the other side clear also.

After that there is nothing to add, unless it be, as David Kessler wrote in reply, that Barley itself had come to 'the end of an era, which began when Redcliffe Salaman installed himself in your village, and will end with your removal to Dorset'. Every English village has its own history. That of the Hertfordshire village of Barley has in recent times been peculiarly distinguished.

7

Barley: The Last Five Years 1959–64

It is no doubt a truism that the more we write the less we know. James Parkes, therefore, has become Harry Houdini. Whenever it appears that we have got him securely tied up, he breaks our bonds and comes to the surface in a place we did not expect. He gets away every time.

After three years of serious illness, and despite the continuing anxiety over the Institute, the reader is likely to find the subject of this study either the same old James, or the same old Harry Houdini. Whichever, he has every appearance of being back to his infuriatingly normal self. There: he has done it again! Take his response to an invitation to the wedding of Dr Gillian Jeffries, daughter of his very old friend W.A. Jeffries, in March 1962. 'Knowing how busy people are on such an occasion', he wrote to the bride's father, 'I enclose a stamped and addressed postcard on which it is only necessary to cross out the irrelevant lines.' The postcard is type-written; the young couple were required to indicate a choice of wedding present by ticking one of three alternatives: *Common Sense About Religion* or *A History of the Jewish People* or that they 'could not bear either book'. They chose *A History of the Jewish People*. Six months previously, in September 1961, I recall being given as a wedding present Michael Howard's *History of the Franco-Prussian War*, though not by the author. None of us, at any rate, got another set of napkin rings. What does the anecdote of the wedding present postcard tell us about James? Was he being sensible? Or was he insensitive? Did the young couple laugh off the postcard and stick in a pin with their eyes closed? Or did they solemnly ponder their choice? Would they have dared to say they 'could not bear either book'? It is impossible to know. The Great Escapologist keeps his secrets.

If he is a mystery to us he was not to his nephews Aldus and

Andrew. The first contact between Aldus and his uncle that I have come across was in January 1949. Aldus sent a letter, perhaps a 'Thank You' Christmas letter, during the writing of which, said his mother, he 'spent a long while giggling over the Latin names in his butterfly book and failing to pronounce them'. Aldus's letter has not survived, but James' reply to it has; it is long and incomprehensible to the non-lepidopterist; its schoolboy humour no doubt amused the eight- or nine-year-old Aldus. Not until August 1957 was there further literary contact. James and Dorothy were going on holiday and regretted not being able to see Aldus: could he come to Barley early in September? They wrote as if he had not been before. Probably James' breakdown prevented Aldus coming that year, but he came in the Autumn of 1959, when James wrote to his mother and father, Edwin and Nancy Barker, that he had learned to pronounce his name 'with an "A" as in ballast, and not as in "call"'. By that date, November 1958, Edwin and Nancy Barker had moved from a rectory in Hampshire to the Rue Crespin in Geneva, where Edwin was working for The World Alliance of Young Men's Christian Associations. Aldus was at Steyning Grammar School, his younger brother Andrew was at Christ's Hospital. A three-way correspondence ensued, its object being a motoring holiday for Aldus and Andrew with James and Dorothy. The holiday, to which the boy's parents were to contribute financially, was to be spent visiting churches in East Anglia; it was finally arranged for a week in April of the following Spring. Aldus had already been accepted for Oxford to read Natural Science. Andrew, who had 'a passion for medieval screens and the suchlike', had two years still to do at school. Both boys seem to have appreciated as well as enjoyed the week. They began at the Swan, Lavenham, went on to the Crown, Framlingham, and ended the week at James and Dorothy's favourite hotel, the Anchor, Walberswick. They clearly liked taking the boys about their 'beloved Suffolk': 'We certainly enjoyed having them with us ... Boys are, when nice, so very nice at the ages of your two, and they are nice!!!'

Another who appreciated James Parkes did so for entirely other reasons; nor could he have been more unlike the two English schoolboys, who 40 years later seem as anthropologically distant as the Solomon Islanders once did. This was the irascible Czech Jewish scholar Paul Winter. Paul Winter was born in 1904 and died in 1969. He graduated in Law from the University of Prague in 1931, practised his profession in Czechoslovakia until 1939, escaped in 1941 to join the Allied Forces in North Africa, and came to England in 1948. He became a British subject and in 1961 published a book *On the Trial of Jesus*. James once summed him up: 'Paul is at the same time the gentlest and most courteous of visitors and the most *farouche* and impossible person when you are trying to help him financially. Various Jewish sources have tried to help him, only to be very violently insulted.'. Indeed, they were. Paul Winter maintained that there was only one Jew in England 'with whom I was on speaking terms': that was Leon Roth. He was difficult to help for the straightforward reason that he could not help himself. It is testimony to James' character that he persevered with a scholar, who (as if by some marvel of nature) seems to have been displaced from Prague at the time of the Golem to London in the era of Eden, Macmillan, and Lord Home, artificial creations of a very different kind.

James was in communication with him from 1954 at the latest. Paul Winter's letters are both hilarious and sad; they certainly make a change from most of the others in the Parkes Papers. An edition ought to be made of them; it would demonstrate just how difficult post-Shoah life could be for one who experienced it indirectly; and how grim and unwelcoming a place Britain was for a professional the British professions wanted nothing to do with. As for British Jewry's treatment of a European Jew: the edition would be enlightening on that sore topic too. Let it be said at the outset that there was one other Jew beside Leon Roth whom Paul Winter admitted on another occasion had helped him. He was not British: it was none other than Leo Baeck. By 1954 Paul Winter had turned himself into a Biblical scholar. I am unable to assess his learning, but it seems to have been prodigious. His own assessment tended to be along similar lines, that is, when it was not of the following sort: 'The attached paper, "Luke 2:49 and Targum Yerushalmi", which I am sending you with my best regards, will make my name a stench in the nostrils of all righteous people, Christians and Jews, and if there are any righteous men outside those two camps, to them too.' I cannot resist mentioning two other papers of Paul Winter's, not only in homage to a scholarship of another, more scholarly age, but because their titles signal so clearly the kind of scholar he was. The first was called 'Mongenes Para Patros' and was published in *Zeitschrift für Religionsung Geistesgeschichte*, volume 5. Being of 30 pages, it evidently was not an occasional paper. The second was entitled 'Zum Verständnis des Johannesevangeliums'; it was published in *Theologische Literaturzeitung*, obtainable from J.C. Hinrichs, Scherlstrasse 2, Leipzig. These were two of what Paul Winter termed his 'more consequential papers'.

In February 1955 James described Paul Winter to an American friend as ' a curious Jewish refugee scholar over here':

> who is leading a very difficult economic existence because he is a first class scholar in a very limited field. His subject is the examination from the Jewish point of view of the New Testament. This is scarcely a basis on which to earn a living and he has to take on all kinds of curious jobs from night watchman onward to keep body and soul together.

In June 1955 having had news of an award of a research grant Paul Winter wrote to Bill Simpson that he did not know how much it was for:

> But I hope it will be enough to enable me to give up my present job, and never to have to take on jobs such as I had, neither to work again in the Goods Yard of Paddington Station nor in the shop of a baptised Jew who believes in the holy trinity of pounds, shillings, and pence. I hope that I shall have a chance to do work that I like. And perhaps even enjoy LIFE. I feel today like a boy. And I am not a bit ashamed!

In 1959 James was reading Paul's 'Notes on the Trial of Jesus' and showing the erudition we have possibly taken too much for granted in this study:

> I found your description of the career of Pilate fascinating, but did he not achieve canonisation? It is a long time since I read the Ethiopian Synaxary in the *Patrologia Orientalis*, but I have a vague memory that it included Pilate.

He was right. 'Yes', replied Paul Winter, 'Sir Pontius *IS* a saint in the Monophysite Church of Abyssinia.'

The book itself, *The Trial of Jesus*, appeared early in 1961; a lengthy correspondence regarding where it might be reviewed and who might review then ensued. Paul was at his most vituperative: 'I have picked out *three instances* of my experience with "English Jews". They were not people from Petticoat Lane, but in all three cases I had to do with some of the Koryphäen des englischen Judentums. I could name *other* cases'. James in recommending the book talked of its author as 'very learned and rather tragic', whose 'concern with the deeper issues of the Trial raises the book out of the ranks of merely destructive criticism into being something which wins respect even in spite of some of its views'. There was talk of getting Arnold Toynbee to review it, but unfortunately he turned out to be in America. Eventually H.R. Trevor-Roper reviewed it in the *Sunday Times*. It made, said Paul Winter, 'an immense impact'. He went on:

> Such is life. Funny. In the decade and a half which I have been in England, I wrote more than 850 letters to prominent gentlemen of Jewish faith in this country. In some 300 cases, I enclosed off-prints of some article I had published somewhere in a periodical. Over 800 of these letters remained without reply. The other recipients replied, and gave me the addresses of some other Jewish gentlemen to whom I might write, and I did so, till I ran out of postage stamps. Only <u>one</u> of the people to whom I had written and who are alive today ever wished to see me and talk to me: Leon Roth. Rabbi Leo Baeck was another, but he is dead. Yes, a long story.

That summer he made the first of numerous visits to Barley. He liked the peace and quiet and the dog. He may even have watched the television, which had been acquired the previous winter. It looks as if he spent Christmas there. In December 1961 he wrote:

> The whole atmosphere of your house is so different from anything I know here in London ... The people whom I met while I stayed with you, John McNeilage, and Dr Wood-Legh, and Dr Cleobury, to say nothing of you yourselves, are so quiet and serene and cheerful that it is quite a matter of wonder to me that such people still exist in this world of ours.

Paul Winter found another home in the convent of the Sisters of Zion at Notting Hill. After his death, James hoped that Sister Theodora of the convent and Mrs Joan Lawrence of the Council of Christians and Jews might rescue Paul's papers from his lodgings: 'When I visited him the whole room was filled with every conceivable kind of material, and I expect it continued to increase as long as he was working.' There were no relatives and no other friends.

The book James published in these years (apart from *A History of the Jewish People* and *Common Sense About Religion*) was *Antisemitism*. It was a reshaping of *An Enemy of the People: Antisemitism*, published in 1945. The new version, published in 1963, has an odd chronological structure, chapters skipping about in time, and it would not be unfair to describe them as discrete essays on a variety of themes, chiefly but not entirely on antisemitism, three of the twelve chapters being about prejudice in general; two others are entitled 'Israel and the Arab World', and 'The Surviving Jewish Community'. Forty years later it remains an admirable book for beginners. It is also admirably Parkesian. I will take three examples. First, there is his salutary emphasis on the non-Jewish victims of Nazism: 'It is unfortunate that the figure of six million has been fixed in the world's memory as though it were the total of all Hitler's civilian victims.' It is no less unfortunate now than it was in 1963: with the Americanization of the Shoah, three million Poles and 15 million Russians seem to have been forgotten. As for the Belorussians, who remembers their terrible suffering? James was no less perceptive on Nazi racial planning, which he gives its proper name of depopulation: 'Had all Hitler's plans been carried out there would have been even more victims ... Truly Hitler's Germany required a wide *Lebensraum*.' A limitless one we would say today, 40 years of scholarship having amply demonstrated the utter nihilism of the Nazi worldview.

Secondly, he is thoroughly well informed about Israel. We might expect him to be, yet on what was happening there and how it would impact on the future political development of the state he is particularly acute: 'What is a surprise, alike to the European and the native born, is that within less than twenty years of its foundation, Israel is passing from a European to an Asiatic state, with a population the majority of whom have no knowledge of the two millennia of Jewish European experience.'

This was due to the influx of Jews from the Arab states, their younger profile, and higher birth rate: 'The abnormality of Jewish history has reappeared in a totally unexpected place!'

Thirdly, he is prescient about the erosion of plurality and the abiding necessity for minority cultures:

> The vastly more powerful trend today is towards a worldwide uniformity based on the mass media of cinema, broadcasting and television. Unchecked and unbalanced it could lead humanity in a not very distant future to become one unrelieved, grey, uniform *lumpenproletariat*. All those separate traditions which make for variety and distinction are more valuable today than they have ever been.

Had James lived to see corporate business intent on making us not only *lumpen* but also *kindlich*, I think even he might have begun to question whether God was still interested in us. Or perhaps, because in his later years he considered humankind still to be at a childlike stage of development, he would have seen our present state of imposed imbecility as signal evidence that God had not deserted us, though how he would have squared that with St Paul's admonition to put aside the things of childhood I cannot imagine.

Yet, it is presumptuous to talk of James needing to 'square' anything. It is as ridiculous as telling Houdini that he will not escape this time. James was not exactly the bundle of contradictions most of us are; he was, nonetheless, entitled to be as inconsistent in the way great men are proverbially meant to be. Unless, we want to say he was consistently good. He was good enough to do almost anything for almost anybody, or so it seems when leafing through the Parkes Papers. He and Dorothy 'put themselves out' for others on a regular basis. When Leah Levinson came during Pesach there were matzos on the table; 'I know of no two people to whom I became attached in such a short time', she wrote after what was her first visit to Barley. When Nada Yousif Rizk, an Arab Christian from Haifa, needed money to pursue a second degree at the University of London, it was James who was written to by the Registrar of Bedford College, where she had taken her first degree, and James who wrote to Victor Gollancz to ask him to find some money. The money was forthcoming. Nada duly got a very good degree in

Arabic at the School of Oriental Studies. The Registrar wrote to James in August 1960: 'Without your help I should certainly not have succeeded in getting sufficient assistance to enable Miss Rizk to carry out her project.' James even tried to get Jews into his Club, the Athenaeum. Both Norman Cohn and David Kessler wanted to become members. David Kessler certainly did not succeed. Was it 'neo-Nazism' that had kept him out? James thought it was, although he did not say whom he thought were the neo-Nazis among his fellow clubmen.

Whether he was politically inconsistent who can say? It was evidently possible to combine socialist principles with membership of the Athenaeum. It was also the case that he was falling out of step with the Labour Party. His disillusion was once again prophetic. After the 1959 election he wrote to Hans Ree:

> I think that the Labour Party will go on having inquests about its failure for a considerable time. For the extent of its failure, I suspect that the behaviour of certain trade unions during the period of the election was largely responsible. But that is only a superficial explanation. I have a suspicion that if you are going to have an election on a purely selfish and materialistic basis, the Tories will always win. In this election both parties based their case entirely on their ability to give people more material possessions.

Politics as 'More For You Is Good For You' was anathema to a 'Less For Me Is Good For Me' person like James. Moreover, politics reduced to bread and circuses was no good for the nation. Nor has it been. It is strange to think of James Parkes surviving into the age of Margaret Thatcher, who more than any other single political figure is responsible for the destruction of the public values he set such store by. In their day politics was still a serious matter. Here is James writing to Tom Sargant in January 1962:

> The political world presents a distressing image; for I am not much comforted by the idea of exchanging Mr MacMillan for Mr Gaitskell. The turning of a serious political proposal like unilateralism into a wildly emotional assault on his virginity seemed to me so disgusting as to end any idea I might have of wanting to go back to politics.

Unilateralism may be right, and may be wrong; but at least it is a serious proposal and I have seen it discussed seriously only once.

Or is it that politics is always disgusting to the onlooker with a sensitive soul and a sharp nose?

If he was right about the decline of the Labour Party he had known since he was a boy, he was equally *au fait* with the imperialist posturing of the United States. He wrote to the editor of *The Times* on 26 October 1962:

> Sir, In the present attempt to find a basis for negotiations between the 'mighty opposites' is there not a danger that Cuba itself be overlooked? Dr Castro ended a typical 'colonial' regime, such as was once possessed by Britain, France, Belgium or Holland in various parts of the world. All Cuba's most important assets belonged to Americans. Like other revolutionary leaders, he was heavy-handed in his actions. The U.S.A. has met the new situation only with a bullying hostility. She has made no secret of her desire to isolate and ruin the Cuban government, and was openly considering the invasion of the country. Ought Cuba to have relied on her own capacity to meet the economic blockade, the political isolation and the threat of military invasion by a world power like the U.S.A? Was it unnatural that she should turn to the only other world power big enough to protect her? Surely part of the negotiations must be a guarantee by the U.S.A. that she will call off her attempt to isolate and destroy the Cuban government.

There has still not been such a guarantee. Yet, if he believed international politics was as straightforward as he suggests here, he had forgotten Romans, chapter seven: the good is knowable, but even good men are incapable of doing it. And then, there is Africa.

In November 1963 James wrote a long letter to the Bishop of St Albans; he was enclosing a donation in response to the bishop's appeal on behalf of the Diocese of Kaffraria; typically, his theme was one that had been neglected because it was political dynamite. 'It seems to me increasingly regrettable', he writes:

that our attitude to White South Africa is almost exclusively negative condemnation. It is painfully true that the whites of present South Africa are pursuing an impossible policy, but it is also true that they have no other home. The sin that was committed against the Africans of stealing their land, was committed three or four hundred years ago. But the whites have Europe, North and South America, Australasia, and it is quite unreasonable that they should claim the right to stay in possession of substantial portions of land, and most of the mineral wealth, of Africa as well.

Here are resemblances with Israel, though James seems unaware of them, as he does of those in his second paragraph:

Somebody has got to have the courage to put before the white world the proposition that they owe it to the unfortunate whites innocently living in parts of the world belonging to other peoples and races the opportunity to resettle in the 'white' continents at the white continents' expense, and that the white and industrial continents owe compensation for what they have taken. This is a very long-term idea, and ought to come from the Christian element in the white world before the situation hardens anymore.

The 'white' continents: what has become of them? James went on to say that 'it would be ridiculous for someone like me to put forward the idea. I have no authority, and am associated much too exclusively with Jewish–Christian relations. I am also much too old.' A man without authority: whose fault was that? He concluded:

I have no doubt whatsoever that in the end this has got to be done, and that this is ground-root realism. I have seen so many of the causes I was fighting for in the SCM in the '20's, and was told were 'utopian idealism', become political actions by the '50's, that I am not deterred by the fact that, at first presentation, the same will be said about this.

Had he lived a few years longer, he would have seen the 'political actions' of the 1950s obliterated by the 'political realism' of the 1980s. James took as self-evidently inviolable the public utilities destroyed by private interest in that and the following decade. One man's 'ground-root realism' is 'utopian idealism' to his next-door neighbour, especially if the latter has bought shares on the stock market.

Africa and Utopian Realism also feature in a letter he wrote the Rev. T.P. Strachan in June 1961. The context was religious. 'Our Christian relations with Judaism', he said, 'are the most striking example of what we are very slowly beginning to realise to be our relations with other religions':

> Rejecting alike the views that 'all religions are equally good' and that 'all religions except Christianity are, if not devilish, completely man made', we are yet being forced to the position that, if Christ is of universal significance, then he must be able to be understood and interpreted *directly* out of all human experience and not only out of the Hellenistic experience which is the background of our traditional Gentile Christian thinking ... I regard our ability to allow the Jews to find Jesus of Nazareth out for themselves as a test case of our ability to recognise the same right in Asia and Africa. It is not going to be easy; and it may be heartrending, as we see others making the same mistakes that we of Europe have made, or even being uninterested in what seems to us most important. In the case of the Jews we have to deal not merely with the objective acceptance of Jesus into Judaic Semitic thought, but with the prior issue that the historic Christ of the Churches has to be divested of his responsibility not only for creating antisemitism, but for his complete failure to produce any signs of a messianic age of righteousness and peace within the 'Christian' civilization which claims allegiance to him.

Was it not Utopian to consider that Jesus might be 'objectively' accepted into Judaism? Is religion ever objective? Reasoned argument would demonstrate that Jesus of Nazareth was not responsible for the creation of antisemitism, and that the writers of the Gospels were, but reasoned argument in religion has never won a single convert. The complete absence of messianic signs within Christendom had been a stumbling block to Jews since the thirteenth century at the latest; how, after the Shoah,

James could expect Jews to believe otherwise is testimony to the ivory tower quality of some of his thinking. Yet his realism consists of his assessment of the difficulties: he will not allow them to be impossibilities. That is the measure of the distance between him and myself; between his nineteenth-century liberal Humanism and my twentieth-century socialist-Christianity.

James ends his letter to the Rev. T.P. Strachan by asking if he has come across Charles Singer's book *The Christian Failure*. 'It contains', he says, 'something of the feeling I am trying to describe. I knew Charles Singer very well, and I know what agony that book cost him.''. Charles Singer had died exactly a year before, in June 1960, and was no doubt on James' mind. Theirs had been a long friendship and a fruitful association. In what was probably the last letter Charles wrote to James, in which he thanked him for sending a recent piece published in the *Jewish Chronicle* ('I agree with everything'), he was in valedictory mood: 'You have ploughed a very difficult furrow but have ploughed it straight and narrow.' The letter was of 6 April 1960. Just over two months later, on 12 June 1960, Dorothea Singer was writing to tell her 'very dear Dorothy and James' of the painless death of her husband. A few days later she wrote again to thank them for 'a beautiful bouquet ... and still more for the precious life-long friendship that has meant so much to us both and does mean so much to me'. Dorothea also mentioned the possibility of a biography of Charles:

> Would you perhaps jot down your impressions and record of how you and the bishop of Chichester impelled him to write *The Christian Approach to the Jews* and I think also *The Christian Failure* ... You will I know of course tell me quite frankly your reaction to my asking this. It may well be that his printed work and his influence on men's minds are all the biography that is needed ...

They are wise words. Still, we persist in writing and reading biographies. There seems all too often prurience in our curiosity for salacious detail, and a need to discover in the subject of the biography if not feet of clay then an Achilles heel.

If James had an Achilles' heel it was ideological. Here it is. 'I am bowled over', he wrote to David Kessler on 12 December 1959, 'by finding that Samson Raphael Hirsch considered it absolutely fundamental to Jewish orthodoxy to accept that the whole oral law was in existence, and nationally taught and accepted, before the written Torah was delivered to God by Moses at Sinai.' He goes on:

> I had never met this idea before ... the case is completely altered if Jewish orthodoxy demands acceptance of the idea that before Sinai the whole oral law existed, was nationally known and taught. For, if that be the belief, then it creates a Jewish 'heilsgeschichte', introducing an action of God in relation to the people of Israel which is irrelevant to other people. For such a religious attitude on the part of the children of Israel in the middle of the second millennium BCE is entirely outside anything which we know of the religions of that period among other peoples. ... It has always seemed to me of the greatest importance for any religion which believes in a God who reveals himself, and at the same time is the God who has created the whole of this world, that his revelation should be in real history, and not apart from the history of the rest of his world. This to me is an essential part of the Christian doctrine of the Incarnation ... I had believed the same doctrine to be metaphysically true of Judaism. For it seemed to me that the rabbinic doctrine of Torah in complete accord with the Scriptures (e.g. Deut. 30, 11ff.) was an insistence that the will and purpose of God was totally revealed in his world and therefore totally understandable by his world, if 'the heart was directed towards heaven.' But there is nothing which persuades me that the whole body of Talmud and Midrash, together with all the other rabbinic writings, was totally comprehensible in the second millennium BCE. That, I feel, would imply a special creation apart from the rest of us, who change, develop, and are influenced by historic happenings and experience.

Alas, it would. The historian had run full tilt into a theologian who cared nothing for history, an a-historical theologian for whom timeless revelation has abolished it. It is no wonder James was bowled over: Judaism is *the* religion of history. 'Put quite bluntly', James continued:

> the experience of the Jews, if growing out of their history, and related to events of which we have historical records, is of universal significance. On this basis I as a non-Jew recognise a Jewish claim to be a chosen people, for the choice is a responsibility which is significant to me. If the chosenness of the Jew has no relationship to history, of which I, as a non-Jew am a part, then it is a denial that I and the Jew are equally the object of the divine love of one God. We have different gods, and each is irrelevant to the other.

There was the rub. There was the Achilles' heel. If Jews did not need Christians, indeed needed no one else at all, had he laboured in vain?

If the Torah was beyond Time, came before it and lasted beyond it, for presumably the Torah could survive anything, even the advent of the Messiah, then much of what James had been doing bore a resemblance to the spoons tinkling at polite tea parties described by T.S. Eliot. Not *all* of what James had been doing, it goes without saying, his single-minded, often single-handed, campaign against antisemitism going far beyond the merely conversational, having had a far greater impact on our thinking than the poetry of Mr Eliot. Was James downcast? There are no signs that he was. There is every indication that his Christian devotion continued to be (as W.H. Auden said of his own attendance at church), a discipline and a comfort. James and Dorothy attended St Edward's Church in Cambridge during these years. 'We found there all the fellowship which we had lacked at Barley', he wrote in *Voyage of Discoveries*; 'I used to preach ... and usually read the lessons.' When all else fails, the liturgy remains. In that respect it is like the Torah, always changing and always (miraculously) the same.

8

The Final Years: Iwerne 1964–81

Old Hores Manor, Barley, was sold at auction on Wednesday 8 July 1964. One of the four photographs in the sale catalogue is of the front elevation of the house: seated at the open window of his study James is hard at work. By August 1964 James was hard at work in a study elsewhere: the location had changed; the work continued.

James and Dorothy found the cottage they wanted at Iwerne Minster, Dorset, in March 1964. It was not so much a cottage they were after as a church. James wrote a number of letters to an old friend the Bishop of Salisbury, and to the Rector of Boyton, near Warminster, a member of the Modern Churchman's Union, recommended to him by that organization's secretary. The correspondence was all about finding a church where James and Dorothy would be happy. 'We want to go somewhere', James wrote to the bishop, 'where we can really share in the life of the Church, and also in the life of our parish church – a thing we have never been able to do at Barley.' They found the right church and the right churchman at Iwerne. Among the clergy whom the Rector of Boyton mentioned there was 'a reputedly good Riponian' at Iwerne. He was the man for James and Dorothy. 'We rang him up', James wrote to Dr Ellis Taverner on 9 March, 'and asked if we could come and see him after breakfast the next day. "No, you cannot", he said, "because I shall be celebrating Communion." We replied that we would like to join him, and so our first contact with Iwerne was through the Church, and through him we found just what we were looking for.' To the bishop on 10 March he wrote that they 'liked the Vicar very much, we liked the church, and the atmosphere of the village; there is plenty of young life around with Bryanston and Claysmore schools, we liked our neighbours, and, finally, we liked the cottage'. The cottage, 'Netherton', 100 yards from the Iwerne War Memorial on the Shaftesbury to Blandford Road, was 200 yards from the church.

That was one matter quickly settled. Another that never was, despite the initial generosity of Southampton University, was the Parkes Institute. The Parkes Library was formally opened on 23 June 1965. Norman Cohn, ever hopeful of getting into the Athenaeum but ready 'to set the wheels in motion at the Saville' should he be disappointed, was not 'free to attend', being 'fully occupied with some visiting Americans at that time'. He had learned that James 'was among the electors responsible for the appointment of Geza Vermes to the Readership at Oxford', and was 'delighted to hear of the appointment'. If James was still able to exert influence in High Places, at Southampton he was unable to do very much. Geza Vermes had attended the opening of the Parkes Library in June; in July he wrote asking James to remind its Governors to send him his expenses. James replied: 'I will see what I can do at Southampton. I am no longer in the position where I could just take up a cheque book and sign a cheque on behalf of the Parkes Library.' He was no longer his own master. In January 1971 James informed the distinguished French scholar Bernhard Blumenkranz:

> I wish it was possible to invite you officially over to Southampton University to give a lecture, but the Parkes Library has just not got to the point of organizing activities of its own. One might say that it is having a still lengthier progress towards birth than an elephant. All university development is difficult in this country at the moment and the Parkes Library really needs a Director of its own to get it firmly on its feet and adequately using its material.

No director was appointed in James' lifetime. He was beginning to discover how different English universities were from those he had known in Europe 40 years before. One cannot imagine a European or American university behaving with philistine miserliness to a gifted resource similar in kind to that of the Parkes Library. Most of the twentieth-century libraries and institutes set up in our a-cultural and anti-cerebral country have been set up by refugee intellectuals, like Aby Warburg and Alfred Wiener; that said, a number of their fellows moved to the

United States, where their talents were better appreciated and properly rewarded.

In 1974, a decade after the opening of the Parkes Library, James set out in a long letter to Beres Bland, Southampton University's Librarian, his and Dorothy's 'difficulties', which 'had become completely unacceptable'. Where had 'the fatal mistake' been made? The university had taken the books and archives and had looked after them 'superbly':

> But the 'Parkes Library Limited' was not primarily books, but work, and that through no fault of its own, the university has left to us – *but we are bereft of all the help and support which we had from being a recognised institute*, and being able ourselves to devote ourselves to positive work, and our modest salaries to ourselves. The house and garden were maintained by the institution. The daily round of housework and cooking were done by the institution. If there were guests, and so often there were, they were the guests of the institution ... Now all these things have to be done by our two selves, and to a great extent at our own expense, and it takes all our time. And to an ut-terly unexpected extent we are still involved in the same complex web of concern with our subject as justified the creation of the institute.

It might be said that it had been their own fault: they ought to have declared that they had retired, should have 'refused all invitations to review, to write, and to speak'. Yet, James wrote, their 'going on working was inevitable'. Equally inevitable was that they could not help 'hoping that someone will arise in Southampton to carry on the torch'. That was the essence of the matter. James had hoped that the university would be 'the needed pioneer' in the 'very disciplined and unsentimental dialogue' that was crucial in a world that would 'go on disintegrating' until a new civilization was constructed out of the ruins of the old. James put his faith in universities: 'There is no place other than the universities where both the men and women and the knowledge are automatically together.' It is too easy to say that he was misguided; in 1974 it looked as if universities had life in them; it would take 20 years before the vitality of the 1960s was knocked out of them. In the longer run their capitulation to the non-ethical world of corporate business, a surrender that would have appalled James and Dorothy, might engender a counter movement; perhaps one day universities of the sort James believed in will do what he wanted them to do: be the agents of a truly global culture, not one determined by businessmen in Houston, Hong Kong and the Channel Islands.

He was, however, impatient when the question was that of a director for the Parkes Library. In the event James would had to have lived to be 100 in order to have seen the first one appointed. Money was apparently the problem, or rather the lack of it. A sad exchange between James and the University Vice-Chancellor in 1978 illustrates the division between bureaucratic and imaginative minds. In February of that year James expressed a hope 'that the Parkes material will ultimately form the basis of an autonomous Institute of the university'. Everything should be done to encourage a 'future wealthy donor'; meanwhile, might the Marks and Spencer connection once again be brought into play? In June, when the remaining files and archives at Iwerne were to be handed over, James expressed his concern that the university have 'on its staff someone who is continuously and actively engaged in preserving, arranging, increasing and developing the material which it possesses':

> During the fourteen years which we have spent at Iwerne Minster we have been constantly asked for information, help, or advice on antisemitism; usually the issue was raised directly at Iwerne, and Southampton University was not involved. But the University must now take over complete responsibility; and, while nobody has my experience, someone must as quickly as possible acquire enough understanding of the subject to know where to look for information, and to help and advise an enquirer ... There is nothing equivalent to the collection of material which I amassed over nearly fifty years of concern, so far as I know, anywhere else in the world. I do hope therefore that it will be possible to make an appointment this summer ...

The Vice-Chancellor thought otherwise. He expected James, not the university, to provide the money for such a post. In July James replied: 'Can we get this one straightened out?' It was vital, he wrote, 'that there is at Southampton University some person whose business it is to know what the Parkes Library contains, but also to keep abreast of new material as it appears anywhere, know new personalities as they emerge, so that its unique possessions can be made available wherever and whenever wanted'. The Vice-Chancellor's response began with the hope that 'we are not working at cross purposes', and went on directly to demonstrate that they were. He used a word favoured by bureaucrats to halt further argument: 'ideally'; in contrast to James' idealism was the reality that 'present funds' were inadequate even to support an archivist for a whole year. There was no Parkes Institute in James' lifetime.

James kept meticulous financial accounts during the first ten years at Iwerne. He and Dorothy seem to have lived well within their income. In 1966–7 James earned about £230 from royalties, just over £400 from reviewing and broadcasting, and together he and Dorothy received nearly £650 from rents and dividends. He had a pension of £584 from the Parkes Library, and she one of £250; their joint state pension was £364. The expenses of a visit to Israel were almost entirely met by the Parkes Library, and other expenses refunded by the Parkes Library came to more than £250. James estimated his total income for that tax year at £2,957. Expenditure amounted to £1,545. The cost of running a car came to more than £200, secretarial services amounted to £85, and travel within the country and hospitality totalled £126. They appear to have lived as frugally as ever. As we might expect, clothes do not feature. Yet, nor do cigarettes: had he given them up? And where are the household expenses? In the end, like all financial documents, these accounts drawn up for taxation purposes obscure just as much as they reveal.

Although James did not include lecturing (along with reviewing and broadcasting) as contributing to his fees of £400 in 1966–7, he quite rightly charged for this demanding service. When he gave a lecture at Bryanston School in 1969 the fee was six guineas. He had to ask for it. In his diplomatically phrased request to the Headmaster he was obliged to put the case of every lecturer who has found himself expected to perform for nothing:

> I write to you in some embarrassment! A little while ago I was asked to come and talk to your sixth about the problem

of Israel and the Arabs, and did so. Now I have received a very appreciative letter from the master who invited me thanking me for it. I had not bargained about a fee when I accepted the invitation, nor had a fee been mentioned. But I admit that I had assumed it. And the position is that, apart from the fact that I have to earn my living, it is not fair to give lectures free which a number of my friends, who come to me for briefing in this particular field, rightly charge an economic fee for giving ... Of course, if it is specified in advance that it is to be a free lecture, then one knows what one is doing in accepting. But, if nothing is said, the presumption in these days ... is that the labourer deserves his hire.

What is the presumption in our day? When lecturers 'in these days' are asked by journalists to give them a briefing, how often is it the presumption on the journalist's part that it will be given freely? In my experience it is every time.

On the other hand, 'in these days' James would have been given a *festschrift* and had a biography written about him. In 1978 Dorothy endeavoured to interest Martin Gilbert in writing the biography; nothing came of her endeavours. The *festschrift* was probably the idea of Sister Louis Gabriel, whom we shall meet again under a variety of names; in 1971 the project fell through 'owing to publishing difficulties'. No one, apart from Professor Goitein, appears to have had any enthusiasm for it. By the 1970s James was becoming a forgotten man, his work on antisemitism a thing of the past. His pioneering had been all too successful.

A dog that had had its day? If so, there was plenty of bite in the old dog still, or, bearing in mind the Lithuanian folk tale – where a wolf gave up killing and led a holy life – the old wolf. The story goes that all went well until, as he was loping down the road one day, a gander came flapping up to him. The wolf wrung the gander's neck. 'Geese should not hiss at saints,' said the wolf. 'I had believed my modesty to be capable of meeting any situation', James wrote in December 1965 to Lowell Streiker of the Department of Religion, Temple University, Philadelphia, 'but to find so learned a scholar as yourself apparently unaware that I have contributed somewhat, both in your country and in my own, to the Jewish–Christian dialogue, has rocked it to its foundation.' To Rabbi Harry Richmond of Brooklyn in August 1965 he was more polite; it is clear, however, that, unlike the Lithuanian wolf, he has only just kept sarcasm in check; his English remained as polished as it had been since his schooldays:

> I am embarrassed. If you publish the manuscript as it stands, I am not the right person to produce a Foreword. If I am an appropriate person to write forewords, then it is to a different sort of book. After a whirlwind tour of the world and history you say that the present age needs religion. There is no point in me writing a Foreword. I am a cleric and it is obvious that an elderly clergyman would agree; I have nothing to contribute. A Foreword by one of the Beatles would be much more to the point. The reader might find it exciting that a Beatle also thought the Age needed religion.

Malcolm Johnson was another who was roundly castigated. He had written a page-length piece on 'Christianity' in the Christmas 1965 number of *World*, a publication of the Council for Education in World Citizenship, and was himself a member of the United Nations Association. After Malcolm Johnson had replied to an earlier letter of criticism, James dealt him a final blow:

> Dear Mr Johnson, Thank you for your letter of the twelfth. No, it certainly does not satisfy. You should be a sufficiently experienced writer to know that I am not concerned with what you 'meant or implied', but with what you conveyed to a well-informed reader. I am concerned with one unnecessary (and false) accusation, and with one statement for which there is absolutely no Gospel justification, but is entirely invented by yourself (I know that bandying texts is unprofitable, but it is quite clear from all the Gospels that the arrest at night was to prevent a popular demonstration in favour of Jesus. Cf Mark 11, 18; Matt. 21, 46 and Luke 19, 48 and 20, 19) and preposterously justified by saying that it rests on 'a first principle of New Testament theology' ... I am aware that it is an entirely negative gesture, but I have cancelled my subscription to the association, which dates, I think, from 1921. Yours truly ...

Reading Malcolm Johnson's piece, we might consider him hard done by. But the wrath of the righteous manifests itself fearsomely. For Solomon Zeitlin, who had written *The Rise and Fall of the Judean State: a Political, Social, and Religious History of the Second Commonwealth*, published by the Jewish Publication Society of America, he had no time at all. He wrote to the editor of the *Jewish Chronicle* in June 1967: 'I really cannot restart my career as a reviewer with that idiot Zeitlin!!'

An irascible old saint perhaps, but not one who had lost his sense of judgement. This did not apply where politics were concerned, however: it had always been weak. In May 1974 James and Dorothy were booked for a holiday into the White House Hotel on Herm in the Channel Islands. The booking had been made in the previous year. In March 1974 they cancelled. James offered two explanations. The first was that Dorothy's doctor was against it, 'because my wife's walking capacity has been seriously diminished of late ... Instead we shall go to the New Forest to the hotel with which we are already familiar at Bramble Hill', a building, incidentally, of which he had written a brief history published the previous year. The second was the risk of civil war in Britain. In February 1974, before the doctor's report of the following month, he had written to the Booking Secretary at the White House Hotel:

> The state of the country is such that it throws into doubt the possibility of our getting over to Herm for a nice peaceful holiday. If one party gets in we are likely to have roaring inflation, so that pensioners could not afford to come, and if the other party gets in we are likely to have next door to civil war. I leave you to guess which party would produce which ...

With his old Guernsey friend John Ozanne, to whom he wrote on the same day, he spoke more plainly: 'events at the present moment have cast doubt on our ability to get to Herm in May. My suspicion is that if the Tories get in we shall be near to civil war for quite a time, whereas if Mr Wilson gets in we shall be living in a ramping inflation as he gives way to every trade union.' What is it that Proust says about the impossibility of prophecy: 'We picture the future as a reflexion of the present projected into an empty space, whereas it is the result of causes which for the most part escape our notice.' Could anyone in 1974 have predicted the politics of Margaret Thatcher?

Historians are happier with the past than with the future. James wrote about Vietnam to *The New Christian* on 31 January 1967. He opened with the recent British past:

> Nothing ... provides a reasonable argument that the war which the Americans are waging in Vietnam can possibly achieve the objectives they desire. Our folly in Suez, lasting a few days and causing only a few casualties, has cost us the friendship of Egypt and the confidence of the Arab world possibly for half a century. Military victory cannot any longer achieve the protection of the noblest civic values. This is partly because of the horrific nature of modern war, but more because all the propaganda advantages are on the other side. The Egyptians told lies about us during the Suez campaign; the Communists are telling lies about the Americans. But it is the lies which remain in men's minds, when one can attach one of the effective contemporary clichés to them. Like us, the Americans are 'imperialists' and 'aggressors', and bombs will never persuade people that they are noble and altruistic liberators ...

Bombs are persuasive in only one direction: those on whom they fall become more convinced of the rightness of the cause for which they are being bombed. James then enunciated some other compelling home truths, any one of which would have tempted Norman Mailer, had he been younger, to write a novel entitled *Why Are We in Afghanistan?*:

> The hard fact is that we have got to discover a new way of overcoming what we believe to be evil or destructive in another people. If the Americans had spent wisely – and the word needs underlining – a tenth of what they are spending on war, they might begin to convince an Asian nation that they had something worthwhile to offer. But it would require infinite patience, constant forgiveness, inexhaustible willingness to be misunderstood – in fact all the virtues in the Christian hierarchy. I doubt whether there is an alternative, and, if we are not willing to pay that price, we can only tell the potential victims that we cannot avert their fate by force.

Will 'imperialists' and 'aggressors', whether they are Russian, American, or Chinese, never learn? Where are the Medes and Persians, the Greeks and Romans after a thousand years? Back far beyond where they began.

Old men, even old saints, are said to forget. James did not forget Guernsey Gache. He had eaten it as a boy and in December 1969 wrote to Maison Le Noury in St Peter Port asking them to send him some Guernsey Gache for Christmas. 'May I add', he wrote, 'that I used to have my lunch with you every weekday sixty years ago when I was at Elizabeth College. I still remember your delicious steak and kidney pie and your entrancing cream cakes!' Alas, there was no Guernsey Gache to be had, not off the premises at least: 'sometimes they were over ten days in the Post and were naturally quite uneatable on arrival', wrote a representative of Maison Le Noury. 'We are glad', he (or she) continued, 'that you still have such happy memories of our Cakes and Pies.' Is that what it all comes down to in the end: the cakes and pies of boyhood? Possibly for Marcel Proust; certainly not for James Parkes. Three days after he had written to Maison Le Noury, he wrote to one of his oldest and truest friends, Guilfoyle Williams:

> My dear Guileful, I do not think that at present we are called to be either optimists or pessimists about the future. I like the saying of Hillel that it is not for us to see the end of the work, but neither are we free to desist from it. I find the implications of our present situation far too complex to make pessimism or optimism in any way meaningful. On the other hand, I have no intention of stopping writing and talking so long as I can do it. So do not be too depressed.

In this regard Proust and Parkes were of one mind, for to each of them to stop writing meant to cease living. For Marcel Proust, as for Primo Levi, an end to remembering meant an end to life. That may be the universal case. For James Parkes, aged 73 in 1969, that end was ten years in the future.

Meanwhile, he was almost as active as he ever had been. There was not time to be depressed. A description of all he did becomes a list: writing to the *Bournemouth Times* about a local Nazi and getting himself into the paper under the hoary old headline HE WAS ON HITLER'S BLACKLIST; suggesting to the West

Wiltshire Water Board that more elastic washers on household taps would save water; protesting in a civilized fashion (but utterly ineffectively) at the closure of the Iwerne Co-op; trying to help the pathetic George Kelly, who lived with his family in a caravan, and who was unable to help himself; and counselling Miss Christina Dewdney of Shirley, Southampton, when she thought she might convert to Judaism (he wrote to Edgar Samuel, who shared in the counselling, 'It must be unusual for an Anglican cleric to help a full Christian to become a Jewess, and for a devout Jew to persuade her to remain a Christian'). He and Dorothy were, on a reduced scale, as hospitable as we have come to expect them to be. One of their visitors was Clem Brouard, the son of a Guernsey friend of a friend. Clem came to Clayesmore Preparatory School, 'three minutes' along the road from the cottage, in January 1975. He came to Sunday tea in February, and wrote the following letter of thanks:

> Dear Rev. Dr. J.W. PARKES, I am righting this letter to thank you for taking me out on Sunday the Second and to thank you for the good Stamps. And I RELY had a nice time. From Clem.

Clem was not the only one who had 'a nice time'. George and Shirley Him came for their first visit in April 1971. George wrote immediately afterwards:

> Dear Reverendissime and Reverendissima, This is first to tell you how much my wife and I enjoyed our expedition to Parkestan where the general atmosphere is exciting, stimulating and invigorating. I felt deeply sorry that, trying to be polite, we left before being literally thrown out – Wilton House proved to be a very poor substitute for Netherton – just stone and no spirit ... In the meantime, my wife and I are circulating your assorted beautiful stories, particularly the one about the hat and the French visa.

James as good storyteller we have encountered before; James as advisor on 'O' level scripture examinations we have not. While on holiday in Guernsey in Spring 1973 he helped Marie, probably the daughter of their hosts, with her Old Testament questions. Marie got a grade C overall; she was more than happy with it. There was, however, one activity where diminishing physical powers restricted him: he had to have help in the garden. From 1975 the boys of Claysmore School supplied the necessary manual labour.

Where he continued indefatigable was in letter writing. Between July and December 1975 he wrote about 240 letters, if the number of pink carbon copies in the Parkes Papers for those six months may be depended on for a total. He evidently had letter-writing days. On 25 November, for example, he wrote 11 letters, including one to Clem Brouard apologizing for not having had him for tea and enclosing a £1 book token, another to Rosemary Reuther, and a third to the Rev. Canon Peter Schneider at Sudbury in Suffolk: 'This is just a brief note. Yes, we will be able to loan you £100. When do you want it?' On 4 December he wrote ten letters, one of them to Martin Gilbert about 'your excellent Atlas of Jews in the ME. As usual it is full of information but, as usual, I wonder whether there is not more you could have done.' On 16 December he wrote 16 letters; on 19 December he wrote a further nine. Who at this point was doing the typing, who was supplying the 'secretarial services'? There was surely too much for Dorothy to cope with unaided.

There were numerous old friends to keep up with, as well as to see from time to time: the McNeilages, for instance, came to stay, and James and Dorothy were due to return their visit at Barley; possibly they did so more than once. Kay Wood-Legh was another old friend who stayed in touch. Miss Wood-Legh had been 'blind since she was a girl'; this did not prevent her writing medieval history of a distinguished kind: she had a succession of secretary-companions. After the move to Iwerne was made, Dorothy became concerned on Kay's behalf. 'James and I have been (more largely than is generally realised) her "home" background. This we cannot provide any longer.' Her fears were not, I think, realized: Kay Wood-Legh continued to manage very well. She was an independently minded woman (as James indicates in *Voyage of Discoveries*), who preached one March evening in 1965 at Ripon Hall, Cambridge, and who bequeathed £4,000 towards the foundation of Lucy Cavendish College. Her letters to James and Dorothy from Germany in September and October 1964 suggest to me that Kathleen Wood-Legh deserves a biography of her own.

There were also newer friends, like Sister Louis Gabriel. She and James seem to have encountered one another in 1961. A letter James wrote to the *Jewish Chronicle* in that year which referred to his condemnatory review of a book written by a Roman Catholic priest, had an 'unexpected result', he wrote many years later; it brought about 'a firm alliance between our work at Barley and the beginnings of Roman Catholic understanding of Judaism through the Sisters of Zion'. The Convent at 17 Chepstow Villas in Notting Hill became the Study Centre for Christian–Jewish relations, and Sister Louis Gabriel, active in Germany and at Rome in the 1960s, was a firm supporter of James and his work. By 1968, when she was teaching at a university in Washington, D.C. she had become Professor Dr Charlotte Klein. She wa, however, unhappy in such surroundings, reported Paul Winter in the same year. By 1973, as Sister Charlotte, she was back at 17 Chepstow Villas. From there she wrote to James about the difficulties with, and demise of, his *festschrift*.

And then there was Dr Karol Brzoska. He wrote to James from London on 29 September 1965:

> This letter I think would be a surprise for you. You did not expect it. But you certainly remember the years 1929 or 1930, when you lived in Geneva, Switzerland. In that time I had the honour of being introduced to you ... I have met you several times. I remember we have discussed, inter alia, several aspects of the Jewish problem which interested you that time. I remember also that I have been invited to you for dinner. We were four at the party ... We sat at candlelights, and the dinner was gorgeous, and – what was remarkable – all was prepared by yourself. The final chapter was the magnificent tea, served in your library in the very fine, genuine, china ... Afterwards we exchanged letters from time to time, till the World War II came and broke our relations. During the unfortunate uprising in Warsaw 1944, my house was burned down and I lost all my belongings ... Now I am in London for several months. I received a scholarship granted by the British Council and I intend to study here the problems of international finance. I am addicted to these problems. One day when strolling along the streets of London I happened to perceive in one bookshop a book of yours: The History of the Jewish People (a

blue Pelican). It reminded me at once of our meetings in Geneva. So I decided to write to you. I think it would be very pleasant to meet you again.

They met at the Athenaeum for dinner on Monday 8 November 1965. James had written to say that Dr Brzoska did not have to dress for the occasion (can this truly have been 1965 and not 1925?), and Dr Brzoska had said how happy he was to meet there. 'I am very anxious', he wrote on 26 October, 'to see this famous club. May be I am wrong and my ideas about clubs are naïve or obsolete but I still think that the clubs have played an important and rather advantageous role in the foundation of British culture. Didn't they?'

On the day immediately following the dinner Dr Brzoska wrote a long letter of thanks:

> I wish I had a better command of my English to convey to you my impressions of our yesterday's meeting. To me they were extremely pleasant. Looking at you I turned my mind back to those nice days 35 years ago ... I remember you from that time as a very interesting personality, given devoutly to a peculiar object of study, but preserving at the same time broad general interests and distinguished by impeccable, amiable manners ...

So much for the young James Parkes, 'given devoutly' to the study of antisemitism: it is a telling phrase. Dr Brzoska also had a good deal to say on the subject of the English Club; it is worth pausing to listen to a Polish view of the matter, as it is an antidote to the lightly dismissive view taken by the English themselves:

> Entering the Athenaeum Club, I must confess, I felt a deep emotion: a great deal of British politics has been formulated here during many generations. And all this has had an impact on the history of the whole world. Don't be too rigorous with me, please. May be my opinions on the clubs and their role in the cultural and political life of Great Britain are too subjective and naïve. I am not ashamed of it. They form a part of my convictions about the absolute necessity of preparing, and even breeding, people prede-

termined to occupy important posts in the life of their country. Oxford and Cambridge Universities belong here. Clubs, I guess, belong here too.

Yes: it *was* 1965. Lord Hume *was* leader of the Conservative Party. James Parkes *did* dine at the Athenaeum. 'I can only deplore', went on Dr Brzoska:

> that nothing of this kind has been known in my country during my life, and germs (of germs) of such ideas have been purposely killed and destroyed by wars, wanton occupation and by human stupidity. I feel melancholic thinking about it the more so as I have in mind my own frustrated life, in which years have been spent in efforts to save the bare life, to preserve my human dignity and the independence of my thought. Years spent in an indifferent surrounding, narrowminded and full of prejudices, childish and suffocating ... Dear Dr Parkes, I sincerely apologize for this outburst of emotions. Believe me, in spite of this melancholy I remain a born optimist. This has saved me in extremely perilous situations. I am always looking forward with hope.

So there it is, the authentic voice of old Poland: Dr Brzoska was born in Warsaw in 1908, graduated in Law from Warsaw University in 1932, received his doctorate (summa cum laude) from that university in 1938, and was economic advisor to the President of the Republic in 1945–6. Better the old Poland than the Poland that succeeded it in 1946; better Old England (Clubs, School Ties, Oxford and Cambridge) than the New England of celebrity culture and corporate control. But: better for whom?

Three years later Dr Brzoska wrote again. It was a sad letter. His mother and father had died. He was alone and 'utterly exhausted and depressed'. It was like many other letters from Poland in the years of Soviet occupation. He sent a Christmas gift: it was December 1968. The 'modest gift' was a book 'on Jewish wooden prayer-houses in Poland'. James replied early in 1969 thanking him for it. The book is in the Parkes Library: take it out and remember Dr Brzoska.

The last letter that James wrote, or rather the last that I have come across, was to a very old friend, Hélène Vogel. She had written a moving account of the death of her husband Theodore in a letter of August 1978. James may have responded before the letter I have before me, which is of 9 January 1979, as he makes no mention in it of Theodore's death. After thanking Hélène for a 'book on Aix in two superb volumes', he becomes uncharacteristically reflective:

> We are very well considering our ages and we are trying to reduce our commitments and actually 'retire' from our relations with the Jewish/Christian problem which has occupied us for so many decades. Fortunately, Dorset is a lovely County to retire to and we shall have no lack of interest and of beauty surrounding us, even if we are not concerned with Jewish/Christian relations. But, alas, I think my travelling days are over and I do not see the possibility of my getting down to you again unless something special happens – but memories go on and la Rolane will always have a place in mine.

Is 'uncharacteristically' fair? It may be thought so. Nonetheless, it is a haunting paragraph. It is also revealing: why should Dorset's interest and beauty be linked, if only semantically, to the closure of their work on 'Jewish/Christian relations'? By 1979 James and Dorothy had been in Dorset for 15 years. Twice the 'work' is mentioned. It is as if James cannot let it go. Probably he found it hard, perhaps impossible, to do so. Unless a biographer's subject discusses his inner life, the biographer has to remain ignorant of it. James never mentions his. One begins to wonder if he had not always been too active to have much of one. In 1979 he was face to face with inaction, face to face with the beauty of Dorset, face to face with death. Is it any wonder that he was reluctant to let go of Jewish/Christian relations? Had they not been his prop and stay for more than 50 years? He had come to need them more than they had him.

Moreover, his beloved Provence, the La Rolane of his youth, was now among those paradises which Proust tells us are lost long before we die and in which we feel ourselves lost too. James described it in the early chapters of *Voyage of Discoveries*. Or he had tried to. He had not the right sort of eye (as his drawings show), nor the right kind of pen to give his recollections the vividness a reader will for a long time remember. *Voyage of*

Discoveries was written during the first years at Iwerne. The contract with Gollancz is dated 13 August 1964; the final text was delivered on 1 April 1968; the book was published in 1969. It was originally longer by four chapters. Three of these, chapters XVI–XVIII, were about Israel; copies are in the Parkes Papers. A copy of chapter XV appears not to have survived. What was it about? In a letter to Hugh Harris of 2 April 1968 Dorothy writes that she and James 'still love Dorset – and it is on that note the book ends', but the published version cannot be said to end on such a note. The title also changed. It was originally called 'Voyage of Explorations: A Life Enjoyed'. The sub-title became the main title of chapter XIV. Evidently, endings presented something of a challenge. As for the book itself Dorothy considered it 'a Parkesian version of Gulliver's Travels' and 'so very Jamesian'. Philip Toynbee, in his damning review thought it a 'misleading book'. When I first read it, I thought it both misleading and disappointing; after subsequent readings, while still thinking it a disappointment I no longer believe it misleading. Philip Toynbee ended his review with the thought that James was 'a good and effective man', who had 'not mastered the delicate art of autobiography'. *Voyage of Discoveries*, however, is not misleading because James Parkes could not write autobiography; nor is it a disappointment for that reason. What is disappointing has been to learn that the self-congratulatory James of *Voyage of Discoveries* is the authentic James Parkes. I ought to have known better: an English gentleman of James' generation, even one from the Channel Islands, was not likely to have been prey to self-doubt.

At Iwerne James not only wrote an autobiography and, until 1979, thousands of letters; he also wrote a good many pamphlets, articles, and occasional pieces. Some of his earlier work was revised and came out in new editions; some of his earlier papers were collected and republished. There does not seem to have been much rethinking, but rethinking is not to be expected of a scholar in his seventies. Nevertheless, James' last thoughts on antisemitism, on Israel, and on theology require more than simple reiteration.

When he wrote a new introduction to *The Jew in the Medieval Community*, republished in 1976, there was no need for him to do much other than to review work done since its first publication in 1934, and to outline his intentions for the subsequent volumes, which were never written. The new introduction was also separately published as Parkes Library Pamphlet 22, entitled *Christianity, Jewish History and Antisemitism*. The themes are familiar: they have been discussed above in the proper place, and one, the most important, will be revisited shortly. There are, however, two issues new to us, which James only mentions in passing; because they raise important questions about his understanding of antisemitism they need immediate attention.

The first concerns the myth of ritual murder. James says that in his third volume he would have dealt with 'false accusations spread by the ignorant and credulous local clergy [of the Middle Ages], and revived in our own day by both Catholic and Protestant antisemites ... Ritual murder, the poisoning of wells, the world plot against Christians and Christendom'. Leaving aside the manner in which these accusations were spread – the phrase 'ignorant and credulous clergy', for example, needs definition and qualification – it is the ritual murder accusation that concerns us here. Did James believe that sometimes such an accusation might be justified? In a letter of 8 January 1968 to Mortimer Cohen of New York James seems to be saying so:

> Thank you very much for your article on Ritual Murder ... I had hoped to make a more detailed study of the subject in the third volume of my History of Antisemitism, which was never written. I wonder whether some of the medieval cases are not either Purim accidents or connected with the use of blood in witchcraft. In neither case would a religious *ritual* act be involved ...

In the last 30 years a great amount of work has been done on the subject of ritual murder accusations. The abuse and murder of children in the Middle Ages, mainly by their parents, seems to have been about as commonplace as it is now. All of the instances in which the murder of young males was held to be the responsibility of a Jew or Jews have been shown to be false. When children died in what we might call the normal course of events, either through the negligence or the sheer ill will of their parents or other relatives, Jews were never accused. Apart from one possible early Byzantine case, the 'Purim accident' idea is a non-starter. The notion of a boy's blood being used for witchcraft purposes by Jews is equally nonsensical, as nonsensical as the notion of Jews wanting consecrated hosts for such purposes and paying Christians to get them: what would Jews do with what they did not believe to be the Body and Blood of Christ? The idea of ritual murder was to be found only in the minds of Christians.

The second issue is that of the inevitability of modern antisemitism. James said that his fourth volume 'would have provided the background which explains the nineteenth-century paradox – that is the century in which emancipation became obviously inevitable, and, for totally different reasons, modern political and racial antisemitism became inevitable also – the theme of volume 5'. The inevitability of anything is hard for the historian to take. The inevitability of modern antisemitism is particularly hard for the historian to accept, however happy he is to share James' view that the Church of the second century and churchmen of the third and fourth are in some sense responsible for it, for if medieval antisemitism is partly, probably mainly, their doing, modern antisemitism is not. It had its own political and racist inventors. There is good reason for going back to the Gospels when the Final Solution is being debated, and there are equally good reasons for concluding that it was not inevitable until Hitler invaded Soviet Russia.

If in these two areas we have detected flaws in James' approach to the history of antisemitism, they do not detract from his reputation as a modern innovator in its study nor do they from the celebration of him as a 'Great Pioneer' by the publication of a volume of essays edited by Alan Davies, which appeared in 1979. *Antisemitism and the Foundations of Christianity* was dedicated to 'James Parkes a Great Pioneer of this subject And a courageous foe of antisemitism On the occasion of his eightieth birthday'.

The most important of the themes touched on by him in *Christianity, Jewish History and Antisemitism* was one that had occupied him for 40, perhaps for 50, years. It has been dealt with above, yet because James continued to be occupied by it until the end, and because it is still an issue not fully addressed by the Christian churches, it requires further comment here. The title he eventually gave an essay dated June 1976, outspokenly defines the topic: 'The Bible in Public Worship: A Source of Antisemitism'. The title it replaced, 'The Christian Liturgy and Antisemitism', was manifestly too neutral. The theme was one that had re-engaged him the previous year. In a January 1975 review of Rosemary Ruether's *Faith and Fratricide*, after describing the proposals she had put before the American Association of Theological Schools, he had written that what was wanted was 'a simple sentence: "What shall we do about reading to our laity in the liturgy those passages in the New Testament which present Jews and Judaism erroneously?"' In June, he reviewed Franklin Littell's *The Crucifixion of the Jews*. It was, 'an unfortunate book ... badly produced ... written too hastily and in too emotional a whirlwind ... [It was] unquestionably sincere but that [was] no substitute for serious argument ... emotion has no place in the necessary analysis of history ... In this case it has led the author to miss the central problem.' 'The real challenge' James wrote, 'with which antisemitism, culminating in the Holocaust, confronts Christendom is that it is perpetuated, and will continue to be perpetuated, by the liturgical reading of the New Testament as "the word of God" in the public worship of the churches':

> The New Testament does not envisage any survival of the Jews as a people, for it claims that Christians have taken over the Old Testament promises. Neither does it envisage any legitimate survival of Judaism, for the church has acquired a "new covenant", and the old is rejected. The Jews should all have become Christians, and there is no suggestion that Jews and Judaism are a natural part of the contemporary world. But that is not all. For in the liturgical reading of the Gospels and epistles, passages are read as the word of God which inevitably invite hatred and contempt by their false descriptions of Jews and Judaism. That is the colossal challenge which all the churches have ultimately to face.

In July 1975, writing to George Appleton and commending to him *Antisemitism and the Christian Mind* by Alan Davies, he put the same point in more general terms: 'I think it is a very important book. He distinguishes those who reject antisemitism and deplore the Holocaust, but do not otherwise alter their traditional view of Judaism as rejected, from those who see the need for fundamental rethinking.'

Rethinking, however fundamental, is not much good without action. What action, for example, had the Anglican Church taken? James addressed this issue in 'The Bible in Public Worship':

> Incredible as it may appear to any Jewish or Christian spectator, the liturgical commission of the Church of England, in its third, and current, revision of the Communion Service in 1973 proposes that a third reading of Scripture be added from the Old Testament, at the end of which the reader *may* say 'This is the word of the Lord', and he *may* say the same after the passage from the epistle, but he *must* say 'This is the Gospel of Christ' after any reading from the four Gospels. The introduction of liturgical fundamentalism in a church in which it is doubtful if there is even one fundamentalist among the bishops shows how deeply rooted the idea of an infallible 'word of God' is in the Christian tradition.

Nevertheless, one could be 'thankful' that there was a tendency, 'as lectionaries are revised, for the worst passages in the New Testament, or the least estimable incidents in the Old, to be omitted'. There was still a very long way to go: 'the background of the nearly two millennia of unreformed lectionaries' had to be squarely faced. Omitting the most offensive passages would 'not change the picture to a new and positive acceptance of Jewry as a legitimate contemporary neighbour, and Judaism as a legitimate contemporary approach to the same God'. That, however, was not 'the whole story'. 'The rejection of Jesus by the Jewish communities to which he himself preached' had formed in the subconscious 'even of a Christian saint the feeling that the Jews had made their own bed: they must lie on it'. 'This I am sure', he concluded, 'is the final contribution of the continuous picture of the Jewish people and their religion in the liturgy of every church':

> It is this feeling that 'they have made their own bed: they must lie on it', which explains the silences of the churches, and Christian bodies, fifty years ago about Nazi antisemitism and the holocaust, and today about Israel. This explains the lack of any protest at the Yom Kippur war. This explains why Christian statements avoid direct mention of Israel while they readily mention the Palestinians ... The

result is that there is constantly a defence of the rights of Palestinians, but never a defence of those of the Israelis.

An unreformed lectionary and an unreformed liturgy had produced not only antisemitism but also anti-Israelism.

On this point James is at one with a number of other commentators on antisemitism: Robert Runcie, Friedrich Heer, Daniel Goldhagen, Sigmund Freud. Robert Runcie, speaking on the Fiftieth Anniversary of Kristalnacht, said that 'without centuries of Christian antisemitism Hitler's passionate hatred would never have been so fervently echoed'. Friedrich Heer in the introduction to his path-breaking book *God's First Love* wrote that 'Auschwitz stands on fifteen centuries of illustrious church tradition'. Daniel Goldhagen, in *Moral Reckoning: the Catholic Church and the Holocaust in History and Today* has identified Christianity as the single greatest source of antisemitism in the world. Sigmund Freud considered antisemitism endemic to Christianity because there was 'an unconscious psychological truth' within it, or rather two such 'truths', the obvious Oedipal one being underpinned by that of Cain and Abel. Antisemitism in a word, one coined by Yosef Hayim Yersushalmi, is 'interminable'. Freud might also have believed, though I have no confirmation of it, that the Torah rather than turning into the Holy Ghost, became Mary the Mother of God. James seems to have neglected both the Mother of God and the Father of Modern Psychiatry.

Is antisemitism 'interminable'? James seems to have believed that the grave damage caused by the 'fall out' from two millennia of liturgical Bible readings would continue indefinitely, unless, that is, something fairly root and branch was done about it. He was right in the assumption that little of that nature would be done. But is it any longer necessary? At the opening of the third millennium there are so few churchgoers in Western Europe that barely one person in a thousand hears the Bible being read. It is unlikely that many more than that read it outside church. Western Europe is ceasing to be Christian; when (and where) Christianity no longer has any cultural and religious significance, will antisemitism wither away and die? What then, it might be asked, of the United States and Africa, where Christians abound and the Bible continues to be read and heard? I know nothing of Africa, but I understand that in the

United States it is the fundamentalist version of Christianity, which James so much abhorred, that is dominant. How antisemitic is it?

It is not only that Western Europe is becoming, if it has not already become, non-Christian; it is becoming, or has already become, anti-Christian. While eschewing prophecy, all the signs are that Christians will at a later date become a persecuted minority, the victims of pogroms conducted by their ignorant and ill-informed fellow citizens, perhaps orchestrated by non-Christian local authorities. What are these strange people up to behind closed church doors? Why do they not behave as we do outside them? They have to be up to no good. They cannot be tolerated. Christmas is a commercial celebration. Easter is a business festival. At any rate, antisemitism should be gone by then.

Meanwhile, religious fundamentalism appears to be on the increase. James, born and bred in a different age, never could take it seriously. In his later years, nonetheless, he was obliged to give some attention to fundamentalist Judaism, when Orthodox Jews became critical of his work. Ten years before, he had been 'in trouble with the rigidly orthodox' after a lecture at the Anglo-Israel Association. 'Poor darlings', he wrote to Israel Sieff on 28 November 1966, 'they are a trial!! We have known Jakobovitz since he was a yeshivabachur. We don't think he knows what the word "toleration" means, though he is personally a man of complete integrity and considerable charm.' In the same month and to another correspondent, Rupert, probably a former teacher at Claysmore School, he wrote:

> I am at the moment engaged in a potential conflict with Jewish orthodox fundamentalism, as represented by the new Chief Rabbi, whom we knew as a young idealistic student, and who now looks a somewhat self-satisfied and portly middle-aged pundit. I shall be very interested, once you begin to get into touch with the Moslem atmosphere of Kaboul, to know how you react to a system of thinking which is so static, after living in an atmosphere as fluid as the England of the sixties. I wonder where the young Afghani finds his fluidity, for the young are young all over the world, at least that was my experience when I was concerned with university students during the twenties and thirties. But I do not remember at that time that

Afghanistan had entered into the international orbit.

It has now: into the international orbit of fundamentalist terrorism. One wonders whether James would have reckoned the 'fluidity' of the 1960s one cause of the rigidity of the young 40 years later – Moslem, Christian and Jewish. The 'potential conflict' of which James wrote to Rupert, was actual enough for Caesar Aronsfield to express his sympathy 'after the disgraceful attacks upon you by some Jews':

> Indeed I must take care not to pretend that this is an affair which concerns you more than me and other Jews. For my part, I am feeling thoroughly ashamed and humiliated. Those detractors are, in my opinion, the exact counterpart of the antisemites, as much 'enemies of the people' as those whom you discussed in your book ... I can only hope that you will not feel unduly hurt but rather draw renewed comfort from the fact that among those who are free from bigotry and petty spleen, your stature as a scholar and a champion of the Jewish cause in its widest sense is unchallenged.

James replied that he was 'not at all distressed – except by the narrowness of the poor dears'.

Among the 'poor dears' was Dayan Grunfeld. In December 1966 he wrote to James thanking him for his lecture, 'Unexpected Israel'. It was a 'masterpiece' with which he could not agree. James, he said, had probably read 'much more on the non-orthodox side than on the orthodox side'. If he were to read the 180 pages of Dayan's Introduction to the Horeb:

> I am quite sure it will then become clear to you why ecumenism is a much more difficult problem in the sphere of Judaism than in the sphere of Christianity. After all, the various Christian denominations *have* a common basis, i. e. they believe in the Divinity of the founder of the Christian religion. Such a common basis of belief is however lacking between orthodoxy and the non-orthodox trends of Jewish thought because the latter do not accept the divine origin and binding force of the Torah, nor the contemporaneous revelation and equality of written and oral law.

After other reflections, he offered the following conclusion: a refusal to recognizse 'any trend of thought which rejects the traditional conception of Torah min ha-Shamaim as a legitimate trend within Judaism is not orthodox rigidity as you say, but simply a statement of historical fact': one would suppose that the two (orthodox rigidity and historical fact) are perfectly compatible. The courteous, even affectionate, non-meeting of minds continued into the New Year. James duly read the Introduction to the Horeb; he could not, 'alas, accept your position theologically'. The Torah for him was 'a continuous revelation from the Divine. You may say that is not your interpretation of *min ha-Shamayim*, but the words express exactly what I mean also.' Was the difference between them, therefore, one of words only? Not in the least, for, leaving aside the gulf in thinking that yawns between the concept of a once for all Torah and the idea of one that is continuously being revealed, there was a world of difference between their two approaches, as there always must be in religion between fundamentalists and liberals. This is how James described the difference:

> I do not believe that Judaism can afford much longer to refuse to accept the discipline of theology. ... Traditional Judaism is standing in a bleak atmosphere of semi-understood rationalism and the scepticism of fear. It asserts in a most uncompromising way that God acts in history and in the contemporary scene, but it pays no attention to its critics or to its religious alternatives. ... Judaism cannot legitimately refuse to answer the questions which are raised by many genuine enquirers. Jakobovitz offers to stretch out his hand in friendship to those with whom he disagrees. But the kind of disagreement which the traditionalist is proclaiming to the most sincere reformer ill consorts with any friendship worthy of the name. I am distressed and oppressed by the situation.

He was right: fundamentalists offer friendship only on their own terms, which are the familiar ones of no give and all take.

There is an interrelated problem identified by James in the final letter between them of 8 March 1967. 'I think', he wrote, 'my problem can be pinpointed by an article which you will probably have seen some weeks ago in the *Jewish Chronicle*':

> There were two opinions about dialogue with Christians. I forget who was for it, but dear Edgar Samuel was against it. He was prepared to join with Christians in any social or political problem, but his loyalty to Judaism was entirely a Jewish affair, which he could not discuss with a non-Jew and which he did not attempt to impose upon a non-Jew ... How can I possibly admit Edgar Samuel's argument? ... To admit [it] would be to deny the common humanity of Jew and Gentile. It was at Sinai that the way of life for all nations of the world was revealed to Israel. But traditional Judaism today is not visible to the non-Jewish world as a life-giving stream in the desert of our international relations; it is seen by them to be concerned with matters which, however innocent in themselves, are not the things the world needs to recover its vision of a divine society.

Such was, of course, a Parkesian view of things, a view that took the brightest (and highest) view of the Jewish contribution to the history of the world:

> If I saw the non-Jewish world successfully dealing with its needs, if I was content with the pronouncements of the Christian Churches, or the problems and demands of our national and international life, then I would be satisfied to leave Edgar Samuel the tranquil enjoyment of a beautiful and satisfying way of life. But I do not see the situation in this way. I see the two fundamentally Jewish rabbinic conceptions of life by the *Mitzwoth*, and the corporate responsibility of continual interpretation, as two modes of living which cannot be replaced by generalizations, by fixed codes, or by imposed authority. They represent values which are needed, and I see no other place than the people of Sinai from which they are likely to come – or divinely intended to come.

The world needs Jews and Judaism; it cannot exist without them. James Parkes knew this; Jews knew this; non-Jews admit it less readily. Indeed, most Christians in the past had thought the opposite: the world would be a better place without Jews. In the Shoah 'Christians' attempted to put the idea into practice. What James did not account for was the post-Holocaust and post-Modernist reaction of Jewry. It was the natural reaction of those whose whole way of life is under dire threat, in the case of Jews during the Shoah and of Jews in Israel under the threat of extinction, and it is the opposite posture to that desired by James: instead of an expansive openness, the besieged dig their heels in and cling all the more tightly to what has been their rock and support throughout the ages. Such a siege mentality does not exclude aggressiveness. If the besieged are organized and armed, it may court it: the best form of defence is attack. Fundamentalists, Jewish, Christian and Moslem, are more than dogged resisters; they can become, do become violent proponents of a cause that must not be lost.

Which brings us to the second of our three themes: Israel. James was as occupied with Israel in these years as he had ever been. More precisely, he was concerned with Israel on an almost daily basis between the move to Iwerne in 1964 and the publication of *Whose land? A history of the peoples of Palestine* in 1970. During the years 1964–9 he wrote *Voyage of Discoveries*, including the discarded chapters XVI–XVIII on Palestine; he was also much in demand as what he called 'a backroom boy' during and after the Six Day War of 1967. His letters of the second half of the 1960s reflect his interest and commitment. He was impressively well informed and just as impressively acute in his judgements on the past, the present and the future. Some of the following is to be found in condensed form in the last few pages of *Voyage of Discoveries*, not least his 'sadness' at the unwillingness of the 'traditionalists' among Jews to listen to a Christian; they are 'caught' he says 'like the continental Protestants in a rigid neo-orthodoxy', and for them 'it is intolerable, or at least impertinent, that a Christian should publicly criticise their practices or beliefs'. Nevertheless, and at the risk of repetition, James' sound sense on Israel, even if (or possibly because) it gives offence to 'traditionalists' of all persuasions, will be re-examined briefly here.

First, the past, always more of a difficulty than the present, which is the reason for it being the preserve of historians and not of journalists and politicians. James was more even-handed with Arabs and Jews than he has been portrayed earlier in this study: had he learned more? Jews and Arabs, along with the British, were equally responsible for the catastrophic events of 1946–8. He wrote to Rabbi Balfour Brickner of Fifth Avenue, New York, in August 1969:

> The immense output of pro-Arab propaganda has convinced even benevolent readers that the statement that the general Arab population was urged – even ordered – to leave by higher Arab authorities is not true, and that much more responsibility lies on the Israeli military than was first admitted. My own position is that there is much more mixture in the motives. I think there is no doubt that in some of the later fighting, when attitudes had hardened, the Arab population was given no choice by the advancing Israelis – I think this was true, for example, in Ramleh and Lod. In the earlier fighting, when Irgun members were involved, there was the same violence. I once had a temporary map-maker who turned out to be a member of Irgun, and he told me in 1947 that his movement intended to clear as many Arabs out of the country as possible as soon as fighting began.

The fate of the displaced Arabs he sets into a context not hitherto noticed and worth citing here from the unpublished chapter XVII of *Voyage of Discoveries*:

> We have to set the Arab refugees in the perspective of the very much larger number of refugees who formed the tragic human debris of the Second World War, of the independence of India, of the return of Germans to western Germany, and of the advance of the frontiers of communism. To none of these millions of non-Arab refugees were these alternatives [of return or compensation] offered. None were allowed to return, however innocent. None were compensated. And in every case the main problem has long ceased to exist, and the great majority of the refugees has been incorporated into the societies which gave them refuge.

It is a comparison worth making, even if he may have been speaking too soon with regard to India and Europe. Still, as a good historian, James knew nothing is ever settled for good, especially when the settlement achieved is bad. He also made another comparison, not often made and for that reason alone worth pondering:

> There is no justice in considering the flight of the Arab pop-

ulation which was created by the war of 1948 without considering the flight of the Jewish population, equally ancient, equally authentic, from all the lands of the Arab world, the 'oriental' or 'sephardic' Jews who now constitute more than half of the Jewish population of Israel, and who, in almost every case, were expelled, or 'encouraged' to depart, with no more than they could carry with them. Apart from a very brief period, when international funds were used to meet their needs, these Jews, whose numbers are approximately equal to those of the Arab refugees, have been supported entirely by their Jewish brethren, and are being, slowly and with many problems on both sides, incorporated into the State of Israel. They make nonsense, in 1969, of the pretence that Israel is a 'European imposition' into an otherwise homogeneous 'Arab' world.

There was and is no going back for them. They are the truly besieged because, unlike American, South African, or West European Jews, they are in the last ditch. It is these Middle Eastern Jews, whose culture was not discernibly different from that of their 'Arab' neighbours, who have so drastically altered the political complexion of Israel over the past 50 years.

James also has more to say on Jewish terrorism. In December 1968 in a long letter to a Mr Rockovitch of Leytonstone, who had sent him a 'Memorandum on The Revolt', he was as interesting on the attitudes of leading British figures as he was on the activity of Irgun:

> Terrorism inspires anger and disgust, and what one has to weigh in the balance is that the Jewish terrorism of 1946 caused a number of leading pro-Zionist figures, such as Churchill himself, to dismiss, or at any rate to reduce, the appeal to sympathy after the Holocaust. There was less protest against our abandonment of the Mandate than one might have thought. Consequently I would not myself attribute any decisive role to Begin and the Irgun. Our decision was based on Middle Eastern oil and strategy, when viewed by a totally unsentimental and ruthless Prime Minister, such as was Attlee by all accounts, and an unsympathetic Foreign Minister, as was Bevin. It was 'clearly' our interest to conciliate the Arab world, and, once the

strategists had decided that a British presence in Palestine was of no importance, I suspect that we would in any case have withdrawn, possibly with more generosity and dignity, very soon. After all, the Mandate was officially declared unworkable as early as 1937.

As for Jewish terrorism, the Jews *'being human*, it is not in the least surprising that a terrorist movement emerged from the anger, frustration, and hostility which accompanied the last decade of the Mandate' and:

> Jews *being Jews*, one can be thankful that the terrorist movement was not much more violent than it was, and that it did not enjoy a greatly increased popular support – as it would have done among any other people with so great a burden of grievances ... I believe that in a historical perspective, the verdict would be that the emergence of the Irgun and Stern gang was inevitable; that, for terrorist groups, their record was more honourable than many others; that their re-absorption into a free Israel was more skilfully handled than one might have expected. One must, after all, compare the various fields in which terrorism has operated in the twentieth century. I think particularly of the Irish situation at the end of the first war.

One has to agree: the Black and Tans behaved more outrageously than did the Irish terrorists of their day. Memories are not so much short in politics as inconsistent: they come and go when it serves the purposes of politicians to make them come or have them go. Fortunately, James did not have to come to terms with the random terrorism of the twenty-first century; no doubt he would not have been surprised at the emergence of the suicide bomber in Islam: such a phenomenon would have fitted into his view of that religion as a 'Black and White' one.

He remained consistent in his view that Palestine had never been 'an Arab country': 'the Palestinian Christians, for example, have probably been Christians for 17 or 18 hundred years, have spoken Arabic for a thousand, and have called themselves "Arabs" for less than fifty', he told Miss Shifra Strizower of Monash University, Australia, in a letter of 15 May 1970. 'In 1905', he informed the audience at a lecture he gave on a weekend course about Jerusalem held at Missenden Abbey in December 1970, 'at the beginning of Zionist settlement in the land you have 40,000 Jews, 13,000 Christians, 7,000 Muslims. I don't think you can escape the conclusion of that.' It was the continuous Jewish presence in Palestine that was a cornerstone for him. The continuous Christian presence mattered to him less. Understandably: he was not very fond of the modern Christians of Palestine. The Missenden Abbey audience was told of his 'particular sadness' at the Christian hierarchy in Jerusalem coming out 'on the side of Jordan ... there was no voice of protest from that very considerable Christian body at the desecration of the Jewish Holy Places in the Old City and the refusal of Jewish access to the Wailing Wall'. As for the medieval, crusading Christians in Palestine, see the next paragraph.

What then of the Muslims? In their case we have arrived at the present. Not that James was uninformed about the history of Islam. When he got around to answering an August 1964 enquiry of the Rev. David Brewster of 45 Walton Street, Chelsea, in March 1965, he was happy to relate the close company Mahomet had kept with Jews and the hopes he had held of their conversion: 'As you know the original prayer-direction in Islam was to Jerusalem not to Mecca ... Jerusalem came to be venerated because of its being the site of the Jewish Temple.' The latter had been 'deliberately desecrated' by the Christians; they had 'made it into the city dung-hill'. It was to Canon Warren of Westminster Abbey, however, that he imparted his thoughts on contemporary Islam in January 1969. He believed it to be 'the main heresy of western monotheism':

> Judaism and Christianity have both refused to 'tidy up' their doctrine of God. It is left full of paradox and incompleteness – in Christianity explicitly, in Judaism implicitly, – and consequently it is always capable of change and development. But the early medieval theologians of Islam committed the disastrous mistake of elaborating a completely logical definition of the omnipotence of Allah which has effectively prevented those tentative re-examinations which prelude reform. They left no loophole by which any change might enter. Dialogue with Islam is therefore a special case, which will need most careful handling. I have a feeling that more may be done outside the Middle East in

the preliminary stages, and that any creative change will only gradually filter into the Arab world.

Has he not been proved right? He went on to ask for Canon Warren's 'verdict on this feeling of mine', for the canon had much greater experience in such matters. 'I have this concrete reason for asking for it', he wrote, because 'I am always seeking to persuade those interested in the Parkes Library at Southampton University that it would be an ideal place for the first tentative steps at 'trialogue'. He has been proved right here too. He concluded the letter to Canon Warren with one of his rare statements on Eastern religions: 'Incidentally as a Deity imprisoned exactly within the terms of human logic is the central heresy of the West, so the central heresy of the East seems to me the tendency to think of matter as illusion.'

Given his public defence of Israel, the abuse he received for it (in July 1967 even in a letter published in the *Church Times*), and his uncomplimentary judgement on Islam, is it any wonder that he was worried in 1972 about Palestinian terrorist activity at Netherton? The police were reassuring, especially when it came to the possibility of letter bombs at Christmas. A few months earlier, in May 1972, they had not, however, let him off a parking-fine; he got quite a ticking-off from the Chief Superintendant of the Dorset and Bournemouth Constabulary: 'The period of time was fifteen minutes. You could have allowed your wife to alight and enter the shop and arrange to pick her up later.' So far as one can tell this was James' sole contravention of the law.

On the future of Israel he was not sanguine; the Middle Eastern Jews there presented problems, as well as an opportunity, he told his Missenden Abbey audience. A unitary state, 'made from the present ingredients', he said in a letter to the *Guardian* of 25 September 1970, was not the answer. Eastern and Western Jews in Israel had 'problems to solve before they became a creative community'; the Arab world was divided; and 'Christian divisions are notorious':

> The wisest way forward is for Jewish and Muslim communities, in both of which a total social and political discipline arises from a religious faith, to allow the Christians real equality, and then, at a stage of tranquillity beyond what we can at present envisage, for there to be a federation – or

confederation – of the different elements into a state which could bring an immense contribution to the growing unity which the world desperately needs.

In 1970 there were still many Christian Palestinians; now there are virtually none; having been forced out by the intense pressure for all Arabs to become Muslims, like so many peoples before them (Jews, Armenians, Palestinians), they are scattered in a diaspora. The ethnically clean nation state, although genetically unreal, and which James so much detested, seems to be the only solution acceptable to contemporary politicians; plurality, whether of peoples, cultures, or religions does not suit them. It does not suit corporate America either: a single-minded (as well as a simple-minded) consumer is what suits capitalism's modern moguls. What has happened to Poland since the seventeenth century is instructive: there has been an inexorable move towards one faith, one people, one culture: since the Counter Reformation one faith; since 1919, but particularly since 1939 (or 1945), one people; since 1989 (or 1945) one culture. It is odd that James did not see the direction in which this wind was blowing. It was because he wanted peoples to live together that he covered his eyes in shame, preferring not to look at a world running mad after slogans like Ireland for the Irish, Germany for the Germans, Turkey for the Turks, Poland for the Poles, Israel for the Jews, and (God Forbid) England for the English.

Good sense seldom prevails in history. History is mostly a matter of the lack of it, Palestine being the perfect illustration of the phenomenon: non-sense *in extremis*. James' utterly sensible scheme for the 'interreligionization' of Jerusalem has stood no chance. The last sentence of his last lecture to the Missenden Abbey weekenders, added in his own hand to Dorothy's typescript, captures his failure to understand the history of his own times: 'It may be a long time before justice is really done, but when it is, it will be rooted firmly in the history this book [*Whose land? A history of the peoples of Palestine*] has described.' The kind of justice James wanted, the justice we all want, is not rooted in history. It lies well outside it.

If James pinned his hopes on history and not on its closure, this does not make him a bad historian. On the contrary, good history is all in the writing and James wrote good history. No more than two or three quotations are needed in order to demonstrate the fact. The first is from a letter of 1 July 1970 to Nicholas Herbert of the Times Education Service:

> When I was writing on the subject [Palestine] twenty-five years ago, I made a point of meeting as many as were alive of the people involved and it is nonsense to pretend that they were all double-dealing politicians with no sense of decency. But it was evident among them all that they regarded the whole field as open, and their language is an expression of good will rather than a very precise commitment to a particular line of action. I asked Amery, for example, what he had in mind when he defined the rights to be safeguarded in the Balfour Declaration as 'civil and religious'. His reply was that he had no more in mind than to choose a euphonious phrase. Even Sykes is worth discussing with his son, Christopher, for he was in no sense a double-dealing and hypocritical politician. But it is difficult for us in 1970 to reconstruct the political atmosphere of 1918. Nor does subsequent Arab history suggest that the planners in 1918 were completely wrong in wondering whether the Arab people should yet evolve for themselves a stable and creative independence.

The non-sense of history does not stem from the stupidity of its protagonists, although one is tempted to believe it derives from their cupidity; generally, politicians like the rest of us reckon to be doing the right thing; unfortunately one man or woman's right thing is not always the next man or woman's: it is this collision between perceived right things that makes history the tale of woe it largely is. When 'accidental' complications also arise, through no fault of individuals or institutions, is it any wonder that the world has always been headed for a dead end? The sort of 'accidental' complication I have in mind is one pointed out by James in his letter to Nicholas Herbert: 'It is one of the unnoticed complications of the whole issue that there is no Moslem stretch of territory corresponding to the Jewish and Christian Holy Land.' This is not to say that all historians have the even-handedness, the integrity, or the charity of a James Parkes; the interpretation of the past is hampered by those who write history with other ideas than those in mind. In August 1969 in a letter to the Rev. Roland de Corneille of

Toronto James discussed one of the more mischievous of those ideas:

> Incidentally, I don't know if it has yet reached Canada, but over here we are going to have a new stick to beat the Israeli with, a debunking of the friendship with the Arabs of T.E. Lawrence. There are splendid quotations to make your flesh creep. The only snag is that Lawrence was an extremely complex personality, and that quotations can be adduced to whack the first lot. And snag number two is that what the Arabs demanded in 1917–19 could not have been granted even by the archangel Michael, and Lawrence knew this as well as anybody.

When historians resort to the tactics of journalism, what hope is there for history? The desire to discover feet of clay, like the allied desire to make a name for oneself, only impedes understanding of the complexities of a past so different from the present that one must tread with excessive wariness. Moreover, the past begins yesterday.

Our closing quotation of this section raises another matter pertinent to James as an historian of the Holy Land. In 1968 the Fellowship of Reconciliation published a pamphlet entitled *Israel and Palestine*. It so upset Dorothy that she resigned from the organization, and so angered James that he wrote a letter of protest to the secretary of the Peace Committee at Friends House:

> It is not merely that the pamphlet is disgracefully ignorant both of recent history and of contemporary facts, but the approach denies everything I have associated with the Society of Friends for nearly fifty years. Men and communities are presented as a set of mechanical marionettes jerked about, with no reference to any moral interest or challenge, without any suggestion of difficulties or uncertainties, by a set of Marxist clichés such as 'imperialism' and 'colonialism' and so on. None of the human values which I had believed to be fundamental to a Friend have any part in this abominable production. It is not that it is 'pro-Arab' or 'pro-Israeli'. It is that neither Arabs nor Israelis are presented as human beings.

Alas, it is a trap easily fallen into: even if one is endeavouring to walk warily: James would undoubtedly have been critical of my use of the cliché of 'capitalism' in this book about him. I hope, nonetheless, to have presented him as a human being and not to have made of him a 'mechanical marionette'.

The third of our themes, theology, will not detain us long, despite the close attention that we must give to James' latter day ideas about reincarnation. About God and Man he remained hopeful to the end. In a lecture published as a Parkes Library Pamphlet in 1979 and entitled *Walk about Zion and go round about her* he wrote of the inevitable movement towards 'a single world civilization'. 'This', he went on, 'can be a spiritual horror, if it means the domination of the mass media in every field':

> But if we can reproduce the symbiosis of the Arab caliphate, it becomes a world of fascinating and inexhaustible richness ... This [would be] to realise the difference between the somewhat pathetic Arabs of today and the Arabs of a thousand years ago in the great centuries of the Ummayyad and Abbasid dynasties of the Arab caliphate. Instead of the stagnation, exclusivity and intolerance of today, Jew, Christian and Muslim, Greek, Persian, Kurd, and Arab brought their contribution to the literary, theological, philosophical, and scientific culture pulsating through the region.

No doubt he romanticized the past and demonised the present: it is something we all tend to do. As to the future, while most of us cannot picture it in any other terms than as an extension of the present, James could look beyond post-modernity ('a spiritual horror ... the domination of the mass media in every field') to an utterly transformed world, where cultural diversity and racial tolerance would suit us all: he was more apocalyptically-minded than he liked to think. It is simply that James did not put his new thoughts into old phrases; the reign of Anti-Christ is not how he described the contemporary scene. He might as well have done. For 'Western man', he wrote in the oddly titled Montefiore Memorial Lecture of 1972, *Religious Experience and the Perils of its Interpretation*, 'the whole sense of living within a secure and stable world has vanished; and in the collapse of the traditional supports of society the failure of religion has certainly been a very important factor':

Today we are confronted with a situation to which, *mutates mutandis*, the only historical parallel is the period of the Dark Ages which followed the fall of the classical civilization. We may not have to fear Norse invaders and their ruthless massacres, but the extreme complexity of our society makes us equally defenceless before the intelligent criminal, the terrorist and the guerrilla.

The guerrillas have departed, if only for a while, the terrorist and the intelligent criminal remain, indeed have gone from strength to strength. In the early twenty-first century intelligent criminals confront terrorists in virtually every corner of the planet. The rest of us, the rest of us who do not consider it all an illusion, look on in appalled fascination and pray that the Messiah will come either for the first or for a second time.

James did not do that. What he did was to put his trust in universities and his hope in the young. The latter is essential; the former is a measure of the central place taken by universities in the radical thinking of the later 1960s and early 1970s. In the final pages of *Voyage of Discoveries* James wrote that his sympathies were 'all with the young ... The future this civilization offers them is intolerable by any aesthetic, psychological or moral standard.' What he called in those pages 'an intolerable dehumanization' has become even more unbearable, and the only question is to what extent are universities to blame for a lamentable state of affairs. In the 1972 Montefiore Lecture James said that 'universities could play an irreplaceable role in the building of the spiritual as well as the scientific foundation of a new age':

> The remedying of both the political and the environmental errors of the past will obviously stretch the intellectual understanding and intuition of the coming generation to the full. It is only in a fully developed university, with all its facilities for research as well as for teaching, that the tools exist for moulding a new society.

It was wishful thinking: instead of moulding society, universities have been moulded by it. Succumbing to the blandishments of big business, universities have exchanged independence for subservience. Not having bothered to learn that in supping with the Devil a phenomenally long spoon is a necessity, they have lost what spiritual influence they once had. Business studies, business management, business ethics, all tell the sorry tale of demoralization; management is an amoral pursuit, there are no ethics in business, and in studying them one necessarily becomes dehumanized. The young have been the unwitting casualties of this movement towards the anti-social. It is clear that a revolt of the intellectuals is required. One has been called for in the United States. Were James still alive he would be the first to enrol.

The reincarnated James Parkes it would have to be. His ideas about the Eternal were enunciated in a sermon he preached in Salisbury Cathedral in November 1967, published in the March–April 1968 issue of *For Health and Healing*, the magazine of the Guild of Health, and in a paper called 'A Contemporary Theology of Survival', published in *Inward Light*, in 1972. There were two starting points. The first was the knowledge that 'we are all one', which, he said, psychology and sociology demonstrated. Had he lived a little longer, he would have been able to add genetics to his short list. The second point of departure were the deaths of his brother and sister in the First World War; in recalling their unfulfilled lives he remembered all the others:

> I think of all my contemporaries at school – less than half of my own Sixth Form survived the First World War. I think of all those who, through economic conditions or the places in which they were born, had but the most limited opportunities for the fulfilment of the simplest human qualities; and it is very natural, in a generation which has seen so much suffering and untimely death, which has become so conscious of the extraordinary limitations of life – for example, of an Indian or a Chinese peasant – that the subject of reincarnation should be constantly at the back of one's thoughts.

Where did these thoughts lead him? They led him to a form of reincarnation that met the problem of 'lives which are incomplete, deformed, frustrated, or destroyed prematurely':

> Its roots lie in the divine society which I believe will be the culmination of the human odyssey, and which I believe has been foreseen in the divine planning, with the same atten-

tion to detail which the Creator has shown in his whole creation. I do not envisage that in this divine society each of us individually will have become a combination of Einstein, Beethoven and St Augustine, but rather that each of us will become perfect members of a body perfect.

His own temporal life, that of 'a middle class Englishman, fortunate in having been able to choose my career, happy in my religious convictions and experience, and in my relations with my contemporaries, happy also in having lived into my seventies', was an unpromisingly 'small foundation on which to build eternal life'. On the other hand, he was a personality, 'with an identifiable aesthetic, moral, and intellectual approach to life; with a mind which approaches a subject in an identifiable manner and possesses identifiable capacities, interests, and limitations; and at the centre of all this a temperament which is also identifiable and analysable'. It was 'this temperamental, intellectual, and spiritual equipment, in the precise form in which I possess it', that had appeared many times before. 'So', he wrote', 'it is conceivable to me that I am part of a greater personality':

> and that that personality has had other lives, with – let us call it – other genes. Thus all the lives are parts of one whole – it is not made up of casual relationships, it is not based on physical relationships, it is a relationship of quality and character. In that way I can think of the survival of my own brother and sister and all my contemporaries whose lives were cut short in the First World War, or those who were cut short in the Second World War, and so on. That they bring all that they knew, all that they built, into a fuller personality of which they are a part.

Unless I have misunderstood the enunciation of these thoughts, there seems to be a problem about WHEN the 'divine society' of 'perfect members of a body perfect' occurs. Is it always in occurrence? If it is, and we enter it after dying a fulfilled and elderly middle-class Englishman, our personality resurfacing in the body of a Chinese woman or a Durham miner, does the 'divine society' then exist 'within' that of (for want of a better phrase) the natural world? If that is so, what of the natural world perfecting itself, James in other places being confident that when we childish creatures have grown up, then and only then will perfectibility be achieved, the responsible Creator having promised us as much. Is, in other words, eternity already in being so that time has no need to come to an end? Whatever the answer, one can surely detect here, albeit in an altered if not a novel form, an age-old view of eternal life, current in the Medieval West before the twelfth century and still sound doctrine in the Eastern Orthodox Churches, of the non-survival of the individual soul.

As had ever been the case, all James' attention was focused on hope. 'What a change it would make', he wrote to a correspondent at the time of the Salisbury sermon, 'if the ordinary decent man or woman was not afraid of dying, but, as the body wore out, looked with joy on the discarding of it':

> For what is the appalling alternative? Medicine will soon assure most of us of a physical centenarianism, brainless, spiritually disintegrating, an appalling cost and curse to all younger people, who, as they contemplate (unwillingly and only by compulsion) a geriatric ward, have to reflect that they too will one day be like that, spiking the chances of their own sons and daughters, not to mention grandchildren, by mere physical hanging onto property, controlling choices, creating burdens whether they would or not, since the state will have to pay out as long as the doctors can keep a 'something' alive, perhaps with a borrowed heart, a borrowed liver, a kidney machine.

It never does to predict what medical research will do next, nor for that matter what the state will do when confronted with too many pensioners living for longer than it can afford to pay them, but with every passing day James' geriatric Dystopia becomes more recognizable. Yet, he seems to be missing his own point about 'personality'. Surely, it is not the old body the 'ordinary decent man or woman' wants to discard, but those mental characteristics that have prevented him or her from being the 'personality' he or she might have been without them. One does not want to become a combination of Epstein, Thelonious Monk, and St Theresa of Avila, but one might want to cease being oneself.

And therein lies the yawning theological gulf between James

Parkes and myself. James, as we can detect from the above, thought his 'personality' worthy of resurrection, apparently without much if any purging. I have less hope, not only about myself but also about mankind in general. William Faulkner writes of one of the characters in *A Fable* 'having to perform forever at inescapable intervals that sort of masturbation about the human race people call hoping', and of another observing that 'We can't be saved now; even He doesn't want us anymore'. James Parkes never gave up hoping; I, on the other hand, rather think God might have.

We have said that no window can be opened into his soul. We have also said that the communion service of the Church of England meant much, possibly everything, to him. In this last phase of his life he continued to conduct communion services in local churches, just as he had always done. 'What matters', he wrote to a London priest, who had greatly displeased him by saying that theology was beyond his limited range, 'is the idea of God which is proclaimed in the local sermon and liturgy.' We can see how much it mattered to James, when in the final decade of his life he was faced with an idea of God not to his liking in the 1970 revision of the 1662 communion service. 'I have just got series 3, and I am shattered!' he wrote in the *News Letter* of the Modern Churchmen's Union. In a series of short papers composed during the first half of the 1970s he took issue with the revised service and in so doing presented his own novel idea of the Eucharist. We will approach that idea by way of others, hardly less novel.

'I am not by nature conservative, let alone reactionary', he began a 1972 piece on 'The 1662 Communion Service', 'but nothing would make me use the proposed alternatives of Series 2 or Series 3. If the service of 1662 were made illegal, then I would celebrate it at home, and offer a "house church" to those who agreed with me.' He said that the 1662 service seemed to him 'as perfect an unfolding of the deepest, truest, and most "contemporary" relationship between Creator and creation' that he could imagine, and that, apart from the time taken in the actual administration of the bread and wine, 'to read *and mean* the whole service takes me about 35 minutes':

> If I had a parish, I would like to train the congregation to add another five minutes for two silences. The first would

be in fellowship with the 'angels and archangels and the whole company of heaven' as they join us in praise of forgiveness and renewal before the prayer of Humble Access. The second would follow the administration and include the Lord's Prayer to be said privately by the communicants.

It is notable that his communion service was what we might call a 'low' one: no choir, no hymns, no chanting. In the same piece James reiterated an antipathy already familiar:

> I dislike the theme one encounters too often 'Dear God, please run the world properly so that I can have a quiet time and get to heaven'. I would like more guidance and sensitivity, on courage and patience in God's service, and less – Oh, *much less* – wailing for mercy. It is now common for my good Dorset neighbours to wail it to a pretty tune in Greek (which they can't pronounce).

No doubt, they would have known better had they had James as their trainer. The theme of 'wailing for mercy' he took up again in a piece published in *The Times* on 30 January 1973. 'Surely', he wrote, 'it is time we gave up thinking of God as an oriental sultan to whom we must wail continuously for mercy? What an intelligent creation should ask of a responsible Creator is patience, courage, sensitivity, faith and understanding.' Yet, all Series 2 offered was 'a litany as an alternative prayer for contemporary humanity'. To all its petitions the only response is "Lord have mercy". We don't propose to do anything about anything. It was the passivity that disgusted him most, but the unspecificity of the prayers also 'got his goat': the woolliness of Anglicanism is one of its most depressing features.

What he also took exception to in other papers of 1973 and again in what might be called a definitive paper of June 1976 was something the 1662 service had also stressed. This was the idea of Jesus as an 'obedient adolescent', 'sent' or 'given' by God:

> This sentimental picture is heightened still further by references to 'an only begotten son' which inevitably invites a parallel to the strain and potential tragedy involved in only sons in human families. *I am absolutely convinced that the whole picture is totally false*, and is accepted only because it

> has always been accepted. If it were presented to any devout and intelligent being for the first time, it would be unhesitatingly rejected as a piece of blasphemous sentimentality ... I am sure that one of the most important emphases which needs to be changed if Christianity is to be the corner-stone of a new age is the New Testament emphasis on Jesus as an only son being sent by a father. I am of a generation which saw so many only sons killed, and heard so many sermons in which the sacrifice of the parents was given a divine pattern, that I have perhaps too much revolted against the picture of the lamb, the adolescent crown prince, as a piece of sentimental delusion. Jesus was, as a man, an adult of thirty, as divine, was responsible for his own actions and decisions. He was not sent: he came.

James appears to have forgotten the Old Testament, at any rate as a source of the idea of sacrifice; 'sentimental delusion' it may have been, but it has its literary if not historical roots, and roots are hard to dig out. Jesus, we are not in the least surprised to learn at this late stage, was 'responsible' for what he did and said; however childlike or adolescent we all are, he was an adult. Does he resemble the thirty-year- old James Parkes perhaps, the James Parkes of 1926, the James Parkes who had been through his 'forty days' in the wilderness during the First World War, who had 'lost' his family, who had recently become the servant of others? In one sense it is absurdly reductive to think so: James Parkes was too considerable a thinker to put himself into his thinking; yet, in another sense, are we not all drawn to see ourselves in the heroes and heroines we have chosen? Do we not 'identify' with them? Is God not made in our own image?

Such speculation must give way to fact: we have arrived at James' idea of what a 'responsible' Jesus thought he was doing at the Last Supper and the institution of the Eucharist. James believed that 'its central explanation' had been lost, 'probably through the setting of the early Gentile church among the mystery religions of the eastern Mediterranean world':

> I am convinced that Jesus was saying to his faithful disciples: 'take this bread and wine as the physical symbols of the spiritual relationship which I still have with you. When

you consecrate it, as I am consecrating it now, it will be for your physical and spiritual strength and healing. But it will be even more. You have henceforth to be the body in which I am present. Take my body as the reminder/evidence that I desire you so to be. Likewise, take my life-blood as the reminder/evidence that I am living with you and in you.'

There is probably nothing novel in this: how can anything new be said about something that has exercised theologians from St Paul's day onwards? It is in the framing of the idea of 'Christ in You' and in the consequences James draws from such a responsibility for Christians that the novelty lies. 'We do not receive the sacraments', he went on, 'only as a profound spiritual preservative, they should also convey a unique physical responsibility.' Note not only the Christian's responsibility, but also and particularly that it is a 'physical' responsibility.

In a letter to the editor of the *The Modern Churchman* of 31 March 1976 he expressed the same idea in an even more remarkable manner: 'Jesus is saying to every generation of his followers "you have to give me my body", "you have to give me my voice", "you have to give me my human power". "Take this bread and wine as the symbol of the actual human body and the life-blood you must provide me".' It is an invigorating and a powerfully enabling proposition: our physicality is offered to Christ who, having given his up for us, has none of his own. What was the relevance of such a proposition to Mrs Jones at 7 The Minnows? There are two similar statements; both are worth quoting. Here is the first. 'The culmination of the Last Supper is, I am sure, to be taken literally. Jesus is saying':

> Because it is necessary and inevitable that this my body of flesh and blood must pass from you, and because it was my physical presence which was again and again essential to what I said and did, I am hereby transmitting the responsibility for the physical presence to you, and through you to all generations. From my position in heaven (to speak metaphorically) I desperately want to help Mrs Jones at 7 The Minnows. I know what she needs. But I cannot knock physically on her door, and that is essential for her. I must rely on you to do it.

The communality of Christianity and the sociability of the Eucharist have seldom been more clearly articulated.

Here is the second quotation. Christ had lived, had made 'use of so temporary a vehicle as a human body ... He had healed [and] he had taught where his physical presence gave him contact':

> That is the underlying significance of the Last Supper. It is the physical presence, and the physical voice and touch, which in the sacrament of the Eucharist he conveys to his followers for all generations by the bread and wine by which his own body had been sustained. Doubtless it is the risen and eternal Christ who seeks to reach his creation through the physical activities of his followers. But it is the incarnate God who inspires us to go to meet the needs of Mrs Jones at 7 The Minnows. For he knows by experience that Mrs Jones needs a physical presence for her healing or comforting.

Whatever one thinks of James' Eucharistic theology, the physicality, or as we might prefer to say the materiality, of Christianity is perfectly adumbrated. Christianity, like Judaism (and no doubt because of it), is a religion of doing.

One is bound to wonder what James made of the 'Sharing of the Kiss of Peace', given once more a central place in the Communion service by the revisions of 1970. As the ritual asserts the essentiality of 'the physical voice and touch', it is specifically about Mrs Jones of 7 The Minnows, Mrs Jones being the very lady in the neighbouring pew with whom one shares the kiss of peace.

It is time to take leave of this extraordinary, sometimes extraordinarily infuriating man. We should not do so with his and Dorothy's disappointment at the failure of the Parkes Library to turn into the Parkes Institute, or the Parkes Centre as it has now become. 'Our greatest disappointment', Dorothy wrote in 1974, 'has been the complete lack of interest of the theological faculty in what we are doing. Howard Root does not answer letters, and nobody at Southampton has any inkling of the possibilities, and the field of work, James is pioneering in.' Disappointment comes both naturally and inevitably to the old. By 1974 also, the universities were changing; theology was becoming a subject few staff or students cared about. It was on the brink of being replaced by 'vocational' subjects, suitable for a 'vocational' age: media studies, cookery, nursing, dress design, golf course management. By 1978, when James, having been hospitalized for a time, returned to Iwerne 'very alert ... but physically frail' and incapable 'of any sustained effort', university departments of theology had almost everywhere disappeared. After 1979 James did not, it seems, write anything more. He died in 1981. He left an estate of just over £25,000. In a brief last will of 4 May 1978, he bequeathed it all to Dorothy, who survived him. Not much else did. He was already being forgotten while he was still alive; when he was dead what was there for a forgetful age to remember?

Coda: James Parkes and the Shoah

For the *Scotsman* of 24 May 1961 James wrote a remarkable piece entitled 'The mentality of persecutor and persecuted'. Its first two paragraphs demand to be quoted in full:

> I look out across my roses, now bursting into flower, past the ordered ranks of iris, over the hills green with new corn, to the distances of the fens and the sparse towers of Cambridge. I am fortunate that everything in my view is man-made, normally and authentically man-made, from the new ranges of colour in my roses and iris, to the elaborate draining of the fens – the work of many centuries – the clearing of the hills, and the seed corn, selected with a world-wide skill and patience.
>
> For it balances the evidence that comes to me daily from the Eichmann trial in Jerusalem which is also man-made. It is not the product of national insanity or the drugs of future warfare. And it is 'normal' in the sense that the murderers, spectators and victims are nothing other than the men, women and children, families and neighbours, such as I would meet if I walked down my village street. Ordinary men did and watched these things and went home to supper, played with their children, listened to music, while their victims went to death.

No one else in 1961 would have been capable of writing like that, of making the direct connection between Barley and Auschwitz. Is this where Christopher Browning got the phrase 'ordinary men', a phrase he has made famous? Forty years after the Eichmann trial everyone has become a know-all about the Shoah. Very few of us knew anything at all about it in 1961.

James went on in the essay to discuss a variety of other issues thrown up by the trial, most of which have been discussed by Tony Kushner in a paper called 'James Parkes and the Holocaust': this appeared in *Remembering for the Future: The Holocaust in an Age of Genocide*, edited by John Roth and others and published in 2001. The paper is in part a response to another, 'The Domestication of Violence: Forging a Collective Memory of the Holocaust in Britain, 1945–6', by Dan Stone, published in *Patterns of Prejudice* in 1999. I do not intend to rehearse here their differences about the response of James to the news of the Final Solution as it became publicly known in Britain in the latter part of 1942, and about the recognition he gave in his subsequent writing to the importance of the catastrophe that had overwhelmed European Jewry. That I think will be made sufficiently clear in all that follows. Nonetheless: three markers ought to be placed at the outset.

First, James found the topic almost unbearable. As we have noted before, he wrote to Bill Simpson in May 1964:

> There are two subjects on which I admit I cannot talk and argue. I can only write, because I care about them so much that I break down and weep. One is the holocaust and the other is the complete indifference of the Christian world to the real roots of Israel and its real justification, and, indeed, necessity.

Secondly, we need always to have in mind, as the quotation serves to remind us, that James did not dwell on the past, or, for that matter the present; he looked always to the future; in so doing he was more positive about mankind than almost anyone else who has written about the Shoah. His sanguinity, as we have called it in the body of the book, had a sound philosophical basis, which we should always have in mind when pondering the question of what might be termed James' humility regarding the Shoah. He expressed this philosophy in a letter to Dr Beate Isserlin of 3 May 1967: 'If you believe that religion is the most important thing in life, then you cannot be surprised at awful things happening where there is no religious foundation of existence.' So anti-humanistic a position seems uncharacteristic of him; of the younger James it might have been, but the Shoah had undermined his humanism. This is evident in the *Scotsman* piece. 'The evidence', he wrote, has given me a new respect for my Christian forefathers.' They had:

continuously proclaimed the sinfulness of man and his need for grace and redemption. This thing is in us as human beings; and it can dominate and lead us into the acts of cruelty and obscenity which have reduced men and women throughout the world to tears ... If I need to lavish the superlatives of horror on the story I only indulge in escapism by separating myself artificially from those who did such things, or watched them done unmoved. But to say 'these but for the grace of God were my acts' may seem an unpleasant kind of inverted bravado, as though I could not possibly mean it. Yet it is nearer the truth than either dissociation or the concentration of hatred on the Germans.

He was, in other words, intent on seeing Nazi murderers and torturers as 'civilized' like himself. Killing in the twentieth century was not 'as difficult as it used to be'; men and women, for a variety of reasons, were more capable of it. James was of course wrong: he would not have killed Jews nor stood by while they were being killed. He was religious; the murderers and torturers were not. That is where he was right: in an environment 'where there was no religious foundation of existence', as was the case in Nazi Germany, atrocity becomes an everyday feature of life. The Shoah made clear to James, as never before, the absolute necessity for 'a religious foundation of existence', and because God was a responsible God he would in due time see that his creation arrived at such a foundation. Hence James was sanguine, even we might say, in the face of the evidence.

Thirdly, there is what I have called in the previous paragraph his humility in the face of the Shoah. Humility is not a contemporary virtue; it is certainly not practised by many of those who study the Shoah. As we have seen, James did not want to distance himself from the murderers and torturers. On the other hand, he had no wish to indulge in a voyeuristic recital of the horrors perpetrated on the victims. As early as May 1940 he wrote to a Mr Sargent that he looked forward to the end of the war when 'the emphasis will, I hope, shift from the bestialities of Nazi antisemitism to the realities of the Jewish problem, in which race plays no part'. It was those 'bestialities' that offended him so deeply. I can remember the time when the debate about using photographs of atrocities was a real one. Nowadays these obscene pictures are a commonplace in glossy brochures, on the covers of *Holocaust and*

Genocide Studies, on the walls of Holocaust Museums. They are a measure of our culture's subservience to the pornography of the advertisement. James would have detested such showmanship: the victims have become freaks at a circus and we who stand and stare have become no better than bystanders after the fact. Perhaps we might gloss James' humility: it was reticence before the fact of suffering. How often in current writing do we come across the phrase 'unimaginable suffering' only to have it 'imaged' in the next chapter, the next paragraph, the next sentence? James would have none of this. It was not that nonsense about being silent after Auschwitz that we should think of in relation to his reticence; what he wanted to avoid was a garrulous approach to the Shoah, the one that we have now.

There is another dimension to his reticence. Tony Kushner has used the striking phrase 'moral masturbation' for what so many Holocaust scholars go in for: they get off on the Shoah. He touches a nerve here, the one that connects violence to sex. But without venturing into those infested waters, there is still the matter of secular or anti-religious scholars using the Shoah as a moral fix, as I seem to remember David Cesarani once calling it. If they are also into Trauma Theory what a field day they have in Holocaust Studies. None of this crossed the mind of James Parkes. What did, was the absolute need to honour the victims. At the least hint of their being 'used' one should sound the retreat.

So much is by way of introduction. The other observations to be made about James Parkes and the Shoah are ones that by this time we are likely to have anticipated. He was, for example, thoroughly aware from the start of what was going on. 'The Fate of the Jews' appeared in the *Christian News-Letter* of 6 December 1939. It demonstrates how well informed James was about German plans for the resettlement of peoples in Eastern Europe, about the 'Lublin Reserve', about the deportations of Jews that had already taken place, and about the 'horrible brutality' of the Germans towards both Jews and Poles in the weeks immediately after the invasion of Poland. Because he had made it his business to be properly informed about the treatment of Jews in Germany before 1939, what was done by Germans to Jews in Poland hardly came as a surprise. 'The Catastrophe in Germany', chapter VIII of his *Jewish Problem in the Modern World*, published in 1939, is by far the best account of its subject written by a contemporary:

> The deepest tragedy of the present persecution in Germany is that it is carried through by the deliberate actions of tens of thousands of normal individuals, schoolmasters, judges, doctors, professors, business-men, local authorities, without question and without protest, on the instructions of the Government or the Party; and, in so far as they are aware of what is happening, it is accepted as right and proper, as natural and inevitable by the great bulk of the population ... Conventional explanations, referring to 'gangster rule', 'sadistic leaders', 'economic jealousy', are not enough to account for so extraordinary a situation.

Because he had known what had happened in Nazi Germany before 1939, and knew what was happening in Nazi-occupied Poland in 1939, he was enabled to know with greater certainty than most what was going to happen in a German-dominated Europe. In the December 1939 piece, for instance, he warned of the tragedy that lay ahead for the Jews in the newly acquired Hungarian territory of Ruthenia, while as for the resettlement policies of Himmler in Poland, 'they', he wrote, ' are not intended to lead to anything but the extermination of the Jews [and] the possession of their property'. Here was Aktion Reinhard prefigured. Needless to say, he kept abreast of events after 1939: witness 'The German Treatment of the Jews', published in 1954 by the Royal Institute of International Affairs in volume IV of their *Survey of International Affairs, 1939–1945*, an essay that Tony Kushner has called 'remarkably well-informed'. There was little that escaped James' attention during the war years. He took the *Times* correspondent to task in March 1942, for example, for his comment on the sinking of the *Struma*: that if the government allowed Jewish refugees into Palestine it would be playing Hitler's game by bringing about a reduction in the number of Jews in the countries occupied by him. Two years later, in March 1944, Tom Driberg responded to a letter of enquiry from James concerning antisemitism in the Polish army stationed in Britain by informing him that 200 (presumably Jewish) men had been transferred into the British Army. Who else would have bothered to enquire about so 'peripheral' a matter?

James could always be bothered, and he could always be sufficiently bothered to act. There is no need in a book of this nature to go over old ground: what James called the British government's 'Hush-hush' attitude to Jews, Jewish refugees, and the Shoah itself, was one decried by him, Eleanor Rathbone, and a handful of others. They did all they could to alter it. James, it has to be said, was enough of an Englishman to believe in a 'Jewish Problem' in Britain and to write a paper with that title in the *Modern Churchman* of 15 December 1943. Tony Kushner has called such an attitude 'disturbing'. Yet, whatever concessions James made to public opinion about Jews in the Black Market and Jewish evacuees from London in the English provinces, Britain was not Poland, there was 'none of what Jabotinsky brilliantly called "the antisemitism of facts"': any Jewish problem there was in Britain was a 'Christian problem'. A Christian Englishman's problem it has to be said. Here is James writing to Walter Stuart Best in February 1942:

> I do see something of the problem in the Letchworth train as Royston is a couple of stations beyond Letchworth. It is certainly true you hear a good deal of broken English, and you see a good many painted Jewesses and bearded Jews, and it is probably true to say that there are enough of them to be noticeable to the ordinary public and that the criticism they would attract would not be favourable, but I have never seen anything quite as gross as Mallon describes in the 'Spectator'.

An early twenty-first century reader might indeed find this 'disturbing', but would not a traveller on the Letchworth train in the middle of a world war, an epic struggle that was still far from won, have found 'a good deal of broken English' even more so? We are far more multi-cultural these days. As for those 'painted Jewesses and bearded Jews', what are we to say of them? I suppose that they were an unusual sight on a suburban train filled with suited city clerks and their unadorned middle-class wives and daughters. There would also have been plenty of young men and women in uniform travelling in March 1942. A residue of disturbance, nonetheless, remains: for instance, how can you tell a painted Jewess from a painted Christianess? Even if cosmetics could only be had on the Black Market, did not Christianesses also seek them out? James has more to say about the Black Market in the second paragraph of his letter to Mr Best:

> The thing that worries me about the Jewish question is the special official policy of 'Hush-hush!' At bottom there is no mystery about the Jews and antisemitism flourishes on misrepresentation in a general atmosphere of silence. It is true that there is a painfully high proportion of Jews in the secondary level of Black Marketing, but I believe that the heads of the Black Market are largely, if not exclusively, non-Jews and I doubt whether the Black Market, abhorrent as it is, has anything like the sinister national effect of the apparently respectable group of the 'controllers' of their own industries who sit tight on our production effort, in whose ranks there is not a single Jew.

Was there a 'painfully high proportion of Jews in the secondary level of Black Marketing'? How did James know? Had he seen statistics? Were there any to see?

Infinitely more important than his views on Jews in the Black Market were his regrets that there was 'no Jewish army', or that there had been no appointment of a 'Minister, a Parliamentary Secretary, or whatever the right title might be, for Jewish affairs'. This was a theme that occupied him in the early months of 1942. He wrote to William Temple about it as well as to the government. William Temple's first feeling was 'one of despair with regard to the possibility of any such action'; his feeling, given the pusillanimous stance of the government, turned out to be the appropriate one. Meanwhile, James persevered. Was he perhaps the man for the job? He wrote to Temple on 31 January:

> In a way the suggestion that I, or someone like me, should be put into the House of Lords is fantastic and absurd, but if we consider the House of Lords as, in fact, an admirable but only half-carried-out Senate, the suggestion is sensible, since that is the place where a person with expert knowledge, but without party affiliations or political ambitions, should be able to question the Government and express his views.

Temple, having raised the matter in London, had found 'the atmosphere quite as chilly as I expected'. James replied on 19 February:

> I am dismayed by finding myself in the fantastic position of

not seeing an alternative to someone like myself suddenly advanced to political eminence. At present, my opposite number in Chatham House at Oxford is, I think, consulted on matters concerning the Jews. They don't come to me, because I do not belong to the <u>war</u> section, but to the peace section, so that all the information about the present position is quite strictly withheld from me. I have accepted this, because if I try to muscle in I should have to pay the price of complete surrender of my liberty to say and write what I like. But though Beeley is an excellent man, there is all the difference between someone who wishes not to be unfair to the Jews and someone who really loves them and, however much he may disagree with what they want, will do everything to understand why they want it.

The non-influential James Parkes has been discussed above; there is no need to go over old ground again, except to restate the obvious: it would have been more helpful to the Jews he loved had his voice been one the government felt itself obliged to heed. As it was, it could pay him no notice whatever. In March he wrote a paper on 'Advantages and Disadvantages of a Policy of Silence on the Jewish Question' and sent it to Kenneth Grubb at the Ministry of Information. 'At bottom', the paper concluded, 'the Jews are a sphinx without a secret, and the Jewish question brought into the open light of day, no more difficult than many of the other questions which call for decision before a New Order can be established.' Although the term 'New Order' seems an ill-chosen phrase, the remainder of the paper was on target, although James had lowered his sights from a Minster for Jewish affairs to an Anglo-American Government Commission. Mr Grubb dispatched a grubby reply in bureaucratic idiom: he found it 'difficult to be optimistic about this matter ... it is impossible for me to commit myself to any definite statement of view on the matter'.

James was most active, as we have come to expect, in relation to the future: what should and could be done for the remnants of European Jewry when the war was won? The future was Palestine. That was the crux of two papers he wrote in 1943 and 1944: 'My Solution of the Jewish Question' and 'The Future of the Jews'. En route to the crux James made a number of interesting observations about the Shoah; these we will deal with in a moment. Palestine had long been on his mind. In a letter to Thomas Masaryk of 18 September 1941 he made clear his preference:

> I enclose the notes of what I want to say about the Jews in Eastern Europe in a speech at the end of October. For the resettlement of Jews outside Europe I put forward the idea that Palestine is the only intelligent place ... Is what I say about Europe sense? Czechoslovakia is a good test, for two reasons. Czechoslovakia had all the assets in decency and experience to accept her minorities, and did so. Czechs therefore have the right to protest against my conclusions being generally valid. But if the Czechs say that my conclusions are good, and that it is no question of better Minority Treaties, but of separating nationality questions altogether from social and economic questions, then the argument applies all the more to Poland, Romania etc.

In May and June of the following year, after the failure of his Minister for the Jews idea, he saw Harold Butler, the Minister of Information, and the American ambassador; under discussion were 'the position of the Jews after the war' and Palestine. Did they listen? He is likely to have told them what he wrote in 'The Future of the Jews': 'We must ultimately face the issue that we have got to take a straight political decision about the future of Palestine.' A 'straight political decision' is a fanciful thought.

In the paper he put his finger unerringly on one of the difficulties surviving East European Jews would encounter. 'We have to consider', he wrote, 'whether such Jews as survive will wish to remain in Eastern Europe at all':

> It is true that some of them will have grateful memories of acts of friendship from their neighbours. But will these be enough to counter the general memories which will be forever associated with these last appalling years? What of the many neighbours whom they would have to meet day by day, who stood by and watched their sufferings, who perhaps were quite prepared to share the spoil and are still enjoying properties and positions once in Jewish hands? The Jews are an extraordinarily optimistic people, ever concerned with future opportunities rather than with past

regrets. But will even Jewish optimism be able to rebuild on such a past? We may be faced with a mass desire for emigration ... It is very likely that it will be the problem of resettlement rather than rehabilitation that will press most urgently for solution in the coming years.

Never has the immediate future been more presciently foretold. In 'My Solution of the Jewish Question' he was equally acute about what was to be expected:

There will inevitably be a good deal of resettlement after the war – I imagine no people, for example, will want a German minority – and it does seem not fantastic that there may also need to be some shifting of populations in the Arab world. I do not know whether anything will be done to compensate the Jews of Germany and occupied Europe for the loss of the immense wealth Hitler has stolen from them. It clearly cannot be returned to individuals ...

The Great Plunder: was there any other Christian who in 1943 saw the Shoah with that clarity of vision? I suspect not.

If the reader still doubts what Tony Kushner has termed the 'frighteningly realistic' response of James Parkes to the Shoah she should read the impassioned essay he wrote in January 1943, 'The Massacre of the Jews: Future Vengeance or Present Help'. How would I have reacted to a discovery that the Final Solution was real? How would she have responded to the British government's policy of 'Do Nothing Now' as proclaimed by Anthony Eden in the parliamentary debate of 17 December 1942? Would we have shed a few tears, wiped our eyes, and got on with what we were doing, told one another that it was a terrible business, that the Nazis were capable of anything, that Anthony Eden had been his usually impressive self, that the government's declaration of vengeance after the war was all that could realistically be expected? It is not the fact that most of us do not care to look squarely at the 'frighteningly realistic' that distinguishes us from James Parkes, it is that we turn our backs, shrug our shoulders, and telling each other that we can do nothing because nothing can be done, do nothing. James always wanted to do all he could, because he always believed something could be done. Just as God was always doing something about his Creation, the British government could do something about the Shoah. Having roundly condemned the contemptible behaviour of the Foreign Secretary in the House of Commons, James in the heat of his anger and frustration at the antisemitism of the government broke into underlining and capitalization:

> Not openly in parliament, but privately in discussion with deputations or individuals, high officials have betrayed the reason for this attitude. It is not a pleasant one for British honour. It is that these people are not regarded just as men or women, not even as children, but as <u>Jews</u>. It is said that if we offered unlimited asylum in our own country or the territories we control, it might lead to a dangerous increase of antisemitism. It is even said – as though the idea should terrify instead of rejoicing us – that Hitler might take our word, and send us all the Jews still alive in Europe, several million of them.
>
> *There is only one answer for men who still believe there is any nobility in the cause for which we are fighting*: WE WILL RECEIVE THEM. AND IF THERE REALLY BE THREE MILLION OF THEM WE WILL THANK GOD THAT WE HAVE BEEN ABLE TO SAVE SO MANY FROM HITLER'S CLUTCHES. AND IF THERE BE A JEWISH PROBLEM TO SOLVE WE WILL SOLVE IT AS CIVILIZED MEN NOT AS MURDERERS. OUR HONOUR AND SINCERITY ARE AT STAKE AS MUCH AS THE LIVES OF MILLIONS OF THE JEWISH PEOPLE.

It was an appeal that fell on stony ground. But the stoniness of the ground is another story. Can one man save the soul of a nation? Can one woman? If so, James Parkes and Eleanor Rathbone saved the soul of Britain during that nation's darkest hour.

The man who loved Jews: has not that been said of Oskar Schindler? If it has not been said of Schindler, it has of some other righteous gentile. James has to be one of them; but he would have been the first to say that there had been all too few. The Shoah, that 'incomparable crime', was for him a Christian crime. We do not have to believe that it was a straight path, 'which goes right back from Hitler's death camps to the denunciations of the early Church' to agree with him. If Christians had failed Jews in the Shoah, the Christian Churches had failed Christians as well as Jews:

> Surely as a theologian one can only say that the pathetic futility of the Churches in the face of the contemporary moral tragedy of the world is the direct consequence of their failures – repeated failures – to meet and answer the deepest needs of the Age. It is just because the leaders of the Churches, being prudent and workaday, would not face the fact that opposition to Hitler, within or outside Germany, would probably have led to a million martyrs as well as the burning and bombing of every cathedral and ecclesiastical establishment the Nazis could reach, that six million Jews and probably twice that number of Russians, Ukrainians, Greeks, Yugoslavs, Dutchmen, Frenchmen and others perished.

This uncompromising statement James made to Bill Simpson in May 1963. If he loved Jews, what he hated was moral cowardice. What he demanded of the leaders of the Churches was a spiritual strength they did not have. Preoccupied as much with safeguarding ecclesiastical property and clerical *dignitas* as they were with the bogey of Bolshevism, almost every bishop, including the Bishop of Rome, had been an appeaser. It was a great pity, as James indicated to Bill Simpson, that only synagogues had burned in Germany. Had churches burned there in the 1930s, synagogues might not have done in Poland and Russia in the 1940s, and there may have been many more righteous gentiles throughout Europe

Yet, was it only churchmen who were spiritual weaklings? For James the Shoah was a watershed in the history of Europe: it was the ultimate test for Christian Europeans and it found them wanting. Not only that, it was a failure which most of them had not noticed, indeed the test itself was one they had not even been aware they were taking. In another letter to Bill Simpson also in May 1963, he asked whether succeeding generations would 'face the facts as we know them ... and gain a spiritual strength which we lacked'? Would the impact of the Shoah be 'spiritually felt' in generations to come? Were James Parkes able to see us now, what would be his answer?

Index

Please note that references to J. P. stand for James Parkes

Abelard, 71, 122, 123
Acland, Sir Richard, 27, 155, 157, 160, 162
Adams, C. F., 53
Adams, Luther, 204
Addenbrooke's Hospital, 213–14, 218
'Advanced Institute of Learning', 223
'Advantages and Disadvantages of a Policy of Silence on the Jewish Question' (J. Parkes), 298
Africa, 240, 241
Agobard of Lyons, 120
Allah, 69
American Association of Theological Schools, 264
'An Economic Trinitarianism', 66, 67, 70
An Enemy of the People: Antisemitism (J. Parkes), 236
Anglican Communion Service, 74
Anglican Pacifist Fellowship, 150
Anglo-Israel Association, 267
Anschluss (1938), 133
Anselm, 122–3
anti-Arabism, 206, 207
anti-Christianism, 93
anti-Israelism, 6–7, 204, 205
'Antisemitic riots in the Universities' (J. Parkes), 87–8
antisemitism, x–xii; Anti-Israelism and, 6–7, 204, 205; anti-Semitism and, 80; appearance of antisemites, 4–5; and detective fiction, 7; development, 115; in England, 6, 8; Holy Ghost, sin against, 80; J. P. on, 13, 54, 79, 80–1, 88–90, 91, 94, 102, 114, 120–1, 145, 258; 'natural' nature of hatred of Jews, 121–2; as racism, 132; respectability issues, 6, 7; roots, 88, 120
Antisemitism and the Christian Mind (A. Davies), 264
'Antisemitism in the East End' (J. Parkes), 126–7
Antisemitism and the Foundations of Christianity (A. Davies), 263
Antisemitism (J. Parkes), 236
Appleton, George, 264
Aquinas, Thomas, 19
Arab–Israeli war (1948), 200

architecture (special subject at Oxford), 50
Aristotle, 156
Armstrong, Karen, 18
Army Book 439, 37
Aronsfield, Caesar, 268
Arthur Davis Trust, 217
Artists' Rifles, J. P. as private in, 37
Arts and Humanities Board, xv
Ashbrook, Herbert, 194
Asquith, Herbert, 168
Astor, David, 227, 228
Athenaeum, dining at, 200, 201, 259
Auden, W. H., 244
August 1914 (A. Solzhenitsyn), 36
Auschwitz, xi, 15, 291
A Village in Wartime (J. Parkes), 108

Baeck, Leo, 210, 233
Bailey, Gerald, 180, 181
Baldwin, Stanley, 4, 168
Balfour Declaration, 186
bankers, Jews as, 116, 117, 125
Barker, Aldus (nephew of J. P.), 231, 232
Barker, Andrew (nephew of J. P.), 232
Barker, Edwin, 232
Barker, Nancy, 232
Barley (Cambridgeshire village), x; gardening skills of J. P., 25; house at, 112; final years at (1959–64) 211–44; 'open house' policy, 10; post-war decade, 189–210; Rectory at, 149, 195; Second World War, prior to, 106–44; 'tripod', 189, 226; in wartime (1939-45), 145–88
Barth, Karl, 15, 55, 72, 75, 97, 154, 163; J. P. on, 68, 73, 77, 78, 79–80, 168; theology of, 76–7
Battle of Messines, 40
Bavaria, conference at (1924), 56
Becker, Hans, 56, 60
Beck, Fritz, 106
Bell, Annie Katherine (*later* Parkes) (J. P.'s mother), 21, 22, 24, 29
Bell, George, 133, 134
Bell, Margaret, 9
Bentwich, Norman, xvi, xviii, 9; correspondence with J. P., 148–9
Benvenisti, Meron, 208

Berry, Reverend Arthur, 194
Best, Walter Stuart, 296
Betjeman, John, 150
'Bible in Public Worship', 265
Bierville conference (1928), 82
biographers/biography, 2–3, 44, 74
Birmingham City Museum, brass candlesticks given to, 10
bishops, J. P.'s dislike of, 149, 196–7
'Black Book', 33
Black and Tans, 274
Bland, Beres, 247
Blinken, Maurice, 194
Bloch, Marc, 48
Blumenkranz, Bernhard, 246
Board of Deputies, 128, 129
Bowden, John, 77
Brade, Miss (of Kurrajong, New South Wales), 13
Brants, Jean, 55
Braybrooke, Marcus, xvii
Brewster, Reverend David, 275
Brickner, Rabbi Balfour, 271
British Army, 37
British Committee of European Student Relief, 56
British Museum, 50, 110
Brouard, Clem, 255, 256
Browning, Christopher, 291
Brown, Wilfred, 157
Bryanston School, lecture at, 249
Bryce-Salomons, Mrs, 213
Brzoska, Karol, 257, 258, 259
Buchenwald, 179, 180
Bunting, Madeleine, viii
Burckhardt, Jacob, 98
Burton, Montague, 145
Büsing, Pastor, 133, 134
Butler, Harold, 299
Byzantine culture, 99

Cambridge Review, 170, 172
Cambridge University: degree at, 137; J. P.'s connections, x; Library, 103; St John's College *see* St John's College, Cambridge; Sermon (1941), 147, 170, 172, 173, 174
Cam, Helen, 137
Campbell, Archie (A. K. C.), 34
Canadian Conference of Christians and Jews, 154
capitalism, 163; history, 117–18
Carvalho, Robert, 227–8
CCJ (Council of Christians and Jews), formation, xvii, 145
Chamberlain, Neville, 4, 92–3, 168
Chandler, Andrew, 134
Channel Islands, viii, 20; scholarships, 35, *see also* Guernsey (birthplace of J. P.)

Charing Cross Hospital, 199
China Campaign Committee, 150
Christian aid, 134
Christian Approach to the Jew, committee on, 93
Christian Approach to Jews (C. Singer), 98
Christian Council for Refugees from Nazi Germany, 182; Dorothy Parkes as Secretary of Press and Publicity Committee, 151
Christianity: communality of, 289; conversion of Jewish people to, 93; conversion of J. P. to (1915), 26; Crucifixion, 44; failure of, J. P. on, 17–18, 68; Jesus Christ, 67–8, 70, 71; and Judaism, 14–15; origins, antisemitism linked to, 88; Orthodox, 90; Resurrection, 44, *see also* Church, the; Jesus Christ; Judaism
Christianity, Jewish History and Antisemitism (Parkes Library Pamphlet 22), 262, 263
'Christianity and Jewry' lecture, St Mary Woolnoth church (1943), 183–4
Christian–Jewish relations *see* Jewish–Christian relations
'Christian Liturgy and Antisemitism', 264
Christian News-Letter, 162, 294
Christmas Circular Letter (1954), 13
Chrysostom, John, 168
Church of England, vii–viii, 134; Committee for 'Non-Aryan' Christians, 133
Church, the, 114, 115–16, 165–6; on capitalism, 118; God, language of, 166–7
Civilization of the Renaissance (J. Burckhardt), 99
classics, reading of, 27, 28, 50
Clayesmore Preparatory School, 255, 267
Cluny, Musée, 213
Cohen, Mortimer, 262
Cohn, Norman, 227, 238, 246
Cold War, 52
Common Sense about Religion (J. Parkes), 174, 231, 236
Common Wealth Party, 24, 155, 158; J. P. on, 27, 79, 114; spirituality, 157, 159
Communion Services, 74, 197; revision (1973), 265
conciliabulum, synagogue as, 120
conferences: Bavaria (1924), 56; Bierville (1928–29), 83; Gex (1925), 56; Glion (1929), 75–6; Hopovo (1925), 56; J. P. at, 56–60; Nyon (1931), 94; Oberaegeri (1925), 56, 81; Prussia (1924), 56; student, 56, 57; Swanwick (Derbyshire), 56; Toc H (1945), 190; Warsaw (1924), 56
Conflict of Church and Synagogue (J. Parkes), 63, 85, 94–5, 96, 98, 99, 103, 114, 117, 137, 144, 173; publication, 216

Constantine, laws of, 120
'Contemporary Theology of Survival', 282
Conway, John, 75
cooperative (Parkes' household), 24–5
Council of Christians and Jews *see* CCJ (Council of Christians and Jews)
crafts, exclusion of Jews from, 116–17
Crocker, Ena, 153, 154
Cross, Christ on, 67–8
crucifixion, 123
Crucifixion of the Jews (F. Littell), 264
Cru, Hélène, 56
Cuddesdon Theological College, vii
culture, J. P.'s lack of interest in, 107–8, 109

Dahl, Murdoch, 69
Daily Telegraph, 165
Dante, 116
Darke, Miss, 22
Daube, David, 226
Davies, Alan, 263, 264
Davies, W. D., 14
Dead Sea Scrolls, 13
de Corneille, Roland, 279
de Coudenhove, Baronne, 34
de Groot, Ralph, 15
Deir Yasin Massacre, 188
'Demobilization' (J. Parkes), 53
detective fiction, and antisemitism, 7
Dewdney, Christina, 255
dialectical theology, 76
Dick Sheppard Memorial Club, 150–1
Diocese of Kaffraria, 239
Disgrace Abounding (D. Reed), 123, 124, 132
doctrine of the Trinity, 66
Dodkin, Kenneth, 112, 146
Domesday Book and Beyond (F. W. Maitland), 99
'Domestication of Violence: Forging a Collective Memory of the Holocaust in Britain, 1945–6' (D. Stone), 292
Domus Conversorum, 119
Dorset, J. P. at, 104
Driberg, Tom, 295
Dugmore, Clifford, 136
Dupuytren's contraction, 43

early Christian art (Special Subject at Oxford), 50
East End, J. P.'s visit to, 126
ecumenicalism, 74, 90; Ecumenical Movement, 162
Eden, Sir Anthony, 140, 300
Edgar, Reverend Leslie, 11
Edward I, King of England, 119
Eichmann trial, 291

'Eights Week Invitations' (J. Parkes), 53
Eisendrath, Rabbi Maurice, 213, 214, 215, 216–17, 219
Eisendrath, Rosa, 213, 214
Eisene Front (Swiss Fascist Party), 104
Eliot, T. S., 72, 244
Elizabeth College, Guernsey, 20, 23; library, 29–30; Lower School, 25; Records of War, 53
Emergence of the Jewish Problem, 1878–1939 (J. Parkes), 189
Emerson, Guy, 146
End of an exile: Israel, the Jews and the gentile world (J. Parkes), 189
Enemy of the People: antisemitism (J. Parkes), 189
England, antisemitism in, 6, 8
England's Jewish Solution, 100
Enlightenment, 70
Epistle readings, 98
Erasmus, 156
Eschelbacher, Hermann, 112, 146
Eschelbacher, Rabbi of Düsseldorf, 134
eucharist, 68, 289
Everett, Robert, 9
extermination camps, 201, *see also* Auschwitz; Buchenwald

Fairfield, Zoë, 55
Faith and Fratricide (R. Ruether), 264
Fascism, 127
'Fate of the European Jews and the Palestinian Arabs, A.D. 1933–48' (P. Toynbee), 200–1, 202
Feiwel, T. R., 123–4, 132
Fellowship of Reconciliation, 279
Fermor, Patrick Leigh, 63
festschrift, 250
'Final Solution', xviii, 75, 86, 92, 140, 178, 180, 263, 292
financial problems, 213, 224; annual expenditure, 217–18; Sieff as benefactor to Parkes, 108, 110, 112, 113, 147, 212, 215, 223, 225, 227
'First Lord de Saumarez and his diplomatic work in the Baltic, 1808–1813', 53
First World War, 92; Flanders, 48; J. P. as soldier *see* soldier, J. P. as
Florensky, Pavel, 71, 72, 73
'Fordism', 117–18
For Health and Healing (Guild of Health), 282
Fort Pitt (Chatham), hospitalisation at, 43
Foundations of Judaism and Christianity (J. Parkes), 98
Freud, Sigmund, 113, 266
Freud's Moses (Y. H. Yerushalmi), 2
fundamentalism, religious, 206, 267

Gabriel, Sister Louis, 250
Garbett, Cyril, 165, 170, 171, 172, 173
gardener, J. P. as, 20, 25, 108, 109
Gardiner, Grace, 147–8
Gardiner, John Rutherford (Rector of Barley), 144, 147, 148, 195
gas officer, J. P. as, 41, 42–3, 45
Gas School, Sittingbourne, 42, 102
General Strike (1926), 57
Geneva: 'Incident', 105, 106, 153, 154; J. P. in (1928–35), 10, 54, 62, 65, 81, 82, 100, 104; Rue Crespin in, 232
Gerald Road affair, 160
German Security Police, 153
'German Treatment of the Jews' (Royal Institute of International Affairs), 295
Germany: antisemitism in, 7; Jewish community in/Jewish problem, 75, 91–2, 133; Munich, 130, 131; racial purity, idea of, 86
Geschichte der Juden (H. Graetz), 84
Gex: conference at (1925), 56; 'morning mediations' at (1928), 74; theology and, 76
Gilbert, Martin, 250
Gladstone, William Ewart, 168
Glaister, Norman, 216
Glion conference (1929), 75–6
globalization, 17
God: doctrines of, 66–7, 69–70; J. P. on, 27–8, 31, 32, 67, 68, 69, 78–9, 111–12, 138, 169; language used by Church, 166–7
'God and my Furniture' (J. Parkes), 30, 31, 32
God's First Love (F. Heer), 266
God at Work in science, politics and human life (J. Parkes), 174
God in a World at War (J. Parkes), 112, 174, 175
Goitein, Professor, 250
Goldhagen, Daniel, xi, 266
Golding, Louis (novelist), 184
Gollancz, Victor, 2, 179, 180, 182, 237, 261
Good God, 112, 147, 151, 174, 175
Gospels: Pharisees of, 97, 170; readings, 98, 170; writers of, 241
Graetz, Heinrich, 84
Great St Mary's Church (Cambridge), 165
Great War *see* First World War
Green, Benny, 19
'Growth of Barley' (J. Parkes), 216, 217
Grubb, Kenneth, 298
Grunfeld, Dayan, 268
Guernsey (birthplace of J. P.), 20–38, 47; Elizabeth College, 20, 23, 25, 29–30, 53; Jewish people in, viii; occupation in Second World War, 106
Guernsey Gache (food), 254

Guernsey Magazine, 21
Gugeon, Trevor, 63
'Guild of Happy Carpenters', 54
Gutteridge, Richard, 76, 77, 80

Hadham, John, J. P. writing as, 145, 147, 173–4, 177
Hamlet (W. Shakespeare), 18–19
Hardwick, Ruth, 212
Harland, Irene, 134
Harries, Richard (Bishop of Oxford), vii, viii, xvii
Harwich, J. P. at, 106
health problems of J. P.: cerebral spasm, 199; crisis (1955–57), 211–13; earlier life, 23, 24, 35, 41, 46, 50; heart attacks, 199, 220; hospitalisation, 38, 43, 199, 213–14, 218; mental breakdown, 34, 42; phlebitis, 214
Heer, Friedrich, 266
Heidegger, Martin, 49
Heinrichsbad, 74, 75, 76
Herbert, George, 168
Herbert, Nicholas, 278, 279
Herzl, Theodore, 201
Heydrich, Reinhard, 178
Him, George and Shirley, 255–6
Himmler, Heinrich, 92, 178, 295
Hinrichs, J. C., 234
Hirsch, Samson Raphael, 243
historian, J. P. as, 30, 68–9, 117
History of the Franco-Prussian War (M. Howard), 231
History of the Jewish People (J. Parkes), 231, 236
History of Palestine from 135 A.D. to modern times (J. Parkes), 189
Hitler, Adolf, 49, 77, 92, 120, 123, 131, 152, 180–1; appointment as Chancellor, 85
Hoffmann, Conrad, 93
'Holidays in my Childhood' (J. Parkes), 20, 21
Holocaust and Genocide Studies, 294
Holocaust Memorial Day, 15
Holocaust, the, 125; antisemitism, loss of respectability, 6; and Council of Christians and Jews, formation, xvii; 'Final Solution', xviii, 75, 86, 92, 140, 178, 180, 263, 292; J. P. on, xi, xviii; Nazi era, xviii; uniqueness of, 132
Holy Ghost, 67, 159; and antisemitism, 80
Holy Spirit, 68, 70, 72, 73, 74
Hopovo, conference of Russian Orthodox Church at, 56
Hore-Belisha, Isaac (Minister of War), 145
Hoskins, W. G., 98
hospitalisation of J. P., 38, 43, 199, 213–14, 218
housework, as God's work, 30, 31

Howard, Michael, 231
Huizinga, Johan, 98
humanism, 68, 70; J. P. as humanist, 31, 53, 167, 292
Hume, Alec Douglas, 259
humility, 293
Hunstanton nursing home, 213
Hunter Dunn, Joan (created by J. Betjeman), 150
HUSKY operation (1943), 209

identity, individual (Western concept), 71–2
ill-health of J. P. *see* health problems of J. P.
Influence of the Synagogue upon the Divine Office, 136
Ingram, Kenneth, 157, 159
'Institute solution', 142
intention, 123
International conferences: a handbook for conference organizers and discussion leaders (J. Parkes), 57
International Council of Christians and Jews, xvii
International Missionary Council, 93
International Student Service *see* I.S.S. (International Student Service)
International conferences (I.S.S.), 57
Isis magazine, 40, 51; 'Eights Week Invitations' in, 53
Islam, 69, 70, 173
Israel: Anti-Israelism, 6–7, 204, 205; Arab–Israeli war (1948), 200; foundation of, 200; J. P. and, 236, 240, 249; Six Day War (1967), 271; *Voyage of Discoveries*, unpublished chapters in, 44
'Israel and the Arab World' (J. Parkes), 236
Israel and Palestine (Fellowship of Reconciliation pamphlet), 279–80
Isserlin, Beate, 292
I.S.S. (International Student Service), xvi, 3, 55, 75, 81, 87–8; committees, 64; Cultural Co-operation Secretary, J. P. as, 81; J.P. as employee of, 54, 110; publications, 57, 85; resignation by J. P. from, 63, 102
Iwerne Minister (Dorset), 211, 227, 245–90; financial accounts kept, 249; move to (1964), 271
Iwerne War Memorial, 246

Jackson, Frederick George (Major), 5–6
Jackson–Harmsworth Polar Expedition (1894–97), 5
'James Parkes and the Holocaust' (T. Kushner), 292
Jeffries, Dr Gillian, 231

Jeffries, W. A., 231
Jehouda, José, 82
Jerusalem, 277
Jesus Christ, 67–8, 70, 71, 80, 97, 122, 170, 173, 241, 288–9; killing of, 118, 123; 'Notes on the Trial of Jesus' (P. Winter), 234; *Sepher Toldoth Jeshu* (Jewish Life of Jesus), 120, *see also* Christianity
Jesus, Paul and the Jews (J. Parkes), 96–7
Jew and His Neighbour (J. Parkes), 13
Jewish Academy, 91
Jewish Agency, 189
Jewish Board of Deputies, 128, 129
Jewish–Christian relations, vii, xii, xiii, 19, 44, 94, 173, 240; history, 96, 99, 117, 137; Lambeth Document, xvii, *see also Conflict of Church and Synagogue* (J. Parkes)
Jewish Historical Society, J. P. President of, xi–xii, 199
Jewish Hospitality Committee for British and Allied Forces, 182–3
Jewish Journal of Sociology, 201, 202
Jewish Peace Aims, 146–7
Jewish people: British, 100, 233; Christianity, conversion to, 93; East European, 186, 299; in Guernsey, viii; image of, 117; killing of Christ, culpability questions, 118, 123; in Middle Ages, 114–15; as money-lenders, 117, 125; political hostility to, 118; as refugees, 114; 'wandering Jew', mythic figure, x, *see also* antisemitism; Judaism
Jewish People's Council Against Fascism and Anti-Semitism, 127
'Jewish problem', 81; in Britain, 296; in Germany/Austria, 91; Jewish responsibility, 124
'Jewish problem in Eastern Europe' (J. Parkes), 87
Jewish Problem in the Modern World, 294–5
Jewish Review,' Judaism–Jews–Antisemities: Thoughts of a Non-Jew' essay in (1934), 82, 88, 89, 90
Jewish Student (I.S.S.), 85
Jew in the Medieval Community (J. Parkes), 68, 85, 112–15, 116, 117, 124, 144, 262; non-chronological approach, 118–19; 'political' chapters, 119; quality of writing, 119–20; responsibility of Jews, 124–5; shortcomings, 114; structure of book, 114
Johnson, Malcolm, 251–2
John XXIII (Pope), 206
Jones, Asterley, correspondence with, 164–5
Jones, David, 48
Judaism: and Christianity, 14–15; Orthodox, 90, 267; Palestine and,

202–3; Yahweh, 69, 70
Judaism and Christianity (J. Parkes), 189
'Judaism–Jews–Antisemites: Thoughts of a Non-Jew' (J. Parkes), 82, 88, 89, 90
Judas, 116, 117
Judeo-Bolshevik conspiracy, Hitler's belief in, 92
June 1934 (K. Barth), 77

Karski, Jan, 178
Kelly, George, 255
Kermode, Frank, 7–8
Kerr, Sir John Graham, 153
Kessler, David, 227, 229, 230, 238, 242–3
kings of England, Anglo-Norman, 119
Kirkpatrick, Reverend George, 149
Klein, Charlotte, 257
Kristallnacht, 80
Kushner, Tony, 292, 294, 295, 296, 300

Labour Party, 238, 239
Langmuir, Gavin, xi
language, and theology, 79
Lanzmann, Claude, 119
Laski, Neville, 125–6
Lawrence, Joan, 178, 236
Lawrence, T. E., 6
League of Nations High Commission for Refugees, 103
League of Nations Union *see* L.N.U. (League of Nations Union)
Lebensraum, 236
Lee-Elliott, Rev. David, 38
Lenin, Vladimir, 92, 120
Le Noury, Maison, 254
Les Fauconnaires (childhood home), 21, 22
Levin, Rabbi Aryeh, 12, 74
Levinson, Leah, 237
Levi, Primo, 254
Liberal Jewish Synagogue (St John's Wood), 11
Liddell, Peter, 40, 41
Lieb, Fritz, 73
Littell, Franklin, 264
L.N.U. (League of Nations Union), J. P. as secretary, 51, 52, 53, 56
Loeb, Walther, 193–4
Loewe, Herbert, 83, 146
London, J. P. at (1920s), 54, 62
London Poor Clergy Holiday Fund: Secretary, J. P.'s correspondence with, 10–11
London Society of Jews and Christians, resignation of Ellis Waterhouse from, 187–8
Louis IX, King of France, 119
Lucy Cavendish College, 257
Lukyn-Williams, A. O., 38
Lure of the North Pole (F. G. Jackson), 5–6

Lutheranism, 49, 77, 78

McDonald, James, 103
McGowan, Lord, 164
Mackay, R. W., 155, 156, 157, 162; 'big business technique', 161
McNeilage, John, 38, 64, 112, 189, 226, 235
Magic People (A. Ussher), 2
Magris, Claudio, 1
Mailer, Norman, 253
Maitland, Frederic William, 98
Making of the English Landscape (W. G. Hoskins), 99
Manchester, xiv–xv; Mamloch House, 15
Manchester Hotel Affair, 161
Marks, Simon, 194, 217
Marks and Spencers, 108
'Mary Tudor: A Tragedy in Five Acts', 53
Masaryk, Jan, 186
Masaryk, Thomas, 299
mass, 197
'Massacre of the Jews: Future Vengeance or Present Help', 300
Matthew, 173
Maxstoke Castle (Warwickshire), 38
Melbourne University, architectural drawings given to, 10
Meldreth, church of, 190–1
mental breakdown (J. P.), 34, 42
Meyer, Naomi, 9
Meyer, Sergeant, 184
Milligan, Spike, 41
Missenden Abbey, course given at, 275, 276, 277
Modernity, 28, 169, 176
money-lending, 117, 118, 125
'Mongenes Para Patros' (P. Winter), 234
'Monologue with Freud' (Y. H. Yerushalmi), 2
Montefiore, Claude, xiii; Library of, 228
Montefiore Memorial Lecture (1972), 280
Moral Reckoning: the Catholic Church and the Holocaust in History and Today (D. Goldhagen), 266
More, Thomas, 156, 157, 158
Morison, Samuel Eliot, 208–9
Mosley, Oswald, 128
Motzkin, Dr Leo, 95
'Mrs Motherley's Spring Cleaning' (J. Parkes), 32–3
'Mrs Snooks of Stamford Hill', 7, 8
Munich University, White Rose group (1942), 78
'My Solution of the Jewish Question', 300

Namier, Julia, 191, 192
Namier, Sir Lewis, 18, 100, 101, 102, 192, 193
Napier, Albert, 139

National Christian Appeal, and German Jewry, 133
National Front parties, 88
National Peace Council, 181
National Socialism *see* Nazism
National Union of Students, 56
Nazi era, J. P. as activist during, xviii
Nazism: antisemitism, respectability of, 7; Barth and, 78; conversion of young Germans to, 15; Final Solution, xviii, 75, 86, 92, 140, 178, 180, 263, 292; non-Jewish victims of, 236; racism and, 132, 236
Nazi–Soviet Pact, 169
New Christian, 253
'New Order', 298
Nicholl, Donald, 71
Nicolson, Harold, 121–2
'1662 Communion Service', 285–6, 287
Northern Command Gas School, 42
Not Entitled (F. Kermode), 7–8
'Notes on the Trial of Jesus' (P. Winter), 234
Nyon converence (1931), 94

Oberaegeri, conference at (1925), 56, 81
Observer, 60, 103
Oldfield, Lady Kathleen, 134
Old Hores Manor Barley, 245
Old Testament, 95, 287
On the Trial of Jesus (P. Winter), 233, 235
Open Thy Mouth for the Dumb: The German Evangelical Church and the Jews 1879-1950 (R. Gutteridge), 76
ordination of J. P., 22, 23
Organization for the Social Welfare of Jewish Students in Vienna, 135
Original Sin, 49
Oxford, J. P. at, 50–4, 101; D.Litt, self-nomination for, 141, 142; doctorate, achievement of, 85, 94; Fellowship, 51; friends, lack of, 51; League of Nations Union *see* L.N.U. (League of Nations Union); special subjects, 50
Oxford University, J. P. educated at, x
Ozanne, Christine (cousin of J. P.), 22, 34
Ozanne, John, 252

Palestine: partition decision of U.N., 200, 202; as place of asylum, 145
Palestinians: J. P.'s attitude to, 205–6; plight of, 199–200
papacy, 115–16
Parkes, Annie Katherine (*formerly* Bell) (mother of J. P.), 21, 22, 24, 29
Parkes Centre for the Study of Jewish–non Jewish Relations, xiv, 290, *see also* Parkes Library, University of Southampton
Parkes, David (brother of J. P.), 20, 25;

death of, 41, 42
Parkes, Dorothy (*formerly* Wickings) (wife of J. P.), 24, 43, 61, 63, 184, 191, 198, 199, 212, 218–219, 224; background, 149–50; marriage to James, 10, 64, 145, 149, 152; as pacifist, 150; as secretary, 146, 149–50, 150–1, 182; on Sieff, 215, 219, 221, 223–4, 224–5
Parkes Fund, 214
Parkes, Henry (father of J. P.), 20–1, 23, 25; death, 10, 21, 153–4, 217
Parkes Institute, xv, xvi, 211, 214, 215–16, 223, 246
Parkes Library, University of Southampton, xiii, xiv, 39, 194, 211, 220, 290; expenditure, annual, 217–18; history, 217; official opening, 246; Pamphlet 22, 262; registration, 218, 219, 223; research projects linked to, xv, *see also* Parkes Institute; Parkes Papers
Parkes, Molly (sister of J. P.), 20, 25, 34; death, 44
Parkes Papers, 8, 48, 74, 104, 137–138, 237, 261; arts, lack of mention in, 107; *Evening News*, copy of (1926), 57; *Jewish Student* project, index cards in, 85, *see also* Parkes Institute; Parkes Library, University of Southampton
Parkes, Reverend Dr James: birthplace (Guernsey) *see* Guernsey (birthplace of J. P.); character, strengths and weaknesses, viii–ix, 4, 5, 6, 9, 12, 23–24, 63, 107–8, 109–10; childhood/education, x, 20–36, 40, 53; marriage to Dorothy, 10, 64, 145, 149, 152
Passover, 120
Paton, Reverend William, 186
Peace, 57
Peace Pledge Union, 150, 151
Peel, John, xv
Penney, Mr (headmaster), 35, 36
personality, theory of, 283–4, 285
Petrarch, 71
Pharisees, 97, 170
Philosopher on Dover Beach (R. Scruton), 1
Plato, 156
poet, J. P. as, 33–4, 53
Poliakoff, Leon, 213
political actions, 156, 159, 240
'political realism' (1980s), 240–1
politics, J. P. on, 57, 238–9
Portsmouth Jewish Truth Society, 8
post-modernism/post-moralism, 1
'Post-War Antisemitism' (J. Parkes), 91
'Potemkinization', 206
Powicke, Maurice, 94, 102, 114
Priestley, J. B., 161
prophets, readings from, 98
Proust, Marcel, 3–4, 11, 17, 48, 158, 182, 254

Provence, J. P. at, 56, 57, 260–1
Prussia, conference at (1924), 56
Psalm 84, verse 6, 11

Queen Mary II (ship), xiii

racism, and Nazism, 132, 236
R.A.M.C. (Royal Army Medical Corps), 37
Rassenschaende (J. P.'s dog), 10
Rathbone, Eleanor, 182, 296, 301; portrait, 6
rationalist, J. P. as, 31, 40
Reed, Douglas, 123–4, 125, 132
Ree, Hans, 238
Reformation, 72
refugees, 134; Jews as, 114
Reinhard, Aktion, 295
religion, individualised, 118
Religion and the Rise of Capitalism (R. H. Tawney), 99
Remembering for the Future: The Holocaust in an Age of Genocide, 292
Renaissance, 68, 70, 71; Twelfth Century, 115, 122
Reuther, Rosemary, 256
'Revelation and a Duster' (J. Parkes), 30, 31, 32
Ribbentrop, Joachim von, 131
Richardson, Alan, 177
Richmond, Colin, viii, ix, x, xviii, xix
Richmond, Rabbi Harry, 251
Rise and Fall of the Judean State: a Political, Social and Religious History of the Second Commonwealth, 252
Rizk, Nada Yousif, 237
Robb, Sir Douglas, 59–60
Rockovitch, Mr, 273
Rolleston, William (History Master), 29–30
Roman Catholicism, 134, 170, 197, 206; papacy, 115–16
Rosenfeld, Else, 191–2, 197
Rosenfeld, Fritz, 191
Rosenfeld, Hanna, 193
Roth, Cecil, 137
Roth, Leon, 233
Rowse, A. L., 51
Royal West Surrey Regiment, 38
Royden, Maude, 185
Rubenstein, Ben, 186–7
Ruether, Rosemary, 264
Runcie, Robert, 266

Sabbatai Sevi (G. Scholem), 2
Sacks, Rabbi Jonathan (Chief Rabbi), 17
Sadducees, 170
Saffron Walden discussion club, 16
St Francis, 13, 31
St John's College, Cambridge, 147; Senior Common Room, 137
St Martin's rectory, 22, 23
St Martin's Review, 162, 164
St Mary Woolnoth, church of, 183
St Omer, barracks in, 37
St Paul, 15
St Seraphim of Sarov, 74
St Stephen's, Hampstead, 55
Salaman, Dr Redcliffe (chairman of Barley Parish Council), 146, 148, 153, 230
Salisbury, Lord, 168
Salmon, Isidore, 145
Samuel, Edgar, 255
Sargant, Tom, 238
Saumarez, Lord James de, 53–4
Sayers, Dorothy L., 15
Schindler, Oskar, xviii, 301
Schmal, Franz, 56, 60–2
Schneider, Reverend Peter, 256
scholarships, 35–6
Scholem, Gershom, 2
Scholl, Hans and Sophie, 77
Schonfield, Hugh, 134
Schrayer, Eric and Pearl, 212, 213
S.C.M. (Student Christian Movement), xvi, 51–2, 55, 75, 183; J. P. as employee of, 52, 54, 110, 162; *Peace* publication (1932), 57
Scotsman, 291, 292
Scruton, Roger, 1, 2
Second World War, 52; Barley during, 145–88; Barley prior to, 106–44; European, transformation of, 154; Guernsey, collaboration history, viii, *see also* First World War; Holocaust, the; Nazism
Selly Oak Colleges (Birmingham), 131
Sepher Toldoth Jeshu (Jewish Life of Jesus), 120
Seven Pillars of Wisdom (T. E. Lawrence), 6
sexuality of J. P., 13, 34
Shakespeare, William, 18–19
'Sharing of the Kiss of Peace', 289
Shoah *see* Holocaust
Shoah (film by C. Lanzmann), 119
Sibthorpe, Miss (Honorary Secretary of National Committee for Rescue from Nazi Terror), 178
Sieff, Becky, 147, 217
Sieff, Israel, 102, 103, 174, 189, 194, 229; as benefactor to J. P., 108, 110, 112, 113, 147, 212, 215, 223, 225, 227; Dorothy Parkes on, 215, 219, 221, 223–4, 224–5
Silcox, Edwin, 154
Simon, U. E., 79
Simpson, Reverend W. W. (Bill) (Secretary of Council of Christians and Jews), xvii, 12, 151, 178, 182, 224, 234, 292, 302; ill-health of J. P. and, 216, 218, 220, 222

Index

Singer, Charles, 83, 98, 137, 138, 139–40, 142, 143, 144, 162, 242
Singer, Dorothea, 137, 138, 242
Sisters of Zion, convent of, 236
Six Day War (1967), 271
Smalley, Beryl, 137
Sniderman, Mr, letter to, 81–2
soldier, J. P. as, 22, 36–40; active service phase, 38–9; Artists' Rifles, private in, 37; gas officer, as, 41, 42–3, 45; Lowestoft period, 44, 45, 46; Queen's (Royal West Surrey Regiment), and, 38, 42; second lieutenant, commissioned as, 38
Solzhenitsyn, Alexander, 36, 168
'Some aspects of the Jewish Situation in Europe' (J. Parkes), 86
South Africa, 240
Southampton, University of, x, xii–xiii; Montefiore Lecture, annual, 228; Parkes Library *see* Parkes Library, University of Southampton
Southern Command Gas School, 42
Spencer, Stanley, 49
Spiller, William, 34
spirituality/mystical inclinations of J. P. or lack of, 12–13, 27–8, 31, 39–40, 74; individual soul, non-survival of, 284, *see also* God: J. P. on
Stalin, Joseph, 92; Five Year Plans (1930s), 16
Steyning Grammar School, 232
Still (New Wave band), xv
Stockwood, Mervyn, 190
Stone, Dan, 292
Strachan, Rose, 3
Strachan, T. P., 241, 242
Streiker, Lowell, 250
Strizower, Shifra, 274
Struma, sinking of, 295
Student Christian Movement (S.C.M.) *see* S.C.M. (Student Christian Movement)
Student Movement, 30
Student Movement House (Russell Square), 64; J. P. as warden, 54
'Students and European Politics' (J. Parkes), 87
Student World (World Christian Student Christian Federation handbook), 87
Study of History (Chapter 8), 200–1, 202
study programmes, devising of, 55
suicide bombers, 274
'Surviving Jewish Community' (J. Parkes), 236
Swann, Charles, 3
Swanwick, Derbyshire (C. of E.'s conference centre), 55–6
Sykes, Norman, 212–13
Syndic, Oxford University Press, 100

Talmud, 84
Tatlow, Canon Tissington, 195
Taverner, Ellis, 245
Tawney, R. H., 48, 98
team-playing, J. P.'s shortcomings in respect of, 23–4, 25
Teich, Dr Alexander, xviii, 84, 134, 135, 146
Temple, William (Archbishop of Canterbury), xvii, 23, 36, 52, 55, 67, 73, 81, 152, 216, 297; books by J. P. reviewed by, 174–5; correspondence with J. P., 65, 66, 128–9, 130, 175; on 'scientific categories', 92
terrorism, fundamentalist, 268, 274
Thatcher, Margaret, 238, 253
Theologische Literaturzeitung, 234
theology: Barthian, 76; Dialectical, 77; Eastern Orthodox, 68; and language, 79; Trinitarian, 65
Thomas, Thomas, 38, 104, 105, 112; attack on, 138
Thurstan (twelfth-century Archbishop of York), 115
Toc H conference (1945), 197
Torah, 98, 122, 244
Torah min ha-Shamaim, 269
Toynbee, Arnold, 235
Toynbee, Philip, 43, 108, 153, 200, 201; 'The Fate of the European Jews and the Palestinian Arabs, A.D. 1933-48', 200–201, 202; *Voyage of Discoveries*, critical review of, 22, 38, 107, 261
'Toynbee and the Uniqueness of Jewry' (J. Parkes), 201, 202
Transactions of La Société Guernesiase, 53
Trend, Captain, 42
Trever-Roper, H. R., 235
Trinitarianism, 65, 66, 68, 71, 72, 81
Truth Shall Make You Free (Lambeth Document on Christian–Jewish relations), xvii

Union Theological Seminary, Broadway, 14
universities: Southampton, x, xii–xiii; theology departments, 16
Ussher, Arland, 2
'usury', 116, 117
Utopian Realism, 241
Utopia (T. More), 156, 158

vagabond years of J. P., 60
Vermes, Geza, 246
Versailles, Treaty of, 181
Vikings, 118
Vogel, Hélène, 259
Voyage of Discoveries (J. P's autobiography), viii, 12; on Annie K. Bell (mother), 22; cooperative (Parkes' house-

hold), description in, 24; on First World War, 36; on Guernsey, 20; on Israel, unpublished chapters, 44; Palestinian visit (1946), 206; Saffron Walden discussion club meeting, paper written for, 16; on Singer family, 138; Toynbee's critical review of, 22, 38, 107; village life, 144; William Temple and, 131; written when (1964–9), 271

Walk about Zion (Parkes Library Pamphlet), 280
Walton-on-the-Naze, water-colours of, 29
Waning of the the Middle Ages (J. Huizinga), 99
Warburg, Aby, 246
Warren, Canon, 275
Warsaw, conference at (1924), 56
Waterhouse, Ellis, 187–8
Waugh, Evelyn, 51
Weissmandl, Rabbi Michael Ber, 19
Weitz, Edith Ruth, xviii, 135
Weitz, Rachel, xviii, 136
Weizmann, Dr Chaim, 185
Werblonksy, Alisa and Zwi, 211–12
Whaddon, church of, 190–1
White House Hotel, Herm (Channel Islands), 252
Wickings, Dorothy (*later* Parkes) *see* Parkes, Dorothy (*formerly* Wickings) (J. P.'s wife)
Wiener, Alfred, 213, 246
Wiener Library (London), 227
Williams, Guilfoyle, 254
Winter, Paul, 232–3, 233–4, 235, 236
Wintringham, Tom, 155
Wittgenstein, Ludwig, 19, 170

Wood-Legh, Kathleen (Kay), 133–4, 136, 137, 191, 256
Wood, Taylor, 195
Word of God and the Word of Man (K. Barth), 78
Wordsworth, Christopher, 176
work ethic, 109
World Alliance of Young Men's Christian Associations, 232
World Christian Student Christian Federation, 87
World (Council for Education in World Citizenship), 251
World Union of Jewish Students, 135
World War I *see* First World War
World War II *see* Second World War
Wyclif, John, 101, 137
Wytschaete (quarters in), 38

Yad Vashem, xix, 74, 208
Yahweh (God), 69, 70
Yersushalmi, Yosef Hayim, 2, 266
Ypres Salient, 38, 43

Zander, Walter, 218
Zeitlin, Solomon, 252
Zeitschrift für Relionsung Geistesgeschichte, 234
Zionism, 185, 186
'Zum Verständnis des Johannesevangeliums' (P. Winter), 234
Zusya of Hanipol (Hasid), 11–12